D0340796

ECONOMIC ANALYSIS AND AGRICULTURAL POLICY

Economic Analysis
and
Agricultural Policy

edited by

R I C H A R D   H.   D A Y

The Iowa State University Press

A M E S

Library of Congress Cataloging in Publication Data
Main entry under title:

Economic analysis and agricultural policy.

    Essays in honor of Geoffrey Seddon Shepherd.
    Includes bibliographies and index.
    1. Agriculture and state—United States—Addresses, essays, lectures. 2. Agriculture—Economic aspects—United States—Addresses, essays, lectures. 3. Shepherd, Geoffrey Seddon, 1898-
I. Day, Richard Hollis, 1933–   II. Shepherd, Geoffrey Seddon, 1898-
HD1761.E33   338.1′873   82-15341
ISBN 0-8138-0532-5   AACR2

FOR

Geoffrey S. Shepherd

A DEVELOPER OF APPLIED ECONOMICS,
OF ECONOMISTS, AND OF ECONOMIES

CONTENTS

III. ON RESEARCH, TECHNOLOGY, AND RESOURCES

IV. MARKETS AND ECONOMIC DEVELOPMENT

PREFACE

THIS COLLECTION of essays was assembled to honor Geoffrey S. Shepherd, whose exemplary life as a scholar, teacher, economic advisor, and family man has been a continuing source of inspiration and edification to his students, to his colleagues, and to his friends, whose numbers it seems are legion. Known throughout the world for his research and textbooks in marketing, price analysis, and agricultural policy, Shepherd is equally remembered as a wise and affectionate counselor, whose severest rebuke might be a gentle barb well designed to moderate an inflated ego, but whose most notable influence on others comes through his profound dedication to the search for truth and to the evaluation of human action with pragmatic and good-humored reason.

Shepherd's professional work encompasses virtually every important aspect of agricultural economics. His studies included research on the efficiency of farm production and management, early in his career comparing animal draft and mechanical power and later (nearly a half century before its contemporary relevance) evaluating the economics of gasohol. His middle professional career emphasized marketing, price analysis, and farm policy, contributing influential studies of commodity grading, parity pricing, and commodity stock management. After retirement from his university position Shepherd continued his career as an economic advisor, work that had already taken him to Washington, Germany, and Japan, and now to the less-developed countries in Southeast Asia and South America. The essays collected in this volume reflect a similar scope.

Shepherd's style and working philosophy have formed a continuous, unifying, and influential theme throughout his career. The basic goal of economics is "to point out the consequences of one set of values compared with the consequences of another, so that citizens of the country can choose which values they want to cling to most or what compromises they want to make among values on the basis of reason and facts more than upon emotion and prejudice"; the basic methodology of economics involves the careful identification of a policy problem, a clear perception of the facts associated with that problem, and a rigorous understanding of those facts by means of economic analysis and statistical measurement. At the foundation of this position is a firm belief in democracy, in decentralized, free enterprise, market mechanisms, and in the scholar's ability to facilitate the economy's functioning through careful research and education.

Shepherd set forth his views in two celebrated essays reprinted as Chapters 2 and 3 of the present volume. These views are clearly illustrated in virtually everything he wrote. A relatively recent but prototypical example of their application concludes the present volume in Chapter 24, in which Shepherd outlines a marketing policy for a less-developed agriculture.

The hallmarks of Shepherd's published work are simplicity and clarity. Although he eschewed advanced mathematical and statistical techniques, preferring to emphasize time-honored methods of graphical analysis, his relish for empirical facts and for careful reasoning led him to contribute some of the very early economic applications of regression analysis and to express an admiration for the more advanced methods of economic theory and econometrics. Indeed, while evincing skepticism in regard to the latter, especially when carried to pretentious extremes by academic dandies, he appreciated their pragmatic possibilities, referring with a kind of bemused approval to one of the latest and most authoritative examples of the kind (G. S. Shepherd, *Agricultural Price Analysis,* fifth ed., p. 4). Of course, the "Ames School," of which he was an important member, became famous for its devotion to and effective practice of good economics, and in particular, for its blend of theory, econometrics, and applied quantitative analysis characteristic of Shepherd's own work. It was inevitable that some of Shepherd's students as well as several of his younger colleagues would push as far into the more esoteric realms of theory and methodology as others were pushing into the more practical realms of policy and applied analysis. It is therefore appropriate that the present volume includes examples of both theoretical and econometric points of view.

Upon the occasion of Professor Shepherd's eightieth birthday, a celebration in his honor was organized. In preparation for this festivity, invitations to attend and to contribute suggestions for a book of essays were sent to a list of former students and close personal associates. The response was overwhelming. Letters of congratulation and good wishes poured in from all around the globe. Among them came commitments for a number of essays. It became clear that a volume could be assembled that might effectively serve three purposes: (1) to focus renewed attention on the work and on the methodological approach of Geoffrey S. Shepherd; (2) to provide contemporary scholars, students, and policymakers with a useful survey of representative research in those areas of economic analysis and agricultural policy to which Shepherd himself so effectively contributed; and (3) to provide colleagues and former students an opportunity to recognize Shepherd's work and influence on their own lives by presenting papers in his honor. This volume is the result. It is not comprehensive, and there were colleagues and students who did not learn of the project in time to submit contributions. Still, we hope it might serve its three purposes well.

The essays are divided into four sections: I. On Values, Analysis, and Policy; II. The Quantitative Approach; III. On Research, Technology, and Resources; and IV. Markets and Economic Development. A brief survey of the essays will serve as a preview of the volume as a whole.

I. On Values, Analysis, and Policy. Pure neoclassical economics involves the theory of how scarce resources are and how they should be allocated among competing ends. The latter are taken as given in the theory, but in policy formulation and appraisal the values that underlie the ends toward which means are economically directed are fundamental and require explicit recognition. Such was the position cogently argued by Shepherd in two well-known essays, Chapters 2 and 3. The fundamental purpose of applied economic analysis he proclaimed to be that of identifying or anticipating the consequences that followed or might be expected to follow from specific economic policies, leaving it to the now better informed and educated citizen to choose freely or to compromise among competing values and alternatives.

Various additional perspectives on the role of values and analysis in policy formulation and appraisal follow in the succeeding essays in this section. Kenneth E. Boulding discusses the role of images, the evolution of values, and the relative and dynamic rather than absolute and static nature of values. He illustrates how, because of faulty understanding of "normative science," the consequences of various agricultural policies are very much different from those intended. Lauren Soth reviews the changing fashions in farm policy and the role of agricultural economists in influencing—or failing to influence—the resolution of rural problems. Harold F. Breimyer is concerned with the paradox that analysis must necessarily rely on abstraction and imagery, while suffering from the distortion and biases that such abstraction and imagery necessarily involve. He then outlines salient features of the economy that should be accommodated in the agricultural economist's conceptual tool kit; these include the cooperative aspect of economies, the distinction between depletable and nondepletable resources, and the internal nature or function of business enterprise. Glenn L. Johnson, in what he refers to as an extension of Shepherd's philosophical position, reviews definitions of "normative" and outlines the contribution of the "objective, normative" philosophers to theorizing and policy. After comparing these views with those of pragmatism he emphasizes the need for an interactive, iterative approach to problem-solving research. Some of the issues involved in the role of values and analysis in policy are well illustrated by W. K. McPherson in the concluding essay of this part, which deals with the concept of the family farm as an objective of public policy.

II. The Quantitative Approach. The conduct of policy analysis and problem solving by means of rigorous economic theory, systematic observation, and empirical verification leads inevitably to the use of mathematics and statistics, to mathematical economics, and to econometrics, tools dominating much of the discipline's development during the last half century. Although an advocate of the simple, commonsense approach, Shepherd's insistence on getting the facts and testing hypotheses using the underlying framework of neoclassical theory led to his appreciation of developments in economic theory, empirical estimation, and hypothesis testing using econometric models and methods.

This second set of essays is therefore appropriately concerned with economic theory and econometrics. It begins with a historical survey by George G. Judge of the development of statistical methods of estimation and inference. These of course have advanced a long way from the period in which the basic working statistical tool was regression and correlation analysis. Nonetheless, Judge reminds us that their purpose remains the same as Shepherd's, a basic quest for "a more effective information base for forecasting and policy analysis." This is followed by an essay in which Karl A. Fox places his own early work on the structural analysis and measurement of demand in the historical, intellectual context, commenting on the roles of H. L. Moore, Henry Schultz, Trygre Haavelmo, Herman Wold, Mordecai Ezekiel, George Kuznets, and many others. He then reproduces his seminal contribution to the simultaneous equations econometric approach. The paper concludes with an assessment of how much subsequent work in the field had been anticipated by other scholars, especially representatives from within the agricultural economics fraternity. This is followed by a chapter by Gerhard Tintner combining two early papers on business fluctuations. It provides an ingenious example of the mathematization of economic theory and its econometric treatment. It is notable in its use of the notion of temporary equilibrium and its emphasis on dynamics.

A concern for dynamics is repeated in the paper by Wen-yuan Hwang, Earl O. Heady, and Reuben Weisz, who compare several complex, "hybrid," recursive programming models for estimating the temporal and spatial aspects of production, prices, income, and other economic variables. It represents a general modeling approach to the kinds of issues that concerned Geoffrey Shepherd in his analysis of the corn price surface and its application in the formulation of regionally differentiated farm policy. Models of the kind presented in these last two chapters involve questions of "aggregation biases" that arise when microeconomic theory is used as a basis for regional and national models. This important problem is discussed and analyzed by Walter D. Fisher and Paul L. Kelley in the concluding chapter of this section.

III. On Research, Technology, and Resources.

III.   On Research, Technology, and Resources. Long known for his concern with the human resources, Nobel Laureate Theodore W. Schultz, who shares with Shepherd an appreciation for good economic thinking and for simple, straightforward style, offers a new essay on one of the primary economic activities, namely research, considering its role in the process of modernizing world agriculture. In particular he estimates the growth and magnitude of research activity and then considers the questions of who should pay for it and how it should be organized. He closes with comments on the harms done research by price distortions and on the importance of understanding the nature of entrepreneurship.

Schultz's wide-ranging essay is followed by three chapters that involve specific studies of technology and technological change. First is a study of the international transfer of technology by R. T. Shand, who focuses attention on the Indian experience with cereal grains. Next George W. Ladd develops a product-characteristics approach to technical change with an application to animal breeding. Then the economics of gasohol is investigated by Robert N. Wisner, building on the work of Shepherd and his collaborators of nearly fifty years ago.

The applications of economic analysis become particularly difficult when the exploitation of a resource produces externalities, involving social as well as private costs and benefits. This is the case with "research." It is also the case with water, where the management problem is rendered particularly acute by the requirements of an advancing economy whose water-polluting activities increase with the increasing use of water in production. John F. Timmons considers these complex issues in his paper, "The Quality of Water: Problems, Identification, and Improvement," that concludes Section III.

IV. Markets and Economic Development. The progress of economic development has led to a growing interdependence among the various countries of the world, developed and underdeveloped. This trend, long in evidence, has been greatly accelerated by the green revolution, which has led to a growing dependence on energy, fertilizer, and machinery inputs produced off the farm and in many cases out of the country. Moreover, population and industrial growth patterns have not been synchronized with agriculture, so that development has involved substantial changes in relative resource endowments and in comparative advantage. World trade in resources, commodities, and capital has correspondingly shifted. In the process new policy problems emerge and some old ones reemerge and intensify. Broadly speaking, the essays in this part reflect, in one way or another, this changing world scene.

In Chapter 19, Richard H. Day offers a new perspective, obtained from a consideration of adaptive, disequilibrium economic theory, on the evolution of crises and structural change in the developing agroindustrial complex. Next, G. Edward Schuh provides a thorough analysis of the growing interdependence of world capital and commodity markets. Then, in a much cited article presented here in an English version for the first time, Professor Arthur Hanau reviews the nature of agriculture in a developing economy and the problems of price and income that often plague the sector. G. Boddez reviews agricultural policy in the European Common Market in an article previously published some years ago but still useful in its consideration of policy in a setting where economic interdependence is institutionalized through economic integration.

In less-developed countries, the marketing institutions (or lack of them) often constitute more severe bottlenecks than farm production. The concluding essays of this volume deal with such problems. First, Frank Meissner considers appropriate marketing technology for the Third World. Then in the final essay of the volume Geoffrey Shepherd shares his views on marketing policy for less-developed countries in a heretofore unpublished essay dealing with his experiences as an economic advisor in Peru. Although the essay was written in 1969, the problems it addresses and the methods of approaching them are of continuing relevance. Though the article is one of the more recent from Shepherd's pen, it deals with many of the issues that concerned him throughout much of his career in what was for him a new setting. Moreover, with its simple, straightforward style, its reliance on good economic thinking rather than on formal analytical tools, and its advocacy of decentralized markets, individual incentives, and the government as a facilitator rather than a provider of services, it is vintage Shepherd, a fitting conclusion to the present volume.

It is said that an editor's job is a thankless task. The purpose of this endeavor, however, is not to receive but to express thanks. So, here is your book, Geoff, with thanks and keen appreciation from all of us. No doubt the greatest rewards of your life have been in its living from day to day, just as the rewards of those mountains you climbed came with the climbing. Still, thinking of the latter adventures there must have been some pleasure for you in looking back, after your descent, to the challenges you have met and conquered. So, perhaps, in a similar vein, you might look back over your professional endeavors to date, noting that the world and some of its people are more civilized because of your efforts, taking some satisfaction in the result.

RICHARD H. DAY

ACKNOWLEDGMENTS

THE PROJECT was made possible and facilitated by many individuals, including of course the authors of the included papers, and in addition by Ray Beneke, Howard Hines, Wayne Fuller, Gene Futrell, David W. Brown, Roberto Lefevre-Munoz, William Merrill, Kenneth E. Ogren, D. S. Panagides, Paul Nelson, and Harry C. Trelogan. Chapter 1 was written by W. Geoffrey and Gordon M. Shepherd, based on interviews and notes provided by their parents. They along with Eleanor and Grethe Shepherd and other members of the family endorsed the effort and provided helpful support from the beginning. Linda Anderson-Courtney assisted the editor and prepared the final manuscript.

Thanks are due the *American Journal of Agricultural Economics* for permission to reprint part or all of the essays appearing in Chapters 2, 3, 5, and 8; to *The Review of Economics and Statistics* for permission to reprint articles incorporated in Chapters 10 and 11; to *Econometrica* for permission to reprint material appearing in Chapter 11; to the International Association of Agricultural Economists for permission to use material on which Chapter 19 is based; and to the Katholieke Universiteit te Leuven for permission to reprint the article appearing as Chapter 22.

ECONOMIC ANALYSIS AND AGRICULTURAL POLICY

1

Geoffrey S. Shepherd:
The Man and His Work

GEOFFREY SEDDON SHEPHERD was born in the county of Kent in the town of Deal, near Dover, on the southeastern tip of England, on November 29, 1898. He was the sixth of seven children of William John and Fanny Elisabeth Hopper Shepherd. His father was first a farmer, and then a butcher in Ramsgate, where Geoff spent his early years.

Life by the sea was abruptly ended when the family sought opportunity in 1908 by emigrating to Saskatchewan, Canada. They homesteaded first near Stalwart, by Long Lake in the middle of the province, and then in the southwest corner, near the Cypress Hills. It is prairie land with its own beauty, but unfortunately marginal for eking out a living from the soil. The family made the transition to farming and cattle raising in this difficult environment, but the odds were always against them, with dawn-to-dusk cultivating and harvesting, droughts, grasshoppers, and long, icy winters. The rugged qualities imbued in Geoff by his childhood there as well as an abiding love for wide open spaces and boundless skies stayed with him throughout his life.

Alone among his siblings and contemporaries of that region, Geoff, with the loyal support of his family, managed to attend high school for a few months in the winter in Regina. In 1918 he enlisted in the Canadian army and was sent to England, where the Armistice came just before embarkation for France. He spent half a year at the "Khaki University" in Ripon, Yorkshire, which whetted his desire for more education. With always precarious finances, he earned a B.S. degree at the University of Saskatchewan, beginning in physics but shifting to economics where he could apply his talents to the problems of agriculture that he knew so well at first hand.

After graduation he returned to the farm to work and save money toward graduate school. A letter from a former classmate, Dennis Fitzgerald, led to an invitation to come to Iowa State College, and he began his studies there in January 1924 on half a $75 a month scholarship. His roomates at the Cranford

Annex on Lincoln Way were Fitz, Bill Murray, and "Cap" Bentley. He received his M.S. degree in agricultural economics in 1925. The department chairman, C. L. Holmes, recommended Harvard for further graduate work. On only a $300 scholarship Geoff completed the required course work there in a single academic year (1926–1927) and ultimately received his Ph.D. degree in 1932 with a dissertation entitled "Fluctuations in the Price of Corn." From 1927 on he was a member of the Iowa State College faculty in the Department of Economics and Sociology.

Qualities of Mind. His interests and qualities were formed and tested by the middle 1920s. Knowing farming well, he was keen to solve its problems, capable of hard and inventive work, and always objective in his research. Early homestead life greatly influenced his later professional work in several different ways. It made him, first, an individualist. The prairie frontier was a hard and lonely—if lovely—place. Each family had to rely on its own efforts to start a farm and make a go of it.

Second, one survived by solving problems, each day and from year to year. Later as an economist, his mind continued to work the same way. His first question was, What's the problem? Then he would test the answer to find out whether the problem was the disease or only the symptom. The problems under investigation grew in scope. Geoff started adult life with the specific, limited problem of how he could make a living on his homestead, then moved to the problems of farmers in the state of Iowa, of the United States, and finally of the world. This was reflected by the series of maps hung in his office— first, the map of Iowa; later, a map of the United States; and finally, a map of the world.

Third, Geoff learned early on to rely on scientific objectivity. Farm life required one to face facts squarely; then, as a physics student, he learned the scientific method. This stayed with him as an economist. He set up hypotheses and tested them against the facts, yielding to no other authority nor to his own cherished beliefs if they did not stand up under the tests. He admitted to no biases. In a preface to one of his books he wrote: "Some authors state their biases in the preface. A scientist should not state his biases; he should remove them."

From the start, Geoff's writing was direct and to the point. His first department head called his style "hammer and tongs." At Harvard he was exposed to helpful criticism and soon evolved the sparse, lucid prose that has since characterized all his writing.

Thus equipped, he entered a field—agricultural economics—that was just beginning a robust growth, characterized (far more than other economics fields) by empirical research and statistical methodology. Yet, like all his best colleagues of that time, he had roots directly in farming. So when the Great

Depression of the 1930s struck farming with great force, it deeply affected his work. The farm crisis posed problems of utmost urgency that required clear and realistic study. It also bred a series of large federal programs to aid farmers that channeled billions of dollars to, and shaped, the whole agricultural sector.

The Depression Years. As a result no doubt of this combination of circumstances, for the better part of three decades of work Geoff sought mainly to probe the causes of domestic farm problems and to identify and correct the faults in some of the government programs. During the 1930s alone he wrote more than thirty pieces, some quite substantial studies, that informed Iowa readers on various topics involving the farm crisis, national agricultural policy, and prospects for improved marketing. The Agricultural Experiment Station of Iowa State College started a series of bulletins in January 1933 entitled "The Agricultural Emergency in Iowa." Geoff wrote three of ten entries in the series. After then being aired in a sequence of radio programs the series was published as a book in July 1933. By the early summer of the same year many remedial measures for rescuing the country from the depression had been passed. A new series of bulletins was started, "Prospects for Agricultural Recovery." The leadoff issue, "The Economic Situation in 1933," written by Geoffrey Shepherd, was published in December 1933. He was also the author of numbers IV and VIII in the series.

The Iowa Farm Economist, a monthly, was launched in 1935, chiefly through the efforts of his colleague, Lauren Soth, then a member of the economics department, later an editor of the *Des Moines Register.* This magazine carried articles on farm economics problems, based on research published in scientific bulletins. It was an important vehicle for Geoff's continuing efforts to inform fellow citizens about the important economic problems facing them in daily life. It was so successful that other departments of the college wanted to be involved, and by 1946 it became *Iowa Farm Science,* and the contents were broadened.

During the 1930s the field of statistics expanded rapidly. Iowa State College brought the great British statistician R. A. Fisher over for a summer session, and George Snedecor of the mathematics department developed the Iowa State Statistical Laboratory into one of the best in the country. Snedecor became a statistician on every agricultural research project on the campus. Geoff and George became good friends as well as colleagues, and Geoff was among the first in agricultural economics—or in economics generally for that matter—to make use of multiple correlation analysis in his research.

During this decade agricultural economics was a rapidly expanding field, largely because of the depression and the growth of government programs to deal with it. The agricultural economists at Iowa State played a leading role in this expansion. They were unusual in having their home within a department of economics, rather than in the division of agriculture as was the custom at many institutions. Thus, they were economists first, as Geoff never tired of telling his students, and they drew strength from this and from rubbing shoulders with colleagues in other sections of the department. During this period Geoff's close colleagues included, in addition to Soth, Murray, and Snedecor, Ken Boulding, Bill Nicholls, and Walter Wilcox; from 1930 on Elisabeth Hoyt and Margaret Reid were on the faculty, and from 1935 to 1943 Nobel Laureate Ted Schultz was chairman of the department.

World War II. World War II changed the focus of Geoff's work from depression and economic recovery to war production and then to the transition to peace.

During World War II, the economics department of Iowa State College put out a series of bulletins entitled "Wartime Farm and Food Policy." Geoff wrote two of the series and provided a substantial revision of a third entry. The series consisted of eleven studies: *Food Strategy,* by Margaret Reid, 1943; *Farm Prices for Food Production,* by Theodore W. Schultz, 1943; *Manpower in Agriculture,* by Rainer Schickele, 1943; *Food Rationing and Morale,* by C. Arnold Anderson, 1943; *Putting Dairying on a War Footing,* by O. H. Brownlee, 1943, with a revised edition, by Geoffrey Shepherd, 1944; *Commodity Loans and Price Floors for Farm Products,* by Geoffrey Shepherd, 1943; *Using Our Soils for War Production,* by Arthur C. Bunce, 1943; *Food Management and Inflation,* by Mary Jean Bowman and Albert G. Hart, 1943; *Land Boom Controls,* by William G. Murray, 1943; *Food Subsidies and Inflation,* by Gale Johnson and O. H. Brownlee, 1944; and *Agricultural Prices after the War,* by Geoffrey Shepherd, 1944.

All during World War II Geoff spent his month of vacation each year working as a consultant with the U.S. Department of Agriculture in Washington. One year he spent several months as chief economist with the Commodity Credit Corporation, then under Jack Hutson. There he worked out a system of different loan rates by counties in Iowa that the CCC used to replace the original flat rates over the state. Other states followed suit.

In the midst of the mobilization period in 1942 a war of a quite different kind broke out in Ames, the celebrated butter versus margarine battle. A colleague, Oz Brownlee, had written a bulletin stating (correctly) that margarine could be as nutritious as butter. This provoked the dairy interests to demand a retraction, and the Iowa State administration, after moderate resistance, acceded. In protest, several members left the department; Geoff, however, decided to stay, continuing the tradition of objective research on economic policy. In doing so he contributed greatly to the department's continuity and strength. The incident reflected some of the pressures—from farmers, food processors, and even the USDA itself—that have always been at work in the field.

Geoff chose to ignore such pressures, going right ahead with his scientific studies and letting the chips fall where they may. This was especially true of his research on federal farm programs. There were many faults in these programs, some quickly removed and others that still exist. Some specialists chose the safe course of ignoring or defending the faults. In a series of papers, monographs, and textbooks, Geoff tried to expose and correct them. Often, economic light could not remove what political forces had created. Yet he did not grow cynical at the persistence of some bad programs. Instead he contributed his research to the discussion and through his teaching helped train a cadre of new agricultural economists in methods of sound policy analysis. The latter task began in earnest after the war.

After the War. After the war Geoff mounted a series of studies on the effects and costs of farm programs. The early policies for stabilizing farm incomes had become distorted, raising prices over the long term. This led to accumulating surpluses, to cutbacks in acreage, and to other wastes, as he had foreseen. Geoff saw, too, that the primary beneficiaries were present landholders, for the programs drove up farm land prices, making it harder for young people to start farming. Taking land out of production with such harmful effects seemed inappropriate. Yet the programs persisted and grew. In a series of studies of parity prices, land banks, and other policy devices, he showed concretely how inefficient and unfair the programs were. The real problem in his view was not too many acres but too many farmers. The need thererefore was to help surplus farmers make the transition to city life and jobs. Geoff perceived that it was small farmers that needed help, not big farmers. This ran against some farm bloc interests and many of his colleagues' views as well.

After 1945 he took a leading part in starting regional marketing study groups, encouraging colleagues to do independent research outside their own states' parochial farm activities. Ten years later he started a national farm policy committee. The response was disappointing. Independent, rigorous analysis of American farm policies never reached the level that Geoff felt was so urgently needed.

Advising Abroad. A second aspect of Geoff's postwar work, both a natural outgrowth of his policy concerns and a refreshing escape from the pressures and mistakes of U.S. farm programs, was foreign advising. In 1949, Geoff took his first foreign job, an assignment to Frankfurt, West Germany, with the U.S. Army. His report, *Long Range Price Policy for Western German*

Agriculture, was published by the Bipartite Control Office, Food and Agriculture and Forestry Group, June 1949. It was not much of a report, he says; he was too green at the job.

On his second assignment, to Japan in 1951, his hosts asked him to assess the best way to set the price of rice—at the cost of production, or parity, or what? Arguing that a parity system was the basis for two evils, he emphasized the likelihood that political pressures would force the parity price up, since a high proportion of the Japanese were farmers, with a consequent distortion in real market forces. The report, *Long Range Policy for Japanese Agriculture,* was printed in English and Japanese. Twenty years later, on a short visit to Japan, it was obvious that the Japanese had not been able to resist the pressures he anticipated. The price of rice in Japan was double the world price, and they could only sell their surplus at that world price, involving a heavy drain on their treasury. At present the problems have only worsened.

In 1957 Geoff served six months in Rangoon, Burma, as a member of a Robert Nathan Associates group. Nothing came of his recommendations for a system of market information on rice supplies and prices in other countries. The Burmese really did not want any advice in the first place; several years later they ousted all their advisors—Russian, American, and others.

Geoff was discouraged about foreign work after Burma, but he took a three-month assignment in Venezuela in 1962 with the Consejo de Biene-star Rural of the Venezuelan government. The new effort turned out well. With the help of two young Venezuelan graduate assistants, he toured the country to evaluate marketing facilities and wrote a report published in English and Spanish, *Report and Recommendations Concerning Food Marketing in Venezuela,* coauthored with Walter Gudel and Cesar Jiminez.

In 1964–1965, Geoff spent a year in Vietnam with the Agency for International Development, investigating the rice marketing system of South Vietnam. Marketing of rice was mostly in the hands of Chinese, who were strongly criticized, partly because of their nationality. Geoff didn't argue for or against them. He simply plotted the Vietnamese monthly price of paddy (rice in the husk) against the wholesale price of milled rice divided by 64% (the average yield at milling). This showed that the operating margin was small, not excessive; it was, in fact, barely enough to cover freight and handling costs. This was Geoff's regular procedure—not to argue or advise, but simply to use a country's own data and let the facts speak for themselves. The report, *Rice Marketing and Price Policy in Vietnam: Problems and Alternative Solutions,* was to be published by the Ministry of Rural Affairs and the Ministry of National Economy. It was half set in print when the war intensified, and the work was abandoned in the ensuing events.

Next came three and one-half years (1965–1969) with the Iowa Universities Group project "Agricultural Development in Peru." Here he was assigned to CONAP, Peru's version of the U.S. Commodity Credit Corporation.

Geoff found, from Peruvian and U.N. Food and Agriculture Organization statistics, that Peru ranked among the lowest nations of the world in average per capita consumption of protein. People with low incomes, of course, consumed still less than the average. What Peru needed, therefore, was not more animal proteins such as meat, milk, and eggs, which people with low incomes could not buy, but inexpensive vegetable (soybean, for example) and fish flour proteins and programs to publicize them among the poor. The title of Geoff's first report reflects well his direct style: *Low Income People in Peru Need More Protein: Here Is How They Can Get It.*

Next, Peruvian farmers—like farmers everywhere—thought that the marketing margins were too wide. Geoff measured the margins and found that they reflected marketing costs more than profits. His report, *Are Marketing Margins for Fruits and Vegetables Too Wide?*, included Peruvian data showing that the number of wholesalers was so large that competition kept their margins low, but that the small number of processing firms were monopolistic. More current market news and grades were needed for the first group, other remedies for the second.

Price control for farm products was the subject of Geoff's next reports, *The Economic and Legal Aspects of Price Controls in Peruvian Agriculture* (with Dale Furnish, a lawyer) in 1967 and *How to Set Guaranteed Prices* in 1969. He also published *Price Policy for Milk in Peru* (with Lorenzo Sousa) and *Price Policy for Beef in Peru*, both in 1968, *Marketing and Price Policy for Beans in Peru* in 1969, and *Is More Storage Needed for Farm Products in Peru?* in 1969.

These reports were all translated into Spanish and mimeographed. His most valuable work may have been his verbal consultations with marketing officials and his training of Peruvian graduate students. Before Geoff left, he had helped establish a system of current market news. Altogether, it was a happy and successful tour of duty.

In Indonesia, in 1970–1971, he was part of a Weitz-Hettelsater team study to provide advice on setting the price of rice and on the location and type of rice drying and storage facilities. Their work took them to different parts of this beautiful country. The report, entitled *The Republic of Indonesia—Rice Storage, Handling, and Marketing Study,* was sponsored by U.S. AID.

In 1972–1973, he returned to Venezuela to work five months for CORPOANDES. This Venezuelan development agency wanted to develop an interior agricultural area around Basinas, but first it wanted to know whether the proposed project would flood the market. The report Geoff prepared, with plenty of local assistance, *Marketing Problems of the Alto Llano Occidental Development Project,* concluded that it would not.

His last assignment was with the government of Paraguay during 1974–1975. The increasing production of soybeans was leading to problems of price setting and storage location. Geoff used the government's own price data to show that what they needed was drying plants, exporting their soybeans rapidly instead of storing them, and replacing their annual price fixing by a system of daily or weekly current price reports. They started doing this before he left.

Teaching and Writing. Soon after his appointment at Iowa State in 1927, Geoff helped organize the beginning courses; Geoff taught marketing, Bill Murray (also doing his first teaching) taught farm management, and John Hopkins taught general economics. As a teacher, Geoff applied the same distinctive approach as in research and writing: start with problems, investigate solutions, and state the answers clearly. He described his pedagogical style in four rules:

(1) When you are teaching a class, start from where they, the students, are, not from where you are. Start with the students' problems and puzzlements, and then help them to find their solutions in your particular field of economics. (2) At the end of each class meeting, write on the board the assignment of readings for the next meeting. At the next meeting, do not begin by lecturing to them on the assignment; ask them what they learned from the assignment—not what they memorized, but what they learned. (3) Be specific. Ask them not what they learned in general, but what they learned in particular. Ask them about specifics—how the law of demand works, or the law of supply. And do not ask the class in general; ask Bill Smith, or Jane Brown. If they did not read the assignment and study it, that will become clear to the rest of the class, and they will not let that happen again. (4) Do not lecture the students. If there is some point in economics that they need to know but is not printed or available, include a mimeograph in your next assignment. Then they can study it and grasp it at their leisure.

When World War II ended, Iowa State was swamped with students, many subsidized by the GI bill. This included many graduate students. The staff was small, so Geoff began to find a number of graduate students assigned to him. He enjoyed working with them. Ultimately, more than sixty graduate students completed Ph.D. or M.S. degrees under his direction, many of whom have gone on to distinguished careers in academia, government, or business. His teaching assignments changed from earlier introductory marketing classes to graduate classes in agricultural price analysis and agricultural price policy.

By 1946 Geoff had finished his three major textbooks, *Marketing Farm Products, Agricultural Price Analysis,* and *Agricultural Price Policy.* Standards in their fields, they went through seven, five, and four editions, respectively, during the next thirty years. There have been translations into several languages, including Spanish, Japanese, and Polish.

The books and his 200 research papers and bulletins are a formidable body of written work. A study in 1953 shows that he was surpassed only by

John D. Black in total number of contributions printed in the *Journal of Farm Economics* from 1929 through 1953. Other prolific contributors of the time were T. W. Schultz, Walter W. Wilcox, and M. R. Benedict. In their variety, volume, and quality, Geoff's writings are truly outstanding among his generation of agricultural economists. Although he had little interest in political office or honors, the esteem in which he was held by his colleagues of the time is indicated by his election as first vice-president of the American Farm Economics Association in 1951.

Some Personal Notes. Geoff was married in 1931 to Eleanor Hawes Murray of Cedar Rapids, Iowa. She had been an editor in the State Department in Washington and has had ample opportunity to apply her talents to a succession of articles and indices, besides contributing her critical judgment to Geoff's writing style. In 1976, Geoff was elected a fellow of the American Agricultural Economics Association, and at the ceremony at Ohio State he brought down the house when he insisted that his "partner person," in the latest idiom, should be with him to receive the award.

Geoff and Eleanor's home at 3425 Oakland Street had been known to generations of graduate students. He is, in fact, a great builder of houses. The house at 3425 was built of cinder block, an innovation in 1937, and he followed it with a cottage built of native lumber in the Black Hills and a house overlooking the Caribbean on Bequia, a little-known island they discovered during their consulting years in South America. These enterprises have seemed to keep alive the homesteading spirit in Geoff, and he has enjoyed them immensely.

Apart from his professional work, Geoff's life has revolved very much about his family, and he has found great reward in his five children and ten grandchildren. His personal habits have always been modest to the point of abstemious; besides the daily walks across "little Siberia" to and from the office, he liked nothing better than an outing devoted to chopping wood with friends like George Snedecor, Ken Boulding, or Bill Murray (with a loose child or two roped in as well). He enjoyed tennis, and at one time fancied himself a mountain climber; this career lasted one year and two peaks, beginning in 1950 with an ascent of the Grand Teton and ending the following year with Mount Fuji during his visit to Japan. In matters spiritual, Geoff, raised a Baptist, has searched for what he terms an "empirical, objective basis" for religion. Unitarianism came the closest, and he served as president of the Ames Unitarian Fellowship and was the keynote speaker at a regional summer assembly in the 1950s. Among family and friends Geoff is a prolific reciter of verse, humorous and classical, much of it learned in his youth, and also has talents for sketching and for picking out chords on the piano; these personal qualities reflect his abiding sense of humor and an artistic sensitivity, part of his intuitive feel for things, and they have lightened his more sober approach to professional and intellectual problems.

Summing Up. Taken as a whole, Geoff's life work is instructive in several ways. It illuminates the growth of his field, as he and others shaped it during the turbulent 1930s and 1940s. Faced with such problems and pressures, he trusted in objective research, and he brought calm study to the subject at local, regional, and national levels.

He also displayed courage in treating issues of political importance. And when some policies proved intractable to economic light, he simply let his analysis stand and went sensibly on to other matters. In moving into foreign consulting, he brought the same practical skills that had clarified U.S. agricultural problems and policies. In the end, he showed that many economic issues are common to all countries.

The integrity of his work, tested in many settings, has been remarkable. So has been the warm personal support he has given his many students and colleagues. In these and other ways, he has been a model for scholars and friends in many fields.

I

On Values, Analysis,
and Policy

2

What Can a Research Man Say about Values

GEOFFREY S. SHEPHERD

RESEARCH MEN in economics continually run up against the problem of value judgments. Economists can show on an objective basis, using marginal analysis, what is the optimum allocation of productive resources—that is, the allocation that will maximize the production of the goods and services demanded by consumers, with a given distribution of income. They can show the same thing concerning the distribution of an individual's income, given his wants for the different goods and services. But economists generally take the position that they cannot show on an objective basis what is the optimum distribution of income among the individuals in a society, nor what is the best structure of wants for any individual.

The reasons given for this position are two in number: (1) Appraising the distribution of income among individuals requires interpersonal comparisons of utility, which cannot be made objectively. (2) The structure of wants for any individual depends upon his value judgments, which lie outside the field of economics.

Accordingly, economists find it difficult to determine objectively how far the nation should go along the road of economic efficiency, for example, if increasing efficiency decreases security, or how far social security should be carried if it reduces incentive, or—in agricultural economics—how far stabilization programs should go in reducing instability.

This exclusion of economic science from problems involving value judgments is not merely an academic matter. Billion dollar programs depend

This paper first appeared as Journal Paper No. J-2810 of the Iowa Agricultural Experiment Station, Ames, Iowa, Project No. 1241. It is reprinted here with slight modification from the *Journal of Farm Economics,* vol. 38, 1956, pp. 8–16. The author is indebted to his colleagues John Nordin and Earl Heady for constructive comments.

upon these judgments, and millions of jobs—sometimes including the job of the research man himself. But most economists maintain that science can say nothing about value judgments. I have some questions to raise about this position. That is the purpose of the present paper.

Orthodox Position. First, we may state the generally accepted orthodox position of most scientists concerning values. Here perhaps are the clearest and strongest statements of this position (Robbins 1940):

> Economics is the science which studies human behavior as a relationship between ends and scarce means which have alternative uses (p. 16).

> The economist is not concerned with ends as such. He is concerned with the way in which the attainment of ends is limited. The ends may be noble or they may be base (p. 25).

> Economics cannot pronounce on the validity of ultimate judgments of value (p. 145).

> Economics deals with ascertainable facts; ethics with valuations and obligations. The two fields of inquiry are not on the same plane of discourse (pp. 97–98).

Many scientists in other fields hold similar views. "Scientific positivists" express their views somewhat as follows:

> Scientific method reports what is, not what ought to be; it can discover social pressure, but not moral obligations; it verifies statements about the desired, and the most efficient means for securing it, not about the desirable in any further sense [Murphy 1943, p. 145].

> Reason . . . can tell us whether our estimates of value are logically consistent, and inform us concerning the causal means best suited to further the ends we have in view. The means are properly judged as good, however, only if the ends are good, and on this point "reason" has no jurisdiction, for "ultimate ends recommend themselves solely to the affections," or, as a more modern version of the same doctrine would say, to the primary "drives" which determine what the organism desires and on what conditions it can be satisfied. And since the means derive their goodness only from the end they serve, we can see why Hume should conclude that, in the field of morals, "reason is and ought to be the slave of the passions" [Murphy 1943, pp. 97–98].

Another statement agrees with this:

> Though knowledge is undeniably power, the moral ends for which that power is used cannot be determined by the science of human relations any more than they can be by natural science [Ridenour 1948, pp. 354–55].

And still another:

> The sense of value that is the basis of choice and freedom lies in a realm that science does not touch . . . freedom in its most essential sense is something of the spirit, and . . . this something of the spirit is beyond the realm of Science [Compton 1952, pp. 5, 10].

That is to say, according to the orthodox view, science can appraise means, but not ends. It cannot make value judgments. For instance, it cannot objectively put a higher value on freedom than on security, or vice versa; that is up to the individual. Science cannot help us to make ethical judgments. Science can tell us how to get to where we want to go, but it cannot tell us whether we ought to want to go there in the first place. It cannot say: this is good, and this is bad. Science says: if you don't like spinach, that's all there is to it. *De gustibus non disputandem est.*

Science and Ethics. The preceding section is full of words like "ends," "values," "good," "should," and "ought." These concepts lie in the field of ethics. "Ethics . . . is not concerned mainly with bare facts but with values . . . not with the actual character of human conduct but with its ideal, not so much with what human conduct is as with what it ought to be."[1]

The student of this field of ethics soon finds that science has a good deal to say about what ethics is, even if science cannot help us make ethical judgments.

Cultural anthropologists tell us that ethics is not something that is already in existence and waits merely to be discovered, like Pluto, or the laws of gravitation, or America in 1492. It is not something that was here before we came, and will be here long after we have gone, like the earth under our feet. Ethics is rather something that we build up as we go along. Ethics is what we want it to be. It is not objective; it is subjective.

These scientists point out that revelation, religion, conscience, superstition, magic, or authority based on any of these, is not a solid basis for ethics. They say that the real basis of ethics is deep-seated human longings and aspirations. This is the only basis that stands up under the test of rational thought. The best system of ethics is the one that most fully satisfies these human longings and aspirations over the long run. "Good" is that which satisfies human wants. "Right" is that which promotes their satisfaction; "wrong" is that which hinders it. We "ought" to do that which will most fully satisfy human wants.

Most deep-seated human wants are common to all men, but many—monogamy, for example, or polygamy, or polyandry, or top hats—are determined by the culture in which men live. Our culture endorses monogamy; one of the books in our college library is entitled *Isn't One Wife Enough?* (the author, surprisingly, is a Young). But some Tibetans think it selfish for one husband to have a wife all to himself. The Arapech, on the other hand, consider it noble and self-sacrificing to have three wives each (Mead 1955, p. 57). I am informed that the natives in one part of Africa used to fish naked. The missionaries were horrified and got the natives to wear clothes; and what happened? The natives caught cold in their wet clothes, and many died. Their original system of ethics was better for them than ours.

Ethics, therefore, is not something that is absolute, eternal; ethics is relative to our culture, relative to our time and place. It differs from culture to culture at any one time, and it differs from time to time in any one culture. There is no absolute standard of right and wrong.

> The diversity in moral standards is so great that no man could act rightly according to any specific moral code that has ever gained wide acceptance without offending against some of the precepts of other codes which are felt to be no less binding for those who accept them. Hence, in this sense what is right for one is wrong for the other, and there is no common standard acknowledged by both, in terms of which this difference can be adjudicated [Murphy 1943, pp. 154–56; see also Benedict 1934].

There is no evidence, either, that the universe, or man, is teleological in nature, driving or being driven purposively toward a predetermined end—to "one far-off divine event, to which the whole creation moves" (Simpson 1949).

These pronouncements about ethics are based on empirical data, subjected to scientific scrutiny. But when we ask scientists if they can help to build the subjective, relative, want-satisfying system of ethics that they have prescribed, they retreat into their orthodox bomb shelter. Science, they say, cannot deal with ethical problems at all. Ethics, as the *Encyclopaedia Britannica* says in the quotation given earlier, deals "not so much with what human conduct is as with what it ought to be." It deals with the morally right and wrong. And scientists tell us that these matters lie outside the field of science.

They agree that the basis of ethics is human wants. But they bow themselves out of the field of wants, on these grounds: I want sugar in my coffee; you don't; and he doesn't want coffee at all. Now, they say science shouldn't attempt to say that I or you or he should want sugar or no sugar or no coffee at all. Look what happened to Prohibition: science showed that alcohol is injurious, but Prohibition had to be repealed because people didn't want it.

Nobody in this democratic United States, they say, would want a scientist dictator to tell us that we've got to have Prohibition whether we want it or not. If a man wants something, no amount of reason will convince him that he ought to want something else. Wants are basic. Reason is and ought to be the slave of the passions. Science can say nothing about wants, and therefore it can say nothing about ethics, which is based on wants.

Obsolescence of Philosophical Concepts. It seems to me that this is all wrong.

We as scientists *can* deal with ethical problems if we examine our ethical concepts, most of which were developed in a prescientific age, and bring them up to date.

In earlier times, men appealed to revelation, or divine authority, or both, or to some assured "categorical imperative" conjured out of air. But in an age of science, men are learning to build their systems of ethics on more solid, testable, pragmatic grounds.

In this endeavor we are hampered even in our own thinking by the normal cultural lag in the use of words and concepts. Our concepts are lagging behind our progress.[2]

Ethics used to be thought of as a set of rules of behavior, existing in nature independently of mankind, as it were, like the moon. And there was presumed to be some obligation upon each individual to measure up to these rules of behavior. Men ought to be ethical. Why? Because it was right to do so, and men ought to do right.

This appeal to some external ethical code and an assumed obligation to live up to it may have been useful in early times, but it has outlived its usefulness today. In our present age of science, there is less inclination to accept any code handed down by revelation or authority and more inclination to test any code by operational criteria and build it up on a pragmatic basis. We ask: Why ought we to do this or that? How do we know what we ought to do? How do we know what is good and bad? What does good and bad mean in an age of science? What obligations do we have? What does obligation mean today? What is a pragmatic basis for ethics?

The answers to questions of this type are plain: In an age of science, "good" means good to satisfy human wants. "Bad" means the opposite. And "ought" is a term that is no longer quite relevant. There is less inclination now for men to exhort each other that they ought to do this or that. The United States now does not rely on a moral obligation for each citizen to be patriotic and bear arms for his country. Instead, Congress considers the country's military needs and pays men well enough to induce them to go into the army or navy or air force voluntarily—not under any moral compulsion, but just as they would into any other paying job. Beyond that, in time of hot or cold war, men are not urged to volunteer; they are drafted, in sufficient numbers to swell the voluntary army to an adequate size to meet the emergency.

Similarly in the field of public welfare. The term *noblesse oblige* used to be employed to refer to the obligation of the rich to take care of the poor. But the term is no longer used in today's democratic society. Instead, taxes are levied. These taxes are mostly progressive, not on moral grounds, but on such economic grounds as ability to pay. The country does not rely on a general belief that a man ought to pay his taxes; it relies on the police power of the state. Moral obligation based on religious authority is replaced by legal compulsion based on pragmatic grounds.

Values Lie in the Realm of Science. We saw earlier that the basis of ethics is the fullest satisfaction of deep-seated human wants. When ethics is freed from its ancient aura of the supernatural, all there is left is fundamental human wants—and that is enough. That is all there is to go on, and that is all there needs to be.

But these wants are not sacred, immutable, and unconditional, as the orthodox scientific view holds. For many wants conflict, and they cannot all be satisfied in full measure. If a man wanted only one thing, unconditionally, there would be no place for the use of reason. Reason would then indeed be the slave of the passions—or more accurately, the slave of the one overriding passion. But it is obvious that a man wants many things, and that some of these wants conflict. They cannot all be satisfied in full measure. The degree of satisfaction of each has to be determined by the use of reason, on some such grounds as the equivalence of marginal satisfaction.

Ethical Values are Built Up. A profound philosopher, a lifelong student and teacher in the field of comparative religion, concludes that "there are no peculiarly religious values" (Haydon 1929, p. xii).[3] In that same sense we may say that there are no peculiarly ethical values. That is, there are no values handed down to us from above. There are only values that we build from the ground up, out of our lives and cultures. And in this building up, science has an important and indeed essential part to play.

In this context, a research man does not attempt to say that another person or group of persons ought to do this or that; he only says that if the person or group does this or that, such and such will happen. He leaves the person or group free to choose among these consequences according to his values.

These values, however, are not sacred or immutable. They are subject to the same sort of analysis as means. If a person values freedom more highly than security, the scientist does not say that he ought or ought not to do so. The scientist merely points out the consequence of that value judgment. Freedom beyond a certain point means anarchy; security beyond a certain point retards progress. If a person then says, "But still I like to go through stoplights," the scientist does not say, "That is your value judgment, and science can say nothing about it." Instead, he attempts to educate the man to change his values, pointing out that the man's actions will result in damage to other cars and persons; and if that does not change the man's values and his actions, the judge takes away his license in an attempt to stop his driving altogether. If that does not do the job, the judge puts him in jail.

This can be put into more rigorous terms, using the concepts of production-possibility curves and indifference curves, along with the concepts of means and ends. My good colleague and friend, Earl Heady, has done this recently in a diagram that measures profits up the vertical axis and nonmarket goods along the horizontal.[4] He points out that farm management education can help a farmer shift his production-possibility curve upward; sociological education can help a farmer shift it to the right. Either of these shifts can put the farmer on a higher indifference curve but neither of them affects the indifference curves themselves.

I believe now that research men can go one step further.

To my mind, research men not only can appraise (in the sense of "show the consequences of") the means (the production techniques the farmer is using) and show how the adoption of new techniques would move the farmer's production-possibility curve up where it would be tangent to a higher indifference curve, but can also do the same sort of thing for the ends—that is, for the values that determine the position of the indifference curves. Research men can show a farmer how he can adopt different values and change indifference curves.

Let us take a simple example. The farmer may like to get in his car and go roaring down the road at 100 miles per hour. But education teaches him what damage that is likely to do to the machine, to others, and to himself; he soon learns to change his values (which determine the position of his indifference curves) accordingly. He changes his own set of values himself. He makes the change as the result of educational activities. He is free to retain his old values; but if he does so, he will not remain free (in another sense) for long. He may lose his driver's license or land in jail, or in the hospital, or under the sod.

Or consider the farmer's wife. Perhaps she is one of those people who just loves to eat. Do nutritionists then say, "That is her value system, and science can say nothing about it, and furthermore science should not try to do anything about it"? They do not. They bombard her with nutritional and health education about the consequences of obesity—its shortening effect on life, for example—in a strong effort to get her to change her values (Swanson et al. 1955, pp. 18–22). The wife who loves to eat, who values eating highly, learns to value eating less highly.

Or, to come right down to agricultural price policy, we observe that farmers want price stability, but we do not conclude that, since that is their value judgment, economic science can say nothing about it. We observe that farmers want freedom and progress as well as price stability, but we do not conclude that since those are value judgments too, economic science can say nothing about how those conflicting values can be reconciled. Instead, economists and statisticians get together and construct parity indexes and compute parity prices that move up and down with inflation and deflation. And when the bases for those parity prices become obsolete, research men cudgel their brains and come up with modernized parity. Still later they come up with flexible price supports, pointing out that these provide a workable measure of stability and freedom and progress too.

Research Men Can Appraise Ends as Well as Means. I think one can safely say that the ultimate end of all research and education is to change the student's reactions, indifference curves, and values from those of a primitive savage to those of a civilized man and to give him the training that will enable him to attain those values as fully as his intelligence and the level of technology permit.

But in a democracy, scientists do not try to impose their system of values on their audience. A dictator does. A dictator makes up his mind what he wants and imposes what he wants on the people. A religious man tells people what they ought to do, in the light of some eternal moral principle from on high, as a compulsion or obligation imposed upon people from above that they ought to obey. But research men and educators in a democracy help people make up their own minds and change their own values, in the light of scientific information concerning the consequences of alternative value judgments and of the training in objective evaluation that science provides.

Research men, then, far from having nothing to say about values and morals and ethics, have a great deal to say about them. They can help people appraise ends—appraise in the sense of "show the consequences of"—just as well as they can help them appraise means. They are doing it every day. Wants and desires furnish the drives to action, but science and reason test these drives and modify and channel them into systems of behavior that enable men more fully to satisfy those desires under conditions of civilization. Science and reason are hampered by tradition handed down from earlier times, hindered by emotionalism and retarded by ignorance; but they are the solid basis for values. One of the legitimate purposes of research and education is to show the consequences of alternative value judgments, as well as of means, and thus help people to change their values in directions that will enable them more fully to satisfy their wants.

Footnotes

1. *Encyclopaedia Britannica,* "Ethics."
2. "Ethical theory began among the Greeks as an attempt to find a regulation for the conduct of life which should have a rational basis and purpose instead of being derived from custom. But

reason as a substitute for custom was under the obligation of supplying objects and laws as fixed as those of custom had been. Ethical theory ever since has been singularly hypnotized by the notion that its business is to discover some final end or good or some ultimate and supreme law. . . . It long seemed as if rational assurance and demonstration could be attained only if we began with universal conceptions and subsumed particular cases under them. . . .

"Two ethical consequences of great moment should be remarked. The belief in fixed values has bred a division of ends into intrinsic and instrumental [or in current terminology, into ends and means] of those that are really worth while in themselves and those that are of importance only as means to intrinsic goods. Indeed, it is often thought to be the very beginning of wisdom, or moral discrimination, to make this distinction. Dialectically, the distinction is interesting and seems harmless. But carried into practice it has an import that is tragic. . . . No one can possibly estimate how much of the obnoxious materialism and brutality of our economic life is due to the fact that economic ends have been regarded as *merely* instrumental. When they are recognized to be as intrinsic and final in their place as any others, then it will be seen that they are capable of idealization, and that if life is to be worth while, they must acquire ideal and intrinsic value. Esthetic, religious, and other 'ideal' ends are now thin and meagre or else idle and luxurious because of the separation from 'instrumental' or economic ends. Only in connection with the latter can they be woven into the texture of daily life and made substantial and pervasive. The vanity and irresponsibility of values that are merely final and not also in turn means to the enrichment of other occupations of life ought to be obvious. . . .

"The other generic change lies in doing away once and for all with the traditional distinction between moral goods, like the virtues, and natural goods like health, economic security, art, science, and the like. . . . Inquiry, discovery take the same place in morals that they have come to occupy in sciences of nature. Validation, demonstration became experimental, a matter of consequences" (Dewey 1920, pp. 161, 166, 170, 171, 172, 174).

3. Mr. Haydon was head of the Department of Comparative Religion at the University of Chicago.

4. Earl O. Heady, *Fundamental Economic Framework for Farm and Home Planning Programs,* February 17, 1955, dittoed.

References

Benedict, R. 1934. *Patterns of Culture.* New York: Houghton Mifflin.

Compton, A. H. 1952. "Science and Human Freedom." In *Symposium on Human Freedoms.* Cedar Rapids, Iowa: Coe College.

Dewey, J. 1920. *Reconstruction in Philosophy.* New York: Holt.

Haydon, E. 1929. *The Quest of the Ages.* New York: Harper.

Mead, M. 1955. "What Is Human Nature?" *Look,* April 19, p. 57.

Murphy, A. E. 1943. *The Uses of Reason.* New York: Macmillan.

Ridenour, L. 1948. "The Natural Sciences and Human Relations." *Proceedings of the American Philosophical Society* 92(5):354-55.

Robbins, L. 1940. *The Nature and Significance of Economic Science.* New York: Macmillan.

Simpson, G. 1949. *The Meaning of Evolution: A Study of the History of Life and of Its Significance for Man.* New Haven: Yale University Press.

Swanson, P., E. Willis, and P. Mairs 1955. "Overweight—A Problem among Iowa Women." *Iowa Farm Science* 9 (11):18-20.

3

What Can a Research Man Do in Agricultural Price Policy?

GEOFFREY S. SHEPHERD

WHAT ARE THE OBJECTIVES of price policy research, and how can research in this field be conducted most effectively?

This is an important question. Billions of dollars are involved in agricultural price programs, and the subject is so explosive that more than one state experiment station director has refused to handle it, on the grounds that it might incinerate him.

It seems to me that the objectives and procedures involved in agriculture price policy research can be most clearly set forth by comparing them with the objectives and procedures in a related field, agricultural price analysis.

The objective of research in the field of price analysis is comparatively simple. Research in price analysis deals with the kind of question a child might ask about a bug—what makes it move? The objective in price analysis is to explain why prices move; it is to ascertain the factors that *cause* price variations and to measure in quantitative terms the relations between these factors and the variations in prices. A further objective in some cases may be to ascertain and measure the *effects* of these price changes on income, production, consumption, etc.[1] The procedures usually applied are simple and multiple graphic and mathematical correlation, simultaneous equations, etc., guided by economic theory and a knowledge of the characteristics of the commodities whose prices are being analyzed.

This paper first appeared as Journal Paper No. J-2707 of the Iowa Agricultural Experiment Station, Ames, Iowa, Project No. 1241. It is reprinted here with slight modification from the *Journal of Farm Economics,* vol. 37, May 1955, pp. 305–13. The author is indebted to his colleagues John Nordin and Earl Heady for constructive critical comments.

Objective of Research in Agricultural Price Policy. Many would say that the objective of research in agricultural price policy is much the same as the objective of research in price analysis. They would say that the objective of agricultural price policy is simply to measure the effects of specific price programs that have been set up to implement specific price policies. This objective is implicit in the titles of two major publications in the field of agricultural price policy that have appeared in recent years (Johnson 1952; Gray et al. 1954). On the face of it, this objective is merely a specialized branch or extension of the "further objective" of price analysis given in the preceding section (to measure the effects of prices on income distribution, production, consumption, etc.) to the measurement of the effects of a price *program* on these things.

But inspection reveals the fact that in the two publications cited, the authors go further than the titles alone imply. One of the later sections in Johnson's bulletin is headed "Evaluation of Existing Control Programs Must Be Based on Beliefs and Convictions," another is headed "Various Beliefs Which Have Determined How Programs Were Operated and Benefits Distributed," and yet another is headed "Present Program Could Be Modified to Eliminate Certain Administrative Difficulties, Pass Gains in Efficiency on to Consumers and Retain Stability Features." Thus the study goes on to consider evaluation and modifications of the program. Similarly one of the later sections of Gray et al. is headed "Appraisal of Market Restrictions as a Method of Increasing Producers' Incomes," and another, "Policy Proposal." Most of the books on agricultural price policy similarly include appraisals and new proposals. Some authors have gotten into trouble by recommending programs that differed from the programs advocated by farm organizations in their states.[2] This is the sort of thing that gives experiment station directors the willies and keeps the USDA out of agricultural price policy research entirely.

On the basis of some experience and observation in the field, I believe that the best solution of this problem is not merely to try to "keep out of trouble" by keeping out of appraisals and proposals, but rather to do the job, including appraisals and proposals, in the light of a clarification of the objectives and procedures in price policy research such as that attempted below. I do not offer this as a means for pussyfooting—quite the contrary. I offer it as a means for doing the job in good objective scientific style, so that nobody has to do any pussyfooting.

Objectives and Procedures. A suggested set of objectives and procedures for effective price policy research is outlined below.

1. *Outline the Price Problem.* The first step in price policy research is to start out with a statement of the "problematic situation"—the variability of

prices or income, the level of prices or income, or whatever it may have been—that caused the particular price policy to be developed in the first place. This step is comparatively simple.

2. *Ascertain the Objectives of the Price Policy.* The next step is to ascertain what the objectives of the price policy are. This does not mean stating what the research man thinks the objectives should have been or should be now. It means stating what the framers of the policy had in mind, entirely independent of what the research man thinks they should have had in mind, and entirely independent of what the research man thinks the objectives should have been.

This distinction between the objectives in the minds of those who framed the price policy and the objectives in the mind of the research worker is not always clearly recognized by the research worker himself. It was not clearly recognized by the North Central Regional Research Committee on agricultural price policy in 1953 when they were asked to appraise the "Summaries and Suggestions Received" by the secretary of agriculture on agricultural price policy. Some of the members were not sure whether their job as research members included appraising price policy. Those who were willing to appraise price policy agreed that before they could proceed to appraise, they needed a statement of the objectives of the price policy, so that they could measure performance against intention. Accordingly, they drew up a statement of the objectives of agricultural price policy and promptly fell into disagreement about it. They disagreed over the goals of price policy, and they disagreed over the question of whether or not agricultural economists should be making statements as to objectives in the first place.

Here is part of the statement of objectives that was drawn up at that time:

> We believe that it is essential that a statement of basic objectives precede and condition the selection of programs and methods to be used in implementing agricultural policy.
> Furthermore, the programs selected should be appropriate to these objectives and consistent with more general economic policies of the government, such as monetary and fiscal policy and foreign trade policy.
> Our price policy should be such as not to destroy nor seriously interfere with the functions of prices as means of directing production and consumption. It should enhance the effectiveness of prices in performing these functions.

It seems clear to me now, although it was not clear then, that we were arguing about the wrong set of objectives. We were arguing about *our* objectives for agricultural price policy—what we thought the objectives should be—when what we should have been doing at that stage was to argue about what the objectives were in the minds of those who framed the policy and set up programs to carry it out. When we appraise a plow, we do not condemn it because it cannot fly. We appraise it with reference to how it does the job it was designed to do, to turn over the sod and bury the trash. If we find that burying the trash leaves fields susceptible to soil blowing, we would not condemn the plow. We would instead point out to farmers that if they want to retard soil blowing—if that is their objective (note: not if that is *our* objective)—then a one-way is a better implement for them than a plow. If they do not want to retard soil blowing, or if their soil does not blow in the first place, then the plow is the best implement. But the decision depends on the farmers' objectives, not on ours.

It is not easy in all cases to determine just what the objectives were in the minds of those who framed a price policy. Even when public statements were made when the policy was set, those statements are not always clear nor always free of playing to the gallery. Henry Wallace's statement of the purposes of the CCC in 1936 is clearer than most:

> By the ever-normal granary I mean a definite system whereby supplies following years of drought or other great calamity would be large enough to take care of the consumer, but under which the farmer would not be unduly penalized in years of favorable weather. During the past seven years, weather, prices, and supplies have swung so violently from one extreme to the other that it is time for all thoughtful men and women, whether living on the farm or in town, to consider what action may be taken to promote greater stability [Wallace 1936].

This statement was followed a few years later by a more specific pronouncement. It referred to the three "fundamental functions of the CCC [Commodity Credit Corporation] loan program: namely, to protect and increase farm prices, to stabilize farm prices, and to assure adequate supplies of farm products."[3] The hearings that are usually conducted before legislation is passed, and occasionally the statement of the objective in the law itself, are sometimes useful. An economic historian may provide useful interpretations.

In some cases, the objectives that are stated are not the real or primary objectives. The stated objectives of the original ever-normal granary were the stabilization of supplies and prices. There is good reason, however, to believe that the primary objective was rather to raise farm prices and thus increase farm income—to "stabilize them upward." But there would be opposition from consumers to this objective, whereas everybody is in favor of stabilization. Not until 1940 was the price-raising objective spelled out loud in the CCC quotation given above. In cases like this, the original statement alone does not tell the whole story. Judgment is needed here to determine what the objective really was. But it is the research man's judgment about what people had in mind, not his judgment about what he believes the objectives ought to be.

3. *Compare Performance with Objectives.* After the original objectives are set forth, the next job is to measure the effects of the program and compare them with the objectives. This is a big job, and a complicated one. Its purpose is to show whether the programs attained their objectives, and at what

cost. Did the corn loan program stabilize corn supplies and prices, and livestock production and prices? If so, to what degree, and at what cost? This is strictly a job of statistical measurement.

4. *Estimate the Effects of Modifications of the Program.* The next step is more difficult. It is to estimate not what the effects of the programs were, but what the effects of specified modifications of the programs, or even entirely different programs, *would have been* if they had been put into effect. What would have happened if the CCC had used more flexible loan rates? If it had used outright purchases and sales, instead of loans? If it had done this or that other thing? This step could also include projecting estimates of this sort into the future.

5. *Estimate the Effects of Alternate Policy Objectives.* The final step is to estimate what the effects of specified alternative *policies* would have been, and would be in the future. What would have happened if different policy objectives had been adopted—if stabilization about world price levels rather than about parity levels had been the goal, or if raising the longtime level of prices, or of income, to meet monopoly in other parts of the economy had been chosen?

This is the most difficult step of all, and the one that has been most likely to get the investigator into political trouble. It seems to me, however, that the investigator does not need to stay out of this sort of work on that account, nor does he need to get into political difficulties when he goes in.

What he does need to do is to handle this job as scientists handle all their scientific jobs, as scientists, not as salesmen.

It is not our job as agricultural economists to say what the objectives of agricultural price policy *should be*. It is not our job to set up *our* objectives of agricultural price policy. It is not our job to say that we think that the objective of agricultural price policy ought to be high rigid prices or low flexible prices or some other prices.

When I hire a heating engineer, I do not hire him to tell me what kind of heating system he thinks I ought to have. I hire him to tell me the various features and costs of different heating systems, so that I can make up my own mind according to whether or not I have cold feet or sensitive ears or a large or small pocketbook.

As agricultural economists, as scientists in a democracy, our job is not to tell people what we think they ought to do. A physicist does not tell us we ought to use uranium 235 to cause an explosion. He tells us that if we use that element under very special conditions we will cause an explosion; if we use something else, we will get some other result. Then he leaves it up to the military, and ultimately to the people of the United States, to decide what result we want.

Similarly, as agricultural economists our job is to show impartially what the effects of high rigid prices would be and what the effects of low flexible prices would be. If the voters decide that they want the one, it is not for us to say that they should want the other.

They may be wrong. If so, our job is not to try to convince them that our views are correct as such. Our job is to educate them in the true sense of the word (not in the propaganda sense) until they see the economics of the matter more clearly and make the correct judgment themselves. They do not want our opinions as to what they ought to do. They want our technical estimate of what will happen if they do this, and what will happen if they do that.

Thus when farmers ask us at the end of a discussion meeting, "What do you think? Are we barking up the wrong tree in trying to get parity prices?" they do not really want to know what we think. And we do not reply that we think this or that. For when farmers ask a nutritionist what he thinks about antibiotics, they do not really want to know what he thinks. They are not interested in his mental processes. Instead, they want to know what the facts are —what effects antibiotics would have on their livestock. The nutritionist does not tell them what he thinks. Like any scientist, he takes himself out of the picture. He simply tells farmers what facts his experiments have revealed and leaves them to make up their own minds about whether or not to use antibiotics, in light of the facts, not in the light of his opinions.

Similarly, we do not reply to farmers that we think this or that about parity prices. We ask them, "What is it you want to accomplish? What is the goal you want to reach?" and we show in as factual a manner as our analyses and data permit what will happen under parity prices or some other prices implemented by loans or other means. We show them how effective the means are for attaining the ends they seek.

A More Productive Approach in Price Policy Research. What is involved here, I believe, is nothing less than the whole fundamental approach to economic analysis.

One approach is well represented in the recent writings of two of my good colleagues: "We economists are almost all honest men; we are all sincere in our quest for roughly the same goals (adequate production, decent farm income, and maximum possible individual freedom); why then do we arrive at such widely different recommendations? A main reason is that we start with completely different assumptions as to the nature of man and society. So we inevitably arrive at different 'answers' " (Mitchell 1953, p. 21).

That is to say: In economics, the answers you arrive at depend upon the assumptions you start out with. Different economists—different answers.

This bothers me. If it were true, it would raise a question of whether economics is a science or not. For one of the characteristics of a science is that the answers depend on the facts, not on the investigator's beliefs. Different investigators get the same answer.

Another colleague (Schickele 1952) starts out to deal with land tenure problems by outlining what he calls two different theories of land tenure, the "family farm theory of tenure" and the "farm business theory of tenure." These two theories place different emphasis upon various aspects of farm tenure and lead to conflicting conclusions with respect to certain specific tenure conditions.

He presents these two theories in turn, starting out in both cases with the same paragraph: "This theory consists of the following general propositions. The welfare of the nation and of the rural community is best served if:"

Then come the general propositions. Under the family farm theory, these propositions are, for instance: "[Welfare is best served if] farmers own and operate their farms as independent entrepreneurs. Farm units are not larger than the farmer and his family can operate without depending upon a substantial year-round hired labor force."

These general propositions contrast with those that make up the farm business theory of tenure: "[Welfare is best served if] free market forces are allowed to determine the tenure status, size of farm, and family income for each farmer.

Schickele points out the essential difference between the two theories. The family farm theory stresses the distributive equity, social status, and security aspects of community welfare, while the farm business theory emphasizes the production efficiency aspects of economic welfare.

Up to this point, one might merely raise a question concerning Schickele's use of the word "theory." A theory is an explanation of phenomena, confirmed by factual evidence. What Schickele calls theories, Mitchell calls assumptions; I would call them preconceptions. Schickele then goes on to say that a scientist regards any theoretical proposition as a hypothesis constantly subject to test for verification, modification, or abandonment. But then he adds:

> But the ideologies out of which theories are conceived are not amenable to such empirical testing. They are believed or disbelieved. A theory can only be tested in terms of its own conceptual structure. . . . Beliefs cannot be verified objectively. . . . The empirical outcome of the struggle between conflicting beliefs is determined primarily by the sociopolitical order of society, by the relative power positions of the respective groups. Whether actual events in American agriculture will move in the direction of the family farm or the farm business tenure theory will depend largely upon the relative power of the two groups holding these conflicting beliefs, in the formulation of public policy affecting tenure.

Willard Cochrane supports Schickele's approach. He says flatly:

> All research is conducted on premises. . . . I agree with Clyde that you cannot test preconceptions or assumptions and different analyses and con-

clusions. Premises, preconceptions or assumptions take two forms: (A) beliefs about the facts; and (B) beliefs about justice, equity or what is good. You can't test (B) and you assume (A) for the reason that given the present state of knowledge you can't know (A).[4]

These things are said in all honesty of conviction, but they seem to me to divert intellectual inquiry into a blind alley.

Philosophers have a name for this approach. They call it rationalism. It does not have a very high rating among scientists and philosophers.

> The fourth unacceptable way of seeking knowledge [the other three were revelation, authority, and intuition] is that of traditional rationalism, which, basing itself at the start on certain fundamental and mathematical or logical assumptions, builds up from them through rigorous deduction a closely interrelated complex of ideas into a coherent whole. Rationalism . . . has grave shortcomings in that it submits neither the original propositions, which may be selected through intuition, nor the final conclusions, to experimental verification [Lamont 1949].

It seems to me that this traditional rationalism approach is completely unscientific. It is more likely to end up in disaster than in any addition to scientific knowledge. If I start from an assumption that there is no such thing as gravity, and step out of my window, I will soon learn the folly of that approach. Is it not better for scientists to start with observed facts, such as that most objects fall to the ground, and go on from there to measure the rate of all and to discover the reasons why some objects do not fall—unbiased by any assumptions to predetermine their answers?

Start with a Problem, Not with an Univerifiable Belief. Instead of starting from assumptions—as Mitchell does, as Schickele does when he starts from beliefs that cannot be verified objectively, and as the ancient astronomers did when they said, "Seven is a major number, so there must be seven planets"—is it not more scientific to start without any propositions about the planets and simply to count them?

Rather than say that "beliefs cannot be verified objectively," I would say the opposite. Myrdal (1944, p. 1027) states unequivocally, "A person's beliefs . . . can be objectively judged to be true or false and more or less complete." I would say that the essence of scientific inquiry is to test (verify or disprove) beliefs.[5] Galileo did not say: "Everybody believes that the earth is fixed and that the sun revolves around it. Beliefs cannot be verified or disproved objectively. I can only observe objectively what beliefs are held by what groups and leave the motion of the earth to be decided by the relative power of the different groups." He proceeded instead to construct hypotheses and test them without regard as to whether they were generally believed or not. It is true that when he published his conclusions, which conflicted with popular beliefs at the time, he got into trouble. But his views were scientifically correct, and eventually they changed popular beliefs.

The approach outlined in Schickele's paper starts from the wrong point of departure. It makes me feel like the Kentucky mountaineer, trying to tell a passing stranger how to get to Smithville, and ending up finally by saying, "If I wanted to get to Smithville, I wouldn't start from here."

Research on any subject, it seems to me, should begin, not with un- provable premises or assumptions or propositions, but with a problem. Then it should set up alternative hypotheses (tentative solutions to the problem) and proceed to get the data that will test the hypotheses.

> Thinking begins in what may fairly enough be called a "forked-road" situation, a situation which is ambiguous, which presents a dilemma, which proposes alternatives [Dewey 1910, p. 11; 1949, pp. 107-8].

> Thinking begins not with premises, but with difficulties; and it con- cludes not with a certainty but with an hypothesis that can be made "true" only by the pragmatic sanction of experiment . . . our social ills are to be handled no longer with majestic abstractions like individualism and socialism, competition and cooperation, dictatorship and democracy, but with restricted inquiries, specific analysis, careful formulation, patient ex- perimentation, and piecemeal renovation [John Dewey 1946, p. 297].

Thus, research in land tenure should start out, not with propositions that welfare is or is not best served by family-sized farms, but with specific and limited problems, such as: What is the most efficient (lowest cost) size of what farm, livestock farm, etc.? (the answer would be different for each commodity and for each major climatic division). And what are the sociological benefits of family-sized farms and of different forms of land tenure?

Similarly, research in agricultural price policy would not start out with a proposition that welfare is or is not best served by free market prices, but with an inquiry into the different results of different programs and policies. When these results have been determined and presented as clearly as possible, the voters can judge intelligently how much of each end (efficiency, security, etc.) they want, according to their systems of values.

Notes

1. This is what is done for example in Fox (1951, pp. 65–81).
2. A recent example is Clyde Mitchell's run-in with the leading farm organization in Nebraska, reported on the editorial page of the *Des Moines Register,* October 4, 1954.
3. *Report of the President of the Commodity Credit Corporation,* 1940, p. 4.
4. Letter to the author, October 21, 1954.
5. "A legitimate task of education is to attempt to correct popular beliefs by subjecting them to rigorous examination in the light of the factual evidence" (Myrdal 1944, p. 1031).

References

Dewey, J. 1910. *How We Think*. Boston: D. C. Heath.

_____. 1949. *The Theory of Inquiry*. New York: Holt.

"Dewey, John." 1946. In *Encyclopaedia Britannica,* vol. 7, p. 297. Chicago: Encyclopaedia Britannica, Inc.

Fox, K. 1951. "Factors Affecting Farm Income, Farm Prices, and Food Consumption." *Agricultural Economics Research* 3 (3): 65–81.

Gray, R. W., V. L. Sorenson, and W. W. Cochrane. 1954. *An Economic Analysis of the Impact of Government Programs on the Potato Industry of the United States.* Minnesota Agricultural Experiment Station Technical Bulletin 211, June; North Central Regional Publication No. 42.

Johnson, G. L. 1952. *Burley Tobacco Control Programs.* Kentucky Agricultural Experiment Station Bulletin 580, February.

Lamont, C. 1949. *Humanism as a Philosophy.* New York: Philosophical Library, Inc.

Mitchell, C. C. 1953. "Parity Price Supports and Controlled Inflation." *Farm Policy Forum,* June.

Myrdal, G. 1944. *An American Dilemma.* New York: Harper and Brothers.

Schickele, R. 1952. "Theories Concerning Land Tenure." *Journal of Farm Economics* 24 (5): 734–43.

Wallace, H. 1936. *The Agricultural Situation,* vol. 20, no. 4. Washington, D.C.: USDA, BAE.

4

Normative Science
and Agricultural Policy

KENNETH E. BOULDING

On the Scope and Principles of Normative Science. Normative science may be defined as the attempt to apply the scientific ethic and method to the problem of human valuations, to try to answer such questions as, What do we mean by things going from bad to better rather than from bad to worse? It is not yet recognized as a respectable discipline, but a good deal of it is already in existence in various places. Economics, of course, has made an important contribution to it in welfare economics, cost-benefit analysis, and the theory of value. The other social sciences also have important contributions to make, especially in terms of the study of the overall evaluation of large systems. Out of this, certain broad principles are beginning to emerge.

Human Valuations. The field of normative science consists of the study of human valuations. Whether there are ultimate valuations in the universe we can only surmise, although images of valuations that are presumed to be independent of individual human values are themselves a part of the structure of human valuations and must be studied. The question, for instance, as to whether there is something that could be called "nature" that has values of its own is a question that we cannot answer, although we can study human beliefs that nature has values and the effect of these beliefs on human valuations themselves. Environmental values, for instance, are human values applied to the total state of the world. If, for instance, we take steps to protect endangered species it is because humans value these species, not because "nature" values them.

This paper was presented as the fourth James C. Snyder Memorial Lecture in Agricultural Economics, Purdue University, March 30, 1978.

Value and Image. Human valuation is a process by which human beings, in their minds, order their images of different states of the world in which we identify certain states as being better or worse than others. We can describe this by a "goodness function," $G = f$ (the relevant state of the world). G is what is perceived as going up when things get better and going down when things get worse. The relevant state of the world may differ for different purposes, as indeed may the concept of G itself, depending on the range over which we are making these valuations. Thus, if A and B are two different states of the world, I may say that A is better than B for me but is worse for my country, or it may be worse for my country but better for the world.

Coordinating Diverse Values. The valuation structures, that is, the goodness functions, for different individuals tend to be different. Even if our perceptions of states of the world A and B are similar, I may think A is better than B, and you may think B is better than A. The very existence of society, however, implies that these different valuations are coordinated by various processes. This does not mean that they become the same. Ongoing social processes, however, depend on the methods and institutions by which diverse valuations are coordinated. I have distinguished three major categories of these processes, which I have called the three Ps: prices, policemen, and preachments. "Prices," of course, is the market and the complex system of exchanges. Particularly when money becomes a medium of exchange, this is a very effective way for the coordination of different values. Its great virtue indeed is that it economizes agreement and permits coordination without eliminating the differences among values. In the market nobody has to buy what they do not want. The teetotaler can buy tea and the boozer can buy liquor. On the other hand, what is produced for the market—the distribution of resources among different occupations—is going to depend very strongly on the aggregate of these valuations.

"Policemen" is a symbol for the political process of legitimated threat through the law and the legislative and judicial apparatus for formulating and enforcing the law. The methods of coordination here are widely diverse, ranging from tyranny, in which the values of the tyrant are imposed on the society, to parliamentary or congressional democracy, in which there is agreement on decision-making rules such as majority rule and the degree of permissible bribery and corruption, with actual decisions worked out according to these rules. This may also involve complex political culture such as log rolling, public interest groups, and persuasive activities of various kinds.

The third mode of coordination, "preachments", is a symbol of the moral order or ethos, the process of critique of individual valuations and preferences. Any subculture has such an ethos. Persons who do not conform to it are apt to leave the subculture, either voluntarily or by forcible expulsion. Methods of persuasion vary from the raised eyebrow and the edge to the voice to thundering denunciations and ringing declarations. Larger societies impose a larger ethos on the subcultures of which they are composed, encouraging some and discouraging others. On the whole, the moral order dominates the other two coordinating processes, although there are strong interactions among the three forms. Exchange and political institutions can only persist as long as they are regarded as legitimate, that is, in conformance with the moral order. And the loss of legitimacy is inevitably followed by a disappearance of the institution. Slavery, capital markets in the socialist countries, and empire are good examples of this; as these institutions lost legitimacy they could not be sustained.

The Structure and Evolution of Values. Individual human valuations are primarily learned, although they do have some genetic base and they change by an essentially evolutionary process of mutation and selection. Mutations take place when old value structures are challenged, often by prophetic figures like Buddha, Jesus, Mohammed, Marx, or Veblen. Sometimes these new valuation structures survive, prosper, and multiply; sometimes they do not. It is a little hard to identify the species structure of human values. They do, however, tend to inhabit the human mind in the form of clusters of propensities, and it is not inconceivable that we might be able to classify these clusters into species— "puritan," "sybarite," "chauvinist," "gentle"—and even derive some mutational origins for them.

These mutations take place at a number of different levels. There is, first, the level of simple preferences. These are very largely learned. We grow up on the whole learning these from our own culture, but sometimes they change through dissatisfaction or inconsistency, as, for instance, in religious or political conversion or in less dramatic changes in life-style and tastes, some of which simply come from aging and maturation. Almost everybody's preferences at sixty-eight are rather different from what they were at eighteen, although there are also strong continuities through life.

The second level is that of ethics, involving the critique of preferences, which may be done internally or may be done through external communication. When I say, "I think your preferences are miserable" (or "splendid," as the case may be), I am talking ethics. This takes many different forms. There is, for instance, to use eighteenth century language, the critique of the passions by reason, in which persons may say to themselves, "I want this desperately, but I know if I get it it will be bad for me." This is the kind of remark that is also frequently addressed to others. There is an even higher level of criticism, a second order ethics, which is a critique of ethics itself, in which I say, "I think your ethics are miserable"—or "wonderful"—as the case may be.

What the survival functions of these value species are is very little understood and would be a large field for research. Some value structures thrive and others decline within a culture without perhaps changing it very much overall. Others thrive or decline because the culture that possesses them thrives or declines. The whole process of interaction is extremely complex and value structures often survive by a kind of piggyback principle, in that they become associated with other structures that do have survival value. The dynamic system here is obviously complex.

Value Relativity. The concept of evaluation as involved in the ordering of different images of the state of the world implies that in evaluation we are always thinking in terms of alternatives rather than in terms of absolutes. It would seem clear that we do not prove anything by showing that something is bad; we always have to show that the alternative is either better or worse. Unfortunately, this is a proposition that is by no means universally believed, and a great deal of human activity involving people who are self-consciously virtuous is aimed at showing that something is bad without spelling out the alternatives. The reason for the survival of such activity is probably another fundamental value, the high value we place on a satisfactory personal identity. Denunciation of evil, even without regard to alternatives, is a fine way of making people feel good.

The Interaction of Value and Fact. A sixth proposition is that images of "fact" and images of value continually interact in the dynamics of change in the cognitive and evaluative content of human minds. The distinction between fact and value indeed is not at all clear because facts are valued, and values are facts profoundly affecting the dynamics of images of the world of fact. We might think of a "fact" as an image of the world that is not changed by our evaluations of it. Thus, it is a "fact" that if I jump off the Empire State Building I will get into serious trouble at the bottom, no matter whether I value these events as good things or bad things. Our values, however, by affecting decisions, help to determine the facts of the future. Furthermore, our evaluative structure acts as a filter in the translation of our information inputs into images of the world, where we tend to filter out information that is not in conformity with our general value structure. This is "wishful thinking." It is also true that our evaluative structures are profoundly affected by our image of fact. Or we tend to upgrade the possibly attainable, even after failure, as in a sport, failure often spurs us on to renewed effort and still higher values for accomplishing the arbitrary.

Value and Decision. The next proposition is that evaluations make their impact on the future course of the world through decisions. Decision involves contemplating an "agenda" of alternative images of the future that are believed to be realistic; that is, into which we can proceed without hopeless uncertainty. These images of the future represent alternative states of the world, which we then proceed to write into the argument of a goodness function. We then order these according to the valuation field in which we are making our decisions, and we select the one that is "best." This, of course, is the familiar principle of maximization, which always involves these evaluative processes. Which one of the futures we think is best may, of course, depend on the field of valuation in which we are making decisions and the role we are adopting. Thus, the president of the United States may decide as he looks over a field of choices that item A would be best for himself, B would be best for his party, C would be best for the country, and D would be best for the world. Which he chooses depends on his valuation field and on the role in which he visualizes himself. Decisions will be changed both by changes in valuation structures and by changes in the "agenda," the images of the future about which we are making decisions.

Evaulating Action. Another question is whether a critique of decisions is possible according to some principles of human valuation, either before or after the event. After the event, decisions are criticized by regret. In the light of its realized consequences, the decision maker decides that either the agenda was wrong—the images of the future were unrealistic—or the valuation principle that selected the decision was wrong. It is very odd that there seems to be no word in the English language for the opposite of regret, for the sense that a decision turned out to be unexpectedly good. Perhaps it is a tribute to the rarity of this phenomenon. Decisions might also be regretted by people other than the decision maker, and these regrets may be coordinated through any of the three methods outlined above. The Ford Motor Company presumably regretted having decided to produce the Edsel, mainly because a lot of other people who might otherwise have bought the Edsel also apparently regretted that decision. A considerable number of people must have regretted having voted for President Nixon, and this regret was expressed in his eventual resignation by political processes. Some people may even have regretted having been Prohibitionists when the consequences of that decision became clear.

The problem here is that we are never quite sure what we are regretting. We do not really know that a choice that we did not make would in fact have been better than the one we did. It may be easy to perceive bad decisions but it may be very hard to perceive the alternatives.

The Pathology of Valuation and Decision. A final point is that, while we cannot hope to develop an analytical framework that will give us the "right answer" in all cases of conflict of human valuations, we can almost certainly identify what might be called a pathology of valuation and decisions in terms of social structures and situations that tend to lead to bad decisions. Important examples are situations like "tragedies of the commons," externalities, and "prisoners' dilemmas"—all of which have the common characteristic of a social situation in which what is a good decision for an individual turns out to be bad for the whole group or society when everybody follows the same bad example. Another situation subject to criticism is the critique of the goodness function itself in terms either of variables that are not considered in it, or variables that are used as imperfect surrogates for others. This occurs where we find variables to which we would give a high value if they could be identified but which are hard to identify. We then tend to latch on to variables that we hope are closely correlated with the ones we are really interested in and that are more easily identifiable. When these correlations are mistaken, so that an increase in the surrogate variable, for instance, does not increase the "real" one, we get into the problem of imperfect surrogates.

Agricultural Policy. Agricultural policy is a very interesting field in which to apply these principles. It is primarily in the political mode of coordination of values, but there are very significant relationships both with the market framework, which produces much of the political dissatisfactions that result in policy, and also with the moral order, which provides the underpinnings for the political values. The political demand for agricultural policy arises mainly because of a perception that farmers are both virtuous and poor. The first of these, of course, arises out of the moral order; the second out of the economic or the market order. Consequently, agricultural policy has been conceived mainly as an instrument of redistribution and economic justice. Its effect, however, as we shall see, is usually extraordinarily different from its intention.

Poverty, Productivity, and Rural Migration. The perception that farmers are poor is an interesting example of perception that is fairly accurate in the aggregate but very misleading when we look at the distribution of the aggregate. There is a great deal of statistical evidence that people in the agricultural sector of the economy receive incomes substantially below corresponding returns to capital of equivalent risk and labor of equivalent skill in other sectors of the economy. The evidence for this is so universal that we need not belabor the point. At many times and places agricultural income has been roughly half the income of comparable resources in other sectors.

The phenomenon indeed is so universal, particularly in developing societies, that there must be a fairly universal reason for it, and indeed there is a somewhat simple one. Agriculture is an occupation in which historically there have been large opportunities for an increase in productivity, especially of land and labor. The increase in labor productivity is particularly significant because agriculture produces commodities with relatively inelastic demands in terms of both price elasticity and income elasticity. Hence, increase in labor productivity results not so much in an expansion of the industry as in a transfer of labor out of it. We see this spectacularly in the United States, where the proportion of the labor force in agriculture may have been almost 90 percent 200 years ago, 50 percent in 1880, and is 4 percent today. The proportion of land in agriculture has also diminished somewhat, but for much more complex reasons, among which the increase in yield per acre from agriculture has been a minor though not necessarily an insignificant factor.

It is a very fundamental principle that in the absence of direct coercion there is only one way to move people from one occupation to another, and that is to have the occupation out of which they are to move less attractive than the one into which they are to move. When in addition the rural population tends to have a higher natural rate of increase than the urban population, this factor is intensified and relative rural incomes are decreased even more. The relative poverty of agriculture, therefore, in an expanding and developing society is necessitated by the need for getting people out of it; and the harder it is to get people out of it, the lower will be the incomes from agriculture relative to those outside it. We have, therefore, this ironic dynamic in which technological improvement in agriculture diminishes the returns to it, which are only recovered as people leave it; and the more easily they leave it, the less the relative decline in return to it will have to be in order to insure the necessary movement.

In the United States the decline in the proportion of people in agriculture has been going on now for almost 200 years, if not longer. It has been particularly noticeable in the last 50 years. There was a period of rapid technological change in agriculture between about 1840 and 1880. Then there was a period of relatively slow technological change from the 1880s until World War I, which resulted in an improvement in agriculture's terms of trade. This is why the period 1909 to 1914 is still regarded as a golden age! It was a golden age produced by the relative technological backwardness of agriculture in the preceding generation. Then, especially from about 1930 on, we have had an extraordinary technological change in agriculture, coupled with a very large migration out of it. At least 30 million people in the last 40 or 50 years have moved to the cities, creating the urban problem (which consists mainly of displaced rural people), but also contributing to the doubling of per capita real income. It is mainly the people displaced from agriculture by technological change influencing the rise of labor productivity who have made the color televisions and the other goodies that have contributed to the rise in per capita real incomes. It is the coordination of values by market mechanisms on the whole, therefore, that has created what is perceived to be a political problem of poverty in agriculture. Aggregates and averages are very dangerous, however, because within an average there may be sharp differences in the distribution. The proposition "farmers are poor" should be amended to read "some farmers are rich, some farmers are very poor, some farmers are in between."

The Policy Response: Parity and Paradox. In the United States, the response to this situation is the demand for parity, a classic example of a surrogate objective. It started with the development of statistical indicators in the Bureau of Agricultural Statistics in the early years of the century. First were developed indicators of prices farmers pay and prices farmers receive. Then somebody got the idea of dividing one by the other and parity was born, parity being an index of agriculture's terms of trade, that is, how much farmers get per unit of what they sell. The period 1909 to 1914 was about the most favorable from the point of view of agriculture's terms of trade, and this became the golden age, the ideal of policy. One hundred percent of parity simply means a return to the terms of trade of 1909 to 1914. Out of this came price supports, the "land bank," a substantial "grants economy" toward agriculture, food surpluses, Public Law 480, a tobacco quota, and other exercises of the finger-poking state.

The critical question is, What state of the world did the people who formulated and voted for our agricultural policy really have in mind that they regarded as better than the state as it would have been without these policies? Certainly in the prevailing goodness function some kind of redistribution toward farmers was in the picture as being good. Improving terms of trade, however, is a very peculiar form of redistribution. It tends to redistribute to the rich rather than to the poor, for it is the rich who have a lot to buy and sell, and this has been the overall consequence of the parity doctrine. This of course was never stated, because we have an underlying political value system in which redistribution to the rich is highly suspect as likely to move things from bad to worse rather than from bad to better. The parity doctrine and price supports have certainly had the effect of redistributing toward the rich farmers, not the poor ones. It is possible that this was a secret and unacknowledged objective of agricultural policy; it could never have been a public and announced objective.

There are some parallels between the parity concept and the "just price" of the medieval scholastics. The just price was supposed to be that which would return the conventional and appropriate income to the producers. The relation between price and income, however, depends on productivity, so that in conditions of changing productivity of various industries, even if there is a set of just prices, they will change in accordance with the change in productivity. The parity principle based on terms of trade in 1909 to 1914 cannot conceivably be justified as a just price when agricultural productivity has increased so much more than productivity in industry, or still more than the productivity in the service trades. When there is an increase in productivity the relative "just price" under any criterion declines, so that justice in this sense at least would demand a parity price adjusted by productivity.

Furthermore, any manipulation of the price structure, even in the supposed interests of economic justice, will tend to redound to the advantage of the rich, whether we look at cheap education at state universities, Medicare, or parity prices in agriculture. In the first place, the rich are those who know how to take advantage of shifts in the relative price structure. It is one of the reasons why they are rich. In the seond place, it is the rich who have a lot to buy and sell and who will succeed, therefore, in being subsidized. The only way to help the poor by manipulations of the relative price structure is to distinguish very sharply between the poor man's goods and the rich man's goods and to subsidize the former or tax the latter.

When we look at redistributional absurdities like the tobacco quota, the case for a normative critique becomes almost overwhelming. The tobacco quota by now is a subsidy to the inheritors for the most part of people who owned land that happened to be producing tobacco in 1934. Farms with a quota in the tobacco areas now sell for many times more than a similar neighboring farm that did not happen to be producing tobacco in 1934. It is hard to justify this redistribution under any principle of economic justice whatsoever; yet once it is established it is very hard to change, simply because many people by now have bought tobacco farms at these inflated prices and are presumably earning no more than a normal rate of return. To abolish the quotas now would tax these people very severely for their error in judgment in assuming that tobacco quotas will go on forever.

The Dynamic Consequences of Agricultural Policy. When we look at the overall consequences of our agricultural policy, however, we see that in dynamic terms it has been astonishingly successful. When I was at the University of Michigan I taught a course in agricultural policy, more or less as a course in the pathology of economic policy, on the thesis that there was hardly anything you could think up to do wrong that we hadn't done. As the years went on, however, it began to dawn on me that, in spite of the fact that we had done everything wrong, we had had a great success, and that the development of the American economy since the 1930s had been dependent in no small measure on the extraordinary rise in agricultural productivity that these policies seem to have engendered.

The reason for this, I suspect, was a completely unanticipated side effect of the policies, that price supports removed an important element of uncertainty from agriculture and that it was this diminution in price uncertainty, not the actual level of supports themselves, that led to the extraordinary willingness of American farmers to invest in expensive labor-saving equipment and to adopt new ideas, new crops, and new methods. Under conditions of high uncertainty the sensible thing to do today is what you did yesterday, for the risks of change are greater than the risks of not changing. Even if change has some probability of high payoffs, if there is any probability of catastrophe the change will not be made. It is uncertainty more than anything else that limits investment, the rate of change, and therefore the rate of development. This almost accidental result of diminishing uncertainty was the key to the fantastic development of agricultural productivity.

On the whole, therefore, our agricultural policy looked like a redistribution somewhat at the expense of poor farmers who were displaced and forced into the ghettos, although one could argue that even they were better off in the ghettos than they would have been sharecropping in Mississippi. Perhaps, therefore, it was rather at the expense of old city residents whose cities deteriorated—all this for the benefit of practically all of us whose income has been increased. There is a good deal of evidence that the proportional distribution of income has not changed much, so this increase in income has been very widely distributed. We about halved the amount of poverty in this country in the last generation, mainly because the poor got twice as rich along with everybody else, not because we redistributed income. A substantial part of the poor getting twice as rich, however, has to do with the increased productivity of agriculture and the ability, therefore, to displace poor farmers and laborers from agriculture to produce at least some poor men's manufactured goods. This is an example of what I have called the law of political irony—that almost everything that you do to hurt people helps them and everything you do to help people hurts them. Agricultural policy produced many examples.

Some other aspects of agricultural policy can be treated very briefly. One objective of policy has been a preservation of the family farm, yet there has been a noticeable though not spectacular increase in corporate farming, and the family farm itself has become the foundation for a hereditary rural aristocracy with the increase in the capitalization and size of the family farm as a result of technological change. The family farmer is now a professional, operating with capital equipment worth perhaps a half million dollars on land worth up to a million dollars or more. The only sure way to become a family farmer is either to be the only son of one or to marry an only daughter. As the real rates of interest have risen, the problem of paying off other children—if we have equal inheritance of estates among children—becomes almost insuperable, and one would expect increasing numbers of children of family farmers to abandon the family farm or to turn it into a corporate enterprise. Thus, monetary policy may have more impact on the family farm than anything done in the Department of Agriculture.

The development of rural electric associations—another offshoot of the New Deal of the thirties—which have a degree of subsidized financing, again tends to subsidize the large farmer rather than the small, but also tends to subsidize the rich exurbanite perhaps even more than the farmer. The impact of the Bureau of Reclamation in providing subsidized irrigation may actually pervert agricultural practices and lead to the wasteful use of water. And the 160-acre limitation has been a remarkable producer of subterfuge in the face of a technological pressure for larger farms.

A Reassessment through Normative Science. This above discussion is merely illustrative of the way in which normative science might be applied to the problem of clarifying the evaluation of a social constellation even as complex as agricultural policy. If we were to do it more systematically, there is little doubt that even in the present undeveloped state of normative science some extremely interesting conclusions would emerge. Suppose, for instance, that we began such an inquiry with an investigation of those human valuations that are relevant to the agricultural sector of the economy. This would mean taking a look at market valuations—what people buy at what incomes, and what people sell, including their services.

The next step is to look at the variables and the characteristics of the goodness functions of people whose decisions may be significant for the agricultural sector. It is particularly important here to try to identify any variables in the goodness function that tend to be overlooked. What are, for instance, the nonmonetary values of rural life? Can we specify these a little more exactly, and specify them also to the extent to which they are "goods" or "bads"? The measure of the value of any particular item in "the relevant state of the world," that is, the argument of the goodness function, is the rough magnitude of its first differential with regard to goodness. That is, when a particular item in the state of the world goes up by one unit, does goodness go up by a lot (in which case the item is a high good)? Does it go up by a little (in which case it might be a moderate good)? Does it not go up at all (in which case the item is indifferent)? Does it go down (in which case the item is a bad)?

Another factor to investigate is the interrelationships among items in the goodness function. When one goes up, does another go down? These are sometimes hard to trace. Thus, the spaciousness of rural life may be offset by its loneliness. We also have to be on the lookout for nonlinear relationships, which are very important. The law of diminishing marginal utility or marginal goodness is extremely general: The more of anything we have the less of a good it will become. If we have too much of it, it will become a bad. We can certainly investigate this for many aspects of the agricultural sector.

Then we come to the central problem of the coordination of different values, particularly the pathologies that may be involved in these different methods of coordination. We have already observed how market coordination in a situation of constantly increasing agricultural productivity will create inequity for agriculture unless there is very rapid migration out of it. All too often we think of these things only in static terms, and one of the very important aspects of normative science is the development of dynamic models of all these situations.

The political coordination of differing valuations with regard to agriculture is an extremely interesting problem. How is it, for instance, that agricultural subsidies have increased almost proportionately to the decline in the agricultural vote? It is very strange that the political power of agriculture seems to have increased with a diminution in its size. This requires a much better theory of political power than we now have, and it has to be related also to the moral order that underlies the political structure.

With regard to the moral order, we need to know much more about the power of symbols. Why did parity, for instance, become such a significant and important symbol—as it indeed still is, as witness the recent farmers' movement—which has renewed demands for parity? When parity is a clear absurdity, what other values is it riding along with? It is obviously an example of the piggyback principle. It is not clear what is riding on what's back. It is probably true that only a symbol can kill a symbol. Up to now we do not seem to have produced any symbol of equity as effective as that of parity, and this is a serious defect in the moral order.

The development of more accurate images of the future is a very important task for normative science, particularly with ecosystems of great complexity where a cause and effect concept simply breaks down and the results of decisions are often extremely surprising to the decision maker as well as to others. One of the real puzzles is why economics has been so remarkably unsuccessful in developing any kind of popular image of the importance of relative prices and the impact of the relative price structure, in spite of the long tradition it has in this field; whereas it has been extremely successful in putting over an image of macroeconomics and persuading people that budget deficits are wonderful and that the national debt is an asset. Agricultural policy is a strange mixture of a highly pathological explicit process coupled with extraordinarily successful unintended side effects in terms, we have suggested, of uncertainty reduction and productivity expansion. Could we elevate the side effects to a major political symbol? Normative science certainly cannot answer that question but it can at least ask it.

It is the dynamics of the moral order that ultimately underlie all the large-scale dynamics of society, particularly in regard to legitimacy and acceptability. This is as true of the market as it is of political processes. Market processes can lose their legitimacy, which is always a little precarious. We tend to regard the market as abstract and a little dirty, and we somehow regard the free gift of outgoing generosity as far superior to the calculating, moneymakingness of exchange. If the legitimacy of the market is lost, the moral order will force the political order to restrict or even destroy it. Similarly, the political order cannot function without an underlying legitimacy derived from the moral order. Yet we understand these processes of the dynamics of the moral order, especially the dynamics of legitimacy, very little, and a further study of this is an important prerequisite to the successful development of a normative science.

No science can discover the truth; it can only eliminate error and search for new errors to eliminate. Normative science is no exception to this rule. Nevertheless, it can help to eliminate errors in valuations, and where error is clearly costly there are payoffs for eliminating it. It is not enough, however, to have a perception of error confined to a scientific priesthood. These perceptions must be translated into terms and symbols that can be widely accepted. Parity is a beautiful example of how a perfectly valid scientific concept can become a symbolic error. Perhaps the challenge to science is to develop further concepts, indicators, and indices that can become symbols of more realistic and highly developed norms.

5

Agricultural Economists and Public Policy

LAUREN SOTH

IN ANNUAL CONCLAVES of scholarly associations, it is standing operating procedure for the members to ask themselves about their role in workaday society. Being devoted to teaching the young and searching for new knowledge, living in semicloistered retreats, professors and researchers must require mutual reassurance that they are doing things that are worthwhile in the real world.

Self-examination is healthy. I feel that I am following an honored tradition in the American Agricultural Economics Association by undertaking a discussion of the topic. But at the outset I must say that agricultural economists have less trouble with the deprecating question, What good are we? than most people in the academic disciplines. They have had another hang-up, as I shall explain.

Agricultural economics in the United States has been almost wholly a pursuit of the land grant agricultural colleges and the U.S. Department of Agriculture. It grew naturally out of the soil and climate of this public educational federation, where practicality was the watchword. Agricultural economics came out of dirt farming, as they say on the political campaign circuit, crops and soils technology, animal husbandry, farm management, and, later, marketing of farm products. Many of the early agricultural economists started their careers as teachers of animal husbandry or farm management. They did not first study economics and then specialize in the economics of agriculture. By and large, it was the other way around.

The nature of the origins of the agricultural economics profession led to a

This paper is a revised version of Mr. Soth's Fellow's Lecture presented to the American Agricultural Economics Association on August 17, 1976. The author wishes to thank Jimmye S. Hillman, James T. Bonnen, Harold F. Breimyer, Emery N. Castle, John A. Schnittker, and Robert K. Buck for comments and suggestions in the writing of this paper.

feeling of inferiority among its early practitioners. I often sensed, when I was taking graduate work in economics and doing extension jobs in farm outlook and public policy questions, that agricultural economists at Iowa State and in the USDA were touchy about their lack of grounding in formal economics. Some of them flaunted their practical knowledge of farming or of agricultural markets and made light of the theories in textbooks. Others tried to prove themselves legitimate and worthy members of the profession of Adam Smith, David Ricardo, and Alfred Marshall.

The circumstances under which agricultural economics began to develop as a separate field of study gave the profession an advantage in the practical world of politics and business. Unlike the workers in most social sciences, including general business economics, the agricultural economists really knew their industry. Moreover, their innocence of theoretical economics enabled them to appreciate the power relationships of the market and to see the wide gap between the textbook principles and the way the economy actually functioned.

Agricultural economists have had more influence on the formation and the carrying out of public policies for their industry, I should venture, than the economists specializing in any other single industry. In the 1920s, when agriculture was suffering from the plunge of prices after World War I, agricultural economists provided the intellectual leadership in designing plans for government action and for structural reforms of the marketing system. W. J. Spillman, Henry C. Taylor, M. L. Wilson, Henry A. Wallace, E. G. Nourse, and John D. Black are names that spring quickly to mind. These were the idea men behind the export debenture plan, the domestic allotment plan, the McNary-Haugen bill, the farm cooperative movement, and other proposals for helping farmers contend with overproduction and low prices.

The prevailing diagnosis of the cause of the farm problem at this time was loss of foreign markets. Farmers had expanded production to sell abroad in the golden years of the early 1900s, so the reasoning went, and then increased output still more to meet the needs of World War I. The setbacks to foreign sales in the 1920s resulted in commodity surpluses. Farm relief plans generally focused on aspects of the foreign trade situation. Agricultural economists called for lower tariffs on manufactured goods to stimulate imports and furnish dollars to foreign customers for U.S. farm products. They urged export subsidies for farm products, two-price plans such as the McNary-Haugen bill, and the export-debenture scheme.

These early agricultural economists were unabashed political economists and partisans for farmers. They pushed the American development theme as espoused by the founding fathers and reflected in the Morrill Act, the Homestead Act, and throughout our public policy. In his *Agricultural Reform in the United States,* John D. Black defined the objectives of national agricultural policy as "first, to hasten the improvement in the rural scale of living; second, to check the present rapid rate of migration to cities; and third, to maintain a somewhat larger proportion of our population on the land than otherwise would be the case" (Black 1929, p. 60).

Black was the principal designer of what was then called the domestic allotment plan, a plan for retiring temporarily part of the land used for major crops. The aim was to reduce output and raise prices of farm products. When prices sagged drastically in 1930, 1931, and 1932, this plan became widely accepted among farm groups. In his one speech on agricultural policy in the 1932 presidential campaign, Franklin D. Roosevelt gave a fuzzy endorsement of the idea. After the election the New Deal Congress approved the first Agricultural Adjustment Act. That has been the fundamental system of supply management ever since, and though it is in abeyance at the moment and the political language has evolved to "set aside" instead of annual allotments, the essentials of the system are the same as those forty-eight years ago.

Black was advocating methods of supporting farm income that he thought would keep people on the farm and that he considered a desirable national objective. Two of his three objectives for farm policy had to do with maintaining a larger farm population than would prevail without a federal action program.

As it turned out, the domestic allotment plan had the opposite effect. It helped farmers who were in a strong financial position to acquire more land; price supports enabled the big farmer to gain substantially in competition with the small operator. Ironically, the allotment and price programs were criticized at first, by many agricultural economists as well as conservative politicians and businessmen, for protecting the outdated, inefficient, small farmer and blocking modernization of the industry. Some naive critics of "farm subsidies," such as the *Wall Street Journal,* have continued even in recent times to charge that the farm programs inhibit efficient, large-scale farming.

It is true that, on its face, the legislation promises certain advantages to small farms, and all farm laws religiously proclaim their purpose as upholding the family farm. But the real effects were quite diffcrent, as became obvious to those who looked at the facts after World War II, instead of basing their opinions on legislative preambles and theory.

There then arose a heresy within the professional agricultural fraternity of the land grant system, including some farm economists. The heretics repudiated the ancient Jeffersonian doctrine about the virtues of the family farm.

Even into the 1930s, farm policy reformers sought to preserve independent, small-scale farming and rural communities. They did not seek a change in the structure of agriculture but in mechanisms to improve its functioning. The philosophy of the Morrill Act, the Homestead Act, and the Country Life Commission of Theodore Roosevelt dominated the land grant colleges. The purpose of research and education was to raise the farm family to an urban living standard—not to drive people off the farm but to keep them there. Extolling the virtues of rural life was part of the ritual of extension work.

But the new technology was seen to be depopulating the farms as it reduced labor requirements. Making a virtue out of necessity, agriculturalists began to laud modernization and consolidation of farms and the "release" of farm workers for nonfarm work.

Geoffrey Shepherd was one of the first agricultural economists to emphasize the effect of new technology in reducing farm population—and thus in increasing the per capita income of farm people. In his book *Agricultural Price Policy* Shepherd wrote, "There is a tendency in some quarters to deplore the movement of young people off farms to better paying jobs in town. But if this movement did not take place, incomes in agriculture would fall to bare subsistence levels. The movement off farms is the only thing that keeps per capita income up."

The family farm ideologists came in for condescending smiles, if not contempt. It was time to recognize farming as a business and not a way of life. Agricultural economists began to talk about farm population adjustment as a "final" solution of the farm surplus problem. It was not a problem of overproduction but of too many people sharing the national farm income. Instead of trying to restrain farm output to increase farm income, what was needed was continued reduction of farm population to increase the individual shares.

At the same time, after World War II, as Brandow (1977) has lucidly explained in his review of the literature on commercial agricultural policy, agricultural economists turned to the demand side as an explanation of the farm problem. The lesson of World War II had been that when the economy was in boom, with full employment, prices of farm products were high and farmers were prosperous. Most importantly, young people leaving farming areas could get jobs in the cities. The farm problem was not really a farm problem but a problem of general economic stabilization on a rising trend of growth.

Shepherd did not fall into this pit. He was alert to the instability problems of agriculture caused by variable weather and the low price and income elasticity of demand for food in the aggregate. He wrote persuasively on the advantages of public measures that would help stabilize farmers' returns (rather than prices alone)—especially for corn and livestock.

This analysis was happily in harmony with the "permanent adjustment" theme. It also furnished timely justification of the conventional land grant doctrine that full-speed-ahead infusion of new technology was all to the benefit of farmers and the rest of us. The same rationale was comforting to those who wanted to "get the government out of agriculture" and let free markets reign.

The technological faith had been questioned by a few farm radicals and a few dissident farm economists who made the logical connection between excess supply and new methods that increased production. So it was nice for the true believers in science to hear other respected economists rebut this by arguing that the farm problem was caused by weak demand for farm products. The free marketeers did not consider government financing and investment in new farm technology an intervention in private business—only "artificial" meddling in what they regarded as natural markets.

Unfortunately for the final solution proponents, it soon became apparent that full employment and continued rapid reduction of the farm population were not enough to keep farm income high. The overproduction tendency seemed not just a matter of weak foreign and domestic demand; it seemed to be chronic, if irregular. Even with high employment, prices of farm products and the net incomes of farmers often were below satisfactory levels.

G. S. Shepherd, along with T. W. Schultz, R. K. Froker, Karl Brandt, W. H. Nicholls, Howard Tolley, and others, explored proposals for compensatory payments to farmers in lieu of price supports. The economists were attracted to a plan for stabilizing farmers' incomes without interfering with commodity markets and thus avoiding unmanageable surpluses.

Agricultural economists attributed the farm problem first to loss of foreign markets, then to slack domestic demand. They were slow to appreciate the consequences of the technological revolution in farming. The application of science to agriculture was regarded as a "given" in the farm economics equation—beyond economic study. The land grant college–USDA system, in all its parts and roles, was based on the idea that technological efficiency is an ultimate good. There could not be too much or too fast a drive for getting more output per man, per acre, or per unit of capital.

Alone among the agricultural establishment scholars, a few economists braved the theologians of technology to ask whether the push for technical advance might be too impetuous. They asked whether the overcapacity of agriculture could be the result of letting technology get ahead of social adjustment. They suggested that priority in public expenditure for rural communities ought itself be subjected to scientific analysis.

Willard W. Cochrane wrote about the "treadmill" of farmers—forced to adopt new machinery and other inputs to keep costs down, but seldom realizing a benefit in aggregate income. The concept that farm people and rural communities bear a heavy burden for introducing new technology at a rapid rate also has been expressed eloquently by Earl Heady, Luther Tweeten, and many agricultural economists since the 1950s. John A. Nordin[1] dealt with the issue as a welfare economics problem, considering farmers' interests both as producers and as consumers. Similar studies might still be useful on the consequences of rapid technological development in agriculture upon rural communities and their small business firms, schools, and other institutions, though in many parts of America today it appears that agricultural adjustment has reached at least a temporary halt.

Considering that these questioners of the dogma were themselves employees of the land grant system, they deserve praise for courage. Nearly all criticism of public agricultural research policies has come from within, not from agricultural economists in the private educational, research, and business institutions, where you might expect it to originate. Instead, the outsiders (including the major farm organizations) mostly have beaten the drums for all-out production research, that is, the development and application of new technology for agriculture.

Agricultural economists inside the sytem were the first to point out that farmers taken as a group did not benefit from the introduction of new methods; only the first users did. They dared to challenge the time-honored experiment station sales argument to legislatures that an increase in corn yields increased farmers' aggregate income. Public spending for agricultural improvements benefited the American consumer and the foreign buyers, not the farmer. Agricultural economists showed that the bypassed farm operators, hired workers, and small towns in rural areas benefited least of all, or not at all, from new farming technology. The discernible effects of these studies on public policy are small so far, but I am confident that they will ultimately be substantial.

Agricultural economists have brought to bear on the intellectual front the nonfarm or nonagrarian concerns that are becoming apparent on the political front. The farmer in the last 200 years has felt that interests outside farming—the middlemen, bankers, railroads, and manufacturers—were making the main decisions about his business. He has had to take the other fellow's price, both as buyer and as seller.

Actually, in this century government farm policies have been largely left to the farmer and his organizations, including the land grant institutions; farm lobbyists have been able to get most of what they wanted. The decline of farmers in number and proportion of the voting population did not weaken their power in government, despite reapportionment. Yet the farmer's instinct about being at the mercy of outside interests is not far off the mark. Government policies have been beneficial to the elite of commercial agriculture and to the business interests selling to and buying from them, but often not to the majority of people in farming.

The political atmosphere regarding food and agriculture has changed in the 1970s. The rise in food costs to consumers, the deterioration of rural community structure, the trend to industrial agriculture, and the migration of displaced rural people to cities have attracted a wider constituency for farm policy.

Agricultural economists as partisans and political activists contributed heavily to the nation's farm policies of the first half of the twentieth century.[2] As "pure" economists, more segregated from the political scene today, their influence has diminished. Agricultural economics undoubtedly has become more scientific, more scholarly, and more knowledgeable about the farming business. The more you know, and the more detached from politics, the less likely you are to attract attention and stir opinion. The more specialized you become, the less effective you are in the political economy. As our studies have become more intensive, more detailed, with greater use of mathematical techniques, they have inevitably become narrower. The impact on public affairs is remote, long delayed, and indirect.

I do not say this is a bad thing; I do not belittle the mathematical tools merely because I do not understand them. I must admit, however, that the remark of Joan Robinson, who refuses to use equations, gave me some satisfaction. She said, "I don't know math, so I am obliged to think."[3] If I were to criticize the budget of research in agricultural economics, I should be more inclined to adopt another criticism of American economists made by Joan Robinson. She said they are floundering because they still have an ideological bias toward the free market, which she says is a theoretical concept that does not exist.

Scientific, mathematical studies about the economic details of agriculture no doubt help us understand the industry. But to the extent that they rest on assumptions about pure economic science, they are illusionary and not helpful in the formation of public policy.

I read recently an interesting paper by Paul McCracken (1976), professor at the University of Michigan and longtime member of the President's Council of Economic Advisers. McCracken believes an economic adviser ought to try to keep his own values and political judgments separate from his advice on economics. I guess everyone would agree with that. But it implies that there is such a thing as economic science that can be divorced from politics. That I doubt.

McCracken tells about an incident in 1961 when he and other advisers were asked to report about the domestic economy and the balance of payments. One of their recommendations was that the gold reserve requirement be reduced or removed while the issue was quiescent, rather than waiting until the Federal Reserve's gold holdings were on the verge of becoming deficient. Kennedy said he understood the economic logic and the economic cost of delaying a decision, but he would have to pass. He said such legislation would have to come before Senator Harry Byrd, and he did not want to start his administration by raising the gold issue with the senator.

McCracken said he and the other advisers performed correctly as advisers, but the president, looking at the larger domain for which he was responsible, chose not to take their advice. McCracken said he understood that pure economics had been adulterated in Kennedy's decision, and he had no reason to think the president was wrong.

I agree on this kind of separation of economics and party politics. But in the larger meaning of political economy, McCracken and his associates took into account more than pure economics in their assessment of the gold reserve question. They had to consider the power factors in banking and government, among others.

In dealing with agricultural policy, as with money or other economic policy, it is impossible to consider economics as a pure science. Economics itself is more complicated than any physical science. It deals with pesky human behavior. It embraces the power of large organizations more and more. We deceive ourselves and our clientele when we claim to be only "humble technicians" bringing to bear an antiseptic economic analysis on a public policy question.[4]

On the whole, agricultural economists have been broad enough to see beyond economics in public policy and to see that economics is more than demand and supply curves.[5] I could provide a long list of current AAEA members who have made large contributions to the agricultural policies of this country. But I am a coward. I am afraid I would leave out a deserving stalwart or two and offend them, while offending others by including certain names. So I will not give you my list. Anyway, you all know the people who have served as economic policy advisers in the executive departments, as directors of policy studies for Congress, as members and directors of presidential commissions, and the authors of influential books and articles. It should be easy, at least in this instance, to support without documentation my claim that agricultural economists have been more influential in economic policies for their industry than other specialized economists have been for theirs.

Nevertheless, the "generalists" of agricultural economics like Geoffrey Shepherd, John D. Black, Howard Tolley, Theodore W. Schultz, and Frederic V. Waugh are scarcer in the ranks of the profession these days. It may be argued that the early "political" agricultural economists were wrong in the counsel they delivered; they, like everyone else, underestimated the rate of farm technological advance and consequently the side effects. Yet they were effective in transferring the current knowledge about agricultural economics into the political arena. Today the country needs more "bridges" of their type between the compartmentalized experts of agricultural economics and the real world.

Geoffrey Shepherd has been especially proficient at this interpretive work, putting into readable language complex ideas; recognizing the influence of noneconomic factors on agricultural policy; and, above all, seeing the nub of a problem in clear light.

In his 1967 presidential address to the AAEA, C. E. Bishop, who was then director of the National Advisory Commission on Rural Poverty, said, "Those of us who work in the rural social sciences have not perceived the significance of the growing urbanization of rural America." He said farm economists had been preoccupied with the problems of the farm firm and had given little or no attention to economic problems much more important to the majority of the rural population.

Bishop asked that economists study the effects of farm programs on income distribution in agriculture and the effects of technology on the structure of rural communities. He said, "In order to increase our usefulness in coping with problems of economic structure and public policy, we must break the bonds of pure competition and extend our analysis to problems that transcend market phenomena" (Bishop 1967, p. 1007).

Nine years later I think one can say that the agricultural economists have been shifting in the direction Bishop advised. With consumer organizations becoming more vocal, with environmental concerns becoming imperative, and with foreign policy once again rising to the forefront of agricultural policy, the trend toward a broader approach to public policy will continue. The public has awakened to the connections between farm policy and foreign policy, food prices, protecting the environment, and the rural-urban structure of society. The public says, in effect, that farm policy is too important to be left to the farmers, since that means in practice the big farmers and agribusiness.

The public is no longer willing to accept without question the assertions of the agricultural establishment that the United States has the purest and most nutritious food supply in the world. Nor is it ready to leave soil and water management to the establishment. Even the issues of rural crime prevention, public welfare, education, rights of minorities, and collective bargaining of farm workers will not be left to rural areas. As Bishop said, the rural society is becoming urbanized; its isolation is ending. The farmer and his community have been brought into the mainstream of the nation.

Don Paarlberg said, "The biggest issue of agricultural policy is . . . who is going to control the agenda. . . . The old agenda is concerned primarily with commodities and specifically with influencing supplies and prices in the farmer's interest. . . . The new agenda differs radically . . .: Food prices and specifically how to hold them down . . . ecological questions . . . rural development, primarily a program of the 80 percent of the rural people who are nonfarmers . . . civil rights . . . collective bargaining." Paarlberg also said the agricultural establishment should not just "repeat the honored rhetoric" but should recognize that the new constituency would have to be served.[6]

I agree with him. Moreover, I think the nonfarm pressures on agricultural policy will be beneficial to independent family farming and to a healthier rural society.

Agriculture's own institutions, developed for an earlier time and for a different farming structure, are incapable of meeting the requirements for public policy on rural affairs today. The very success of the scientific advances in farming tended to freeze the institutions in place. The fact that the benefits of scientific advance were not being shared equally within agriculture and between agriculture and the urban sector tended to be ignored by the land grant system, the commercial farm organizations, and agribusiness.

There seems to be a law of nature that successful human organizations resist change until they have lost effectiveness and are replaced. Bonnen, our honored president, has frequently alerted us to what he has called "the Decline of the Agricultural Establishment." In a speech fourteen years ago Bonnen said that "the commercial agricultural power structure has reached a state of extreme organizational fragmentation . . . and these fragmented elements are themselves contributing greatly to a general erosion of the political power which together they exert."[7]

The politics of farming in the 1920s and 1930s had to do with a fairly homogeneous farming community. That community has been splitting apart from the effect of the technological revolution. Farmers' organizations have been splitting into agribusiness firms and commodity groups. The colleges of agriculture and the USDA have tended to become associated with large farming interests and the suppliers of farm inputs and the buyers of farm products. The close association of the USDA with the pesticide industry and international grain companies has been notorious. Regulation of pesticides has been taken away from the USDA, and the regulation of grain inspection is being reformed.

Agricultural economists have been the leaders in calling to public attention the neglect of low-income farm families and hired farm labor, the effects of government programs on the farming structure, and the impact of technology on rural America. But the challenge laid down by Bishop is still pertinent if one judges the profession by what appears in the *Journal of Agricultural Economics*. Public policy issues still receive secondary attention, especially those policies that affect the general public.

For half a century the principal public policy question concerning food and agriculture was how to deal with production overcapacity; in the next half century the central problem could well be scarcity. High food costs and instability of prices will be public policy targets. Agricultural economists will find themselves in a different position with respect to farm policy formation than in the past. We need more work on food and nutrition policies, foreign policy, national energy and environmental policies, and on the structure of agriculture and rural communities.

Perhaps I could be accused of bias, but I am confident that the members of the AAEA will rise to the needs of the occasion as they have in the past.

Notes

1. John A. Nordin, Contribution 78-338-S, Kansas State University, Kansas Agricultural Experiment Station.

2. Among the many good books recounting the impact of farmers' political movements on government policy that tell of the contributions of early agricultural economists are those by Saloutos and Hicks (1951), Benedict (1953), and Hofstadter (1955).

3. Soma Golden, "Economist Joan Robinson, 72, Is Full of Fight," *The New York Times*, March 23, 1976, pp. 33, 42.

4. Randall (1974) stated perceptively: "Conceiving the economy as a system of mutual coer-

cion, it becomes impossible to avoid the moral dilemmas which confront anybody involved in the public sector or in social decision making. If an action taken in any public agency tends to increase the power of some people while reducing the power of others (i.e., to make some people better off and others worse off), its distributional consequences cannot be attributed to some inevitable and inexorable economic law. Rather, these consequences are the result of a decision of which that agency should be conscious and for which it must take responsibility" (p. 229).

5. "What, then, is the normative significance of a supply curve, a demand curve, a price? Very little, I suggest, since all of these things are very largely dependent on the structure of power within an economy, and the structure of power can be changed by political action as well as by what we have come to think of as economic changes. Economic data such as prices and supply and demand curves can be used in a normative context only if the current structure of power is assumed optimal" (Randall 1974, p. 229, note 9).

6. Don Paarlberg, speech at the National Public Policy Conference, Clymer, New York, September 11, 1975.

7. James Bonnen, speech at the Great Plains Agricultural Council Meeting, Bozeman, Montana, July 28, 1966.

References

Benedict, M. R. 1953. *Farm Policies of the United States, 1790–1950.* New York: The Twentieth Century Fund.

Bishop, C. E. 1967. "The Urbanization of Rural America: Implications for Agricultural Economics." *Journal of Farm Economics* 49:999–1008.

Black, J. D. 1929. *Agricultural Reform in the United States.* New York: McGraw-Hill.

Brandow, G. E. 1977. "Policy for Commercial Agriculture, 1945–1971." In *A Survey of Agricultural Economics Literature,* vol. 1, edited by Lee R. Martin. Minneapolis: University of Minnesota Press.

Hofstadter, R. 1955. *The Age of Reform from Bryan to F.D.R.* New York: Alfred A. Knopf.

McCracken, P. 1976. "Reflections on Economic Advising." Los Angeles: International Institute of Economic Research Original Paper No. 1.

Randall, Alan. 1974. "Information, Power, and Academic Responsibility." *American Journal of Agricultural Economics* 56:227–34.

Saloutos, T., and J. D. Hicks. 1951. *Agricultural Discontent in the Middle West, 1900–1939.* Madison: University of Wisconsin Press.

Shepherd, G. S. 1947. *Agricultural Price Policy.* Ames: Iowa State College Press.

6

The Images Agricultural Economists Think By

HAROLD F. BREIMYER

We cannot help trying to understand the world
we are living in, and we need to construct some
kind of picture of an economy. . . .
Joan Robinson (1977)

The complexity of the real world often defies
such properties as clarity, unity, consistency, and
generality.
Theodor Heidhues (1979)

Analysis and Image. Agricultural economists have long had trouble knowing who they are and what they do. They are less than fully confident about how to define the universe to which they address their introspective and analytical skills. At times they seem more pragmatically resourceful than scientifically fastidious. Their unsureness may be traced to the clouded legitimacy of their discipline. Agricultural economics as a field of knowledge and inquiry sprang from an unlikely mating of elegant (general) economic theory with barnyard farm management. Hybrid vigor may accompany the genetic potpourri.

This essay is not directed, however, at a definition of agricultural economists' talents, the epistemology of their discipline, or the research techniques employed. It targets another relevant aspect of the scientific process applied to the economics of agriculture seldom remarked on, namely, the nature of the images of the universe to which agricultural economists address themselves.

This essay draws heavily on a piece written for *Looking Ahead,* a publication of the National Planning Association. See Breimyer (1979).

The heart of the message offered here is that agricultural economists necessarily examine simplified images rather than the complex reality of the agricultural universe. They do so out of constrained necessity; they have no alternative. The necessity arises from the limitations of the human mind. The real world, or any sector of it, is too big and complex for even the most brilliant human being to comprehend. The only recourse is to simplify. In the terms of logic we "abstract." In another paper devoted to the subject (Breimyer 1979) I wrote, "We reduce the economic world in its infinite complexity to small-scale models that fit within our comprehension." This is the way it must be. "No other course is possible," I added, "other than to creep into a shell of ignorance and futility."

The process of abstraction bears an analogy to model building, and in a sense image and model are analogous terms. More precisely stated, though, models are one logical step subordinate to images. Econometricians construct their sets of equations upon the images they have previously formed.

Nor does the computational wizardry of computers alter the case. Calculations are not the equivalent of comprehension; furthermore, the computer potential remains finite in the face of an infinite universe. Essentially, abstraction is confined to the image.

No novelty is claimed for these reminders about implicit limits to understanding, although the literature of agricultural economics is hardly studded with them. Almost a generation ago Kenneth Boulding (1956) wrote about his "*Image* of the world." he emphasized the personalizing of "knowledge," itself defined as what a knower knows. More recently Herman Daly (1973) couched similar ideas in the phraseology of paradigm and paradigm shifts. Taken from Thomas Kuhn (1969), these relate to prevailing conceptualizations about a corner of the universe as accepted, or set, by the scientific community. Kuhn notes that any given formulation is relinquished reluctantly: "to abandon one paradigm in favor of another amounts to a scientific revolution" (Kuhn 1969, p. 2).

To recapitulate, in a true sense economists analyze a make-believe world. It is a tiny world of their own imagining, their self-created microcosm. Its first requisite is that it fit within the human brain.

The Danger of Distortion. The first inference to be drawn regarding the image-creation process is that it must be as free as possible from distortion. Random accidental error is the easiest to deal with. It cannot be entirely avoided, but statistical error terms at least suggest its probable magnitude.

More subtle, however, is the possibility of ideological bias. This introduces the issue of objectivity, about which Emery Castle (1968) and Alan Randall (1974) have written, as have I (Breimyer 1967).

Supposedly, scientists disinfect themselves ideologically before they undertake their inquiries. Economists put on the counterpart of the hospital gown. The heart of the scientific revolution was indeed a confidence that scientists could work accurately from observed phenomena, in place of relying on "revealed" knowledge.

No expose of agricultural economists, favorable or unfavorable, will be offered here. On the whole their record is not bad. Only a few individuals, I have suggested, are "as quick as Faust to sell their souls; not many cater that deferentially to special interests." Agricultural economists' greater sin is the one of which Kuhn accuses the scientific community, namely, overcommitment to a favorite image (paradigm, model). I put it that agricultural economists err as they "stick too closely to a doctrinal allegiance" (Breimyer 1979). It's almost a Pygmalion complex. An economist, having drawn his favorite model of the universe, becomes enamored of it. Thereupon the tendency is to fit new observations to the model, instead of modifying the model to conform to the observations.

Value-Laden Criteria. It may seem paradoxical, but if in the scientific tradition we want our images of the economy to be derived by value-free abstraction we encounter the dilemma that the most exalted stage in analysis, the making of welfare judgments, can be arrived at only by setting up welfare criteria that are value laden. Manifestly, the higher the level of aggregation, the more do value criteria invade the welfare calculus.

Moral principles entering welfare judgments may be the most precious element in all human relationships. The late John Brewster provided an invaluable service to agricultural economics when he specified the principles or values that have most characterized U.S. agriculture. His terms such as the creed of self-integrity, the democratic creed, the work ethic, and such social values as economic growth and social stability are now part of our lexicon (Madden and Brewster 1970).

Agricultural economists may nevertheless be ingenuous regarding the prevailing value system. We may endow our visualized public with more enlightenment, beneficence, public spirit, and democratic or even puritanical values than are deserved. More citizens than will admit it are antidemocratic. Not a few are essentially aristocratic or plutocratic. Economic justice is usually subscribed to in a vague way, yet specification is difficult and contentious. Various examples of value conflicts could be named.

A Cooperative Economy. What are some of the ingredients a conscientious agricultural economist should put into his conceptual image? Of what timbers ought he build his shanty miniature of the Big House?

First of all, the economy is cooperative.

This epigram is more potent than it may appear to be. It reminds us that agricultural economics is essentially dichotomous. One-half relates to the institutional terms of cooperativeness and puts agricultural economics in close connection with sociology and political science; the other carries all the stuff of a mechanistic production function extended to distribution of product. The division between the two is sharp and sometimes acrimonious. It evolves from the dual origin of the discipline, and it helps explain the problems of identity noted at the beginning of this essay.

In sober reality, though, the two divisions are not logical equivalents. The mechanistic portion is secondary. The effort to make income distribution mathematically determinate and therefore institution-neutral may be laudable, but it is impossible to achieve. A decade ago James Buchanan told agricultural economists their first concern was with the behavioral and institutional aspects of their field. Economics as a social science, he said, "is more than applied mathematics." Rather, "Economists, as professional social scientists, should possess a comparative advantage . . . in their expertise in a particular sort of human behavior and in the institutions that emerge from that behavior." Economists (including those specializing in agriculture) should give their attention to the "theory of markets" and should go "beyond these confines . . . to explore man's never-ending quest for more complex and elaborate forms of voluntary cooperation." The ultimate stage is study of "institutions of all kinds, including the political," and "collective decision-making" (Buchanan 1969).

The Resources We Employ. An interesting irony in the agricultural economic tradition is that economics is routinely defined in terms of employment of scarce resources, and yet the heroic achievements in economic growth, for which economists ask a share of credit, amount to making resources less scarce.

A more honest phrasing is that some resources are employed in order to make others more plentiful. In our national tradition, human resources have been directed to converting physical resources into forms contributing to creature comfort.

Of the two resource categories, human and physical, during the first two centuries of our national history the physical have been regarded as the more abundant. Human ingenuity has been applied to "work" them and deliver the product.

The human psyche is invariably more circumspect toward that which is scarce and useful than toward the plentiful. So it is that education has been exalted and put in the public domain, whereas physical resources have been denied consistent protection and have largely stayed in the private sector.

Our third century has opened on a different note. Events of the 1970s reminded us not only of the ubiquitousness of scarcity, but of its pain. The economics of physical resources has suddenly gained stature. Its politics has climbed to the forefront of national debate even though at the decade's end these issues were mired in indecision.

It may be significant and in some respects ominous that public education now attracts diminishing support. Efforts to assure quality of public school education at elementary and secondary levels, an obsession just after Sputnik, seem to be losing momentum. Private schooling is resurging. Significantly, public education tends to conform to democratic values, but private education is class stratified. Higher education too is in some trouble. State universities fight for both status and funds, and a growing portion of their research depends on privately contracted financing.

Depletable (and Depleting) versus Nondepletable Physical Resources. Definitions of depletable and nondepletable resources are familiar. Depletable include the fossil fuels, mineral ores, and rocks. The nondepletable category is less exact, as some resources such as land, water, and ocean beaches can be retained undepleted yet are subject to diversion of use as well as permanent damage. In strict language, "nondepletable" should be phrased as "potentially sustainable."

"The two kinds of resources differ in the nature of their scarcity. Nondepletable resources, even if protected, become scarce due to pressure put on them, primarily by a growing population. Depletable resources become scarce as their supply is progressively exhausted" (Breimyer 1979, p. 6).

The economics of depletable and of nondepletable resources differ intensely. Concepts in agricultural economics are at the core. As Ricardo taught everyone who would listen, the pressure of population on a fixed (therefore nondepletable) resource yields rent to all enterprises except the few at the margin. Rent is an unearned return. The ancients called it tribute. The economics and the social explosiveness of the factor return of rent are part and parcel of all instruction in the economics of agriculture. If it is played down because of its dolorousness, a demerit goes to the erring instructor.

Also part of received economic theory nowadays is the contrived rental return generated in imperfect competition, so well delineated more than a generation ago by Sraffa, Chamberlin, and Robinson. This is the whole meaning of differentiation of product, as Campbell labels its soup differently from Heinz and Cadillac its automobiles separately from Chrysler. University professors are not innocent. On the contrary, they use their degrees and all possible accoutrements to justify preferential treatment by deans and presidents. (Insofar as they enter collective bargaining, they imply collective differentiation but internal homogeneity.)

What about depletable resources? So long as a nation regards them as inexhaustible they have no economic status. All enterprise and valuation are confined to the process of extracting, processing, and delivering them. So it has been in the United States until recently.

It is not so now. It is not so notably for the fossil fuels. A new teacher came on the scene in the early 1970s, named OPEC. The OPEC nations instructed the world in the economics of attaching a reservation price to a depletable resource. That reservation price contains a sizable element analogous to rent.

The degree of similarity or difference between the income share arising from reservation pricing of a mineral and rent on land need not concern us here. Lewis G. Gray (1914) examined the subject perceptively many years ago.

In two articles (Breimyer 1974, 1978), I have called attention to the significance of reservation pricing, especially as it bears on the cost of industrial raw materials utilized in the technology of modern farming.

Agricultural economists will henceforth be burdened with learning more about the nature and consequence of reservation prices of depletable resources. Not the least of the issues will be the terms of recovery of their monopolistic portion. In the economics of agriculture, part of the rent has been captured for society by means, first, of land taxes reflecting market value, and, second, of graduated income taxes. The latter have the advantage as a social instrument in that they can tap the rent that comes from fiat arrangements such as trademarks for industrial products (and, for that matter, the licensing of physicians and even the protective cloak the Ph.D. degree gives university professors). At the time this essay was written, public debate over social collection of part of the reservation price of domestic oil was couched in terms of windfall profits taxes.

The Nature of the Economic Unit. Of all aspects of the big, wide world that economists must reduce to conceptual and computational manageability, none is more basic than the nature of the enterprise unit.

It long was fashionable to assume that units were neutral so long as they stopped short of monopolistic properties. On the consumption side the unit was the household, and in production the firm. The former remains a reasonbly discrete unit, although institutional delivery of some consumption items (as food eaten in restaurants or school lunchrooms) obscures many of the empirical consumption function data taken from family behavior. Also, the literature of recent decades has acknowledged, however reluctantly, that households are not exclusively "economic men."

The business firm is another matter. Paul Nelson (1958) published a virtual diatribe saying that the larger business firm of our age is remote from the firm of classical theory.

Is the firm essentially a legal entity? A management unit? Is it defined technologically? P. J. D. Wiles (1961) stresses the idea of sovereignty. How do private and public influences bear on sovereignty?

In my writing (Breimyer 1976), I have objected to regarding the firm as passive. I renounce earlier (pre-Nelson) bland doctrine that the firm has "no more id than a rag doll." The respect lately accorded Herbert Simon, Nobel Prize winner and perceptive writer on managerial economics, amounts to scholarly penance for economists' earlier neglect.

My judgment is that the larger business firm is midway in metamorphosis. Aside from trends toward conglomerate ownership and franchise linkage, two sharings of sovereignty are notable—those with counterpart firms in an industry via perceived common interest and those with government by the avenue of regulation. For years I have predicted a private-public codification of trade practice rules, happily simplifying the present melange, but the idea has won little acceptance (Breimyer 1977b).

The nature of the firm takes on special meaning in marketing, where the unique and vital function of value determination is carried on. In an exchange economy composed of private enterprise units the determination of value—as converted to price—plays an instrumental role. It directs economic activity. Apart from oversight reserved to the state, two kinds of firms come into existence. One is the trading firm, the purest example of which is the commodity exchange. The second is the market firm that negotiates value in connection with transfer of ownership of its product. In the latter case value determination is more or less incidental to the firm's other economic activity, yet it attracts public scrutiny because of its strategic importance.

Because of the complications of combining value determination with operational functions (as assembly or storage), Professor Bakken (1953) has urged confining marketing, conceptually and definitionally, to the process of exchange.

Determinants of Price and Returns. The note just offered about the nature of the firm as a value-determining instrument is unconventional, not in its substance but in its location. Ordinarily, economists examine economic forces at length and measure them with precision before they vouchsafe a comment on the institutional framework for putting a dollar tag on product. Moreover, economists operating in the neoclassical tradition are enamored of the concept of equilibrium, borrowed from the physical sciences. That blissful state is supposedly arrived at as an outcome of vicious, virtually carnivorous, aggressions. Oskar Morgenstern (1972) once wrote a parody on the paradox. Capstone to the paradox is that the most stable state of economic affairs may be not equilibrium among balanced adversaries but dominance by one firm, or by two or three firms that would rather connive than fight.

The literature of competitive models exceeds anyone's 5-foot-shelf limit and will not be developed here. Three comments nevertheless are relevant to our images of a competitive economy.

The first is the heroic hope that factor and product price, product flow, and therefore income generation can all be arrived at simultaneously. The biggest potential obstacle is the opportunity to affix a reservation price to any physical resource, giving rise to unearned rent.

The second is the well-known tendency of business firms to employ non-price methods of competition. The implication for the moment is not their welfare consequence but their indeterminacy. It's an image that does not allow direct solution. Economists do not like that!

Third is the substantial part now played by transfer payments. They, even more than rent, are not directly related to employment of factors of production. Professor Boulding is the best-known publicist of this complicating feature of today's economy.

Today's economy is significantly flawed by allowing the facile determination of value and income that economists find so attractive. The temptation to create an unrealistic but analytically manageable image is hard to resist.

The Image of Agriculture. My closing comment calls attention to a double image of agriculture about which I have written. Agriculture today combines its agrarian tradition, which is as old as Abraham, with a technology as modern as laser beams. The two are each empirically verifiable yet almost incompatible. The agricultural economist is therefore pulled and hauled between choosing one to the exclusion of the other, for ease of communication, or trying to encompass both, braving the frustrations.

The two images are described in my *Farm Policy: 13 Essays* (Breimyer 1977a). Agrarian agriculture features the resource of land, the biology of living things, the imperiousness of climate, the sociology of the work ethic, and other values commonly (if sometimes mistakenly) attributed almost exclusively to agriculture and the economics of distribution of surplus value (rent).

Industrial agriculture brings high productivity but industrial-type problems in managing it, susceptibility to environmental restraints on certain materials (notably applied chemicals), and perhaps above all the extreme monetization of risk.

The agrarian root is credited with the entrepreneurial structure known as the family farm. An industrial agriculture is more likely to convert to the business unit of manufacturing and commerce, as indeed has been done in large commercial feedlots and egg cities.

In brief summary, the burden of this essay is only that image building in agricultural economics is implicit and inescapable, and that it is seldom neutral. It is not neutral with respect to the viewer's capacity to view. Bias in viewing may be accidental, interest shaped, or merely reflective of personality.

What kind of an economy do we indeed have? What kind of agricultural economy? What modifications are emerging? And to the agricultural economist who hopes to shape and not merely record, what kind of agriculture, what kind of economy, what kind of world do we want?

The intellectual process of seeking answers involves image building. We should take care to do it well.

References

Bakken, H. H. 1953. *Theory of Markets and Marketing.* Madison: Mimir Publishers.

Boulding, K. E. 1956. *The Image.* Ann Arbor: University of Michigan Press.

Breimyer, H. F. 1967. "The Stern Test of Objectivity for the Useful Science of Agricutural Economics." *American Journal of Agricultural Economics* 49(May):339-50.

_____. 1974. "Agricultural Economics in a Less Expansible Economy." *American Journal of Agricultural Economics* 56(November):812-15.

_____. 1976. *Economics of the Product Markets of Agriculture.* Ames: Iowa State University Press.

_____. 1977a. *Farm Policy: 13 Essays.* Ames: Iowa State University Press.

_____. 1977b. "Rules, Roles, Economic Reality, and the American Dream." Third Gardiner Memorial Lecture, New Mexico State University, April 21. University of Missouri-Columbia Department of Agricultural Economics Paper 1977-22.

_____. 1978. "Agriculture's Three Economies in a Changing Resource Environment." *American Journal of Agricultural Economics* 60(February):37-47.

_____. 1979. "The Nature of the U.S. Economy: An Essay on Parameters and Preconceptions." *Looking Ahead,* National Planning Association, 4(3):3-11.

Buchanan, J. M. 1969. "A Future for 'Agricultural Economics'?" *American Journal of Agricultural Economics* 51(December):1027-36.

Castle, E. N. 1968. "On Scientific Objectivity." *American Journal of Agricultural Economics* 40(November):809-14.

Daly, H. E. 1973. "Paradigms in Political Economy." In *Toward a Steady-State Economy,* edited by Herman E. Daly. San Francisco: W. H. Freeman.

Gray, L. C. 1914. "Rent under the Assumption of Exhaustibility." *Quarterly Journal of Economics* 28(May):466-89.

Heidhues, T. 1979. "The Gains from Trade: An Applied Political Analysis." In *International Trade and Agriculture,* edited by Jimmye S. Hillman and Andrew Schmitz. Boulder, Colo.: Westview Press.

Kuhn, T. S., 1969. *The Structure of Scientific Revolutions.* 2d ed. Chicago: University of Chicago Press.

Madden, J. P., and D. E. Brewster, eds. 1970. *Selected Works of John M. Brewster.* Philadelphia: J. T. Murphy.

Morgenstern, O. 1972. "Thirteen Critical Points in Contemporary Theory: An Interpretation." *Journal of Economic Literature* 10(December):1163-89.

Nelson, P. E., Jr. 1958. "Altering Marketing Concepts to Modern Conditions." *Journal of Farm Economics* 40(December):1511-22.

Randall, A. 1974. "Information, Power and Academic Responsibility." *American Journal of Agricultural Economics* 56(May):227-34.

Robinson, J. 1977. "What Are the Questions?" *Journal of Economic Literature* 15(December):1318-39.

Wiles, P. J. D. 1961. *Price, Cost and Output.* Oxford: Basil Blackwell.

7

An Extension to
"What Can a Research Man
Say about Values?"

GLENN L. JOHNSON

In 1956, Professor Geoffrey Shepherd published "What Can a Research Man Say about Values?" (see Chapter 2). While being a scholarly article, it was not inhibited by unthinking adherence to a particular philosophical position. Instead, it was a free expression of where Shepherd stood with respect to the need for and the possibility of researching values in connection with agricultural policy, farm management, and other problems of the real world. He clearly saw that such research is necessary if we are going to have nonarbitrary, nonauthoritarian decisions made with respect to the practical problems facing society.

In his analysis of the role of values, Professor Shepherd made no direct response to the positivism of John N. Keynes, as reflected for example in the writing of Milton Friedman (1953), although he did explicitly reject the reflection of Keynes's positivism in the writings of Lionel Robbins (1949). He gave some attention to Pareto optimality but clearly indicated that interpersonally valid knowledge about values has to be available in decisions that affect the distribution of the ownership of the means of producing income if such decisions are to be nonauthoritarian and nonarbitrary. The article contains few, if any, references to the pragmatic institutionalists such as Kenneth Parsons (1949), John Timmons (also at Iowa State), Leonard Salter (1948), or John R. Commons (1934). However, there are numerous references to the interdependence between the values of means and "more ultimate" or intrinsic values. These references tend to reflect the pragmatic presupposition that knowledge

This paper first appeared as Michigan Agricultural Experiment Station Bulletin No. 9280. The author is indebted to James Bonnen, Larry Connor, Lester Manderscheid, and Allan Schmid for helpful comments and criticisms.

of values and positivistic knowledge not having to do with values are interdependent. The pragmatists are often vague about the distinction between values in exchange and intrinsic values—in fact, they tend to reject the idea of intrinsic value. As we will later see, Professor Shepherd's article is also somewhat ambiguous on this issue.

While his article's emphasis on the role of values departed sharply from widely held points of view concerning research methods in the 1950s, which prevail to the present day, it must be pointed out that he had then, and still has, a great deal of company. Practical economists who research and make decisions on practical problems typically disregard the constraints of specialized philosophies on their ability to work with values. Such agricultural economists are found in the employment of national, state, and local governments as well as in international agencies such as the World Bank, the UN Food and Agriculture Organization, and the Asian Development Bank. They are also found in the private sector, whether their firms be multinational, national, or local. A concern with values is, therefore, of immediate relevance for applied economics.

Professor Shepherd's scholarly article does not cover the works of what I term "the objective normativists." I refer here to G. E. Moore (1903/1956), C. I. Lewis (1955), and related philosophers. In this article I attempt to extend, in a way that I hope will be acceptable to Professor Shepherd, his excellent work to include the contribution of the objective normativists. I will first define "the normative" and strengthen Professor Shepherd's case for researching it. I will then incorporate the contributions of the objective normativists into Professor Shepherd's framework. I will conclude with a brief discussion of the interactive, iterative nature of problem-solving research.

The Need to Work on the Normative. This section is best introduced with a definition of what I mean by the word "normative." Fritz Machlup (1969) has catalogued the confusing array of definitions that economists use for this term. In this paper, I define normative as meaning "knowledge having to do with the goodness or badness of conditions, situations, or things." The normative, as I use it here, does not mean "what ought to be" as, obviously, not everything that is good ought to be done or ought to be brought into existence because resource constraints prevent us from doing everything good. Instead of being able to do everything good, we are faced with the need to choose the best among alternative goods in view of what has to be sacrificed in order to obtain them. Conversely, it is not always wrong to do bad. Economists are keenly aware of the need to minimize losses, i.e., to minimize the bad—to do the least bad that can be done in the circumstances faced. Sometimes a bad "ought to be." It is clear that a distinction must be drawn between good and bad, on one hand, and "what ought to be" or prescriptions, on the other.

Society faces many issues and problems at all levels, internationally, nationally, subnationally, and locally. Other problems are faced in the private sector. Issues now before us include poverty, environmental quality, minorities, energy, population pressures, and food production, to mention only a few. Solving the specific practical problems associated with any one of these issues in a nonarbitrary, nonauthoritarian way requires objective, interpersonally valid knowledge of goodness and badness of conditions, situations, and things per se. This involves more than finding out who regards them as good and bad. Decision making even at the farm level is similar because the farm family typically includes a number of decision makers and affected people—man, wife, and concerned children, at least. Particularly in arranging for the intergenerational transfer of property, farm management consulting requires interpersonally valid knowledge of goodness and badness, including the degrees thereof.

Values also lie at the basis of much applied economic analysis. For example, the expected utility hypothesis, which is in vogue in the field of farm management, requires objective measurements of utility functions that are normative whether or not interpersonally valid. In another area, we find resource and developmental economists currently very interested in project evaluation and design analyses. Use by project evaluators of internal rate of return, net present value, or benefit/cost ratios is basically normative. Also, planning research at national, subnational, and local levels involves selecting the "best route" to follow through time and in space in developing an economy or parts thereof. Decisions as to the "best path" cannot be made without knowledge of goodness and badness. Even the concept of production—as the creation of time, form, and place *utility*—is normative.

In closing this section it seems desirable to note that price, income, and expenditure data are all normative—they deal with values, in this case monetary values. Though we commonly make the distinction between monetary and nonmonetary values, there is an unfortunate tendency among some economic researchers to regard prices as being nonnormative or positive simply because they are easily quantified and measured. This unfortunate tendency probably arises from positivistic brainwashing that has convinced such persons, consciously but more likely unconciously, that anything quantifiable and measurable cannot be normative! But it should be remembered that prices are values in exchange that reflect the underlying values of the parties involved.

The Potential Contribution of the Objective Normativists to Professor Shepherd's Point of View. Professor Shepherd's freedom from philosophic inhibitions makes him somewhat of a philosophic eclectic. Because he is not inhibited by the positivists (see the section of Chapter 2 entitled "Values Lie in the Realm of Science"), he is able to use contributions from the normativists. Similarly, because he knows about the pragmatists, he can use and advocate their approach without necessarily being constrained by the complexity of pragmatism. Certainly he has command over the methodologies of positivism and is able to use them. The conditional normativism of Gunnar Myrdal (1944) and of so many of Professor Shepherd's agricultural economic colleagues was also well known to him and he could practice it without foregoing the advantages of normativism, positivism, and pragmatism.

Currently, there is a move toward formalization of the kind of eclecticism that Professor Shepherd appears to practice. This move toward formalization grows out of the work of the pragmatists, the systems scientists, and the cyberneticists and out of increased recognition of the advantages of eclecticism.

Professor Shepherd's original article, while advocating normativism, does not, in my view, use the contribution of the "objective normativists" to full advantage. It is their contribution that I want to concentrate on because I think it is important for fully establishing and formalizing the eclecticism that Professor Shepherd practices. I believe he will approve of this attempt on my part to extend his eclecticism to include the work of the objective normativists. Such an extension confirms the wisdom of his choice of direction.

The two important objective normativists to be considered are G. E. Moore (1903/1956), who authored *Principia Ethica,* and C. I. Lewis (1955), who authored *The Ground and Nature of the Right.*

Moore argued in his 1903 book that "good" and "bad" are undefined terms whose meaning we know from experiencing good or bad, per se. He argued that goodness and badness are experiential, not definitional. It should be kept in mind that he was not writing about what "ought or ought not be done"; instead, and to repeat, he was writing about value, about good and bad, per se. Concepts of the goodness or badness of conditions, situations, and things go into decisions or prescriptions about what is right or wrong to do. Yet, value concepts are not the same as concepts about what ought or ought not to be done. This point was difficult for me, as an economist, to grasp. The difficulty probably arose from the many years when I and other careless people defined values as "what ought to be done" rather than distinguishing between values, on the one hand, and prescriptions as to what ought to be done, on the other.

Moore's point of view is in sharp contrast to that of the positivists and logical positivists who take it (on the basis of an empirically untested, metaphysical proposition) that goodness and badness are not experienced. I find it ironic that the positivists who place such great emphasis on experience and experiential observations should base their philosophy on an empirically untested metaphysical proposition! I believe that my experiences of, say, the badness of a toothache or the goodness of having grandchildren are as real as my experiences of the color red or the weight of a 42-inch northern pike on the end of my fishing line. Moore was too much an empiricist to accept an untested metaphysical presupposition about the impossibility of having normative experiences. Moore found it to be empirically true that people do have normative experiences; hence he rejected the empirically untested presupposition of the positivists who are (ironically) also referred to as empiricists.

In any event, Moore's acceptance of the reality of normative experiences made it possible to treat research on normative questions in a manner precisely parallel to that developed by the logical positivists and clarified by such linguistic analysts as Wittgenstein and Carnap. Once primitive, undefined normative terms were available, whose meanings are known only from experience, it was possible to convert purely formal logical systems (*analytic* in nature) into *synthetic* statements (empirically descriptive) and to verify and validate them by the same methods used for positive knowledge. (See Carnap's [1953] truth/falsity table and the pages that follow it.)

C. I. Lewis (1955), in his book *The Ground and Nature of the Right,* draws a sharp distinction between the prescriptive and the normative. His distinction is in full accord with the formal structure of economics and is the distinction between the normative and prescriptive used above. In economics, we convert a production function into a value productivity function by multiplying it by the price (value) of the product being produced, regarding the total value productivity function as a "good." We then construct a cost function made up of the sum of total fixed costs and total variable costs and ascribe badness to the costs it represents. We solve for the quantities of the variable factors of production that maximize the difference between the good (total value product function) and the bad (total cost function). These two functions are based on both normative and positive data, the normative data in this case being monetary in nature. The set of quantities of productive factors that maximizes this difference is *prescribed* as what ought to be done by the entrepreneur.

Note that, in the above example, concepts of goodness and badness have been processed through a static decision making rule into a *prescription* as to the right action to take. It is precisely this distinction that Lewis makes between good and bad, on the one hand, and right and wrong, on the other. While our example deals with monetary values, Lewis's point of view is general and applies to both monetary and nonmonetary values. Lewis's general logic covers the welfare or consumption economists who maximize nonmonetary and/or monetary values, as appropriate.

Thus, when the G. E. Moore and C. I. Lewis contributions are combined, an objective way of reaching prescriptions from *both* positive and normative knowledge emerges that is entirely consistent with economics. It is important to note, however, that G. E. Moore's contribution is much greater than that of agreeing (in combination with C. I. Lewis) with the maximizing procedures practiced by economists. That greater contribution is one of objectifying research on normative and prescriptive grounds.

In the positivistic biological and physical sciences, positivistic, primitive, undefined terms are used to transform purely formal analytical systems into descriptive, synthetic systems. Objectivity is attained through application of the tests of correspondence, coherence, and clarity or lack of ambiguity. The formal truth of an analytical system is tested by checking its coherence or logical consistency. Many logicians assert that the formal truth of such systems can be proven, though others, such as Godel, question even that. The empirical truth of synthetic systems, however, is never proven, just not disproven. It is always possible for observers to make mistakes in their interpretation of sense impressions. Realization that synthetic or descriptive empirical knowledge is never beyond question prompted Popper (1959) to assert that falsifiability is important in developing empirical concepts. The importance of falsifiability is as great on the normative as on the positive side, though Popper, as a positivist, ignored the normative side. In the positivistic biological and physical disciplines, experience and the interpretation of sense impressions are used in testing for the *correspondence* between a concept and reality. Here, in order not to overrate the correspondence test in positivism, it is important to note that a concept is never checked directly with reality for correspondence; instead, one concept is tested against another concept, the alternative concept being based upon (1) additional experience or on sufficient "degrees of freedom" so that the tested concept is capable of being falsified by experience and (2) a leap of faith that there is something "out there in reality" (whatever reality is) that corresponds with the impressions on our senses of touch, smell, taste, sight, and hearing.

Moore's stress on the undefined primitive nature of concepts of goodness and badness places empirical normative research on a formal par with empirical positive research. This does not state that it is as easy to make normative as to make positive measurements, though that may be distinctly possible. For instance, it is easy to measure monetary values. Nonmonetary values are also measurable as indicated. Von Neumann and Morgenstern (1947) outlined techniques of measuring utility on the basis of much earlier work by Bernoulli (1738). These techniques were clarified by Friedman and Savage (1948) and are now employed in the current utility hypothesis analyses being carried out by students of decision making in farm management and agricultural finance. On the positive side, we note that there are also severe measurement and observational difficulties encountered in connection with the concepts of the "fundamental particle" in physics or of black holes in astronomy. Thus, the difficulties with observation and measurement on the normative side are similar, in principle, to those on the positive side—the amount of difficulty depends on what is being measured.

The linguistic analysts have stressed the importance of the test of *clarity* almost as a precondition for applying the tests of correspondence and coherence. If a statement, either positivistic or normative, is ambiguous (i.e., has more than one meaning), it is more difficult to falsify or disprove it than if it has only one meaning.

There is some conflict between objective normativism and pragmatism, which can be handled or neglected by an eclectic. Pragmatists are interested in the solution of practical problems faced by real world decision makers, which is something different from being interested in questions asked by disciplinary *normativistic* academicians. The *pragmatic interest is in prescriptions to solve problems.* Prescriptions have to do with what ought to be, which, as we have seen above, can be either good or bad. Pragmatists, as is argued eloquently in a long quotation on page 18 of Professor Shepherd's article, tend to regard positive and normative knowledge as interdependent. However, their position is somewhat ambiguous because of the following: while it is obvious that the prescriptive depends simultaneously on the positive and the normative, the pragmatists may confuse (1) the dependence of the prescriptive on the positive and normative for (2) interdependence between the positive and the normative. Pragmatists are more interested in values in exchange than in intrinsic values. In my own work and in my collaboration with Professor Lewis K. Zerby, a philosopher, I have found empirical instances of apparent interdependence between positive and normative knowledge and instances in which they appear to be relatively independent, such as the positive knowledge of cucumber production functions and the normative knowledge of the goodness of equity, as reported in Johnson and Zerby (1973). This leaves room for both objective normativism and pragmaticism as long as neither excludes the other. We did not, however, find instances in which prescriptions did not depend jointly on both normative and positive knowledge. Pragmaticists reject and accept prescriptive knowledge on the basis of whether or not the prescription "works," i.e., solves the problem. The test of *workability* is a special case of the correspondence test considered earlier, which is logically compatible with pragmatism and objective normativism if not positivism.

Problem Solving as an Interactive, Iterative Process. In any event, it seems important for researchers doing practical research—i.e., engaged in problem solving—to interact pragmatically with decision makers and affected persons. Because decision makers are often replaced through elective or more violent means, it is advisable to *interact* with affected persons as well as decision makers. Interaction is a significant source of information for problem-solving researchers. For instance, decision makers and affected persons can often point out positivistic and normative knowledge relative to the problem being solved that is unknown and unperceived by a problem-solving researcher. Problem solving is an *iterative* process with many feedbacks as a decision maker or researcher proceeds through the steps of problem definition, observation, analysis, decision making, execution, and responsibility bearing (see Johnson and Halter 1961). As information from decision makers and affected persons feeds back into the problem-solving research process, earlier steps in the problem-solving process have to be modified and/or repeated. Even the problem itself may have to be redefined. New observations may have to be made in order to check the positive or normative truth of information furnished by decision makers and affected persons. Then too, the analysis may have to be changed and even the decision rules used in converting normative and positive knowledge into prescriptive knowledge may have to be changed. Executive procedures and the bearing of responsibility may also have to be changed as the result of such feedback. Thus, it is necessary to *iterate interactively* with decision makers and problem solvers.

This iterative process is part of researching the normative when doing problem-solving research. When this process is quantified, as is done increasingly by modern systems analysts (Johnson et al. 1971; Rossmiller et al. 1972, 1978), we approach a quantification of pragmatism. If pragmatism is not taken too seriously in this iterative, interactive process, there is still room for objective normativists to contribute to the accumulation of normative knowledge independently of positive knowledge and for positivists to contribute to the accumulation of positive knowledge independently of normative knowledge. In short, we can follow formal eclectic procedures, which allow for needed *iterative interaction,* without abandoning the eclecticism toward which Professor Shepherd's admirable paper tended.

Objective normativism has a major contribution to make to this eclecticism. With that contribution, what a research man can say about values can be much more objective than without it. I hasten to add that what I think the objective normativists can add to Professor Shepherd's article is mainly detail, for which he has already provided ample space with characteristic foresight and comprehensiveness.

References

Bernoulli, B. 1738. "Specimen Theoriae Novae de Mensura Sortis." Commentarii Academiae Scientiarum Imperiales Petropolitanae, V. Translated by L. Sommer in *Econometrica,* 1954, vol. 22, pp. 23–36.

Carnap, R. 1953. "Formal and Factual Science." In *Readings in the Philosophy of Science,* edited by H. Feigl and M. Broadbeck. New York: Appleton-Century-Crofts.

Commons, J. R. 1934. *Institutional Economics.* New York: Macmillan.

Friedman, M. 1953. *Essays on Positive Economics.* Chicago: University of Chicago Press.

Friedman, M., and J. L. Savage. 1948. "The Utility Analysis of Choices Involving Risk." *Journal of Political Economics* 56(August):279–304.

Johnson, G. L., and A. N. Halter. 1961. *A Study of Managerial Processes of Midwestern Farmers.* Ames: Iowa State University Press.

Johnson, G. L., and L. K. Zerby. 1973. *What Economists Do about Values: Case Studies of Their Answers to Questions They Don't Dare Ask.* East Lansing: Department of Agricultural Economics, Michigan State University.

Johnson, G. L., et al. 1971. *A Generalized Simulation Approach to Agricultural Sector Analysis: With Special Reference to Nigeria.* East Lansing: Michigan State University.

Lewis, C. I. 1955. *The Ground and Nature of the Right.* New York: Columbia University Press.

Machlup, F. 1969. "Positive and Normative Economics." In *Economic Means and Social Ends,* edited by R. Heilbroner. Englewood Cliffs, N.J.: Prentice-Hall.

Moore, G. E. 1956. *Principia Ethica.* Cambridge: Cambridge University Press. (Originally published in 1903.)

Myrdal, G. 1944. *The American Dilemma.* New York: Harper Brothers.

Parsons, K. H. 1949. "The Logical Foundations of Economic Research." *Journal of Farm Economics* 31(November):656–86.

———. 1958. "The Value Problem in Agricultural Policy." In *Agricultural Adjustment Problems in a Growing Economy,* edited by E. O. Heady et al. Ames: Iowa State University Press.

Popper, K. R. 1959. *The Logic of Scientific Discovery.* New York: Harper & Row.

Robbins, L. 1949. *An Essay on the Nature and Significance of Economic Science.* London: Macmillan.

Rossmiller, G. E. 1978. *Agricultural Sector Planning: A General System Simulation Approach.* East Lansing: Department of Agricultural Economics, Michigan State University.

Rossmiller, G. E., et al. 1972. *Korean Agricultural Sector Analysis and Recommended Development Strategies, 1971–1985.* East Lansing: Department of Agricultural Economics, Michigan State University.

Salter, L. 1948. *A Critical Review of Research in Land Economics.* St. Paul: University of Minnesota Press.

Von Neumman, J., and O. Morgenstern. 1947. *Theory of Games and Economic Behavior.* Princeton, N.J.: Princeton University Press.

8

A Critical Appraisal
of Family Farms as an Objective
# of Public Policy

W. K. McPHERSON

A VAST MAJORITY of people throughout the world are convinced that retaining the family farm is a desirable objective of public policy. General acceptance of this concept suggests that it reflects values ranked high among the ultimate ends people strive to attain. This, in itself, is sufficient reason to examine the adequacy of the family farm as an aim of public policy, especially since it is frequently cited as being symbolic of the American way of life.

The Problem of Definition. The phrase "family farm" is used so widely that both popular and scientific definitions must be examined.

Popular definition: The public has never precisely defined what is meant when the words "family" and "farm" are used together. Each individual defines the phrase differently. Farmers think of it as the farm on which they live, or would like to acquire. Others consider it as the place of their youth. The phrase "family farm" meets the requirements of political slogans or dogmas because it implies values held in high esteem by many people, and yet the lack of clear definition precludes the possibility of differences of opinion that might cost votes.

Scientific definition: Social scientists are not in full agreement on a definition of the family farm. A conference called for the express purpose of studying "family farm policy" failed to develop a definition acceptable to all

Florida Agricultral Experiment Station Journal Series No. 64. The article is reprinted by permission from the *Journal of Farm Economics* 34(August):310–24. It was read before the Agricultural Economics and Rural Sociology Section of the Association of Southern Agricultural Workers in Atlanta, Georgia, February 5, 1952.

participants (Ackerman and Harris 1947). More recently one student of the family farm accepted a definition developed by a group of religious leaders (Timmons and Murray 1951). The U.S. Department of Agriculture classifies family farms into four groups by three economic criteria: value of product, value of land and buildings, and work off farm by operator (Bachman and Jones 1950, p. 54). However, most students of family farm policy do not consider all farms operated by families desirable (Ackerman and Harris 1947).

That the family farm has escaped precise definition may be highly significant for two reasons:

First, some concepts defy definition because they consist of an amorphous group of heterogeneous ideas. If this is true of the family farm, more attention must be placed on identifying the components of the concept.

Second, ends are confused with means of attaining ends. This is clearly stated by those who say, "We feel impelled, however, to avoid the common mistake of looking on the family farm as an end of public policy rather than an instrument through which agriculture and rural life can be made a richer and more satisfying experience for those who farm, and a stronger institution in the American economy" (Ackerman and Harris 1947, p. 390; see also Schultz 1950, p. 30). This indicates that these authors believe that the family farm is a socioeconomic institution that has made it possible for people to attain a group of vaguely defined ends.

For these reasons, no effort is made here to define the family farm further. Instead, attention will be focused on trying to find out what farm families really strive to attain.

Assumptions. First, we assume the family farm to be a socioeconomic institution that generally changes to accommodate changes in wants and desires of people, availability of raw materials, and technology used to convert raw materials into useful goods. In other words, the family farm is a dynamic institution whose form and usefulness are constantly changing.

Second, we assume that the ends people attain from the family farm consist of a mixture of political, ethical, and economic values. This is not a new idea but one that has not been examined as scientifically as have the narrower concepts that lie within the confines of single disciplines.[1]

Third, policy is assumed to mean a plan or course of action to attain one or more ends or objectives that a group of people establish as desirable. Here we are primarily concerned with public policy.

Fourth, the ultimate ends of public policy are assumed to be the social and economic well-being of the nation as a whole. This assumption, in effect, rejects the philosophy of agricultural fundamentalism (Davis 1939) and accepts the desirability of an integrated and expanding economy to promote the social and economic well-being of the nation as a whole.[2]

Fifth, in a democracy we assume that individuals endeavor to attain ends that differ both qualitatively and quantitatively and vary with age, educational achievement, political situation, religion, and other factors. In this context, public policy consists of the ends that individuals can agree upon as being mutually desirable.

Analytical Approach. Within this framework, we will examine the family farm, with the analytical assumptions or hypotheses suggested by the late John R. Commons (1950).[3] These are sovereignty, scarcity, efficiency, futurity, and custom. Our attention will be focused on finding out what values families derive from family farms, whether these values are genuinely different from the values other families endeavor to attain, and whether the values people strive for on family farms are more desirable policy objectives than the family farm itself.

Sovereignty. Human beings use social organizations to obtain the advantages and satisfactions of collective action. The family was the first and is still the basic unit of social organization. To obtain the advantages of collective action, families use three kinds of power—physical, economic, and moral—the same tools that all social groups use to govern the action of their members. In the language of modern jurisprudence, duress is the physical power of violence, coercion the economic power of scarcity, and persuasion the moral power of propaganda.

Sovereign states use their monopoly of violence to define and protect property. In America, the sovereign state (first England and later the United States) expanded the institution and encouraged private ownership of property. Even before the Revolution corporeal property was defined to include all physical things that were scarce. The "obligation of contract" was recognized as incorporeal property and established as such in the Constitution. Finally, intangible property was recognized and the right to use it protected.

When the family farm originated in the United States, land was the only type of property that could be readily acquired. At that time, the right to use land enabled a family to satisfy the basic human motivation to possess or dominate and to produce the goods needed to subsist and raise their level of living. Consequently, about 90 percent of the people lived on farms and were able to satisfy these objectives simultaneously. Here we will concentrate attention on three questions:

(1) How effectively does the family farm satisfy the desire to possess or dominate? Farm ownership or the right to use farmland under reasonable tenure arrangements provides families with many opportunities for acquiring or creating things for many reasons. Some are primarily economic and others have little economic value. For example, farmers have a wide variety of op-

portunities to do many things not classified as earning a living. They may improve their homes, hunt or fish, or raise plants and animals because they like them.

(2) Do other forms of property satisfy the desire to possess as well as the family farm? Approximately 33 million nonfarm families in the United States endeavor to use other forms of property for this purpose. Several million of them own homes; others own cabins, boats, books, and paintings, as well as stocks, bonds, buildings, patents, and other forms of property.

Are the values that flow from possession of family farms superior to those derived from the ownership of other types of property? It would be difficult to answer in the affirmative. As civilization progresses, the wants and desires of people increase both qualitatively and quantitatively. To enable people to satisfy them, society creates a larger amount and a greater variety of property, and new forms of social organization to use it. While at one time the family farm was one of a few institutions that enabled people to satisfy their diverse wants and desires, there are now several, which means that families can choose among them to attain particular ends.

(3) Do family farmers tend to value the freedom that landownership provides more highly than improving their standard of living? Farmers endeavor to retain as much freedom as possible. When other groups use powers of coercion and persuasion to gain what appears to be an "unequal" share of the social product, farmers turn to government for protection. The Granger movement, antitrust laws, and parity price legislation are all examples of the farmers' use of the sovereign government's monopoly of duress to protect the freedom and independence provided by landownership and the right to use land.

In contrast, nonfarm families have surrendered some individual freedom to voluntary, nonsovereign governments such as corporations, cooperatives, and labor unions. In return they have received the benefits that accrue from specialization and trade. In other words, they have made what they believe is a reasonable compromise between the satisfactions that flow from freedom and independence and the larger number and variety of satisfactions that flow from group action.[4]

Does this mean farm families value freedom and independence higher than nonfarm families? To some extent it may, but many farm families would gladly surrender some freedom and independence for a larger share of the social product. The rural-urban migration trend demonstrates this. How many nonfarm families are willing to take a smaller share of the social product in return for the independence and freedom many farms afford?

Here we need more information on how highly farmers value their individual freedoms. Do they really value freedom and independence more highly than a larger share of the social product; or is the real problem a lack of opportunity or the inability of some farmers to participate in other forms of social organization? This suggests a series of case studies of why families move from the farm to urban areas and vice versa.

Each family, within the limit of its ability to contribute to the productive process, must decide what constitutes a reasonable compromise between freedom and independence and a larger share of the social product.[5] In this context, those that value freedom and independence highly will create no serious social problem until land becomes more scarce or until they ask for a larger share of the social product than they produce. The only way inefficient producers can have both is through subsidies.

Scarcity. Scarcity[6] originates in the fact that the natural environment does not provide enough raw materials to satisfy all of the wants and desires of people. In capitalistic societies, the institution of property is altered and expanded to cope with the ever-changing problems of scarcity. Since the family farm is based on property rights in land, society will constantly appraise the adequacy of that socioeconomic institution to cope with problems growing out of the use of scarce land.

History provides some clues about how problems growing out of a scarcity of land may be solved. About the turn of the century the public began to realize that all land was becoming scarce and that family farms and fee simple ownership might not be the most desirable use of forest, range, and recreational land. Now there is rather general agreement that the family farm does not maximize the use of all forestland.[7] Similar problems are arising in the use of rangeland.[8]

This indicates that when agricultural land becomes more scarce, the only alternative to family farms and fee simple ownership that we know much about is government ownership. Society has been more ingenious in solving the problems associated with other scarce factors of production. Corporations and cooperatives are man-made institutions designed to utilize scarce capital, technology, and labor. These organizations are far from perfect but in some instances are more desirable than either family economic units or public ownership.[9] In fact, many people think of them along with family farms as being typical of private enterprise.

When agricultural land becomes more scarce, the public will assert a more positive interest in conservation and productivity of soil. The modern concept of conservation is wise use in the long-run public interest (Allen and Foster 1940, p. 421). How well do family farmers conserve soil? The answer is not yet clear. Some find conservation to their advantage. Others deliberately exploit the land.

Of the methods of increasing land productivity, the availability and control of water is probably the most important. With respect to its availability, water now occupies about the same status land did a century ago. Land was then almost a free good, but scarcity was in sight. So it is with water now.

What kind of socioeconomic institutions make the best use of water, and how will they affect the family farm?

Will the public delegate all of the responsibility for conserving and increasing the productivity of the soil to three, four, or five million individual farm families? Certainly the family farmers are in the best position to do the job if they have adequate technical information and if they find it in their own self-interest. The task of supplying the information falls largely on the USDA and the land grant colleges. Yet these organizations have developed much more technical know-how on both subjects than is being applied.

We seem to know more about how to increase land productivity and conserve soil than about arranging social institutions to make them serve both public and private interests simultaneously.[10] Drainage districts, soil conservation districts, and Tennessee Valley Authorities all constitute efforts to accomplish this. Perhaps society should expend more creative energy on developing social organizations that will resolve this problem. Reconciling the short- and long-run interests in scarce land resources is of fundamental importance, and the role of the family farm is not clear.

Efficiency. Problems created by the scarcity of land can be partially solved by increasing the efficiency of using land to produce useful goods. By employing more capital, labor, and technology, people have been able to improve their level of living with a limited supply of land.

The general trend toward specialization and trade is altering the efficiency of family farms. The comparative advantage for farmers in producing raw materials is increasing while their comparative advantage in processing on the farm is decreasing. At the same time, the comparative advantage of specific geographic areas in producing specific commodities is becoming more pronounced. Consequently, the number of economic opportunities for families to produce many things efficiently on one farm is decreasing.

Some students of policy feel that family farms may not be an efficient form of social organization for producing some commodities (Ackerman and Harris 1947, p. 229). Furthermore, current agricultural research indicates that further specialization may be desirable. The time may soon arrive when the only enterprises farm families can operate efficiently will be those making a relatively uniform use of labor throughout the year.

On farms that do not provide sufficient economic opportunities for members of the farm families to work efficiently throughout the year, what are the alternatives? Corporations and estates are frequently suggested. One of the objections to both is that the participants must surrender a considerable portion of their right to use economic and persuasive power as they choose. This in turn is alleged to be undemocratic on the grounds that it would require the formation of agricultural labor unions and make collective bargaining necessary to protect the rights of farm workers.[11] However, if the surrender of some economic and persuasive power is undemocratic and undesirable, then is not the surrender of the power of persuasion by farmers to large farm organizations also undesirable?

We assume here that corporations and estates are not the perfect answer to the problem of increasing efficiency in agricultural enterprises; we explore three alternatives.

INDUSTRIALIZATION.[12] The steady decline in number of farmers and the rapid increase in nonfarm population can be partially attributed to an increase in the productivity of farm labor and partially to an increased number of nonagricultural economic opportunities. Furthermore, the number of farmers working 100 or more days in nonagricultural employment is increasing rapidly. What is happening to agriculture in communities in which erstwhile, strictly farm families are now earning incomes from both agricultural and nonagricultural sources? There are indications that these families enjoy a more satisfactory way of life than families operating small farm units (Bachman and Jones 1950, p. 45).

However, all farm families do not have opportunities for nonagricultural employment. This may not be an insurmountable barrier since (1) businessmen seek new locations with a potential labor supply;[13] (2) there are several nonagricultural enterprises that can be combined with farming such as tourist homes, fishing camps, and gasoline stations; and (3) modern transportation facilities enable farmers to travel considerable distances during parts of the year to maximize income. Perhaps we should be examining industrioagricultural families as a socioeconomic institution.

PRODUCTION PLANNING. Farmers living close to each other have much to gain by planning production together. A marketable volume of a uniform quality of any commodity produced in one community will sell at a higher price than small lots produced over a larger area. For example, egg prices are higher in the areas that produce large volumes of eggs than in those where egg production is low and scattered, when supply exceeds demand. If farmers can work out social organizations that facilitate producing a marketable quantity in a small geographic area and reducing costs of assembling and selling, the farming operation can be made more efficient.[14] This presents the challenge for social scientists to develop methods of production planning that will enable farm families to maximize efficiency through some type of group action requiring the surrender of the minimum amount of individual freedom.

MANAGERIAL AGREEMENTS. The investment required to establish an efficient farm is increasing because real value of land increases when population increases in a fixed geographic area and because more capital goods are required to produce efficiently. To date, the problem of acquiring capital has been successfully met at the policy level by a liberal extension of farm credit at nominal rates. However, serious problems are arising from the difficulties encountered by one generation of a farm family in accumulating enough capital to operate an efficient unit. At the farm level this focuses attention on inheritance laws and the type of managerial arrangements utilized.

Existing inheritance laws tend to break up farms into smaller and often less efficient units. To avoid this, either a farm must be sold as a unit, or one heir must buy out the others by accumulating mortgage obligations, often in addition to encumbrances already on the land. This makes it difficult, if not impossible, for one heir to obtain enough working capital to continue the operation. The only way a family can acquire capital is to reduce their level of living until the principal is paid. Yet one of the criteria proposed to judge the desirability of a tenure situation is: "A person with the necessary training and experience should not be barred from farming because of lack of capital, and capital accumulation should not be attained at the expense of family living" (Ackerman and Harris 1947, p. 10). To what extent can increasing efficiency continue to offset increasing capital costs?

In the past, mortgages, leases, and rental arrangements have served as devices for assembling enough capital to operate a farm efficiently, and much tenure research has been done on these arrangements.[15] However, this approach has definite limitations because of landowners and farmers shifting to newer type managerial agreements such as contracts that specify capital, labor, and management inputs and returns; employment contracts providing a minimum wage and a share of the profits; and employment or retention of professional managers.

Relatively little research has been done on the merits of these agreements, largely because they are not now used widely enough to be "significant" in statistical samples. Yet they may prove more effective as a means of increasing the efficiency of farming than corporations, cooperatives, or family ownership of all of the factors of production. The principal questions are: Is the ownership of land more important than the ownership of other factors of production? And, if not, how can several people owning property of one kind or another assemble it into an efficient production unit and retain participation in management?

Finally, we must recognize that technological, economic, and political conditions are changing rapidly and altering the conditions under which efficiency can be attained. To cope with this dynamic situation and keep efficiency as one policy objective, we must make an orderly change in our socioeconomic institutions and not fix them as a policy objective per se.[16]

Futurity. Our task here is essentially to determine whether or not there are alternate ways of satisfying four futurity values.

SECURITY AGAINST CHANGES IN THE VALUE OF CURRENCY. Until a monetary system that provides a uniform measure of value over time is perfected, security against inflation and deflation will be an objective of most families.

Land values fluctuate with the value of currency. This means that when the owners of farmland are forced to sell at deflated prices, landownership may not be superior to any other type of investment for the attainment of this kind of security.[17]

As security against fluctuations in currency value, landownership does enable farmers to subsist when other social organizations can produce nothing. However, society is now so highly specialized that many nonfarm families would find it difficult, if not impossible, to survive even if they had access to the use of land. Those who could survive on land without the products of all other social organizations would do so at a drastically reduced level of living. In trading some economic freedom for a larger share of the social product, some individuals have probably lost their ability to cope with adversities.

Yet people can make a fuller use of nature by specializing and working together in social organizations. This indicates that landownership or the right to use land has special value as a means of survival only when the economic system fails to function properly. One question remains: Will the nation ever accept the lower level of living that a drastic deflation and a heavy "back to the farm" movement would involve? Many people think not and believe that other means of attaining collective action would be employed.

SECURITY IN OLD AGE. Farm families look forward to the time they can relinquish management to children, rent or lease the land, or sell the farm and retire. This is satisfactory for farmers who have used soil that was productive enough to permit the accumulation of substantial savings in cash or equity in or title to land.

Much land is still productive enough to enable a sole owner to retire outright by selling or renting the farm. This partially explains the high percentage of tenancy in the Midwest where tenant farmer incomes are often higher than owner operator incomes on less productive land. On land with low productivity, farmers find it difficult to acquire security in old age, and those who accumulate savings in the form of land frequently find it necessary to charge rents that are high relative to productivity. Others farm less intensively and reduce their level of living in old age.

Are the alternatives to landownership for old age security more attractive? The many farmers who invest savings in nonagricultural securities believe they are. Some prefer this form of investment to landownership and remain in the tenant status throughout their productive life. In contrast, business and professional men often buy land out of earnings in nonagricultural enterprises.

Both farmers and nonagricultural workers who earn low incomes find it difficult to accumulate savings for old age security. Of these, nonagricultural workers have social security whereas farmers who perform the entrepreneurial function do not. Thus, many family farmers who use land of comparatively low fertility and operate inefficient enterprises really have an inferior type of old age security.

INVESTMENT. A constantly declining land-population ratio increases the value of land with respect to the value of factors of production that are becoming more plentiful. How many farmers have acquired savings from the increased value of land in contrast to the number who have accumulated savings solely from the production of agricultural commodities? Is it in the public interest to reserve this type of investment for family famers? A good case can be made for this on the grounds that farmers assume more risk and uncertainty than nonagricultural entreprenuers. Yet it has never been adopted as public policy.

Another point of view is that large investments are necessary to make land more productive, and nonfarm savings are a potential source of these funds. If this is true, investment in agricultural land by non-farmers can increase the volume of food and fiber produced. Any policy that would limit the freedom of any individual to invest in property of his own choice would restrict the flexibility of the institution of property and the freedom of people to engage in enterprises of their own choosing.

OCCUPATIONAL SECURITY. Farm families value landownership or longtime lease or rental agreements because either will ensure them an opportunity to work. Nonagricultural workers seek the same value through seniority clauses in labor contracts. In some respects, attaining this value retards social and economic progress, especially when it is attained at a cost of decreasing efficiency or of retarding the adoption of new technology. On the other hand, without some degree of occupational security many people cannot obtain other values or ends, such as education for the children or home ownership. The family farm fulfills this requirement in agriculture quite effectively. The questions here are: How much can society afford to pay for it in terms of efficiency? And could other kinds of socioeconomic institutions provide the same values at lower absolute or social costs?

Custom. Custom is a similarity of behavior that continues essentially unchanged. As long as any given form of behavior is rational, it serves society well because it saves the time and energy required for people to formulate a specific plan of action to meet each and every situation. Once established, however, customs tend to lose their rational characteristics due to the everchanging nature of sovereignty, scarcity, efficiency, and futurity values. When customs fail to provide an effective means of coping with new situations, they retard social and economic progress.

Every society and social group develops a web of customs. These customs cannot be changed easily or rapidly because a majority of the group must agree to the change, and the process of breaking old habits and forming new ones is time consuming.

In many respects the family farm is a custom. And farmers frequently ask government protection rather than developing rational solutions to ever-changing ethical, political, and economic situations. In other respects the family farm has contributed much to the alteration of old customs and development of new ones.

Many farm children have broken the custom of family farming by educating their children for other occupations. Our policies of education have facilitated this trend. This process is still going on, but the tempo of economic activity is now so rapid there is not time for many families to follow the procedure. For example, some family farmers are not able to earn a sufficient income to give their children an education that will equip them to alter the custom. As a result, the heads of families often find it necessary to leave the farm at middle age or over—when they find it difficult to enlarge farms, mechanize, change crops, and make other changes required to cope with new ethical, political, and economic situations.

To retain the family farm on grounds of custom alone would constitute a sharp deviation from principles upon which the nation was founded, especially the freedom to apply initiative and enterprise. Initiative is the germ, and enterprise the action of change. If there is any one symbol of the American way of life, it is the flexibility of custom and the ability to change. Yet custom cannot be changed quickly. To leave the family farm out of our policy considerations would be as catastrophic as retaining it in its present form. The solution to this apparent conflict in ends is orderly change—change that can be made without making any group bear an undue burden of the cost of doing things for which they were not wholly responsible. The establishment of ends, rather than the means of attaining ends, as policy objectives will allow society to concentrate more attention on developing socioeconomic institutions to facilitate attainment of these ends in an orderly and satisfactory manner.[18]

Conclusions. This brief and incomplete analysis enables us to draw only tentative conclusions:

(1) Families endeavor to attain a wide variety of values through the socioeconomic institution commonly called the "family farm."

(2) These values have political, ethical, and economic content. Families do not classify values neatly into these categories; hence values reflecting all of

these considerations simultaneously may be more useful than those classified by academic standards.[19] Some values suggested are freedom and independence, conservation of scarce resources, efficient production, security, and orderly change. Other studies along these lines would refine and perhaps extend this list.

(3) The values family farmers endeavor to attain are basically the same as those of nonfarm families. For this reason, serious consideration should be given to adopting these values as policy objectives rather than one of the socioeconomic institutions that has been reasonably satisfactory in attaining some of them. This would enlarge the area of freedom for families to choose among several socioeconomic institutions in attaining their own personal policy objectives and strengthening the democratic process. In effect, this approach would focus attention on inconsistencies in public policy that are the inevitable result of "pressure groups" endeavoring to improve the economic and social status of one occupational group of an integrated and interdependent society.

(4) Difficulties encountered in defining the family farm render it undesirable as a policy objective for administrative reasons. Establishing the family farm as a policy objective calls for a precise definition of the phrase. This in turn would tend to stifle initiative and enterprise to alter the institution and call for more centralized planning to interpret the policy. On the other hand, setting up the values as policy objectives would facilitate individual planning in the public interest.

(5) Using values as policy objectives could stimulate the creation of a more desirable socioeconomic institution incorporating the desirable features of the family farm. For example, farmers may find some division of management responsibilities between two or more families is more desirable than retaining the management functions entirely in one family. Likewise, it may be more satisfactory for families to own only part of the production factors rather than the entire enterprise.

Finally, we must recognize that responsibility for formulating public policy lies with the people themselves. As social scientists we are responsible for providing them with tools to do this. This suggests a need for developing ways and means of presenting policy problems to the public clearly and objectively and stimulating everyone (not just farmers) to think about them. Revival of the town meeting is one suggested means of doing this (Case 1951, p. 1229). Nevertheless, before any educational devices can be really effective we must know more about the true nature of ultimate values people are endeavoring to attain.

Notes

1. Professor Raymond J. Penn, head of the Department of Agricultural Economics, University of Wisconsin, states: "It is unfortunate that many economists have dropped the concept of

'political' in current thinking.'' The import of the ethical values of family farming have been recognized formally by the Home Missions Council, the Federal Council of Churches, and the International Council of Religious Education (Timmons and Murray 1951, pp. 206, 220-21). Also see Felton (1951, pp. 75-77).

2. See the Employment Act of 1946, Public Law 304, for a broad statement of policy objectives of this kind.

3. It may well be that other analytical tools will eventually prove to be more useful. A psychological approach has attractive possibilities. This use of Professor Commons's assumptions does not in any way imply that he would have used them in this way or that he would have reached the same conclusions. In fact, there is one important difference in approach: Commons suggests the use of these tools to interpret economic activity; while I am, in effect, saying that all human action has some economic content, the other components being political and ethical, and that these components are inseparable. It is not known whether Commons would have agreed.

4. See Brant (1942, p. 208) for a similar point of view.

5. We are not overlooking the fact that during the past century both farm and nonfarm families have formed new social organizations for the express purpose of equalizing their bargaining power in the marketplace, in which freedom and independence are traded for a larger share of the social product that in turn provides (or is intended to provide) still more freedom and independence. By operating at all levels of government, both public and private, these social organizations (pressure groups) play an important role in the formulation of public policy. However, the fact that they are organized along occupational lines rather than representing cross sections of public interest limits their usefulness in policy determination because it tends to narrow the area of policy formulation. It may well be that the current trend in centralization of public government is the inevitable result of centralizing private government into occupational institutions.

6. Here we assume the dynamic nature of resources and that scarcity is a relative term. Under this assumption the scarcity of land is especially significant because land provides some unrenewable resources and because the span of time required to renew soil fertility and some of its products is often too long. For an excellent discussion of this see Zimmerman (1951, Chapter I and II). A somewhat different, but not inconsistent, point of view was outlined by McPherson (1948, pp. 95-112).

7. One of the current problems in this field is to develop effective means of increasing the productivity of the timberland that is now owned in ''small'' tracts. Here ''small'' means 5,000 acres or less (*Forests and National Prosperity* 1948).

8. Timmons and Murray (1951, Chapter 7), especially Renne's statement that ''much of the acreage in western range land is not suitable for division into units for single operator control'' (p. 115).

9. It has been suggested that cooperatives and corporations both strengthen the family farm. In some respects they do, but they also represent further specialization and hence decrease the number of economic opportunities on the farm. See the next section of this paper, ''Efficiency.''

10. Professor Penn suggests five alternative approaches to this problem, and V. Webster Johnson six ways of altering the use of land (Ackerman and Harris 1947, pp. 229, 241).

11. For conflicting points of view, see Rainer Schickele (Timmons and Murray 1951, Chapter 2) and A. Whitney Griswold (1948, especially p. 204).

12. It is interesting to note that the World Land Tenure Conference put the first priority on this approach (USDA, Office of Foreign Agricultural Relations Preliminary Report of the Steering Committee, mimeographed, 1951).

13. The author has seen this point amply demonstrated by businessmen seeking industrial locations in the Tennessee Valley. By and large these businessmen are not seeking cheap labor. Instead, they are looking for a number of other things, including labor, that can produce efficiently. In other words, they are seeking ways and means of lowering the unit cost of production rather than lowering wage rates.

14. Marketing cooperatives often have the solution of this problem as an objective but frequently fail to solve it because they do not provide an effective mechanism for production planning.

15. See B. H. Kristjanson and S. W. Voelker (1951). This is typical of a number of very useful publications from different experiment stations.

16. See Murray R. Benedict's comment on efficiency (Ackerman and Harris 1947, pp. 128-29).

17. Liberalizing credit policies of agencies lending public funds does alleviate this problem but at the same time further injects government into economic life.

18. Here we recognize the significance of the observation, "To be interested in ends and have contempt for means which alone secure them is the last stage of intellectual demoralization" (*John Dewey's Philosophy,* Ratner, Modern Library Edition, p. 494).

19. Committee I of the Farm Tenure Conference (Ackerman and Harris 1947, pp. 385–403) does distinguish between political, social, and economic values. This distinction is useful to students of policy, but it is possible to go further and identify some values that a majority of people will agree are desirable policy objectives.

References

Ackerman, J., and M. Harris, eds. 1947. *Family Farm Policy.* Chicago: University of Chicago Press.

Allen, B. W., and E. A. Foster. 1940. *The 1940 Yearbook of Agriculture.* Washington, D.C.: U.S. Department of Agriculture.

Bachman, K. L., and R. W. Jones. 1950. *Sizes of Farms in the United States.* Washington, D.C.: U.S. Department of Agriculture Technical Bulletin 1910, July.

Brandt, K. 1942. "Towards a More Adequate Approach to the Farm Tenure Problem." *Journal of Farm Economics* 24:206–25.

Case, H. C. M. 1951. "Farm Policy Problems in This Era of Tensions." *Illinois Farm Economics,* no. 197, October.

Commons, J. R. 1950. *The Economics of Collective Action.* New York: Macmillan.

Davis, J. H. 1939. *On Agricultural Policy, 1929–1938.* Stanford, Calif.: Food Research Institute, Stanford University.

Felton, R. A. 1951. *Proceedings of the 10th Annual Conference of Professional Agricultural Workers.* Tuskegee, Ala.: Tuskegee Institute.

Forests and National Prosperity. 1948. Washington, D.C.: U.S. Department of Agriculture Forest Service Miscellaneous Publication 668, August.

Griswold, A. W. 1948. *Farming and Democracy.* New York: Harcourt, Brace.

Kristjanson, B. H., and S. W. Voelker 1951. "Legal Aspects of Renting Farms in North Dakota." Fargo, N.D.: North Dakota Experiment Station Bulletin 376.

McPherson, W. K. 1948. "Resource Patterns in Southern Industry." *Bulletin of the Bureau of School Service* 20(4):95–112. University of Kentucky.

Schultz, T. A. 1950. *Production and Welfare of Agriculture.* New York: Macmillan.

Timmons, J. F., and W. G. Murray. 1951. *Land Policies and Problems.* Ames: Iowa State College Press.

Zimmerman, E. W. 1951. *World Resources and Industries.* New York: Harper.

II

The Quantitative Approach

9

On the Theory and Practice of Econometrics

GEORGE G. JUDGE

GEOFFREY S. SHEPHERD has always been a keen observer of economic processes and institutions, one who has long focused on the interesting and basic econometric question of how economic data are generated. His commitment to measurement in economics is documented by both word and deed, a commitment summarized by the following quote by Lord Kelvin, which occurs after the title page in the many editions of Shepherd's classic price analysis book: "Whenever you can measure what you are speaking about, and express it in numbers, you know something about it. But when you cannot measure it, when you cannot express it in numbers, your knowledge is of a meager and unsatisfactory kind."

For many of the questions concerning Shepherd in the areas of agricultural marketing, price analysis, and economic policy, it was not enough for decision and evaluation purposes to know that certain economic variables were interrelated. In addition, he needed to know the direction of the relationship and to be able to estimate its magnitude. As an economist Shepherd was and is acutely aware of the connection between information and decision making; and, in his quest to aid producers, consumers, and governments, his measuring stick for performance was to generate new knowledge and information that would help to make the "best" decisions. In order to fulfill this objective he emphasized and made effective use of both theory and measurement.

In the last half century, measurement in economics has changed from casual empiricism to the use of econometric models, methods, and data systems. In fact, it might be said that we now have an econometric model–building industry, and many in academia, government, and business are involved in the care and feeding of the models at each of the structural decision-making levels. Because of both the magnitude and rate of change in the quantitative economic area, the purpose of this essay is to review and comment on the state of only certain areas of econometric theory and practice. In particular, I will discuss the statistical tools currently available for handling the expanded range of statistical econometric models, for using all of the information available in estimating unknown parameters and testing hypotheses about the statistical specification, and for selecting among the admissible economic and statistical models to describe a set of data; and I will comment on the frameworks available for measuring the performance of various statistical decision rules.

The Ingredients of Economic Measurement. Economic measurement involves three interdependent links in the research chain: the economic and statistical model, the data, and the statistical methods or tools of inference. In each of these categories, the last half century has provided countless examples of progress.

All facets of economic theory have advanced. The last five decades have provided a better understanding of the general equilibrium theory of Walras, the partial equilibrium theory of Marshall, and the aggregative economic theory of Keynes and have provided the basis for "measurement with theory." Recent work would suggest that we are now on the threshold of breaking out of the restriction of having to use as our conceptual base a theory based on position rather than movement.

With respect to data, comprehensive systems have been developed or improved for agriculture and all of the other sectors of the economy. Annual measurements of a wide array of economic variables have been augmented by quarterly, monthly, weekly, and, in some cases, daily data. Sample surveys and even controlled experiments are now being used to expand the data base and to insure more compatibility between the data collected or generated and the corresponding theoretical counterparts. In spite of the advances and the productive efforts of many, much of our data are still collected for administrative rather than research purposes; the experimental design and desired outcome data reflected by our economic models have, in many instances, little relation to the data we must often use; and just as few economic relations are measured without shocks, few economic variables are measured without error.

In respect to measurement tools, in the last half century the Pearson and Fisher beginnings of statistical inference have evolved to a mature science dealing with general questions involving decision problems under uncertainty. Regression and correlation analysis, the backbone of most quantitative ventures in the 1920s, has evolved from descriptive methods to measurement tools with an inferential base. The problem of the simultaneous generation of economic variables has been faced, statistical models consistent with the interdependent nature of economic data have been formulated, and estimating methods have been proposed and evaluated within both a sampling theory and the Bayesian framework. We have been acutely aware of the special characteristics of economic data and have provided statistical models and methods of estimation and testing to handle situations dealing with dynamic relations, with qualitative variables, with combining cross-section and time series data, with models involving random instead of fixed parameters, and even with how to handle or at least mitigate some of the problems concerned with measurement errors and nonobservable variables.

Research in statistical techniques has gone hand in hand with developing computer programs that form the basis for implementation and the development of econometric modeling techniques.

Given this impressive record of achievement, a question remains—one that often concerned Shepherd in his pursuit of quantitative analysis: How can we improve our basis for capturing the parameters of economic relations so they can be used as a more effective information base for forecasting and policy analysis (the descriptive-prescriptive dichotomy) and for testing alternative economic theories? We turn to a partial answer to this question.

Nonsample Information. In searching for quantitative economic knowledge, economic theory or postulation provides one foundation stone. This base point, of course, tells us nothing about the truth or falsity of the propositions. It only suggests that, if we have correctly made use of logic, the conclusions follow from the assertions. In addition, in most research ventures an applied worker, such as an agricultural economist, goes into the analysis with some particular knowledge about the economic processes and institutions for the sector or set of phenomena under study. Many times, for example, through both logic and observation, we know something about the signs of the coefficients in the relation or, indeed, in some cases about the magnitudes of individual coefficients or their linear combination. For example, marginal propensities to consume and marginal products are supposed to be nonnegative and, in terms of magnitude, lie somewhere between zero and one. Particular knowledge about the phenomena under study may permit a more exact statement of this type of nonsample or presample information.

In traditional statistical inference a "correct" statistical model is specified, data consistent with this specification are employed or generated, and the sampling theory (repeated sample) approach to inference is employed in gauging the performance of various rules en route to point and interval estimation. Thus, only the *sample* information is used as the basis for estimation and hypothesis testing. Nonsample, prior or outside, information is not permitted as a foundation stone for inference. This rather puritan state of affairs has been summarized by Tukey (1979) as follows: "It is my impression that rather generally, not just in econometrics, it is considered decent to use judgement in choosing a functional form, but indecent to use judgement in choosing a coefficient. If judgement about important things is quite all right, why should it not be used for less important ones as well?''

Recognizing the incidence of nonsample information, the sampling theory maximum likelihoodlums have rushed to patch up the traditional approach so as to accommodate both types of information. In doing this they have identified three separate ways of introducing *nonsample* information and combining it with *sample* information.

First, they consider the somewhat unlikely, although fortunate, situation when the investigator has *exact* information about a coefficient or a *linear* combination of coefficients. For example, if Shepherd in the 1940s had knowledge that the income elasticity of demand for food was 0.25, he should have been able to use this information along with sample information on prices or quantities to improve his estimate of the price elasticity of demand for food. One way to combine the two types of information is to use this information as a linear equality restriction and solve the usual least-squares (likelihood function) problem subject to this linear restriction. If the nonsample prior information is correct, the resulting point estimates will be unbiased, and their precision will be superior to those estimates that ignore this information. In fact, whether the information is correct or not, the precision will be improved. If the nonsample information is *incorrect,* the estimates will no longer be unbiased—i.e., we have the opportunity of being more precisely wrong.

Recognizing that the case for perfect information may be limited, a second approach involves the use of stochastic prior information. Under this approach, the mean and variance (covariance in the case of joint stochastic restrictions) of the nonsample information are specified by the investigator, this stochastic prior information is combined with the stochastic sample information, and the Aitken generalized least-squares estimator is used to obtain estimates of the unknown coefficients. If the nonsample stochastic prior information is unbiased, the resulting estimates are unbiased, and the sampling precision of the mixed estimator results are improved over the conventional estimator that makes use of only sample information. As before, if the stochastic prior information is incorrect, we are in a position where the estimates may be more precisely wrong. Also, if the investigator is willing to assume that the stochastic prior information is on the average correct—i.e., unbiased—and unbiasedness is the goal, then perhaps one might be tempted to ignore the sample data and work only with a sampling of the stochastic nonsample information, a somewhat novel and perverse approach to inference.

Recognizing that each of the above types of nonsample information may be too demanding, investigator information in the form of inequality constraints that may be combined with the sample information has been proposed. In this form the investigator becomes less precise in the form of the prior information and states that the coefficient or linear combination of co-efficients must satisfy the condition of being nonnegative or nonpositive or perhaps lie between some upper and lower bound. Estimates can be obtained by minimizing the traditional quadratic form for the least-squares or maxi-mum likelihood estimators subject to the specified linear inequality or ine-qualities. Again, whether the restrictions are correct or incorrect, the precision is improved. If the restrictions are innocuous to the extent that—in a repeated sample sense—they are never binding, then the estimates are unbiased. Alter-natively, if they are always binding they take on the same bias characteristics as the equality-restricted estimator discussed above. Therefore, in general, the estimator that combines these two types of information is biased; but, if one can correctly choose the *direction* of the inequality—and bias and variance are weighted equally—the increase in precision more than offsets the loss due to centering around an incorrect mean (bias).

Another approach to using nonsample information that has been growing in importance over the last two decades is the Bayesian approach to inference. In the Bayesian approach inferences about parameter values—say, the parameter vector γ—are based on a posterior probability density function for γ that incorporates the sample information d and whatever nonsample in-formation PI the investigator chooses to use. Bayes's theorem provides the following expression for the posterior density function: $p(\gamma|d, PI) = ap(\gamma| PI) \ell(\gamma|d)$, where a is a normalizing constant, $p(\gamma|PI)$ is the prior density selected by the investigator, and $\ell(\gamma|d)$ is the sample likelihood function. Thus, Bayes's theorem provides a systematic basis for using all the sample and nonsample information. Again, if we may continue the previous Tukey quote, "Perhaps the real purpose of Bayesian techniques is to let us do the indecent thing while modestly concealed behind a formal apparatus. . . . If so let us hope that day will soon come when the role of 'decent concealment' can be freely admitted" (Tukey 1979). Several advantages accrue by using the Bayes-ian approach to inference rather than the sampling theory approach, which seems to use the investigator's nonsample information in a somewhat ad hoc way. The Bayes's posterior density provides an exact finite sample probability density function and thus, in principle, excludes the need for large sample ap-proximations, which are a necessary evil of econometric life for many sam-pling theory statistical models and their corresponding statistics. Also, since the posterior density function is available, one does not have to settle for a point estimate unless one chooses to do so. Finally, in large samples, the Bayesian and sampling theory results converge to a distributional form with the same mean vector and covariance and thus provide a basis for justifying whichever approach one seeks to justify. Of course, although the large sample results converge, their interpretation is quite different. Zellner's (1972) book on Bayesian inference in econometrics provides an excellent road map for this approach to learning from economic data.

On Evaluating Performance. In the previous section we discussed two approaches to inference for the investigator wishing to combine certain judgments with the sample information. Also, within the sampling theory approach, we have reviewed several alternative formulations. Given this feast of alternatives, how is one to choose? In traditional sampling theory the choice between estimators or rules to use in learning from data is made on the basis of certain properties that are defined in a repeated sampling context. Thus, one may judge an estimator or decision rule as to whether it is, for example, unbiased or minimum variance. Thus, if one pursues the godly role of unbiasedness and chooses to stay within the class of estimators that are linear in the parameters, then a widely used measure is to define best in terms of minimum variance and thus choose the one that is best linear unbiased. For the linear regression statistical model, as shown by the Gauss-Markov result, this leads—in estimating the unknown coefficient vector—to the choice: the least-squares estimator or maximum likelihood estimator. This best in a class of one outcome is a beautiful result; and, in applied work in econometrics, the best linear result is repeatedly referred to with great reverence and authority. But why should the applied worker be restricted to rules that are linear, and why should he insist that his estimators or decision rules be unbiased, hitting the target on average? If there are other rules that are biased but have greater precision, missing in terms of the location parameter but having a smaller scale parameter, is there a trade-off in the mind of the user between bias and variance? The relevance of these "on the average" properties in analyzing a particular set of data where the unobserved samples of the imagined repeated sampling process are not possible is far from clear. Whether or not an estimator is best unbiased, the estimated value in point estimation can very inadequately capture the information content of a set of data.

Some who are unhappy with the process of defining a set of conditions or requirements as the basis for evaluating estimator performance have pointed out that many econometric ventures are directed at capturing estimates of the unknown parameters that can be used in a decision or choice context, i.e., quantitative information that can be used as a basis for making the best decision at the firm, household, or government level. If this is indeed true, then it would seem that the theory of statistical decision, based on the analysis of losses due to incorrect decisions, should be used. Thus, the investigator can choose the loss function most relevant for his situation and then evaluate—as Judge and Bock (1978) and others have done—the risk functions of the various estimators. For example, if a squared error loss is relevant for the problem at hand, this leads to a risk or mean squared error measure that combines bias and variance, thus providing a basis for comparing over the range of the parameter space both biased and unbiased estimators.

In the Bayesian approach the complete posterior density function is provided for the parameters of interest. If a point or summary estimate is of interest, it can be obtained in conjunction with the choice of an appropriate loss function. For example, if a quadratic loss is used, the mean of the posterior desity is an optimal point estimate (if it exists) in that it minimizes posterior expected loss. In general, Bayesian estimators minimize average risk (if finite), and they are admissible (no other estimator has smaller risk for every value of the parameter space).

With these approaches and alternative rules, the applied worker has at least a chance to choose the formulation that best fits the problem at hand so that he can make the "best" use of both his sample and nonsample data.

On Choosing the Correct Model. It is interesting to note that, although it may seem reasonable to question the validity of nonsample information, it is traditional not to question the validity of the statistical model reflecting the sampling process for the observations. Thus, the sampling properties for most models are worked out under the assumption that the statistical model is *correctly* specified. Seldom, if ever, are economic data free of measurement error; and seldom, if ever, are statistical (econometric) models correctly specified. Thus, we are in some sense destined to work with false models, and the statistical properties discussed in theoretical econometrics texts and generally alluded to in applied work are seldom, if ever, fulfilled in practice.

This fact has not been lost on econometricians, and much of their effort over the last four decades has been directed toward developing statistical models that permit consistency between the model specified for estimation purposes and the one that actually describes how the sample observations are generated, discovering and mitigating the defects of proposed models. In fact, dissatisfaction of this sort was the main motivation for specifying a statistical model consistent with the simultaneous, dynamic, and stochastic characteristics of economic data—that is, the structural (simultaneous) econometric model. This model made painfully obvious the inadequacy of the conventional regression model for many economic problems and initiated the long trek down the road that ended in an estimator that had good asymptotic and, it was hoped, good finite sample properties. The old E. J. Working problem of how to identify a particular economic relation in a system of economic relations was set out in sharp relief, and a new vocabulary involving endogenous, exogenous, predetermined, and latent variables was introduced. Again, in true econometric style, the simultaneous equation statistical model was assumed to be correctly specified. This means, for example, that the stochastic assumptions describing the random forces at work were correct, and no important economic variables were omitted. Consequently, estimators were specified and evaluated relative to this utopian base. Model specification, while no doubt more realistic, was made much more difficult; or perhaps the possibility for error was more sharply identified. In fact, in order to avoid the unpardonable sin of "least squares bias," correct decisions were required in terms of the number of equations appearing in the complete model, the algebraic form of each equation, the dynamic characteristics of each equation, the inclusion of all relevant variables and their correct appearance in the equation, and so forth. All of this added up to a very large order and meant that seldom, if ever, did the simultaneous equation estimates achieve the objective of consistency or of being asymptotically unbiased.

Unfortunately, even at this date, little information is available on the sensitivity and sampling consequences of some of the asymptotically justified estimators to a range of errors of omission and commission. In addition, since most applied work in econometrics involves limited samples of data, information on the finite sample properties of the estimators is essential. Some limited Monte Carlo and analytical results are available in this area, and we now know that some estimators that are asymptotically equivalent have very different finite sample properties. For example, some asymptotically unbiased estimators have serious finite sample biases; and, under some conditions, the single equation least-squares estimator has a smaller mean squared error than some of the consistent estimators. This, of course, raises somewhat embarrassing questions for those who embrace asymptotic justifications or are hung up with unbiasedness or minimum variance. In the past two decades, Bayesian procedures have been used to analyze simultaneous equation models, and some of the positive aspects of this work are summarized by Zellner (1979).

One bright spot in this model specification error is that, in the last decade, we have gradually learned more and more about the sampling consequences of various forms of errors in specifying the classical linear statistical model and the statistical pitfalls of using some of the well-known model selection procedures. For example, we know that using conventional t or F test statistics as the basis for determining whether to include or exclude a variable(s) in the statistical model leads to what we now call a pretest estimator and that this estimator is, under a squared error loss measure, inadmissible. This means the maximum likelihood estimator is dominated by or uniformly inferior to another estimator whose underlying conditions are normally fulfilled in practice. In addition, all of the ad hoc informal model selection rules that fill the literature (Amemiya 1976) can be expressed in terms of the F test statistic and thus are, in one form or another, pretest type rules and, therefore, lead to estimators that can be beaten.

The restrictiveness of setting up properties to evaluate decision rules and of remaining in the linear unbiased world, in terms of estimator choice, has led some to consider a biased nonlinear alternative. In this regard the Stein-rule family of estimators (Judge and Bock 1978) has been shown, under squared error and a range of other loss functions, to dominate or be uniformly superior to the conventional least-squares or maximum likelihood estimator. Lindley has very cogently summarized this result as follows:

The result of Stein undermines the most important practical technique in statistics. . . . The next time you do an analysis of variance or fit a regression surface (a line is all right) remember you are, for sure, using an unsound procedure. Unsound that is, by the criteria you have presumably been using to justify the procedure.

Worse is to follow, for much of multivariate work is based on the assumption of a normal distribution. With a known dispersion matrix this can again be transformed to the standard situation and consequently in all cases except the bivariate one, the usual estimates of the means of a multivariate normal are suspect [Lindley 1973, p. 422].

These results point up the dilemma faced by the applied researcher who wants to or must choose between alternative models or theories and who uses quantitative results for prediction, forecasting, and policymaking. The process of postdata model evaluation constitutes a rejection of the concept of true models for which statistical theory provides an inferential base. Although for the linear model the least-squares maximum likelihood estimator is the only unbiased estimator based on sufficient statistics, the Stein family of rules leads, under quadratic loss, to a better estimator. Also, as noted above, all model selection procedures lead to pretest estimators (that is, all selection rules are some function of the error sums of squares), and thus better alternatives exist for the estimator used in most applied work.

In addition, this pretest estimator outcome points up the problem of choosing the optimal level of statistical significance for the test, a choice usually handled in applied work in a very cavalier way. On a positive note, the Stein family of rules enjoys good properties from both a sampling theory and Bayesian point of view, and one can abandon the maximum likelihood rules without embracing the Stein result. However, there is certainly little penalty for using the Stein family of rules since they cannot have a larger total mean squared error. Finally, it is important to note that the Stein rules are computationally simple since they are simple functions of the maximum likelihood estimator.

The most favorable situation for the use of the Stein rule is when an investigator wants to estimate the unknown parameters of a linear statistical model, which are known to lie in a high dimensional space, say, H_0. However, the investigator may suspect that a lower dimensional parameter space H_1 may serve as an accurate description of the data generation process. If one uses maximum likelihood on H_0, maximum likelihood on the estimates are unbiased but may have large variance. Restricting the parameter space to H_1 may, as with the equality-restricted estimates above, permit great precision but do this with the expense of large bias. We, therefore, have two end points on the continuum, and the bias-variance dilemma for the applied worker is sharply drawn. In the Stein-rule approach, the data are used to determine the compromise between bias and variance and thus the ultimate nature of the model.

This would seem to be quite a sensible procedure unless one happens to be equipped with the power of magic, mysticism, or revelation.

On Broadening the Range of Statistical Models. Over the last half century, advances in econometric theory and practice have come about by making changes in the amount and type of information used, the specification of the statistical model that describes the sampling process envisioned, and the measure that is used to gauge the performance of the rule that is used for analysis purposes. We have discussed the first two advances earlier, and we have also discussed the statistical respecification that took place when Haavelmo converted the Walrasian general equilibrium system into a simultaneous-equations-system statistical model. Let us now turn to some examples of other statistical models that have been specified or respecified and analyzed so that the applied researcher can cope with a range of characteristics reflected by economic data that we observe, collect, and/or generate.

The focus on simultaneity in the 1940s helped, in one sense, to make econometricians face up to the question of how to specify statistical models that were also consistent with the dynamic characteristics of economic data. Since all economic behavior is not instantaneous—some outcomes occur with leads, lags, and expectations (rational or otherwise)—statistical models to accomodate both infinite (Koyck 1954) and finite (Almon 1965) distributed lags were formulated and their statistical properties evaluated. Interest could focus on estimating the short- and long-run parameters of behavior patterns and the economic consequences of this type of equilibrating mechanism. In this connection the work of Box and Jenkins (1970) increased the range of data generation alternatives one could cope with by treating time series models as a class of discrete linear stochastic processes of an autoregressive-moving average form. Unfortunately, for the applied researcher, in all of these specifications, the appropriate parameterization of the model remains an important and somewhat unsolved problem.

Given the limited availability of time series data, questions naturally arose as to how one might increase the data base for econometric analyses. Since much data exist in both a time series and cross-section form, the debate centered around how one might formulate a statistical model that would permit the use of both types of data—a question not all that different from that considered above on how to combine sample and nonsample data. To cope with this problem, statistical models were formulated that would permit the coefficients to vary, say, over both time and individuals (Griffiths 1974). Although these models permit us to take account of particular microtemporal characteristics of economic data, questions such as when to combine the two types of data and the economic interpretation of the results remain.

Most traditional econometric models are of a fixed parameter form.

However, since many economic parameter systems are nonstationary and do vary over one or more dimensions, the validity of the fixed parameter specifications in reflecting how the underlying economic data are generated is, in some cases, questionable. To resolve this situation, stochastic rather than fixed parameter statistical models were formulated and analyzed (Swamy 1971). In addition, when aggregate data are used, models have been specified that permit the parameters to vary with time, switch from one regression to another (e.g., seasonal models), or vary as a function of other economic and noneconomic variables.

Although at times the world can be quite nonlinear, most conventional econometric models are at least linear in the parameters. To accommodate the situations where parameter systems cannot be captured in the linear net, statistical models incorporating parameter nonlinearities have been specified, computational procedures to obtain the solution to the corresponding nonlinear system of equations have been proposed and evaluated, and the sampling properties of the estimators investigated and procedures for inference have been proposed.

As one final example, consider the fact that not all economic data are available as observable continuous variables, but that some economic data are qualitative (e.g., binary choice models), and that in some cases the sample of data is censored or truncated (e.g., missing data). In order to handle sample data of this type, general quantal response and missing data statistical models have been formulated and analyzed.

In each of the cases noted above, the statistical model has been generalized to take account of the special characteristics of the data generated or collected and to achieve more consistency between the underlying sampling model and the statistical model specified for its analysis. We are now in the happy position of being able to design our statistical model to conform to the way the economic data are generated. In the 1920s, 1930s, and, to some extent, the 1940s—when Shepherd made some of his major attempts to learn from economic data—the investigator by and large had to "make" the data fit a particular linear statistical model.

Some Final Comments. Over the last half century, we made the trek from the casual empiricism of graphic regression to an econometric model-building industry that is concerned with model specification, care, and feeding. Our knowledge of economic processes and institutions has vastly increased, and the data systems that provide the foundation stones for the theory and practice of economics have improved in quantity and quality. In terms of inference or learning from data, many breeds and varieties of statistical models exist, and it is now possible to model a range of economic processes and institutions and, we hope, to achieve a high degree of consistency between the conceptual model and the actual data generation process. Statistical tools now exist for taking account of or using all of the information, and the decision theory framework for evaluating decision rule (estimator) performance provides an action mechanism more in line with the theory of choice basis of economics. There is still a large array of economic models that do not contradict our knowledge of economic processes and institutions. This means there is a degree of uncertainty surrounding each model we put down, and our tools are far from perfect as to how we should use the data to narrow the admissible set.

Structural simultaneous-equation models and time series models of the Box-Jenkins type now permit a more accurate model of some of the data we observe. However, in spite of all of the analytical finite sample work with simultaneous-equation models, some typical longstanding time series problems have not been analyzed. In addition, if we consider the various simultaneous-equation (asymptotically justified) estimators that have been proposed, it is highly likely that they are inadmissible relative to a range of loss functions. Further, in the construction and estimation of structural equation models, there is a large degree of testing and data massaging. The impact of this preliminary testing on the finite sample properties is virtually unexplored. The Zellner-Palm (1974) synthesis of econometric modeling and time series analysis offers one route to improved model specification and estimation.

These comments on the state of the science of econometrics would seem to imply that many of the problems faced by Shepherd in the 1920s and 1930s as he attempted to learn from and use his economic data still remain. Unfortunately or perhaps fortunately, in order to achieve the descriptive and prescriptive goals of understanding, predicting, and controlling the economic processes and institutions that are the outcome of society's experiment, additional improvements in economic theory, data systems, and measurement tools are required. One hesitates to promise success in this venture, but if the past is any indication of the future, there is a firm foundation for optimism.

References

Almon, S. 1965. "The Distributed Lag between Capital Appropriations and Expenditures." *Econometrica* 33:178–96.

Amemiya, T. 1976. *Selection of Regressors*. Technical Report No. 225. Stanford, Calif.: Stanford University.

Box, G. E. P., and G. N. Jenkins. 1970. *Times Series Analysis, Forecasting, and Control*. San Francisco: Holden Day.

Griffiths, W. E. 1974. "On Combining Cross-Section and Time Series Data." Working Paper. Armidale, Australia: University of New England.

Judge, G. G., and M. E. Bock. 1978. *The Statistical Implications of Pre-Test and Stein Rule Estimators in Econometrics*. Amsterdam: North-Holland.

Koyck, L. M. 1954. *Distributed Lags and Investment Analysis*. Amsterdam: North-Holland.

Lindley, D. U. 1973. "Discussion of 'Combining Possibly Related Estimation Problems' " (by B. Efron and C. Morris). *Journal of the Royal Statistical Society, Series B* 35:403–5.

Swamy, P. A. V. B. 1971. *Statistical Inference in Random Coefficient Regression Models.* Heidelberg: Springer-Verlag.

Tukey, J. W. 1979. "Discussion of Granger on Seasonality." In *Seasonal Analysis of Economic Time Series,* edited by A. Zellner. Washington, D.C.: Government Printing Office.

Zellner, A. 1972. *An Introduction to Bayesian Inference in Econometrics.* New York: John Wiley and Sons.

_____. 1979. "Statistical Analysis of Econometric Models, with Discussion." *Journal of the American Statistical Association* 74:628–51.

Zellner, A., and F. Palm. 1974. "Time Series Analysis and Simultaneous Equation Econometric Models." *Journal of Econometrics* 2:17–54.

10

Structural Analysis and the Measurement of Demand for Farm Products: Foresight, Insight, and Hindsight in the Choice of Estimation Techniques

KARL A. FOX

Early Econometric Contributions. Agricultural price analysis is a field of great importance in the history of econometrics, for it was in that field that econometrics achieved its first practical successes. In a 1908 article, "The Statistical Complement of Pure Economics," Henry L. Moore outlined a program to which he devoted the rest of his professional life. He pointed out that although the great mathematical economists Cournot, Jevons, Edgeworth, and Pareto had devoted a substantial part of their work to the elaboration of the deductive phase of economics, each of them had conceived of "an inductive statistical complement of the pure science without whose development the a priori instrument must lack concrete effectiveness." He cited with approval a statement from Jevons's *Theory of Political Economy:* "The deductive science of Economics must be verified and rendered useful by the purely empirical science of statistics. Theory must be invested with the reality and life of fact."

Moore was a theorist in search of data. It was self-evident to him that "the most ample and trustworthy data of economic science" then available were official statistics, particularly the statistics on prices and production of agricultural commodities in the United States. Moore turned his attention to these data, with the somewhat unexpected result that his empirical work had

The section entitled "Structural Analysis and the Measurement of Demand for Farm Products" is reproduced from Fox (1954). Because of space limitations several passages and footnotes have been abbreviated. All such changes are indicated by brackets or in footnotes. Editorial insertions for purposes of continuity are set off in brackets. The author is indebted to Tej K. Kaul for checking the references, and his interpretation of them, in the introductory and final sections.

its first and greatest impact on the emerging discipline of agricultural economics. His books *Economic Cycles* and *Forecasting the Yield and Price of Cotton* furnished the inspiration for much of the work on statistical estimation of demand and supply functions that was carried on in the United States during the 1920s.

As heirs to this tradition, agricultural economists may underestimate its innovative character. Oskar Morgenstern, in his article "Mathematical Economics" in the *Encyclopaedia of the Social Sciences* (1931), devoted all but one paragraph to mathematical economic theorists. The deviant paragraph referred to

> a group of economists who work with mathematical tools in the field of inductive study. They attempt by utilizing statistical data to translate the formulae of theory into empirical equations with numerical values for constants. . . . Really significant work in this field was not done until very recently. A leader and in a sense the founder of a school in this type of research is the American H. L. Moore.

It is significant to note that the *Encyclopaedia of the Social Sciences,* whose 15 volumes were published in alphabetical sequence during 1930–1935, had no article on "econometrics." The word does not appear in the index to the encyclopedia or in Morgenstern's article just cited. In all probability Morgenstern completed his article (under "Economics") a few months before the founding of the Econometric Society in December 1930. Well before that date, U.S. agricultural economists were internationally known for the excellence of their work on the statistical estimation of demand and supply functions. Geoffrey Shepherd's journal articles in this field were concentrated in the early and middle 1930s; he shared its distinctions, contributed to its development, and codified its achievements by writing one of its first and best textbooks, *Agricultural Price Analysis,* first published in 1941 and still in print in its fifth edition in 1981.

Wassily Leontief, now a Nobel Laureate in Economic Science, began his career when U.S. agricultural economists were in the ascendant and has retained the highest respect for their successes in combining theoretical and empirical analysis. In his presidential address to the American Economic Association, Leontief indicted the economics profession for its failure to create an adequate empirical foundation for the highly articulated economic analytics and theory developed over the preceding several decades. But he specifically excepted agricultural economists from his indictment:

> An exceptional example of a healthy balance between theoretical and empirical analysis . . . is offered by agricultural economics as it developed in this country over the last 50 years. . . . Official agricultural statistics are more complete, reliable and systematic than those pertaining to any other major sector of our economy. . . . Agricultural economists demonstrated

the effectiveness of a systematic combination of theoretical approach and detailed factual analysis. They also were the first among economists to make use of the advanced methods of mathematical statistics. However, in their hands, statistical inference became a complement to, not a substitute for, empirical research [Leontief 1971, p. 5].

Apparently, Moore, his student and disciple Henry Schultz, and the agricultural economists were doing all the right things during the 1920s and 1930s to develop demand analysis as "the statistical complement of deductive economics." Moore had read all the works of the great mathematical economic theorists and had spent two terms studying statistics at Karl Pearson's laboratory in England. Henry Schultz kept abreast of the new developments in economic theory by Hicks and Allen, independently rediscovered the now-famous article by Slutsky on ordinal utility, studied statistics under A. L. Bowley and Karl Pearson, and kept up with later developments in mathematical statistics by Jerzy Neyman and Egon Pearson. Ezekiel, Waugh, the two Workings, and Shepherd also related their empirical work to the mainstream developments in economic theory and statistics. Henry Schultz's *The Theory and Measurement of Demand* was, and is, one of the great classics of econometrics. Everything seemed to point toward the further cumulative development of demand, supply, and price analysis as a branch of econometrics characterized by an admirable integration of theory, factual knowledge, and statistical techniques.

This faith in an orderly future was suddenly and severely shaken in the mid-1940s by the appearance of Haavelmo's (1943, 1944) articles introducing the simultaneous equations approach. From 1943 until 1953, this approach was advocated, disseminated, and exposited at various levels and with various degrees of lucidity by some of the most brilliant, mathematically trained economists and statisticians ever convened at a single institution—the Cowles Commission, then located at the University of Chicago.

I became an agricultural economist by accident in 1941. In fact, I did not realize I had become one until October 1942 when, confronted by a job choice between the Office of Price Administration and the War Food Administration, I chose the latter—specifically, the Program Appraisal and Development Division of its Western Region headquarters in San Francisco. A personal recommendation from Harry Wellman opened the way.

From my first day on the job, I was plunged into statistical demand and supply analysis in a policy-oriented setting: Western Region administrators were repeatedly called on to make recommendations on support prices needed to attain acreage and production goals; on price differentials between fresh, canned, and dried forms of fruits and vegetables; and on "cushions" needed in price ceilings to compensate for possible temporary market gluts and low prices for perishable products. When asked for advice, I examined all the published time series that seemed relevant (if possible, on a county-by-county basis), checked the illustrative production cost and yield estimates in R. L. Adams's *Farm Management Crop Manual,* read the enterprise cost and efficiency studies made on actual farms by the California Extension Service economists (Burlingame, Shultis, and Fluharty), phoned the state statisticians in Sacramento (Schiller and Blair) for detailed information on possible pitfalls in interpreting their data, and conferred with Bill Rosenberg and Cruz Venstrom. Bill Rosenberg had personally grown almost every kind of crop that could be raised in the Central Valley; Cruz Venstrom, my supervisor, understood agriculture, Alfred Marshall, and the impatience of administrators with technical jargon. My statistical analyses were done graphically, which forced me to look at and think about every observation in the short time series that seemed relevant to the problems at hand. In brief, I behaved like an agricultural economist.

The accidents that predisposed me toward this behavior occurred in Berkeley during January–May 1941. I wanted to learn something about econometrics, but there was no course in the catalog by that name. So, I selected a portfolio of courses entitled Advanced Economic Statistics (Mowbray), Business Cycle Analysis (Gordon), and Quantitative Agricultural Price Analysis (Wellman and Kuznets).

Mowbray's textbook was Ezekiel's *Methods of Correlation Analysis;* the same textbook was used by Wellman and Kuznets. Gordon asked me to review three books for his seminar: Myrdal's *Monetary Equilibrium,* Tinbergen's *Statistical Testing of Business Cycle Theories,* and Henry Schultz's classic. To understand Tinbergen's methodology I had to read Koopmans's *Linear Regression Analyis of Economic Time Series* and Frisch's *Statistical Confluence Analysis by Means of Complete Regression Systems.* When the going got tough, George Kuznets helped me out. George Kuznets could teach anything he could understand, he understood everything he had read, and it seemed to me he had read everything. Kuznets also directed me to Wold's *A Study in the Analysis of Stationary Time Series,* which greatly clarified the problem of autocorrelation in the residuals from time series regressions.

The writings of Ezekiel and Schultz and the teachings of Kuznets and Wellman convinced me that agricultural price analysis was a high-prestige field, richly interconnected with economic and statistical theory and very much in the mainstream of the econometric movement. In 1945, I transferred to the Washington office of the U.S. Bureau of Agricultural Economics, which had been the innovating center of work in demand and supply analysis in the 1920s. Most of the leading contributors of that decade had moved on, but some, like Ezekiel, Waugh, Bean, Wells, and Elliott, were still in Washington, as were younger economists (Robert M. Walsh, James P. Cavin, R. O. Been, R. J. Foote, Harold Breimyer, Herman Southworth, and others) who had learned from them. The files, the reading room, and the USDA library contained a wealth of unpublished regression analyses, computing instructions for "the Foote method" and "the Waugh method" of multiple regression analysis, mimeographed price studies, and the published technical bulletins by Sewall Wright, Ezekiel and Haas, Killough, and others.

The literature of statistical demand analysis was finite, and by 1951 I had read a substantial proportion of it. I had also updated many analyses done by my predecessors in the BAE and conducted many new ones. Meanwhile, the simultaneous equations movement rolled on, completely oblivious of anything that had been written prior to 1943 and completely impervious to criticism. It was a strange and mystifying episode in the history of economic science, from which some lessons may be derived.

The next section of this paper contains my attempt to reconcile the claims of the simultaneous equations approach with the established methodology and reasoning of statistical demand analysis. It was written in 1952, prior to the publication of classic works on demand analysis by Herman Wold (1953) and Richard Stone (1954). The third section of this paper then views the simultaneous equations movement in historical perspective with the aid of the historian's most powerful instrument—hindsight.

Structural Analysis and the Measurement of Demand for Farm Products. Ten years have passed since the publication of Haavelmo's first article on the simultaneous-equations approach. These years have produced an abundance of theoretical literature and have greatly increased the capital requirements of those who would engage in the measurement of economic relationships. Measurement without theory has (quite properly) been drummed out of the journals. However, measurement *with* theory has been painfully slow to come forward.

This may be due in part to a sort of natural selection, in that those who have been most forehanded in acquiring the new methodology have (with few exceptions) been chiefly interested in methodology per se. For them personally, empirical applications of the new technique may be even less inviting than research using simpler methods. For, to paraphrase Haavelmo, "economists will have to revise their ideas as to" not only "the level of statistical theory and technique" but also "the amount of tedious work that will be required, even for modest projects of research."

There is no point in lamenting the division of interest between methodologists and applied workers. But it appears that the burden of testing the new econometric tools under operating conditions must be taken up by the latter group. Specific cases of breakdown or evidence of poor design may then direct the attention of methodologists toward improving their product or modifying their claims for it. My own experience suggests that the "simultaneous" advertising has been much too derogatory of a long-established competitor.

During the past few years my work in the U.S. Department of Agriculture has involved a considerable amount of statistical demand analysis. The object of this work has almost invariably been to obtain numerical results that "made sense" in terms of the commodities and classes of economic agents involved—that is, results of structural significance. In all but a few cases I have used single-equation methods for estimating the desired coefficients. I accept the proposition that many economic phenomena must be explained in terms of two or more simultaneous relationships. However, single-equation methods appear to be both practically and theoretically appropriate for estimating many structural relationships in the field of food and agriculture.

The first part of this section is an appraisal of the applicability of single-equation methods to statistical demand analysis for farm products. The second part deals with an older and simpler problem in structural analysis, the adjustment of least-squares results for the effects of measurement errors in independent or predetermined variables, the object being to obtain best estimates of the coefficients of reversible (hence, structural) demand functions.

The common element in the two sections is the emphasis upon estimation of *coefficients* or *parameters* as reversible demand relations. The usefulness of single-equation methods for predicting future values of a *variable* (given unchanged structure) has not been disputed by proponents of the simultaneous-equations approach. Their applicability to structural analysis has, I believe, been underestimated during the past decade, and some reaffirmation of their value in this area is needed.

Single-Equation Methods in Demand Analysis. Prior to 1943 practically all statistical demand analysis was carried on by single-equation methods. This is no reflection on the acumen of leading demand analysts in the pre-Haavelmo period. In 1927 Elmer Working had made a clear statement of the identification problem, pointing out that price-quantity observations were points of intersection of simultaneous demand and supply curves and that, in general, the least-squares regression of price upon quantity was an uninterpretable combination of demand and supply coefficients, depending upon the relative magnitudes of the shifts in each curve and the correlation (if any) between them (Working 1927). In the following year, however, Ezekiel argued that "correlated shifts in demand and supply schedules, which Working feared might completely invalidate many price-analysis studies, are not so likely to cause trouble as he thought" (Ezekiel 1928). Only the "instantaneous" adjustments of supply to price within a given time unit could give rise to such trouble, and these adjustments (for farm products) were generally small relative to those in subsequent time periods. Another article by Ezekiel (1933) shows a selection of dependent and independent variables in single-equation demand analyses that is correct from the standpoint of Haavelmo's theory.[1] It also shows an awareness that simultaneous-equation methods of some sort were needed in cases where "values are actually neither dependent nor independent, but are determined by some sort of mutual interdependence."

No sound method of separating demand and supply curves in the truly simultaneous case was suggested until Haavelmo's 1943 paper. But Haavelmo's general theory of econometric analysis includes the single-equation model as a special case. In the next few pages I shall try to show how the simultaneous-equations theory leads me, in many cases, to select a single least-squares equation as an estimate of the structural demand function.[2]

Equation (10.1) is typical of the simpler consumer demand functions for food products:

$$X_1(t) = b_0 X_2(t) + c_0 X_3(t) + d_1(t) \tag{10.1}$$

where X_1 is retail price; X_2 is per capita consumption; X_3 is per capita disposable income; d_1 is a random disturbance, and b_0 and c_0 are "true" values of structural coefficients. In order to show (within the framework of simultaneous-equations theory) that this demand function can be approximated by a single least-squares equation, we must show on logical grounds (or assume) that the disturbances are distributed independently of the explanatory variables, consumption and disposable income. If this is so, we may regard consumption and disposable income as predetermined variables (see note 2). As the disturbances are then reflected only in retail price, the demand function must logically be fitted with price in the dependent position. A demand function with the attributes just described may be called a uniequational complete model (Marschak 1950).

The argument in the next few pages is directed toward showing that demand functions for many farm products probably meet the specifications of the uniequational complete model. It is impossible to show affirmatively that the disturbances in a given case are distributed independently of the explanatory variables, because the disturbances are (by definition) not directly observable. Thus it is *possible* that a noneconomic variable such as summer temperature, which affects consumer demand for lemons, will be correlated with disturbances arising from minor economic factors. Similarly it is *possible* that apple production, though causally determined by weather and by economic influences prior to harvest, will somehow be correlated with nonmeasurable disturbances in the demand function for apples during the subsequent marketing season. But there is certainly no a priori reason to expect that the disturbances will be dependent (in a probability sense) upon the variables in question.

In general, I will argue that relevant variables whose values are determined prior to the current time period or outside a given model may be used as explanatory variables in the estimation of demand functions by the method of least squares. Such variables are independently determined or predetermined in the usual or logical sense in which this word is used. The nonanswerable question of whether the disturbances are distributed independently of the explanatory variables will be disregarded unless some case arises in which there are special reasons for assuming the contrary. Instead I shall concentrate on the answerable question of whether certain variables entering into demand functions for farm products are predetermined in a logical sense, or nearly enough so, to be used as explanatory variables without leading to seriously biased estimates of demand elasticities.

Is Consumption of the Given Commodity Predetermined? For perishable food products, production is very nearly equal to domestic consumption. It will facilitate the exposition to consider first the logical status of production as a variable determined independently of the current price of the commodity, assuming for the moment that production and consumption are identical.

If production is not predetermined, its current value must be influenced by the current values of other endogenous variables, particularly price. This at once implies the existence of a second structural equation in which production is expressed as a function of current price in addition to other relevant variables. As production is now dependent on price, it can no longer be regarded as distributed independently of the disturbances affecting price. A least-squares regression of price upon production (equals consumption) and consumer income would give biased estimates of the structural demand coefficients. Thus, the alternative to treating production as a predetermined variable is the simultaneous fitting of two equations, a supply curve and a demand curve.

For many farm products it is clear on logical grounds that production is a predetermined variable. The production of a crop is the product of planted acreage, which is influenced by economic and other considerations before planting time, and yield, which in any given year is strongly influenced by weather. For livestock products, the question might be approached on a partly statistical basis: What part of the observed variance in production can be explained by (1) variables whose values were actually known prior to the beginning of the current period; (2) variables whose values, though not *known* in advance, must clearly have been *determined* prior to the current period;[3] (3) exogenous or noneconomic variables, such as weather and disease; and (4) errors of measurement? If by such a procedure we can explain 95 percent or so of the observed variation in production we may conclude that, for practical purposes, production is a predetermined variable. The residual variation sets an upper limit to the possible endogenous or jointly determined element in production and to the "disturbance bias" that might be involved in the least-squares regression of price on production.

If production of a perishable commodity is predetermined and if consumption is identically equal to production, consumption itself can obviously be treated as a predetermined variable. But can consumption be so treated under more general conditions?

Consumption of many farm products differs from (predetermined) production due to variations in exports, imports, or stocks, but it is still highly correlated with production. For example, during 1922–1941 the correlation coefficient between year-to-year changes in production and consumption of meat was 0.98 ($r^2 = 0.95$). If the disturbance or unexplained residual in the relationship between consumption and production is random, it seems intuitively clear that the degree of bias in the least-squares estimate of b_0 in equation (10.1) will not exceed the percent of total variance in consumption that is uncorrelated with variations in production.

Thus it appears that consumption may be treated as an explanatory variable in this case also, though perhaps with certain minor adjustments. One of these would be to regard not actual consumption but consumption as estimated from its regression upon production as a predetermined variable. The remaining variation in actual consumption would be regarded as a random disturbance-and-error component attaching to the consumption variable itself. The least-squares regression of price upon consumption would tend to be biased toward zero by the random measurement error component.[4] The bias in this coefficient arising from the disturbances is less obvious and could be either positive or negative, depending upon their correlation with the disturbances attaching to the "true" demand function.[5]

Is Consumer Income Predetermined? If this question is answered in the negative, we are implying that the applicable model includes an equation "explaining" disposable income of consumers as a function of other variables. In Girschick and Haavelmo (1947), disposable income was treated as a function only of predetermined variables, so that the income equation could be fitted independently by the method of least squares. This did not preclude the possibility that disturbances in this equation were correlated with disturbances in other equations.

A more interesting possibility is that disposable income may also be a function of one or more other endogenous variables, such as price and possibly consumption of a given commodity. If this is so, we are immediately confronted with the problem of deriving this equation simultaneously with the demand function (and also with a supply function if the consumption variable is not wholly or approximately predetermined). This alternative should be kept in mind during the following discussion.

In the first place, if the commodity in question is relatively unimportant—that is, if total expenditures for it are very small relative to the national income—even relatively large (percentage) gyrations in the value of the commodity can have little effect on the level of aggregate consumer income.

Pork, beef, and fluid milk are the three most important farm food products in terms of retail value. Expenditures for each of these products are equivalent to 2 or 3 percent of disposable personal income. It is difficult to see how variations in the supply of one of these commodities, operating chiefly through the coefficients of consumer demand functions, could account for more than 2 or 3 percent of the total variation in disposable income. In fact, since the bulk of the variation in disposable income is usually attributed to changes in investment and government expenditures, the 2 or 3 percent figure is almost certainly too high.

Various factors may be cited in support of this proposition. Among these are the relative stability of agricultural production, especially that of livestock products, and the apparently limited degree of competition (in demand) between major farm products on a short-run or year-to-year basis. The fact that consumer demand elasticities for pork and beef may not be far from unity tends to restrict the income effects that might otherwise flow from these commodities. It seems doubtful, therefore, that the "back effects" on disposable income resulting from variations in the price of pork, beef, or fluid milk would stand out above the errors of measurement in the published disposable income series, even if the latter were assessed at not more than 1 percent of the observed variance. If this conclusion is justified with respect to the major farm products, it applies even more strongly to the minor ones.[6]

Are There Two or More Simultaneous Demand Functions? Another somewhat different question may arise in determining whether the single-equation approach is applicable to a given situation. Even though commodity production and consumer income are predetermined, there may be two or more simultaneous demand functions involved in the determination of the commodity price. For example, suppose that a substantial percentage of the commodity is exported. We need to extend equation (10.1) to include some measure of export or foreign demand:

$$X_1 = f(X_2, X_3, X_4) \tag{10.2}$$

where X_4 may be regarded as the net resultant of demand and supply factors in foreign countries. If we fit a single least-squares equation expressing price as a function of total production, domestic income, and net foreign demand, we may have a satisfactory price-estimating equation so long as the relative importance of domestic and foreign markets does not change much. However, if we wish to estimate parameters of the separate domestic and export demand curves, we must attempt to derive them by a simultaneous-equations approach. A simple model is given by equations (10.3) through (10.5):

$$X_1 = f_d(X_{2_d}, X_3) \tag{10.3}$$

$$X_1 = f_e(X_{2_e}, X_4) \tag{10.4}$$

$$X_2 = X_{2_d} + X_{2_e} \tag{10.5}$$

where X_2 = total disappearance (assumed predetermined), X_{2_d} = domestic disappearance, and X_{2_e} = quantity exported. This model is just identified and can be fitted readily by the method of reduced forms.

The above procedure is logically indicated if a major portion of the commodity is exported. Where exports constitute only a small percentage of total utilization we may be content to fit a single least-squares equation—either (10.1) or (10.3)—and make judgment allowances for the biases that may be involved.

Can the Relation between Farm and Retail Price Be Fitted Independently of the Consumer Demand Functions? Another question that arises in demand analysis for farm products is this: Granted that we are permitted to fit a consumer demand function, in terms of retail price, by least squares, can we also fit the relationship between farm price and retail price independently of this equation, again by least squares? Each of the three equations (10.6) through (10.8) implies a marketing structure that would permit the independent fitting of a relationship between farm price, X_1^F, and retail price, X_1^r:

$$X_1^f = X_1^r(1/p) - k \tag{10.6}$$

where p is the product of "customary percentage markups" and k is "fixed charges or costs"; or

$$X_1^f = X_1^r - \Sigma c_i \tag{10.7}$$

where c_i are costs of specific input items or services; or

$$X_1^f = X_1^r - f(c_i, X_2) \tag{10.8}$$

where $f(c_i, X_2)$ is a supply function for marketing services. If food marketing agencies are highly competitive there will be a tendency for the average charge for marketing services to be equated with the marginal cost of providing them. Since total food consumption is reasonably stable from year to year it may also be that we can assume approximately constant unit costs of marketing within the relevant range of supply variation. Equation (10.8), however, provides symbolically for the possibility of a supply function for marketing services that requires margins to vary with the quantities of food moving through the marketing system.

Applications to Pork[7]. The complication that seems most likely in estimating demand functions for livestock products is the existence of a simultaneous supply function. The possible biases in fitting a demand function by least squares in this case may be appraised much as in Fox (1954, footnote 13).

Suppose that consumption is determined simultaneously with price. Then the two structural equations are

$$\text{Demand: } P = (1/b)q + cy + u \tag{10.9}$$

$$\text{Supply: } q = \beta p + \gamma z + v \tag{10.10}$$

where p is price, y is disposable income, q is consumption, and z is an estimate of production based on wholly predetermined variables; u and v are random disturbances. Each equation is just identified. If the variables are in logarithmic form, b is the elasticity of demand and β the elasticity of supply.

The reduced form equations are

$$p = cb/(b - \beta)y + [\gamma/(b - \beta)]z + (bu + v)/(b - \beta) \tag{10.11}$$

$$q = cb/(b - \beta)y + [b\gamma/(b - \beta)]z + b(\beta u + v)/(b - \beta) \tag{10.12}$$

each of which is to be fitted by least squares. Since β will be calculated as the ratio of the coefficients of y in the two equations, our ability to establish a value of β significantly different from zero depends upon whether the net regression of q upon y in equation (10.12) is significantly different from zero.

When we argue that equation (10.9) may be fitted by least squares without significant bias, we are arguing that β is equal to, or close to, zero. If $\beta = 0$, the reduced-form equations become

$$p = (\gamma/b)z + cy + (u + v/b) \tag{10.13}$$

$$q = \gamma z + (0)y + (\beta u + v) \tag{10.14}$$

The corresponding structural equations are

$$\text{Demand: } P = (1/b)q + cy + u \tag{10.15}$$

$$\text{Supply: } q = \gamma z + v \tag{10.16}$$

In the case of pork during 1922–1941, when about 95 percent of the variation in hog production was clearly predetermined, I obtained the following results. The reduced form equations are

$$p = -0.9581z + 0.9707y + u', \quad R^2 = 0.92 \tag{10.17}$$
$$(0.1091) \quad (0.1026)$$

$$q = +0.8370z - 0.0641y + v', \qquad R^2 = 0.91 \qquad (10.18)$$
$$(0.0670)\quad(0.0629)$$

The two structural equations, assuming $ß \neq 0$, are

Demand: $p = -1.1447q + 0.8974y + u$ \hfill (10.19)

Supply: $q = -0.0660p + 0.7738z + v$ \hfill (10.20)

The least-squares demand function is

$$P = -1.16q + 0.90y + u, \qquad R^2 = 0.97 \qquad (10.21)$$
$$(0.07)\quad(0.06)$$

The "supply" function, assuming $ß = 0$, is

$$q = 0.8403z + v, \qquad R^2 = 0.90 \qquad (10.22)$$
$$(0.0670)$$

If the structural demand function is estimated on the assumption that $ß = 0$, we have

$$p = -1.1402q + 0.8974y + u \qquad (10.23)$$

It will be readily seen that the differences between the structural demand coefficients and those of the least-squares demand function are very small in relation to the standard errors of the latter. The supply elasticity, $ß$, is negative and not significantly different from zero.

A similar analysis for beef encounters greater difficulties. While the differences between equations [the structural and least-squares demand coefficients] are larger than in the case of pork, they do not exceed one standard error of the least-squares regression coefficients. [See note 7. Ed.]

Other commodities could be selected for which two or more important simultaneous relationships are quite clearly involved. So far, I have had little opportunity to experiment with such commodities. I have corroborated the simultaneous-equations approach in a negative way for two or three products—that is, logical analysis of their demand-supply structures indicated that single least-squares regressions would give poor results, and they did. So far I have not been able to bring forth positive results from simultaneous-equation analyses of these cases, owing to such problems as the inaccuracy or nonexistence of data, shortness of time periods for which the structures (probably) were stable, and high intercorrelation between logically distinct predetermined variables.

In concluding this section, I would like to make one point that will suggest to experienced price analysts some of the difficulties to be expected in the measurement of simultaneous supply functions: Our ability to establish statistically significant coefficients in the subordinate or less influential members of a simultaneous-equation model will be limited by both specification and data problems. For example, the reduced-form equation upon which depends our ability to estimate the simultaneous elasticity of supply will frequently take the following form:

$$q = k_0 + k_1 z + k_2 y + v \tag{10.24}$$

where z is a combination of the predetermined variables underlying commodity production and y is the disposable income of consumers. The statistical significance of β, the elasticity of supply, depends on that of k_2—that is, we must show a statistically signficant association between the production of a specific commodity and total consumer income *after* the influence of factors directly and obviously affecting commodity production has been eliminated. Since the influence of consumer income upon production operates through the retail price of the commodity and thence, via the marketing system, upon and through its farm price, data, disturbance, and aggregation problems at each of these levels may obscure the relationship between production and income.

The preceding paragraph does not deny the possibility of establishing significant simultaneous supply elasticities for some farm products. It does suggest that the data requirements for the simultaneous-equations approach are more exacting than has been commonly realized and probably more exacting than many of our existing agricultural time series can support.

Adjustments for Errors in Variables. The simultaneous-equations literature generally assumes that all observed variables are measured without error. On this assumption, the unexplained residuals from each reduced-form equation consist only of random disturbances or shocks that affect the endogenous or "dependent" variable.

The standard assumption in least-squares regression analysis is similar except for terminology. The independent variables are assumed to be measured without error, and the unexplained residuals are considered to be a random component of the dependent variable. It was recognized fairly early that if independent variables actually contained random errors the simple regression coefficient of the dependent variable upon each independent would be biased toward zero. If the variances of (random) errors in the independent variables were known, the coefficients could easily be corrected for such biases.

In the 1920s and 1930s some analysts experimented with weighted regressions in an effort to arrive at what are now called structural relations. For example, consumer demand curves are generally thought of as reversible or exact functions, such that the net effect on price of a unit change in consumption should be precisely the reciprocal of the effect on consumption of a unit change in price. But consider the following least-squares equations relating to the demand for food:

$$P_f = -0.004 - 2.00q_f + 0.91y, \qquad R^2 = 0.86 \tag{10.25}$$
$$ (0.49) \quad (0.08)$$

$$q_f = -0.000 - 0.25p_f + 0.25y, \qquad R^2 = 0.66 \tag{10.26}$$
$$ (0.06) \quad (0.05)$$

where P_f and q_f are indexes respectively of retail food prices and per capita food consumption; y is per capita disposable income. All variables are expressed as first differences of logarithms for the period 1922–1941. The first equation implies that a 1 percent drop in price would be associated with a 0.50 percent increase in food consumption; the second implies a consumption increase of only 0.25 percent.

If it is assumed that there are no disturbances due to omitted variables, any unexplained variance in equations (10.25) and (10.26) must be attributed to errors in the data. A "correct" adjustment for such errors would produce perfect correlation between P_f, q_f, and y regardless of the direction in which residuals were minimized. In the present case, one adjustment yields the equations

$$p_f = a_1 - 2.97q_f + 0.95y, \qquad R^2 = 1.00 \tag{10.27}$$

$$q_f = a_2 - 0.34p_f + 0.32y, \qquad R^2 = 1.00 \tag{10.28}$$

Another, equally plausible, adjustment yields the equations

$$P_f = a_{12} - 2.70q_f + 0.92y, \qquad R^2 = 1.00 \tag{10.29}$$

$$q = a_{22} - 0.37p_f + 0.34y, \qquad R^2 = 1.00 \tag{10.30}$$

In each of these pairs, demand elasticity is the exact reciprocal of price flexibility. The two adjustments reflect different assumptions concerning the relative levels of error in the three variables.

However, if the true model is believed to include random disturbances in the dependent variable, an adjustment for errors in variables should not be sufficient to produce perfect correlation between their corrected values. The ideal adjustment would involve subtracting from the observed variance of each variable an estimate of the variance due to (random) measurement error. If the values of each variable were estimated from probability samples, the error variances could be estimated from standard error formulas.

In some other cases, rough judgments as to the levels of measurement error in a series might be formed on the basis of firsthand information as to the method by which it was constructed.

For example, a least-squares equation for eggs, based on first differences of logarithms during 1922–1941, gave the following results:

$$P_e = -0.010 - 1.83q_e + 1.24y, \quad R^2 = 0.80 \tag{10.31}$$
$$\quad\quad\quad (0.48) \quad (0.15)$$

where P_e is retail price, q_e is per capita production of eggs, and y is per capita disposable income. Due to the extremely limited year-to-year variability of q_e, an allowance for relatively small absolute errors in the series accounted for 15 percent of its observed variance; P_e and y fluctuated much more sharply, and the error levels estimated for them accounted for less than 2 percent of their observed variances. The equation adjusted for these error allowances is

$$P_e = -0.010 - 2.34q_e + 1.34y, \quad R^2 = 0.87 \tag{10.32}$$
$$\quad\quad\quad (0.44) \quad (0.13)$$

The adjustments leave 13 percent of the variation in retail egg prices to be explained by other factors or "disturbances."

This type of adjustment is consistent with the assumption of the simultaneous-equations approach that variables can be classified into endogenous and predetermined categories, with the latter distributed independently of the disturbances. The weighted regression adjustment that forces perfect correlation implicitly denies the validity or usefulness of this classification.

The type of adjustment illustrated in the case of eggs could with equal logic be applied to each reduced-form equation derived from a multiple equation model. Such an adjustment assumes that the observed variance of each endogenous variable can be partitioned into error, disturbance, and systematic components. While such partitioning is logically acceptable and could under ideal conditions be accurately done in large samples, it can at best be roughly approximated in samples of 20 or 30 observations.

Remarks. The concept of economic structure is much broader than any particular technique of statistical measurement. I believe that any substantial attempt at demand analysis should start with a description of the structure of economic relationships believed responsible for generating the observed data. Specialized knowledge of the commodities, markets, and statistical series involved is indispensable to such a description. Statistical estimation of each relationship in the complete structure should be guided by this knowledge, and problems of identification and true simultaneity should be met squarely where they exist.

In this I believe I am in basic agreement with leading proponents of the simultaneous-equations approach. However, my own experience with demand analysis for farm products leads me to single-equation estimates in a great many practical cases—more, perhaps, than the simultaneous-equations literature would lead one to expect. To some extent preoccupation with the general simultaneous case has created a reluctance to recognize simpler models where they actually apply. This has led some workers to adopt what might be called "the Procrustean approach" in econometric analysis—the practice of forcing every set of economic data through the same highly elaborate computational routine. This behavior is little more intelligent (and much more expensive) than the primitive type of Procrusteanism that sliced through the most complex set of relationships with a least-squares equation or a graphic flourish. I suspect that different preconceptions as to the nature of disturbances—their magnitude relative to systematic components and the factors that might lead to significant correlation between disturbances and observed variables—also make for misunderstandings between applied demand analysts and those who are primarily interested in methodology. I believe the latter group has devoted too much attention to constructed examples (despite their value for pedagogical purposes) and too little to problems involving real economic data.

While progress in theory is essential to progress in measurement, it seems to me that the latter is the real goal of econometrics. Progress in measurement can be accelerated by teamwork between those who know particular sets of data and the processes by which they are generated and those who have the mathematical resources to develop models and techniques appropriate to the problem at hand. As applied workers have the most to gain by such teamwork, it is only fitting that they should take the initiative in seeking specific aid from the mathematically trained group.

Some Reflections as of 1979. Simultaneous-equation estimation is a family of statistical techniques that proceeds from the assumption that the disturbances in different equations of an economic model are, or are likely to be, correlated with one another. This contrasts with the assumption almost universally made in economics prior to 1944 that the disturbances in different equations of a model were statistically independent (uncorrelated); under this assumption, each equation could be estimated separately by ordinary least squares—a "single-equation" technique.

In principle, Haavelmo's 118-page article, "The Probability Approach in Econometrics," published in 1944, should have been followed by a dispassionate scholarly discussion and careful testing of its merits as a guide to applied econometric research. In practice, the scholarly community had been badly disrupted in Germany since 1933, in Austria since 1938, and in the whole of Europe since 1939. Some economists who might have moderated the discussion were in German-occupied countries and others were working to capacity in war-related activities. Apart from such disruptions, it would be difficult to explain why Haavelmo's article showed no evidence that he had heard of the thirty years of cumulative experience in applied econometric research (much of it in the United States) prior to 1944.

In order to concentrate on the implications of correlated disturbances in equations, Haavelmo and his equally brilliant associates neglected important problems that had long been recognized by applied econometricians:

(1) At any given time, some of the variables that theoretically belong in a model may not yet have been measured; (2) some of the variables that have been measured are subject to substantial errors; (3) high intercorrelation among the independent variables in models fitted to economic time series is more nearly the rule than the exception.

Haavelmo and his colleagues emphasized the following problems, but with little or no recognition that they had been dealt with earlier by others:

(1) The "identification problem" in the case of Marshallian simultaneous demand and supply curves. This problem was formulated and solved explicitly by Marcel Lenoir (1913) and E. J. Working (1927), and it was well understood by Mordecai Ezekiel and Holbrook Working in the mid-1920s.

(2) The identification problem in the general case including both lagged and nonlagged variables. Moore in 1914 was seeking a causal explanation of business cycles in the following sequence: (a) cycles in rainfall in the American Midwest cause (b) cycles in crop production, which cause (c) cyles in crop prices, which *might* cause (d) cycles in other sectors of the economy. Thus, rainfall (an exogenous variable) during the spring and summer determined the size of the crop harvested in the fall and sold during the fall and winter; hence, crop production was a predetermined variable in the demand functions for crops: $P_t = f(Q_t)$. In 1917, Moore also fitted a supply function for cotton in the form $Q_t = f(P_{t-1})$.

Moore contrasted his dynamic approach (which included lagged variables and a strong interest in prediction) with the static, simultaneous approach of Alfred Marshall. Moore's recursive supply-and-demand equations embodied a dynamic mechanism that later became known as "the cobweb model" (Ezekiel 1938). This mechanism was recognized independently and separately by Schultz, Ricci, and Tinbergen in 1930, described by Leontief and by Kaldor in 1934, and discussed in detail by Ezekiel in 1938. The cobweb model is an example of what Herman Wold later called a "causal chain," in which each equation can be estimated separately and without bias by least squares.

The identification problem was also solved and applied to more complicated models, some in economics and some in genetics, by Sewall Wright in 1921, 1925, and 1934.

Haavelmo's approach was brilliantly conceived, but it rested on an untested assumption that nearly all econometric models were of the synchronous type, in which each equation contained two or more endogenous variables, the disturbances in different equations were correlated, and least-squares estimates of the structural coefficients were badly biased. If this assumption were true, it raised the possibility that nearly all results hitherto obtained by single-equation (least-squares) methods were invalid because they had ignored what Herman Wold referred to as the "Haavelmo bias." As of 1945 this possibility was particularly alarming to Wold, for in that year he had nearly finished the statistical side of an investigation of consumer expenditures, all numerical results of which might be subject to the Haavelmo bias.

Wold immediately undertook a critical examination of the traditional single-equation method and its logical foundations. Wold's conclusion (stated in a paper presented at a 1947 meeting of the Econometric Society and published in 1949) was that the traditional method is free from Haavelmo bias when applied to a certain general class of models that was "wide enough to cover most, if not all, dynamic models used in econometric research up to 1940" (Wold 1949, p. 12). Wold cited Jan Tinbergen's pioneer 1939 work in applying *model sequence analysis* or *process analysis* to statistical data in his 45-equation model of the U.S. economy during 1919–1932 and stated that "it is precisely this type of dynamic systems, properly specified, which goes free from the Haavelmo bias" (p. 13). In his later work, Wold repeatedly and forcefully emphasized the importance of "causal chain" or recursive models in econometrics; the cobweb model is the earliest (and perhaps the simplest) representative of the type.

Wold's position was viewed as the correct one by most econometricians who had done serious work with data prior to 1944; few or none of them adopted Haavelmo's approach. A younger group accepted Haavelmo's assumption of correlated disturbances at least provisionally and developed several additional techniques (two-stage least squares, instrumental variables, principal components, and others) for handling the first stage of estimation represented by the reduced-form equations. As experience in applying such methods to data accumulated, it turned out that the estimates in many cases were so close to those obtained by least squares that the differences were not statistically (or economically) significant. It also turned out that the simultaneous methods were more sensitive than ordinary least squares to high intercorrelation among predetermined variables and that specification errors in one equation could substantially affect the estimated coefficients of others. By the mid-1970s, applied econometricians felt free to use ordinary least squares or one of the simultaneous-equation methods, depending upon the characteristics of particular equations and subgroups of equations in a complete model.

Koopmans and Marschak, who helped extend, explain, and popularize Haavelmo's approach, stated that errors in variables were disregarded in order to concentrate on the central problem of disturbances in equations. The computing instructions for applying Haavelmo's concepts to data embodied the assumption that all variables were measured without error, and these instructions were carried forward uncritically into a number of textbooks. As a result, several cohorts of graduate students were trained in the belief (sincerely held by instructors who had done no empirical research) that errors in variables were of no consequence. Only in the 1970s did econometricians trained in this tradition begin to recognize the need for dealing explicitly with errors in variables, a subject treated extensively, and regarded as of crucial importance for applied work, by Schultz (1925) and by Frisch (1934).

Haavelmo's 1943 article contained no references to any other scientist, if we except the mathematician Jacobi, whose name was used in adjectival form. The index of his 1944 article contained nine references to Abraham Wald and five to H. B. Mann, the latter in his capacity as coauthor of a single article with Wald. There were scattered references to other mathematicians and mathematical statisticians and to theoretical works by Frisch, Koopmans, and Marschak. There was no direct reference to empirical work of any kind; Tinbergen's name appeared in two footnotes, but only to identify a theoretical memorandum written by Frisch for a conference to discuss Tinbergen's work for the League of Nations. Haavelmo acknowledged major intellectual debts only to Frisch and Wald.

Haavelmo and his mentors were men of genius, but it was a case of theory feeding upon theory. Moreover, the theory at the front end of this ethereal food chain was that of probability, not economics. Their less sophisticated followers believed that progress in econometrics depended only upon mathematical statistics. The result was a great proliferation of estimation techniques and of textbooks and courses conveying the impression that econometrics *is* estimation.

The young professors remained ignorant of the great tradition of empirical research initiated by Moore and of the books, bulletins, and articles that made its achievements a matter of permanent record. Their students were effectively walled off from contact with this literature. On the other side of the wall were classics by Moore, Schultz, Wright, Ezekiel, Waugh, the Workings, Shepherd, Leontief, Tinbergen, and others. They contain the records of the real econometric revolution, which started from a base in economic theory and sought, by creating its statistical complement, to invest it with "the reality and life of fact." Therein lay the great strength of agricultural price analysis and of Geoffrey Shepherd's contributions to it as scientist, practitioner, and teacher.

Notes

1. See especially Koopmans (1945, p. 460) for a statement on this point.
2. The following pages assume familiarity with the basic concepts and terminology of the simultaneous-equations approach. The basic assumption is that the variables figuring in an economic model or system of relationships can be classified into endogenous and predetermined categories. The current values of endogenous or jointly dependent variables are determined within the model; those of predetermined variables are determined outside the model or prior to the current time period. Statistical residuals are assumed to lie exclusively in the endogenous variables and are attributed to real but minor factors (disturbances) that operate on the endogenous variables randomly and independently of the predetermined variables.
3. For example, the number of milk cows on farms January 1 is causally determined as of that date but is not reported as a statistic until mid-February.
4. [For an explanation of this point, see Fox (1954, footnote 10). Ed.]
5. [The possible "disturbance bias" in the situation under discussion is discussed in Fox (1954, footnote 11). Ed.]
6. In the preceding paragraphs we have rejected, on intuitive grounds, the hypothesis that an equation expressing the generation of consumer income must be fitted simultaneously with the consumer demand function. This hypothesis can also be treated formally. See Fox (1954, footnote 13).
7. [Because of space limitations the section on beef together with a related footnote have been deleted. The case of pork is, however, sufficient to illustrate Fox's point. Ed.]

References

Ezekiel, M. 1928. "Statistical Analysis and the 'Laws' of Price." *Quarterly Journal of Economics* 42(February):199–227.

_____. 1930. *Methods of Correlation Analysis*. New York: John Wiley and Sons. 2d rev. ed., 1941.

_____. 1933. "Some Considerations on the Analysis of the Prices of Competing or Substitute Commodities." *Econometrica* 1(April):172–80.

_____. 1938. "The Cobweb Theorem." *Quarterly Journal of Economics* 52(February):255–80.

Fox, K. A. 1954. "Structural Analysis and the Measurement of Demand for Farm Products." *Review of Economics and Statistics* 37(February):57–66.

Frisch, R. 1934. *Statistical Confluence Analysis by Means of Complete Regression Systems*. Oslo: Universitets Okonomiske Institutet.

Girschick, M. A., and T. Haavelmo. 1947. "Statistical Analysis of the Demand for Food: Examples of Simultaneous Estimation of Structural Equations." *Econometrica* 15(April):79–111.

Haavelmo, T. 1943. "The Statistical Implications of a System of Simultaneous Equations." *Econometrica* 11(January):1–12.

_____. 1944. "The Probability Approach in Econometrics." *Econometrica* 12, Supplement, July, 118 pp.

Jevons, W. S. 1871. *The Theory of Political Economy*. London: Macmillan. 3d ed., 1888.

Koopmans, T. C. 1937. *Linear Regression Analysis of Economic Time Series*. Haarlem: De Erven F. Bohn N.V.

_____. 1945. "Statistical Estimation of Simultaneous Economic Relations." *Journal of the American Statistical Association* 40(December):448–66.

Lenoir, M. 1913. *Etudes sur la Formation et le Mouvement des Prix*. Paris: Giard and Briere.

Leontief, W. W. 1971. "Theoretical Assumptions and Non-observed Facts." *American Economic Review* 61(March):1–7.

Marschak, J. 1950. "Statistical Inference in Economics: An Introduction." In *Statistical Inference in Dynamic Economic Models,* edited by T. C. Koopmans. Cowles Commission Monograph No. 10, pp. 1–50.

Moore, H. L. 1908. "The Statistical Complement of Pure Economics." *Quarterly Journal of Economics* 23:1–33.

_____. 1914. *Economic Cycles: Their Law and Cause.* New York: Macmillan.

_____. 1917. *Forecasting the Yield and Price of Cotton.* New York: Macmillan.

Morgenstern, O. 1931. "Mathematical Economics." In *Encyclopaedia of the Social Sciences,* 5, p. 368. New York: Macmillan.

Myrdal, G. 1931. *Monetary Equilibrium.* London: W. Lodge. Originally published in German.

Schultz, H. 1925. "The Statistical Law of Demand as Illustrated by the Demand for Sugar." *The Journal of Political Economy* 33(October and December):481–504, 577–637.

_____. 1938. *The Theory and Measurement of Demand.* Chicago: University of Chicago Press.

Shepherd, G. S. 1941. *Agricultural Price Analysis.* Ames: Iowa State University Press. Sixth edition, 1968.

Stone, R. 1954. *The Measurement of Consumers' Expenditures and Behaviour in the United Kingdom, 1920–1938: Vol. I.* Cambridge: Cambridge University Press.

Tinbergen, J. 1939. *Statistical Testing of Business Cycle Theories, Vol. I: A Method and Its Application to Investment Activity; Vol. II: Business Cycles in the United States of America, 1919–1932.* Geneva: League of Nations Economic Intelligence Service.

Wold, H. 1938. *A Study in the Analysis of Stationary Time Series.* Uppsala: Almquist and Wiksells.

_____. 1949. "Statistical Estimation of Economic Relationships." *Econometrica* 17(Supplement, July):1–21.

_____. 1953. (In association with Lars Juréen) *Demand Analysis: A Study in Econometrics.* New York: John Wiley.

Working, E. J. 1927. "What Do Statistical 'Demand Curves' Show?" *Quarterly Journal of Economics* 41(February):35.

Wright, S. 1921. "Correlation and Causation." *Journal of Agricultural Research* 20:557–85.

_____. 1925. *Corn and Hog Production.* Bulletin 1300. Washington, D.C.: U.S. Department of Agriculture.

_____. 1934. "The Method of Path Coefficients." *Annals of Mathematical Statistics* 5:161–215.

11

A *"Simple"* Theory
of *Business Fluctuations*

GERHARD   TINTNER

THIS PAPER presents a theory of business fluctuation that is "simple" in the mathematical sense, as defined by Jeffreys (1937). It also can be considered as the simplest possible dynamic generalization of the Walrasian system of general equilibrium. It explains the business cycle as a purely speculative, short-run equilibrium phenomenon.

Roughly speaking, the "simple" theory explains business fluctuations as resulting from the existence of interrelated speculative markets. The buyers and sellers on these markets react not to existing prices but to anticipated prices. All functional relationships involved are assumed to be linear (as first approximations). If anticipations of the buyers and sellers are asymmetrical in

---

This paper incorporates, with slight modification and some abridgement, two previously published papers by the author: "A 'Simple' Theory of Business Fluctuations," *Econometrica,* vol. 10, 1942, pp. 317–20; and "The 'Simple' Theory of Business Fluctuations: A Tentative Verification," *Review of Economics and Statistics,* vol. 26, 1944, pp. 148–57. The first of these was based upon a paper read before a group of the Econometric Society at Chicago in July 1943. The author there indicated his indebtedness to Professor H. Hotelling, then of Columbia University, for advice and criticism. The paper also appeared as Journal Paper No. J-1217 of the Iowa Agricultural Experiment Station, Ames, Iowa, Project No. 557.

Author's note: A French article (Une Théorie simple des fluctuations économiques) was published in *Revue d'Economie Politique,* vol. 57, 1948. See also my *Econometrics* (New York: Wiley, 1952), pp. 72–75. Stochastic aspects of the theory are considered in: "A Stochastic Theory of Economic Development and Fluctuations," in N. Hegelung, ed., *Money, Growth and Methodology* (Lund, 1961); and G. Tintner and J. K. Sengupta, *Stochastic Economics* (New York: Academic Press, 1972), pp. 27–93. See also "A Macro Model of the Economy for the Explanation of Trend and Business Cycle with Applications to India" (with G. Kadekoki and M.V.R. Sastry), in W. Sellekaerts, ed., *Econometrics and Economic Theory. Essays in Honour of Jan Tinbergen* (London: Macmillan, 1975). Applications to Austria are: "Stabilitatskonzepte am Beispiel Osterreichs" (with B. Böhm and R. Rieder), *Empirica,* vol. 1, 1977; "Is the Austrian Economy Stable?" (with B. Böhm and R. Reider), in J. M. L. Janssen, F. L. Pau, and A. Straszak, eds., *Models and Decision Making in National Economics* (Amsterdam: North-Holland, 1979); and "A New Concept of Economic Equilibrium, Deterministic and Stochastic" (with B. Böhm), in O. Kyn and W. Schrettl, eds., *On the Stability of Contemporary Economic Systems* (Göttingen: Vandenhoeck and Rupprecht, 1979).

a certain, well-defined sense, then there is the possibility of periodic fluctuations in prices and quantities. These magnitudes will fluctuate with the same period but with various amplitudes (which may be constant, damped, or exploding) and with leads and lags. Such a movement of prices and quantities is essentially what we mean if we speak of the business cycle (Mitchell 1940).

It is not claimed, of course, that this is in all cases the only possible explanation of booms and depressions. The author has indicated in an earlier publication that a variety of causes may be at work in creating these fluctuations (Tintner 1935). But it is possible that these "speculative" fluctuations are able to explain some of the cyclical phenomena met within our economy (Haberler 1939).

Strictly speaking, the empirical verification of our theory would require a study of all or at least the most important markets. Such a study is not feasible because of the amount of computational work, which, as will be seen, is very great even with only three variables. We therefore shall limit ourselves to the most important markets and shall use for our verification data for stock prices, farm prices, and prices of nonfarm commodities covering the period 1920–1942. All the series are in the form of index numbers; we hope that this fact does not unduly distort the picture.

A model based upon our theory will be constructed and the unknown parameters determined by various methods, keeping always in mind the relationships necessarily implied by our theory.[1] The fitted functions will be subjected to certain statistical tests in the final sections of this paper.[2]

Such a procedure cannot, of course, afford a complete test of the theory. Even if the statistical test were completely applicable, the model used is not unique for our theory. All that can be said is that ours is the *simplest* theory that will lead to the specific model.

The Theory. Assume an economic system consisting of n commodities. The buyers and sellers take into account not the actual but the *anticipated* price. Assume further with Evans (1930, pp. 36ff) that they form their anticipations upon the prevailing price and the price tendency, that is, the rate of change of the price in time.[3] If all relationships are linear (as first approximations), we get, for the demand for the ith commodity,

$$D_i = a_i + \sum_{j=1}^{n} a_{ij} p_j + \sum_{j=1}^{n} b_{ij} \dot{p}_j \quad (i = 1, 2, \ldots, n) \tag{11.1}$$

where p_j is the price of the jth commodity and $\dot{p}_j = dp_j/dt$, its time derivative. The supply of the ith commodity is

$$S_i = a_i' + \sum_{j=1}^{n} a_{ij}' p_j + \sum_{j=1}^{n} b_{ij}' \dot{p}_j \quad (i = 1, 2, \ldots, n) \tag{11.2}$$

The a_i, a_i', a_{ij}, a_{ij}', b_{ij}, b_{ij}' are constants. The Hotelling (1932) conditions are

$$A_{ij} = a_{ji}, \qquad a_{ij}' = a_{ji}'$$

They need not, of course, be strictly fulfilled.

Putting demand equal to supply for short-term equilibrium we get

$$A_i + \sum_{j=1}^{n} A_{ij}p_j + \sum_{j=1}^{n} B_{ij}\dot{p}_j = 0 \quad (i = 1, 2, \ldots, n) \tag{11.3}$$

where we abbreviate $A_i = a_i' - a_i$, $A_{ij} = a_{ij}' - a_{ij}$, and $B_{ij} = b_{ij}' - b_{ij}$.

From general economic considerations, we have $A_{ii} > 0$ (rising supply and falling demand curves). The strict Hotelling conditions imply $A_{ij} = A_{ji}$. If we further assume with Evans (1930, p. 36) that the buyers and sellers anticipate the continuation of the prevailing price tendencies, we have $A_{ij}B_{ij} < 0$.

In order to solve the dynamic system (11.3) we proceed as follows: Let $p_i = x_i + c_i$, where the constants c_i are determined from the system,

$$A_i + \sum_{j=1}^{n} A_{ij}c_j = 0 \quad (i = 1, 2, \ldots, n) \tag{11.4}$$

by $c_i = -(\sum_{j=1}^{n} D_{ji}A_j)/D$, where D is the determinant $|A_{ij}|$ and D_{ji} the cofactor of the element A_{ji} in D. Then (11.3) becomes

$$\sum_{j=1}^{n} A_{ij}x_j + \sum_{j=1}^{n} B_{ij}\dot{x}_j = 0 \quad (i = 1, 2, \ldots, n) \tag{11.5}$$

This is a system of linear differential equations with constant coefficients. In order to find the solution, we study the roots λ_k of the determinantal equation

$$|A_{ij} + \lambda B_{ij}| = 0$$

and arrive at

$$x_i(t) = \sum_{k=1}^{n} d_{kj}\exp \lambda_k t \tag{11.6}$$

where the d_{kj} are constants determined for simple roots of the determinantal equation by the equations

$$\sum_{j=1}^{n} (Aij + \lambda_k B_{ij})d_{kj} = 0 \quad (i = 1, 2, \ldots, n) \tag{11.7}$$

For multiple roots they become polynomials of a degree one less than multiplicity. The λ_k may be real or (conjugate) complex. In the first case, the solutions become exponential functions; in the latter, damped or exploding sinusoidal fluctuations or fluctuations with constant amplitudes. Exponential solutions will arise if the Hotelling conditions are fulfilled and there is further symmetry of the anticipations, i.e., $B_{ij} = B_{ji}$ (Turnbull and Aitken 1932, pp. 110ff).

All prices and quantities sold and bought on the markets will participate in the cycles if some of the roots of the determinantal equation are conjugate complex. They will not participate if the corresponding d_{kj} are zero. All prices and quantities participating in a given cycle will show the same period but may have different amplitudes and leads and lags. This is essentially the phenomenon of the business cycle (Mitchell 1940, p. 92). Hence it could be claimed that our general framework affords an explanation of these fluctuations.

An extension of the theory is possible in the following directions: (1) the coefficients may not be constant but only bounded; (2) the differential equations may not be homogeneous but involve functions of time on the right-hand side; (3) the coefficients may be periodic; and (4) the relationships may not be linear. Some of these extensions probably provide better approximations to reality. It is, however, the purpose of this paper to demonstrate the existence of a business cycle under the minimum of assumptions and to state the theory in the simplest possible terms. Let us proceed then to the empirical evidence.

The Data. The index of stock prices used for the period 1920–1937 is that of Mr. Alfred Cowles;[4] data for the years 1937–1942 are from Standard and Poor's Corporation.[5] The indices of wholesale prices of farm products and of nonfarm products are those of the Bureau of Labor Statistics.[6] For all the indices the base period used is the year 1926. The theoretical model requires the derivatives of these series as well as the index series themselves. The derivatives are approximated by the central difference formula using up to and including the third difference (Whittaker and Robinson 1924, p. 65). Four items are lost in this procedure, two at the beginning and two at the end.

Regressions. Since we are considering a rather long period of 23 years, we can no longer assume that the (linear) demand and supply functions in the various markets stay constant in time. Very important shifts in taste, in technology, etc., occurred in the period that we are studying. We shall try to represent these changes in the manner of Henry Schultz (1938, pp. 140ff), as linear shifts in time. Our differential equations then cease to be homogeneous.

One statistical difficulty that arises is the direction in which to minimize when we use statistical regressions in order to establish our fundamental system of differential equations (Frisch 1934; Koopmans 1937; Roos 1937).

However, since it is clear that the derivatives will have larger errors than the original index series,[7] it seems justifiable to minimize in their direction. Denoting stock prices as S, farm prices as F, and the prices of nonfarm commodities as N, and indicating time derivatives by dots, we have, from (11.3), the following fundamental system of regression equations:

$$\dot{S} = -0.48S + 2.16F - 1.29N + 2.06t - 19.41$$
$$\dot{F} = -0.24S + 0.45F - 0.17N + 0.45t + 0.88 \qquad (11.8)$$
$$\dot{N} = -0.07S + 0.15F - 0.03N + 0.44t - 3.72$$

Here t is time, measured from 1931 as the origin. Only 19 yearly items are included in each analysis, since we lost two years at the beginning and at the end in computing the derivatives.

The multiple correlation coefficients are 0.67, 0.55, and 0.50 for the first, second, and third equations, respectively. All these are significant for 14 degrees of freedom. The level of significance of 5 percent requires a correlation coefficient of only 0.4973. Since we are, however, dealing with time series, there is some doubt about the validity of this test (Davis 1941, pp. 175ff; Tintner 1940a, pp. 93ff).

Mathematical Discussion. The solution of the system of equations appears as

$$S = a_1 + b_1 t + A_1 e^{\lambda_1 t} + B_1 e^{\lambda_2 t} + C_1 e^{\lambda_3 t}$$
$$F = a_2 + b_2 t + A_2 e^{\lambda_1 t} + B_2 e^{\lambda_2 t} + C_2 e^{\lambda_3 t} \qquad (11.9)$$
$$N = a_3 + b_3 t + A_3 e^{\lambda_1 t} + B_3 e^{\lambda_2 t} + C_3 e^{\lambda_3 t}$$

where t is time measured from 1931 as the origin. The magnitudes a_1, b_1, etc., are immediately determined by equating all the constant terms and the terms linear in t in the three equations. Equations (11.9) can then be written as

$$S = 0.1793 - 0.0595t + S_1$$
$$F = -0.4188 - 0.0744t + F_1 \qquad (11.10)$$
$$N = -0.8722 - 0.0864t + N_1$$

The functions S_1, F_1, and N_1 are the sums of the exponentials in the functions S, F, N in formulas (11.9).

They must fulfill the following relationships:

$$\dot{S}_1 = -0.48S_1 + 2.16F_1 - 1.29N_1$$
$$\dot{F}_1 = -0.24S_1 + 0.45F_1 - 0.17N_1 \qquad (11.11)$$
$$\dot{N}_1 = -0.07S_1 + 0.15F_1 - 0.03N_1$$

We assume here that the characteristic equation of the matrix of the co-efficients of S, F, and N of our equations

$$\begin{vmatrix} -0.48 & 2.16 & -1.29 \\ -0.24 & 0.45 & -0.17 \\ -0.07 & 0.15 & -0.03 \end{vmatrix} \tag{11.12}$$

has no repeated latent roots, but that the three roots λ_1, λ_2, λ_3 are distinct. Should this condition not be fulfilled and there are multiple roots, then the constants in the solutions become polynomials of a degree one less than the multiplicity.

The coefficients of the exponential terms in our equations are determined in the following way (Moulton 1930, pp. 246ff).

$$(-0.48 - \lambda_1)A_1 + 2.16A_2 - 1.29A_3 = 0$$
$$-0.24A_1 + (0.45 - \lambda_1)A_2 - 0.17A_3 = 0 \tag{11.13}$$
$$-0.07A_1 + 0.15A_2 + (-0.03 - \lambda_1) = 0$$

This system of homogeneous linear equations has a solution since the de-terminant of the coefficients is zero, λ_1 being a latent root. One of the coeffi-cients A_1, A_2, A_3, however, remains arbitrary. By using the other two latent roots λ_2 and λ_3 instead of λ_1 in the equations (11.13) we can determine B_1, B_2, B_3, and C_1, C_2, C_3. If the roots are conjugate complex, they can be combined to give sine and cosine terms in t.

Since we have one arbitrary coefficient in each set of solutions, we shall have, altogether, three arbitrary constants in the complete solution of our system. These will be found by the method of least squares.

Determination of the Period. We use the matrix (11.12) to determine the period of the fluctuations. This period is intimately related to the latent roots of our matrix. Since Hotelling's methods (1933) are valid for symmetrical matrices only and our matrix is evidently asymmetric, we use Aitken's (1936–1937) ingenious procedures (see also Frazer et al. 1938). These pro-cedures give for the greatest latent roots of the matrix the two conjugate com-plex values of $-0.0510 + 0.4901i$ and $-0.0510 - 0.4901i$.

This corresponds to a sinusoidal fluctuation that is slightly damped, since the real part of the complex roots is negative. The imaginary part gives the period, measured in radians. We see that the period is 12.820210 years. This is not at all a bad approximation considering the very tentative character of our fundamental assumptions and the fact that our rather complex numerical analysis is based only upon 19 yearly observations.

We find the third remaining latent root of the matrix in the following manner: The sum of the diagonal elements of the original matrix (11.14) is equal to the sum of the three roots. The sum of the diagonal element is -0.06; hence the remaining root is 0.042. This represents an exponential trend. It is interesting to note that this exponential trend is a result of the interaction of speculative markets, whereas the linear trends in the formulas (11.12) follow from entirely different causes, economically, which bring about the linear shifts in the demand and supply functions.

The solutions can now be expressed in the following way (by combining the two complex roots):

$$S_1 = k_1 e^{0.042t} + e^{-0.051t}(\alpha_1 \cos t + \beta_1 \sin t)$$
$$F_1 = k_2 e^{0.042t} + e^{-0.051t}(\alpha_2 \cos t + \beta_2 \sin t) \tag{11.14}$$
$$N_1 = k_3 e^{0.042t} + e^{-0.051t}(\alpha_3 \cos t + \beta_3 \sin t)$$

where k_1, k_2, α_1, α_2, β_1 can be expressed in terms of k_3, β_2, and β_3. This follows from the fact that our matrix is zero, if the latent roots are deducted from the diagonal elements.

Concentrating first on the real root $\lambda_1 = 0.042$, we have a solution:

$$S_2 = k_1 e^{0.042t}, \qquad F_2 = k_2 e^{0.042t}, \qquad N_2 = k_3 e^{0.042t} \tag{11.15}$$

This must fulfill the relations (11.13). Hence, we get the following system of equations for the coefficients k_1, k_2, k_3:

$$-0.52k_1 + 2.16k_2 - 1.29k_3 = 0$$
$$-0.24k_1 + 0.41k_2 - 0.17k_3 = 0 \tag{11.16}$$
$$-0.07k_1 + 0.15k_2 - 0.07k_3 = 0$$

The determinant of this system of homogenous linear equations ought to be zero. Actually it is not zero but 4.97×10^{-4}. The error involved is very small. We express k_1 and k_2 in terms of k_3 as follows:

$$k_1 = 0.72K_3, \qquad k_2 = 0.53k_3 \tag{11.17}$$

In a similar way we treat the case of the two complex roots. Assume a solution:

$$S_3 = e^{-0.051t}(\alpha_1 \cos t + \beta_1 \sin t)$$
$$F_3 = e^{-0.051t}(\alpha_2 \cos t + \beta_2 \sin t) \tag{11.18}$$
$$N_3 = e^{-0.051t}(\alpha_3 \cos t + \beta_3 \sin t)$$

Inserting the solution (S_3, F_3, N_3) into the formulas (11.13) we get the following system of homogeneous linear equations in the coefficients α_1, α_2, α_3, β_1, β_2, β_3:

$$0.43\alpha_1 + 2.15\alpha_2 - 1.29\alpha_3 - 0.49\beta_1 + 0.00\beta_2 + 0.00\beta_3 = 0$$
$$0.49\alpha_1 + 0.00\alpha_2 + 0.00\alpha_3 - 0.43\beta_1 + 2.16\beta_2 - 1.29\beta_3 = 0$$
$$-0.24\alpha_1 + 0.50\alpha_2 - 1.17\alpha_3 + 0.00\beta_1 - 0.49\beta_2 + 0.00\beta_3 = 0 \qquad (11.19)$$
$$0.00\alpha_1 + 0.49\alpha_2 + 0.00\alpha_3 - 0.24\beta_1 - 0.50\beta_2 - 0.17\beta_3 = 0$$
$$-0.07\alpha_1 + 0.15\alpha_2 + 0.02\alpha_3 + 0.00\beta_1 + 0.00\beta_2 - 0.49\beta_3 = 0$$
$$0.00\alpha_1 + 0.00\alpha_2 + 0.49\alpha_3 - 0.07\beta_1 + 0.15\beta_2 + 0.02\beta_3 = 0$$

These equations are obtained by equating separately the sine and cosine terms. Their determinant should be zero but is actually -2.52×10^{-7}. The error involved is not significant.

The values of α_1, α_2, α_3, β_1 expressed in terms of β_2 and β_3 are

$$\alpha_1 = -13.83\beta_2 + 41.69\beta_3, \qquad \alpha_2 = -6.28\beta_2 + 22.15\beta_3,$$
$$\alpha_3 = -1.83\beta_2 + 6.28\beta_3, \qquad \beta_1 = -10.74\beta_2 + 44.50\beta_3 \qquad (11.20)$$

Statistical Verification: The Cyclical Movement. The main interest in our theory attaches naturally to the cyclical terms S_3, F_3, N_3 as represented in the formulas (11.18). Certain relationships between the coefficients that must hold true are given in the formulas (11.19). The three functions are damped sinusoidal movements with a period of about thirteen years.

Because of the relationships (11.19) that must necessarily hold true, we have to determine only the two parameters β_2 and β_3 since all the other coefficients of the cyclical movements of the three price index series can be expressed in terms of them (formulas 11.19).

The fact that the relationships (11.19) must necessarily be fulfilled creates some difficulties for the application of the method of least squares. They will be overcome as indicated below.

In this section we shall try only to get a fit for the cyclical movement as such, using the method of least squares. Hence we first fit a linear trend to our original series S, F, and N of the stock price, farm price, and nonfarm price indexes. The linear trend lines are

$$T_S = 0.9716 - 0.003035t$$
$$T_F = 0.8305 - 0.023035t \qquad (11.21)$$
$$T_N = 0.8721 - 0.015035t$$

Denote by S_4, F_4, N_4 the difference of the original functions and their trends:

$$S_4 = S - T_S, \qquad F_4 = F - T_F, \qquad N_4 = N - T_N \qquad (11.22)$$

The mean of the function $e^{-0.051t}\cos t$ over our period ($t = -9$ to $t = +9$) is -0.2647 and the mean of the function $e^{-0.051t}\sin t$ is 0.0211. Deducting these values from the respective functions, we first achieve a fit by the method of least squares separately for the functions S_4, F_4, N_4. We get as our results:

$$\begin{array}{lll} \bar{\alpha}_1 = 0.0936, & \bar{\alpha}_2 = -0.0992, & \bar{\alpha}_3 = -0.0766 \\ \bar{\beta}_1 = -0.2968, & \bar{\beta}_2 = -0.1113, & \bar{\beta}_3 = -0.0429 \end{array} \qquad (11.23)$$

These values of the coefficients are found by fitting successively S_4, F_4, and N_4. From the relationships (11.19) we get three sets of values for β_2 and β_3, resulting from fitting S_4, F_4, and N_4, as presented in Table 11.1.

Table 11.1

Fit of	β_2	β_3
S	−0.0984	−0.0305
F	−0.1100	−0.0357
N	−0.0936	−0.0400
Average	−0.1007	−0.0354

The values found for β_2 and β_3 by fitting S, F, and N are different. Since our fit must hold true simultaneously for the three functions S_4, F_4, and N_4, we take the *averages* of these quantities from Table 11.1. Putting them again into the formulas (11.19), we get values for all the coefficients as indicated in the following functions:

$$\begin{aligned} S_5 &= e^{-0.051t}[-0.08(\cos t + 0.2647) - 0.49(\sin t - 0.0211)] \\ F_5 &= e^{-0.051t}[-0.15(\cos t + 0.2647) - 0.10(\sin t - 0.0211)] \\ N_5 &= e^{-0.051t}[-0.04(\cos t + 0.2647) - 0.04(\sin t - 0.0211)] \end{aligned} \qquad (11.24)$$

These are the functions that represent a fit of the results of our theory to our data.

We present in Figure 11.1 the original stock price series with the trend removed and the curve fitted to the cyclical movement alone (heavy line); similarly in Figure 11.2 we present the farm price index and in Figure 11.3 the index of nonfarm prices. Since we took into account only the cyclical movements and neglected the trend, this cannot be considered a very good test. We shall present a more comprehensive test in the next section where we shall also try to apply statistical tests of significance.

Statistical Verification: A Complete Test. Here we will try to fit the complete set of solutions:

$$\begin{aligned} S_6 &= 0.1793 - 0.0595t + k_1 e^{0.042t} + e^{-0.051t}(\alpha_1 \cos t + \beta_1 \sin t) \\ F_6 &= 0.4188 - 0.0744t + k_2 e^{0.042t} + e^{-0.051t}(\alpha_2 \cos t + \beta_2 \sin t) \\ N_6 &= 0.8722 - 0.0864t + k_3 e^{0.042t} + e^{-0.051t}(\alpha_3 \cos t + \beta_3 \sin t) \end{aligned} \qquad (11.25)$$

We have to fit by the method of least squares our original data S, F, and N. We have to determine the constants k_1, k_2, k_3, α_1, α_2, α_3, β_1, β_2, β_3, keeping

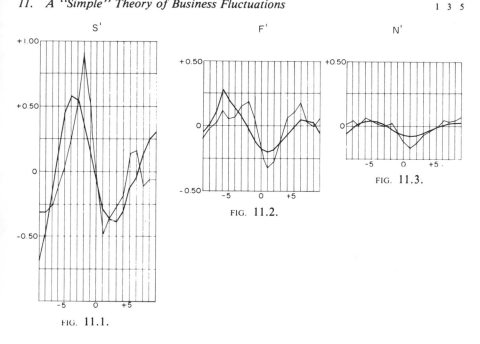

FIG. 11.1.

FIG. 11.2.

FIG. 11.3.

in mind the relationships (11.17) and (11.20) that must necessarily exist between these magnitudes in order to make them possible solutions of our system.

We proceed in our application of the method of least squares in the same
way as in the previous section. That is to say, we shall first fit independently
the functions (11.25) to each series of our data and determine the values of the
above constants. Then we will take averages such that the conditions (11.17)
and (11.20) are fulfilled.

The method of least squares gives us the following three sets of values for
our coefficients:

$$
\begin{aligned}
\hat{k}_1 &= 0.8326, & \hat{k}_2 &= 1.2028, & \hat{k}_3 &= 1.6917 \\
\hat{\alpha}_1 &= 0.1579, & \hat{\alpha}_2 &= -0.0717, & \hat{\alpha}_3 &= -0.0396 \\
\hat{\beta}_1 &= -0.3075, & \hat{\beta}_2 &= -0.1126, & \hat{\beta}_3 &= -0.0427
\end{aligned}
\tag{11.26}
$$

By inserting these three sets of constants in equations ((1.17) and (11.20),
we obtain the values for k_3, β_2, and β_3, which are shown in Table 11.2.

The values of the coefficients in Table 11.2 should be identical. Since they
are not, we take the averages indicated in the last line. Using these averages

Table 11.2

Fit of	k_3	β_2	β_3
S	1.5709	−0.1195	−0.0358
F	1.6706	−0.1100	−0.0343
N	1.6917	−0.1154	−0.0400
Average	1.6444	−0.1150	−0.0367

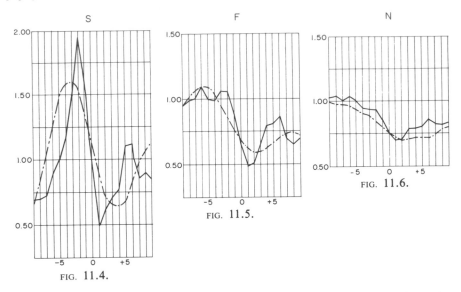

FIG. 11.4.

FIG. 11.5.

FIG. 11.6.

and equations (11.17) and (11.20) we get the following set of functions that represents our fit to the original data, taking into account the necessary relationships that follow from our theory:

$$S_7 = 0.1793 - 0.0595t + 0.8715e^{0.042t} + e^{-0.051t}(0.0604\cos t - 0.3980\sin t) \quad (11.27)$$
$$F_7 = -0.4188 - 0.0744t + 1.1840e^{0.042t} + e^{-0.051t}(-0.0907\cos t - 0.1150\sin t)$$
$$N_7 = -0.8722 - 0.0864t + 1.6444e^{0.042t} + e^{-0.051t}(-0.0200\cos t - 0.0367\sin t)$$

We present in Figures 11.4, 11.5, and 11.6 the original data of our three series together with the fitted curves corresponding to our theory. If the fitting does not appear very successful, it should be kept in mind that we are obtaining our estimates under very rigorous conditions postulated by our theory. In fact, the method of least squares strictly speaking has been applied only in order to obtain the three parameters k_3, β_2, and β_3 out of a totality of eighteen constants that determine the shape of the estimates for S, F, and N. All the other constants have been obtained by other methods. It should also be borne in mind that we never fit a single one of the three series alone but make a comprehensive fit of the whole system.

Various statistical tests can be applied for the goodness of our fit. Let us first use the χ^2 test.

Computing the functions (11.27) and comparing them with our original data, S, F, and N, we get the following values for χ^2: for S, $\chi^2 = 1.2547$; for F, 0.2471; and for N, 0.1051.

In order to evaluate these results, we have to take into account the number of degrees of freedom. Each series consists of nineteen observations. Altogether we have obtained eighteen constants, i.e., the values a_1, a_2, a_3, b_1, b_2, b_3, λ_1, λ_2, λ_3, k_1, k_2, k_3, α_1, α_2, α_3, β_1, β_2, β_3. Hence we have lost 6 degrees of freedom for each fit, and each individual χ^2 in Table 11.2 is based upon 13 degrees of freedom. We secure from Fisher's tables the result that for a level of significance of 1 percent a value of χ^2 of 27.688 is permissible. Hence we would judge that we have in all three cases an extraordinarily good fit, since the empirical values of χ^2 are much below those theoretically permissible.

An alternative test runs as follows: The correlation coefficients between our fitted functions (11.27) and the original data S, F, and N are 0.7004, 0.8634, and 0.9480, respectively; the average is 0.87.

For each individual correlation coefficient, we secure, at a level of significance of 1 percent for 13 degrees of freedom, a theoretical coefficient of 0.6411. In all three cases the empirical correlation coefficients are greater and hence the correlations are significant.

Using the z-transformation of R. A. Fisher, we compute the average correlation coefficient. Here we have 39 degrees of freedom and, at the 1 percent level, a theoretical correlation coefficient of 0.3932. Our empirical value is again much larger than this and the relationship must be judged as significant. This is to say, all our statistical tests indicate it is extremely unlikely that we should get as good a fit as we actually got by pure chance. There is, however, as indicated above, some room for doubt about the applicability of these tests because of possible serial correlation.

We show finally in Figure 11.7 the purely cyclical movements of stock prices, farm prices, and nonfarm prices. These are the movements that correspond to our theory. It appears that there are various amplitudes, and the damping is also clearly exhibited. We also notice the leads and lags that correspond not too badly to the actual movements of the three price series over the period considered.

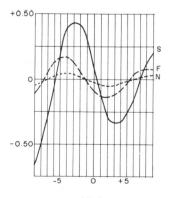

FIG. 11.7.

Notes

1. For similar mathematical business cycle theories, see especially I. Fisher (1922–1923, pp. 1024ff), C. F. Roos (1930, pp. 501ff), G. C. Evans (1930, pp. 106ff, 154ff), E. Theiss (1935, pp. 213ff), B. Chait (1938), and H. T. Davis (1941, pp. 370ff).

2. In attempting an empirical verification, the author has been greatly influenced by the writings of J. Tinbergen (see, especially, 1939).

3. See also G. von Haberler (1939, pp. 145ff) and G. Tintner (1938, p. 145).

4. Alfred Cowles, 3rd, and Associates. 1938. *Common Stock Indexes, 1871–1937*. Bloomington, Indiana, pp. 66ff.

5. Standard and Poor's Corporation. *Trade and Security Statistics* (long term security price index record).

6. From *Federal Reserve Bulletin*.

7. In a random series, the series of first differences has twice, the series of second differences six times, the series of third differences twenty times the variance of the original series. See G. Tintner (1940b, pp. 40ff).

References

Aitken, A. C. 1936–1937. "Studies in Practical Mathematics." *Proceedings, Royal Society of Edinburgh* 57:269–304.

Chait, B. 1938. *Les Fluctuations economiques et l'interdependence des marchees*. Brussels: R. Louis.

Davis, H. T. 1941. *The Analysis of Economic Time Series*. Bloomington, Ind.: Principia Press.

Evans, G. C. 1930. *Mathematical Introduction to Economics*. New York: McGraw-Hill.

Fisher, I. 1922–1923. "The Business Cycle Largely a Dance of the Dollar." *Journal of the American Statistical Association* 18:1024–28.

Frazer, R. A., W. J. Duncan, and A. R. Collar. 1938. *Elementary Matrices*. Cambridge: Cambridge University Press.

Frisch, R. 1934. *Statistical Confluence Analysis by Means of Complete Regression Systems*. Oslo: Universitetes Økonomiske Institutt.

Haberler, G. 1939. *Prosperity and Depression*. Geneva: League of Nations.

Hotelling, H. 1926. "Relations between Two Sets of Variates." *Biometrika* 27: 321–77.

_____. 1932. "Edgeworth's Taxation Paradox and the Nature of Demand and Supply Functions." *Journal of Political Economy* 40:577–616.

_____. 1933. "Analysis of a Complex of Statistical Variables into Principal Components." *Journal of Educational Psychology* 24:417–41, 498–502.

_____. 1936. "Simplified Calculation of Principal Components." *Psychometrika* 1:27–35.

Ince, E. L. 1927. *Ordinary Differential Equations*. London: Longmans, Green.

Jeffreys, H. 1937. *Scientific Inference*. Cambridge: Cambridge University Press.

Koopmans, T. 1937. *Linear Regression Analysis of Economic Time Series*. Haarlem: De Erven F. Bohn N.V.

Mitchell, W. C. 1940. "Business Cycles." *Encyclopedia of the Social Sciences*, vol. 3. New York: Macmillan.

Moulton, F. R. 1930. *Differential Equations*. New York: Macmillan.

Roos, C. F. 1930. "A Mathematical Theory of Price and Production Fluctuations and Economic Crises." *Journal of Political Economy* 38:501–22.

_____. 1937. "A General Invariant Criterion of Fit for Lines and Planes Where All Variables Are Subject to Error." *Metron* 13:3–20.

Schultz, H. 1938. *The Theory and Measurement of Demand*. Chicago: University of Chicago Press.

Theiss, E. 1933. "A Quantitative Theory of Industrial Fluctuations Caused by the Capitalist Technique of Production." *Journal of Political Economy* 41:334–49.

_____. 1935. "Dynamics of Savings and Investment." *Econometrica* 3:213–24.

Tinbergen, J. 1939. *Business Cycles in the United States, 1919–32.* Geneva: League of Nations Economic Intelligence Service.

Tintner, G. 1935. *Prices in the Trade Cycle.* Vienna: J. Springer.

_____. 1938. "A Note on Economic Aspects of the Theory of Errors in Time Series." *Quarterly Journal of Economics* 53:145–49.

_____. 1940a. "The Analysis of Economic Time Series." *Journal of the American Statistical Association* 35:93–100.

_____. 1940b. *The Variate Difference Method.* Bloomington, Ind.: Principia Press.

Turnbull, H. W., and W. C. Aitken. 1932. *An Introduction to the Theory of Canonical Matrices.* London and Glasgow: Blackie and Son.

Whittaker, E. T., and G. Robinson. 1924. *The Calculus of Observations.* London: Blackie and Son.

12

Application of RIP and RAP Models in Evaluating Time and Space Dimensions of Price, Production, and Related Variables

WEN-YUAN HUANG, EARL O. HEADY, AND REUBEN WEISZ

BECAUSE of the differential impacts among regions of agriculture, and of various commodity pricing and economic development policies, there is need for models that can reflect price, income, resource use, and related items over space and time. These models may take various forms. One can be positive or predictive in nature—predicting the response that farmers and regions will take as specific pricing, developmental, or other policies are implemented. Another form can be purely normative in nature—determining the potential production capacity of American agriculture should the world and nation evolve programs to fully utilize its productive capacity while certain environmental or other restraints are in effect. In the case of the first interest, the answer will be based largely on statistical or econometric models that predict future response on the basis of experience from the past as reflected in time series data. But this basis is insufficient for the second interest, where the program of the future has never been experienced in the past. In the latter case, we are interested in physical and resource potentials and not predicted response. However, if the potential is favorable, we can be interested in policies that will cause the response to attain the potential. Hence, there is some need for models that link the normative and descriptive or positive approaches. In particular, we may be interested in a normative analysis of production potential under various regional resource use and environmental restraints, but also on the market and price impacts if these potentials were attained. Too, normative programming models may be better adapted, because of time series data limitations, in expressing the spatial or regional potentials of production and resource use, while the price and market impacts will be a more nearly national outcome in terms of the existing real-world structure of demand as reflected in relevant time series data.

Day's (1963), Schaller's and Dean's (1965), and Sahi's (1972) recursive linear programming models combined normative and positive aspects by use of convenient programming tableaus linked among years by flexibility constraints statistically or econometrically estimated. Positive and normative aspects also have been combined in quadratic programming models (Takayama and Judge 1964; Plessner 1965; Meister et al. 1978). While these solutions are simultaneous, rather than obtained through passing information from one model component to another, they utilize demand functions that are estimated econometrically in the objective function and linear programming models formulated in the conventional normative manner. Generally the recursive linear programming models are used for short-run analyses, while the simultaneous models are used for long-run analyses. In these cases, a programming model is used to complement an econometric model in providing policy variables that could not be specified in the econometric model and in dealing with situations where unprecedented programs are imposed. The RIP and RAP hybrid models described in this chapter are intended to accomplish this task with special emphasis on combining a large-scale econometric model with a large-scale linear programming model involving two-way communication among these major model components.

Recursive Models with One- and Two-Way Communication among Components. In one-way communication models, demand or production levels obtained from an econometric model are fed into the programming model, which is solved accordingly. There then is no similar communication feedback from the programming model to the econometric component. An example of a one-way communication model is the National Water Commission Model (Heady et al. 1972), where demand estimates for the year 2000 were updated from Brandow's econometrically based demand estimates. Another example is the National Water Assessment (NWA) model (Meister et al. 1976; Nicol and Heady 1974), where demand levels for years 1985 and 2000 were generated by the National Interregional Agricultural Projection (NIRAP) system (Quance 1976), furnished by the National Resource Economics Division (NRED) of the Economic Statistical Cooperative Service (ESCS) and communicated on a one-way basis to the static programming model developed at the Center for Agricultural and Rural Development (CARD) at Iowa State University. Numerous examples of these one-way communication models can be found in Heady and Srivastava (1975). The equivalent of one-way communication from a programming model in providing a set of exogenous parameters as a starting basis in an econometric model has been employed in some studies (see Sonka and Heady 1973).

One-way communication models are sufficient for certain purposes, as outlined previously, where the objectives relate to purely normative (programming) results or to predictive (econometric) purposes alone. However, sometimes we are also concerned with the time and spatial attributes of production, prices, income, and related variables. Normally, these problem settings suggest application of interregional programming models to measure potentials linked with two-way communication to econometric models that reflect real-world market sectors. Such models were proposed in Day (1963, Chapter 3) and in Day (1964). See also Mueller and Day (1978).

Hybrid Recursive Models with Two-Way Communication. We review initial efforts on two recursive hybrid models formulated by CARD, and cooperatively by CARD and NRED of the U.S. Department of Agriculture. We summarize the specification of both and detail the nature and some applications of the second. The first is a Recursive Interactive Programming (RIP) model and the second is a Recursive Adaptive Programming (RAP) model. Initial results are promising, although much remains to be done.

Characteristics of a RIP Model. Baum (1977) linked the crop sector of a CARD interregional programming model (Nicol and Heady 1974; Meister et al. 1976), modified to a single land class, with a revised econometric recursive simulation model (Ray and Heady). This model has two-way communication between the programming and econometric components. Within each stage of the analysis, the profit-maximizing linear programming model is solved first to estimate crop acreages and production. The values of these linkage variables are then passed to the simulation model. The simulation model subsequently is run to estimate the values of market sector variables for the same stage in time. The output of the simulation component is used to revise the coefficients in the linear programming model in the preceding stage. They also are used to estimate the net returns coefficients in the objective function, the values of the activity flexibility restraints (the upper and lower limits on crop acreage response by region), the values of the transformation or input-output coefficients, optimal nitrogen fertilization rates, and crop yields in the linear programming model. The RIP model moves to the next stage, starting with the programming model.

The RIP models have several advantages over the one-way communication models summarized earlier: they allow for a two-way flow of communication—one way within each stage and the other way between stages. This is a higher degree of interaction between components than is achieved by one-way communication models. They present less of a computational problem than simultaneous solution models because the feasibility set is not restricted to equality solutions of the econometric model. Finally, they dynamically simulate a sequence of events over space and through time in a nonsimultaneous, or cobweb, solution framework.

The RIP approach also has limitations: a RIP hybrid tends to overestimate production and underestimate prices, if the interest is in prediction of production as well as price. (Many normative analyses are interested in potential production, not actual production, and in expected prices under potential production levels.) This result is forthcoming because the linear programming component attains an economically efficient use of resources. Excess production, as compared with the real world, thus serves as an input in the econometric model and causes an underestimate of prices, as compared with the expected real world. If the concern is with real-world production responses and corresponding prices, biased results are expected. (However, if we are interested in potential production and resource use and the prices that would result accordingly without ameliorating policies, this is no problem.)

Also, the RIP hybrid may encounter infeasible solutions if the econometric component gives an estimated production that exceeds the capacity of regional production. If either of the components has been specified incorrectly, the recursive nature of the model may result in a propagation of errors over time, between stages.

The first problem can be ameliorated by introducing behavioral constraints into the programming component. The procedure of adjusting the upper and lower programming bounds on acreage limitations by region in response to the price impacts produced by the econometric component is one possible method. However, additional research is needed to improve the accuracy of regionally specific acreage (or production) response equations in interregional programming model components. The second and third problems can be addressed in part by incorporating a two-way flow of communications between components within each stage of the analysis. This concept of a corrective-adjustment-within-stage feedback mechanism is equivalent to a self-adaptive control system (D'Azzo and Houpis 1966); it is defined as a model that has the capability of changing values of linkage variables through an internal process of estimation evaluation and adjustment according to a presetup rule. It forms the basis for the RAP model that is described below.

Characteristics of a RAP model. One component of the RAP model, currently being tested, is an econometric model, the Cross Commodity (CC) Forecasting System developed by ESCS (Brandow 1961). The second component is a linear programming (LP) model with several unique characteristics: in the current LP model, the prices utilized in the objective function are local prices for the producing regions of the interregional programming model computed using historical ratios of state to national prices; the national prices are obtained from the econometric model. These local prices also are used in the production response equations that compute local production flexibility constraints for the LP model. For each region, the LP component contains an accounting row that measures the deviation between aggregate U.S. production as forecast by the econometric component and the aggregate contained in the LP solution. Large penalty costs have been assigned to the deviational variables in the profit-maximizing objective function in order to force the LP solution to come as close as possible to the econometric solution.

The econometric model is used as the former component based on the following reasoning: the LP model was originally designed for the purpose of conducting long-range projections and analyses of potential resource use. In contrast, the econometric model was developed to support the short-run situation and outlook process in ESCS. Because the RAP hybrid is intended for use in evaluating the short-run impacts of agricultural policies, the econometric system was selected as the principal component in this hybrid model. At each stage in the solution of the RAP hybrid, the LP model acts in the following subordinate and complementary role. If all of the deviational (production) variables in the LP solution vector are equal to zero, the solutions produced by the two components are assumed to be consistent. In this case, the LP model has validated the results of the econometric component, and the RAP model begins the computations for the next stage in time. However, if any of the deviational variables in the LP solution vector are not equal to zero, then the production forecast by the component is outside the production possibilities region defined by the feasibility constraints in the LP component. In this case, the presetup adaptive feedback mechanism is invoked. Within this stage, the production variables in the programming component become linkage variables from the programming component to the econometric component; they are set equal to the LP solution values. The econometric component is re-solved, producing a new set of prices and a new set of values for other endogenous variables. Then the RAP model goes forward to the next stage of analysis.

Alternative Feedback Adjustment Procedures for RAP Models. The key problem in building the RAP hybrid model is to find the best presetup procedure to adjust the production (or acreage) when the econometric equilibrium solution is outside the feasible region as represented by the resource restraints. Such an infeasible solution is illustrated in Figure 12.1. The production possibility HDE reflects the upper bounds on the feasible region of an LP format with one region and two crops. The econometrically estimated equilibrium solution $A(q_1, q_2)$ is outside the feasible region in the two-crop LP component. Thus, a main task of building the RAP hybrid model is to develop a proper adjustment procedure when the econometric estimated production is outside the production feasible region defined by the linear programming component.

Harrison (1976) suggested an iteration procedure to find the equilibrium prices in a hybrid model. Convergence of shadow prices from linear program-

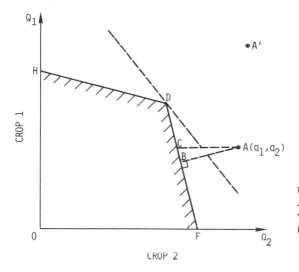

FIG. 12.1. Points *B*, *C*, and *D* are candidates for adjusted values from infeasible solution $A(q_1, q_2)$.

ming is used as the criterion. This procedure is appropriate when both the econometric and the programming components in the hybrid model have a simple model structure and are inexpensive to run. This is not the case for the RAP model.

Figure 12.1 can be used to illustrate four procedures to adjust the econometric estimated equilibrium solution $A(q_1, q_2)$, which is outside the feasible region in a two-crop model. (1) The shortest distance (SD) approach will give the final solution indicated by *B*. *AB* is the shortest distance as measured by the sum of squares of the quantity of the two crops to be adjusted from *A* to the feasible region. (2) The independent adjustment (IA) approach will give the solution indicated by *C*. This approach adjusts only the crop production that is larger than the feasible range (OE). The approach, however, does not adjust the crop production that is less than the feasible range (OH). (3) The maximization approach (MA) ignores the equilibrium solution generated by the econometric model. The approach obtains the adjusted value simply by running the programming component. One of the likely solutions is indicated by *D* in Figure 12.1. (3) The minimum absolute distance (MAD) approach gives the solution that has the least adjustment of absolute values of the production. The solution may be either *C* or *B*, depending on the slope of *DE* as shown in Figure 12.1.

Each approach has its own appeal. It should be noted that it is possible that the SD, MA, and MAD approaches will obtain the same adjusted values when the econometric estimated value is at *A'* in Figure 12.1. The SD approach has the least squares for quantity of production to be adjusted; the IA approach only has to adjust the crop that is outside the feasible region; the MA approach gives the adjusted value that maximizes net return from the production; the MAD approach has least absolute value in adjustment. Furthermore, the MAD procedure gives a solution either the same as the solution of the SD or the solution of the IA. Because of this characteristic, the MAD approach is used in building the RAP hybrid model.

Mathematical Formulation to Illustrate the Essence of the Hybrid Model. An econometric component and a programming component are used to illustrate the essence of constructing the hybrid model. Assuming an econometric component consisting of N equations, the hybrid model is expressed as

$$Y_{nt} = \sum_i a_i Y_{it} + \sum_j b_j Y_{jt-1} + \sum_k c_k Z_{kt} + e_{nt} \quad \text{for } n = 1, 2, \ldots, N \quad (12.1)$$

where Y_{nt} and Z_{kt} denote endogenous and exogenous variables respectively; a_i, b_j, and c_k are coefficients; e_{nt} is an error term. The first I ($I < N$) endogenous variables are linking variables to a programming component, which is expressed as

Maximize

$$\left\{ \sum_i \sum_j [P_{ijt} - C_{ijt}] X_{ijt} - \alpha_1 \left[\sum_i (V_i^+ + V_i^-) \right] - \alpha_2 \left[\sum_i \sum_j (W_{ij}^+ + W_{ij}^-) \right] \right\} \quad (12.2)$$

subject to
   National production balance restraints

$$\sum_j X_{ijt} + V_i^+ - V_i^- = Y_{it} \quad \text{for } i = 1, 2, \ldots, I \quad (12.3)$$

Regional production response balance restraints

$$X_{ijt} + W_{ij}^+ - W_{ij}^- = \beta_{ijt} X_{ijt-1} \quad \begin{array}{l} \text{for } i = 1, 2, \ldots, I \\ j = 1, 2, \ldots, J \end{array} \quad (12.4)$$

Production resource restraints

$$\sum_i \sum_j V_{ijl} X_{ijt} \leq R_{lt} \quad \text{for } l = 1, 2, \ldots, L \quad (12.5)$$

where:

P_{ijt} = Farm price for crop i in producing region j in time period t

C_{ijt} = Cost of production for crop i in producing region j in time period t

X_{ijt} = Quantity of production of crop i in producing region j in time period t

α_1, α_2 = Two arbitrary large constant values satisfying the following conditions: $\alpha_1, \alpha_2 > (P_{ijt} - C_{ijt})$ for all i, j, and t

V_i^+, V_i^- = Positive or negative deviation from econometric estimated production of crop i ($V_i^+, V_i^- \geq 0$)

W_{ij}^+, W_{ij}^- = Positive or negative deviation from econometric estimated production of crop i in region j ($W_{ij}^+, W_{ij}^- \geq 0$)

V_{ijl} = Technological coefficients for using resource l by crop i in region j

R_{lt} = Maximum amount of resource l available in time t

β_{ijt} = Coefficient used to predict the products X_{ijt} from X_{ijt-1}. The value of β_{ijt} is estimated from a regression equation that has independent variables such as expected price and other variables.

The objective function (12.2) is to maximize production net returns and minimize the absolute deviation between the programming solution and values of national and regional econometric estimates. The formulation of minimizing the absolute deviation is described in Sposito (1975). Another form of the objective function, minimizing production costs and the deviation formulated, or minimization of the deviation, can also be formulated.

By properly assigning values for V_i^+, V_i^-, W_{ij}^+, and W_{ij}^-, the model [(12.1) to (12.5)] can be transformed into a national, regional, and simultaneous national-regional hybrid model. The model becomes a one-way national (N) hybrid model by setting V_i^+ and V_i^- equal to zero. The model is a national model because the production in the solution from the programming component is set to the value estimated by the econometric component. The N model usually is used to analyze regional production response to meet a national target quantity of the production. Similarly, the model can become a one-way regional (R) hybrid model by setting W_{ij}^+ and W_{ij}^- equal to zero. The model is a regional one because the national production is determined by summing all the regional production. This R model is useful to investigate possible inpact from regional production expansion. When this R model is structured in such a way that the sum of all the regional production is used in the next time period (stage) the model becomes a two-way communication or RIP model as mentioned earlier.

The model also can be transformed into a simultaneous national and regional hybrid model when V_i^+, V_i^-, W_{ij}^+, and W_{ij}^- are not set equal to zero, or ranges are used to replace these variables. One variation of the NR simultaneous model is to employ a pair of flexibility restraints to give a range for each crop production in each region. The model is a simultaneous one, because the final solution production in the programming component is jointly determined by national and regional estimates. This is the basic structure of the RAP model explained earlier. At each time period, the RAP model checks whether ΣX_{ijt} is equal to Y_{it}. If not (either V_i^+ or V_i^- is not equal to zero), the value of $\Sigma_j X_{ijt}$ replaces the value of Y_{it} and is fed back to the econometric model to adjust the values of all endogenous variables before the RAP model starts the simulation for the next time period (stage $t + 1$).

If the first term (the net profit) in equation (12.2) is set at zero, this RAP model is equivalent to a restricted statistical model that is fitted with least-absolute-value to a series of production data generated by the econometric component.

Model Validations. The RAP test model consists of two components: an econometric model represented by the Commodity Economic Division(CED) of the ESCS Cross Commodity model and a programming model represented by the CARD-NRED LP model. The CED model includes livestock and crop sectors (Teigen 1977). It has 127 exogenous variables and 164 endogenous variables represented by 164 regression and identity equations. These equations are divided into ten groups: retail demand, retail product supply relations in the dairy sector, farm demand for the livestock sector, capital stocks, livestock supply, crop demand, product stocks, planted acreage relations, supply and utilization identity, and index definitions. The crop sector group includes corn, sorghum, barley, oats, wheat, and soybeans. The CED econometric model can be expressed as:[1]

$$Y_{it} = a_{it} + \sum_{\substack{n=1 \\ n \neq 1}}^{164} b_{in} Y_{nt} + \sum_{n=1}^{164} (b_{2n} Y_{nt-1} + b_{3n} Y_{nt-2})$$

$$+ \sum_{m=1}^{127} (b_{4m} Z_{mt}) + e_{it} \quad \text{for } i = 1, \ldots, 164 \qquad (12.6)$$

The CARD-NRED model is a reduced version of the CARD-NWA model (see "An Overview of Data Processing Activities in CARD-NRED LP Model" by Huang, Weisz, and Alt, in Meister et al. 1976). To reduce the cost of the test, the programming component of the model has only one land class (as compared to nine in the CARD-NWA model) and uses land as the only resource restraint. The programming component can be expressed as:

Maximize

$$\sum_{i=1}^{6} \sum_{j=1}^{105} \left[\sum_{k=1}^{kj} (XD_{ijkt} + XI_{ijkt}) P_{ijt} - \sum_{k=1}^{kj} XD_{ijkt} CD_{ijkt} - \sum_{k=1}^{kj} XI_{ijkt} CI_{ijkt} \right]$$

$$- \alpha_1 \sum_{i-1}^{6} (V_i^+ + V_i^-) \qquad (12.7)$$

subject to
   National production balance restraints

$$\sum_{j=1}^{105} \sum_{k=1}^{k_j} (XD_{ijkt} + XI_{ijkt}) + V_i^+ - V_i^- = Q_{it} \tag{12.8}$$

for $i = 1, \ldots, 6$; k_j varies from region to region.
   Regional production response behavior restraints

$$\sum_{k=1}^{k_j} (XD_{ijkt} + XI_{ijkt}) + W_{ij}^+ - W_{ij}^- = \beta_{ijt} \left[\sum_{k=1}^{k_j} (XD_{ijkt-1} + XI_{jkt-1}) \right] \tag{12.9}$$

for $i = 1, \ldots, 5$; $j = 1, \ldots, 105$

   Land restraints[2]

$$\sum_{i=1}^{13} \sum_{k=1}^{k_j} VD_{ijkt} \, XD_{ijkt} \le LD_{jt}$$

$$\sum_{i=1}^{13} \sum_{k=1}^{k_j} VI_{ijkt} \, XI_{ijkt} \le LI_{jt} \quad (j = 1, \ldots, 105) \tag{12.10}$$

where XD_{ijkt} (or XI_{ijkt}) is defined as the quantity of producers of crop i using rotation and tillage practice k on dry (or irrigated) land in producing area j in time period t. The term CD_{ijkt} (or CI_{ijkt}) is the cost of producing one unit of XD_{ijkt} (or XI_{ijkt}), respectively; VD_{ijkt} (or VI_{ijkt}) is the number of acres of land used to produce one unit of XD_{ijkt} (or XI_{ijkt}), respectively. The term LD_{jt} (or LI_{jt}) is total dry or irrigated land available in producing area j in time period t.

   Three sets of endogenous variables are selected as linkage variables to transfer information from the econometric component to the programming component. These three sets (expressed as Y_{it} in the econometric component) are regional crop price P_{ijt}, cost of production CD_{ijkt} (and CI_{ijkt}), and national aggregate crop production Q_{it}. At time period t the values of P_{ijt} and CD_{ijkt} (and CI_{ijkt}) are used to revise the coefficient in the objective function; the values of P_{ijt} are used in the regional production response restraints; the value Q_{it} is used as the value of the right-hand side of the national aggregate production balance restraints.

   The final production $[\sum_{j=1}^{105} \sum_{k=1}^{k_j} (XD_{ijkt} + CI_{ijkt})]$ determined by the programming component is used as the linkage variable to transfer information from the programming component to the econometric component. When the final production (denoted as Q_{it}^*) differs from Q_{it}, Q_{it}^* will be considered a better estimated value of the actual production and will then be used in the econometric component to adjust the value of other endogenous variables in the component. When Q_{it}^* is equal to Q_{it}, no adjustment is performed.

The test for using the RAP model for regional and national simultaneous use encountered a problem because we lacked crop response functions in all producing areas (PA). Published price elasticities of crop supply obtained from POLYSIM (Richardson and Ray 1975) were used to derive the regional responses. The response restraints (12.11) are replaced by a pair of constraints expressed as follows:

$$\sum_{k=1}^{kj} (XD_{ijkt} + XI_{ijkt}) \leq [\overline{\beta}_{ijt}] \left[\sum_{k=1}^{kj} (XD_{ijkt-1} + XI_{ijkt-1}) \right]$$

$$\sum_{k=1}^{kj} (XD_{ijkt} + XI_{ijkt}) \geq [\underline{\beta}_{ijt}] \left[\sum_{k=1}^{kj} (XD_{ijkt-1} + XI_{ijkt-1}) \right]$$

(12.11)

where $\overline{\beta}_{ijkt}$ and $\underline{\beta}_{ijt}$ are respectively maximum and minimum proportionate increase or decrease of production of crop i in PA j from year $t - 1$ to year t. The values $\overline{\beta}_{ijt}$ and $\underline{\beta}_{ijt}$ are determined as follows:
Define

$$T_{ijt}(\phi) = \left(\frac{P_{ijt}}{P_{ijt-1}} \right)^{[\epsilon_{ii} + \phi(SD_i)]} - \sum_{\substack{s=1 \\ s \neq i}}^{6} \left[1 - \left(\frac{P_{ijt}}{P_{ijt-1}} \right)^{(\epsilon_{is})} \right]$$

The first term is percentage change in production of crop i in region j between two time periods, while the second term is the percentage change due to price change of other crops.

If $T_{ijt}(2) < T_{ijt}(0)$, then $\overline{\beta}_{ijt} = T_{ijt}(0) + [T_{ijt}(0) - T_{ijt}(2)]$, $\underline{\beta}_{ijt} = T_{ijt}(2)$

If $T_{ijt}(2) < T_{ijt}(0)$, then $\overline{\beta}_{ijt} = T_{ijt}(2)$, $\underline{\beta}_{ijt} = T_{ijt}(0) - [T_{ijt}(2) - T_{ijt}(0)]$

The term $T_{ijt}(\phi)$ is the percentage change of crop production from year $t - 1$ to year $t + 1$, because of the effect of elasticities of production response with respect to price change. If ϕ is equal to 2, two standard deviations of ϵ_{ii} are added.

Test Methods. Two test methods are used to evaluate the performance of the hybrid model in estimating agricultural production, prices, and level of other agricultural activities, if in fact we are interested in these tests. These two methods are (a) static simulation and (b) dynamic simulation. Each method is applied to the hybrid model and to the CED-CC models, and is compared with actual observation data. In the first method, for each time period actual observed data are used for all predetermined variables (including lagged endogenous and exogenous variables). In the second method, the lagged endogenous variables are estimated recursively and used as input in the next time period. The first method attempts to conduct "ex post" analysis. Results from this method provide information indicating how well the model performs when error from input data is removed or kept at a minimum, while results from the second method provide information indicating how the model can be used for multiperiod simulations (for example, how seriously the error accumulated in previous time periods affects the performance of the model in later time periods).

The years 1969 and 1972 were arbitrarily selected for the static (or ex post test) of the hybrid model.[3] Years 1969 to 1973 and 1972 through 1976 are selected for the dynamic test. However, only the results from years 1969 to 1973 are presented.

Data. The regression coefficients of the econometric component (CED-CC model) were established in 1977 by using historical data from years 1950 to 1977. Endogenous and exogenous data from 1960 to 1977 were also updated.

The data set in the programming component (CARD-NRED LP model) were derived from the 1975 LP data base residing in CARD. Initial data (1968) were derived from this data base. In the static simulation, production costs were adjusted according to a cost index for production, interest, taxes, and wage rates. Projected production costs were adjusted by a constant rate from the test period 1969–1973. Stoecker's (1975) yield function was used to estimate yield for 1969. Constant yields were assumed during the test period. The derived regional to national price ratio (1972–1974) was assumed unchanged. The values of ϵ_{ii}, ϵ_{is}, and SD_i used in the test are shown in Table 12.1. Data in the table were assumed to be constant for years 1969 and 1972 in the test run.

Results of Test for RAP. Each year's simulation of the econometric component determines 164 values for endogenous variables including livestock and crop production, utilization, and marketing activities. The programming component gives spatial or interregional distributions of thousands of crop pro-

Table 12.1.   Crop production supply elasticities with respect to price

Crop	Feed grains	Wheat	Soybeans
Feed grains	0.20 (0.15)	0.03	0.06
Wheat	0.03	0.15 (0.20)	0.02
Soybeans	0.15	0.02	0.35 (0.287)

Note: These values are derived from the data given in POLYSIM (Richardson and Ray 1975). Each value is the sum of acreage and yield elasticities.

Figures in the parentheses represent one standard deviation (SD_i).

Table 12.2.   Ex post simulation results

Crop	Actual	Estimated	Error (%)
1969 national production (*million bushels*)			
Corn	4687	4487	0.27
Soybeans	1133	1116	1.50
Oats	965	959	0.62
Wheat	1442	1453	0.76
1969 Iowa production (*thousand bushels*)			
Corn	1,012,563	1,001,146	1.13
Soybeans	179,850	182,530	1.49
Oats	93,840	108,720	13.69
Wheat	1,320	1,755	32.95
1972 National production (*million bushels*)			
Corn	5570	5444	0.24
Soybeans	1270	1312	3.31
Oats	690	784	13.62
Wheat	1546	1601	3.56
1972 Iowa production (*thousand bushels*)			
Corn	1,212,200	1,154,493	4.76
Soybeans	217,800	215,161	2.92
Oats	70,000	81,362	16.23
Wheat	1,238	1,360	9.90

duction activities and land-use patterns in 105 producing areas. Because of space limitations only key portions of results are presented.

Static Simulation Tests. Results of national and Iowa production of corn, soybeans, oats, and wheat are shown in Table 12.2. In general, in a predictive method, the model performed well in the estimation of corn and soybeans on both national and state levels. On the national level, both cases showed less than a 5 percent error in estimation while on the state level the error was less than 2 percent in 1969 and less than 4 percent in 1972. Oats and wheat are two minor crops in Iowa. The model performed poorly in estimating 1972 oat production at both state and national levels. Although the model performed well in estimating wheat production on the national level, it did poorly on state level estimations. These simulation results indicated, as a predictive basis, that the hybrid model does well in estimating Iowa major crop production on either level while performing poorly in estimating minor crops. However, this poor performance can be improved significantly if more accurate regional crop production response information were available and implemented into the LP component of the hybrid model.

Dynamic Simulation Tests. In conducting the dynamic simulation test runs, one has crop production flexibility restraints in each PA while the other does not have flexibility restraints but does have four Iowa regional production restraints for corn, soybeans, oats, and wheat. In the first simulation run most of the national crop production generated by the econometric component was adjusted by the programming component. This caused a significant discrepancy in estimates of the national crop production and prices between the hybrid model and the CED-CC model. The following information can be drawn from these results (not presented here in order to save space): (1) The hybrid model using the regional restraints (12.11) does not give as good an estimate of aggregate national production and price as the estimates generated by the CED-CC model. The difference is due to the restraint (12.7), which does not sufficiently represent the regional responses. (2) The adjustment mechanism in the hybrid model assumes that national aggregated production can be better estimated by summing the individually estimated regional productions than by estimating national aggregated data as is done by the CED-CC econometric model. This assumption holds only if a set of accurate regional response functions can be formulated. In order to improve the performance of the hybrid model in a descriptive or predictive sense, considerable effort is needed to develop appropriate regional restraints. (3) The time recursive structure, such as the one used by the hybrid model, can accumulate error and pass it on to the next time period. This result was found for corn and soybean prices. To reduce this error, the regional constraints should be formulated as a function of the endogenous variable in the econometric component rather than depending heavily on the previous year's production, as formulated in (12.11). From these findings it is suggested that whenever accurate regional response restraints are not available, the one-way communication model may perform better than any model with a recursive structure between time periods.

In the second simulation run, the regional restraints (12.11) were not included. Instead, four regression equations representing corn, soybeans, oats, and wheat production responses[4] were used as regional restraints for Iowa. These equations were used to generate the RHS Iowa values of the regional restraints. As expected, the hybrid model gave the same estimation of the national production as the estimates generated by the CED-CC model. Meanwhile, a significant improvement on simulation of the Iowa crop production was achieved (as judged by the values of the RMSE). This result demonstrates that if a better econometrically estimated regional response function is used, the hybrid model might give a good estimate of regional production, as well as national production and prices.

Notes

1. When the test equation is used to express an identity, b_{it}, a_{2n}, a_{3n}, and error e_{in} are set equal to zero and some of the b_{1n} and b_{m4} are also equal to zero.

2. $i = 7$ to 13 refers to corn silage, nonlegume hay, legume hay, cotton, summer fallow, and sugar beets.

3. In conducting an ex post analysis, it is necessary to use actual values for all predetermined variables as input data. Although this requirement poses no difficulty in the econometric component, it does pose difficulty in the programming component. The LP component uses extensive-

ly synthesized data that do not have observed values. Furthermore, the ex post analysis also requires forecast values that should be outside the sampling period in which all the regression coefficients in the model were estimated. Therefore, it is an approximation of ex post analysis.

    4. The four regression equations are

$$Y_t^c = 746326 - 13119.56(P_t^c - P_{t-1}^c) + 35297T - 81412P_{t-1}^c, \qquad R^2 = 0.747$$
$$(59289) \quad (177184) \qquad\qquad (7373) \quad\;\; (59485)$$

$$Y_t^s = -53528 + 5.27A_t^s, \qquad R^2 = 0.9345$$
$$(14329) \quad\; (0.35)$$

$$Y_t^o = 027826 + 5.6\ A_t^o, \qquad R = 0.8658$$
$$(13694) \quad\; (0.55)$$

$$Y_t^w = 1286.5 - 590(P_t^w - P_{t-1}^w) + 390.94P_{t-1}^w, \qquad R^2 = 0.4432$$
$$(401) \qquad (278) \qquad\qquad (183)$$

where Y_t^c, Y_t^s, Y_t^o, and Y_t^w = crop production respectively of corn, soybeans, oats, and wheat; P_t^c, P_t^w = national prices of corn and wheat; A_t^s, A_t^o = planted acres of soybeans and oats. Values for these variables are generated from the econometric components in the hybrid model.

References

Baum, K. H. 1977. "A National Recursive Simulation and Linear Programming Model of Some Major Crops in U.S. Agriculture." Unpublished Ph.D. diss. Ames: Iowa State University.

Brandow, G. E. 1961. "Interrelationships among Demand for Farm Products." Pennsylvania Agricultural Experiment Station Bulletin 680.

Day, R. H. 1963. *Recursive Programming and Production Response*. Amsterdam: North-Holland.

————. 1964. "Dynamic Coupling, Optimizing, and Regional Interdependence." *Journal of Farm Economics* 46:442–51.

D'Azzo, J., and C. Houpis. 1966. *Feedback Control System Analysis and Synthesis*. New York: McGraw-Hill.

Harrison, M. J. 1976. "Software Tools for Combining Linear Programming with Econometric Models." *Computer and Mathematical Programming*. NBS Special Publication 502. Washington, D.C.: U.S. Department of Commerce.

Heady, E. O., and U. K. Srivastava. 1975. *Spatial Programming Models in Agriculture*. Ames: Iowa State University Press.

Heady, E. O., et al. 1972. "Agricultural and Water Policies and the Environment." CARD Report 40T. Ames: Iowa State University Center for Agricultural and Rural Development.

Meister, A. D., E. O. Heady, and R. W. Strohbehn. 1976. "U.S. Agricultural Production in Relation to Alternative Water, Environmental, and Export Policies," CARD Report 65, Ames: Iowa State University Center for Agricultural and Rural Development.

Meister, A. D., C. Chen, and E. O. Heady. 1978. *Quadratic Programming Models Applied to Agricultural Policies*. Ames: Iowa State University Press.

Mueller, G., and R. H. Day. 1978. "Cautious Rolling Plans with Forecasting and Market Feedback." In *Modelling Economic Change: The Recursive Programming Approach,* edited by R. Day and A. Cigno. Amsterdam: North-Holland.

Nicol, K. J., and E. O. Heady. 1974. "Models of Soil Loss, Land and Water Use, Spatial Agricultural Structure and the Environment." CARD Report 49. Ames: Iowa State University Center for Agricultural and Rural Development.

Plessner, Y. 1965. "Quadratic Programming Competitive Equilibrium Models for the U.S. Agricultural Sector." Ph.D. diss. Ames: Iowa State University.

Quance, C. L. 1976. *Agriculture in the Third Century*. ESCS, no. 1, May.

Ray, D. E., and E. O. Heady. 1975. "Simulated Effects of Alternative Policy and

Economic Environments on U.S. Agriculture." CARD Report 46T. Ames: Iowa State University Center for Agricultural and Rural Development.

Richardson, J. W., and D. E. Ray. 1975. "User's Manual for the National Agricultural Policy Simulator (POLYSIM)." Research Report P.727. Oklahoma State University Agricultural Experiment Station.

Sahi, R. K. 1972. "Recursive Programming Analysis of Prairie Land Utilization Pattern." Unpublished Ph.D. diss. Winnipeg: University of Manitoba.

Schaller, W. N., and G. W. Dean. 1965. "Predicting Regional Crop Production." Technical Bulletin 1329. Washington, D.C.: U.S. Department of Agriculture Economic Research Service.

Sonka, S. T., and E. O. Heady. 1973. *Income and Employment Generation in Rural Areas in Relation to Alternative Farm Programs.* Ames: Iowa State University North Central Regional Center for Rural Development.

Sposito, V. A. 1975. *Linear and Nonlinear Programming.* Ames: Iowa State University Press.

Stoecker, A. L. 1975. "A Quadratic Programming Model of U.S. Agriculture in 1980: Theory and Application." Ph.D. diss. Ames: Iowa State University.

Takayama, T., and G. C. Judge. 1964. "Spatial Equilibrium and Quadratic Programming." *Journal of Farm Economics* 46:77–93.

Teigen, L. D. 1977. "A Linked Model for Wheat, Feed Grain and Livestock Sectors of the U.S." CED Working Paper. Washington, D.C.: U.S. Department of Agriculture Economic Research Service.

13

Selecting Representative Firms in Linear Programming

WALTER D. FISHER AND PAUL L. KELLEY

The Representative Firm Problem

Definition of the Problem. Assume that an industry is composed of many firms, each producing the same set of several products with the same type of resources, and that one has the data needed to solve for each firm separately the linear programming problem of identifying activity levels that maximize profit subject to given resource constraints. One is interested in determining industry activity levels that will result when each firm is producing optimally— at a given set of prices and costs, or for a number of different levels of prices and costs. If one assumes that all firms in the industry behave, in fact, in a profit-maximizing manner, then summing results over all firms provides a descriptive measure of industry supply response for each product.[1] Without that assumption, one has a measure of normative supply response. The method of programming each firm individually to obtain industry results may be called *microprogramming.*

Since it is often costly, and sometimes not feasible, to solve the many linear programming problems needed to apply the microprogramming method, a shortcut method has been proposed, called the *representative firm method,* or *macroprogramming.*[2] Under macroprogramming firms are

The research for this paper was supported by the Bureau of General Research, National Science Foundation Grant GS-830, Department of Economics, and by Kansas Agricultural Experiment Station, Project No. 542, Contribution No. 432, Department of Agricultural Economics. Extensions and adaptations of Chapter IV and Appendix A from *Clustering and Aggregation in Economics,* by Walter D. Fisher (Baltimore: The Johns Hopkins University Press, 1969) are included here by permission.

The authors gratefully acknowledge the assistance of Mr. James Letourneau, Mrs. Linda Woolf, and Mr. Ming Wu.

grouped into fewer strata, and a "representative firm" is defined for each stratum. For each representative firm linear programming data are constructed as averages (weighted or unweighted) of the corresponding data of the individual firms that constitute the stratum. By "linear programming data," we mean the matrix of cost coefficients (A), the resource availability vector (b), and the net revenue vector (c). Those matrices and vectors are averaged into $\overline{A}$, $\overline{b}$, and $\overline{c}$ for each representative firm. Linear programming problems are then solved for each representative firm and weighted sums or averages of the results are used as estimates for the industry.[3] These aggregates are considered approximations of results that would have been obtained under microprogramming. Differences in the results are called *aggregation error* or *aggregation bias*. The research problem is to determine a system to group or to aggregate individual firms into strata and to determine a system of weights in computing averages so that aggregation errors are as small as possible and that the computational and programming cost associated with macroprogramming is no greater than that with microprogramming.[4]

Recent Literature. The suggestion to use representative firms, or farms in agricultural economics, as a device to reduce computational costs of linear programming when deriving industry supply response functions was made by Hartley in 1962. Tests of Hartley's suggestion applied to specific problems have been made by Sheehy (1964), Abou-el-Dahab (1965), Frick and Andrews (1965), Sheehy and McAlexander (1965), and Miller (1967). Their tests have demonstrated relatively small aggregation errors and substantial savings in computational costs when macroprogramming is used—even when few strata, say 25 percent or fewer of the original farms, are used.

Some effort has also been exerted to determine conditions, theoretically and rigorously, under which *no* aggregation error will result from macroprogramming. Richard H. Day (1963) has shown that if certain proportionality conditions hold among individual farms in a stratum i.e., if all have identical A matrices and proportional b and c vectors—then macroprogramming will result in exact aggregation. Miller (1966) later showed that Day's conditions could be made more general—i.e., exact aggregation is obtained if firms have identical A matrices and, when microprogrammed, their solution vectors are "qualitatively homogeneous" (they contain identical types of activities). Miller's conditions are, unfortunately, defined in terms of microprogramming solutions, rather than in terms of data, as he recognizes. Both Day's and Miller's conditions deal with exact aggregation (no aggregation error) and with identical A matrices for individual firms.

Most of the literature cited above discusses in some detail the problem of selecting strata for representative firms when exact aggregation is not possible, but no strong results or definite recommendations for the general problem are available. The most interesting proposal seems to be that of Sheehy (1964) based on the notion of "most restrictive" resources.[5] However, identifying the "most restrictive" resource, which plays a key role in the proposal, is difficult and not completely described for multiproduct situations.

Developing a satisfactory criterion to group firms into strata for macroprogramming solutions appears to be a major problem. Another problem is how to select a specific set of weights to average individual firm coefficients into aggregate coefficients for representative firms after strata are selected, and the literature offers no consensus.[6]

Objectives. Our objectives were: (1) to relate the representative firm problem to that of aggregating activities and constraints in a general linear programming problem, and to do it for the case of inexact aggregation (i.e., when there may be some aggregation error) where A coefficients of firms in the same stratum may differ; (2) to propose a specific method to select strata and to weight individual firm data to construct representative firm data; and (3) to illustrate and test the proposed method.

The suggested method is evaluated by comparing microprogramming solutions of forty-nine firms with (1) macroprogramming solutions for nine representative firms constructed from data of the forty-nine firms, using the proposed grouping method, and (2) with three alternative methods.

Two limitations are imposed. First, parametric programming at various price or revenue levels is not considered; alternative stratification methods are compared at one fixed set of values of the microdata. Second, the criterion used in judging alternatives is the error in the value of the objective function, profit. As stated above, this function may be thought of as an index of composite output, representing all output commodities of the firms.

Representative Firms and Aggregation

Linear Programming and Normalized Cost Coefficients. Consider first the general linear programming problem: given for a single firm a matrix A of M rows and N columns, a column vector b of M elements, and a row vector c' of N elements; choose a vector x such that the objective function

$$z = c'x \tag{13.1}$$

is a maximum, subject to the condition

$$Ax \le b \tag{13.2}$$

and further subject to the condition that x is nonnegative. Here we call A the *cost matrix* and its typical element a_{ij} a *cost coefficient* (because it states a real cost—the amount of resource *i* needed to produce one unit of product *j*). We call *b* the *resource vector,* *c'* the *net revenue vector,* and the scaler *z profit.* For brevity the problem could be called $\binom{c'}{A b}$.

Now consider the special linear programming problem that arises when the elements of *A* are nonnegative and all elements of *b* and *c* are positive. In terms of the usual examples from production economics, that would mean that all real costs are positive, that all activities yield positive revenue, and that all constraints pertain to resources limited in absolute quantity. That implies, among other things, that there are no "intermediate activities" with negative net revenues and no "balancing rows" with a zero constant term.

It is convenient to deal only with the positive problem and to convert any original problem into a positive problem by performing in order these steps: (1) replace any zero elements in the *b* or *c* vectors with very small nonzero elements; (2) multiply any negative elements in these vectors by −1 and also multiply the corresponding rows or columns of *A* by −1; (3) remove any negative elements in *A* by adding a large enough positive constant to all elements of *A*. It can be shown that the solution to such a transformed problem may be made arbitrarily close to that of the original problem by multiplying certain elements of the solution vector *x* by −1 and by adding a certain constant to *z*.

Now define the *normalized cost matrix A** of *M* rows and *N* columns as the matrix whose typical element is the *normalized cost coefficient:*

$$a_{ij}^* = a_{ij}/(b_i c_j) \tag{13.3}$$

Such a matrix always exists for the positive problem. It may be interpreted as the cost matrix of a transformed or normalized problem $\binom{1}{A^* 1}$, where units of product have been redefined in "dollars' worth" and constraints have been restated as "fractions of available resources."[7]

The solution vector of the normalized problem contains elements, say x_j^*, that represent the profit from product *j*. The solution of the problem before normalization is obtainable by the transformation

$$x_j = x_j^*/c_j \tag{13.4}$$

Previous writers (e.g., Dorfman 1951; Waugh 1951) have presented an instructive geometric interpretation of the normalized problem. Let each resource (and its associated constraint) be represented by (and on) a Cartesian axis in *M*-space. Let each activity and its associated product be represented by a point in the *M*-space whose coordinates are normalized cost coefficients. Then the normalized cost matrix *A** represents a collection of *N* points in *M*-space. For example, for five products and two resources the points can be plotted as P_1 to P_5 in Figure 13.1. The P_j can be called *activity points.* Frac-

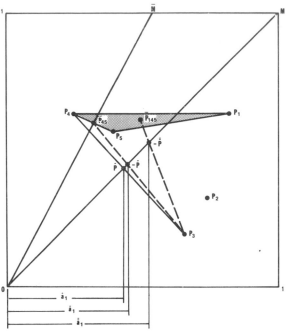

FIG. 13.1. Geometric
representation of normalized
cost matrix A^* in two-space.

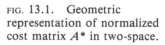

tions of available resources expended in operating any activity j at x_j^* dollars
can be read from the graph by finding the ray connecting P_j with the origin,
moving a distance on the ray equal to x_j^*, and reading the coordinates of the
point at this distance. (If a coordinate exceeds 1, it would require more than
available amounts of that resource to operate the activity at the specified
level.) Likewise, the fractions of available resources spent operating any
"composite activity" (two or more activities operated jointly in specified proportions) at level x_j^* dollars may be found the same way by using a point, say
$\overline{P}_{jk} \ldots '$, that is a convex combination of the P being combined. For example,
$\overline{P}_{45}$ in Figure 13.1 is the composite activity point representing spending equally
on activities 4 and 5; its coordinates are the fractions of available resources 1
and 2 used in spending 50 cents on activities 4 and 5 each.

   The optimal program then is represented by the composite activity point
that lies on the intersection of the "southwest frontier" of all activity points
with the 45* ray,[8] and the profit from this program is the reciprocal of one of
the coordinates of this point. That is, in Figure 13.1, the optimal activity point
is $\hat{P}$, and the profit associated with it equals $1/\hat{a}_1^*$.[9] More generally,

$$\hat{z} = 1/\min_i(\max \overline{a_i^*}) \tag{13.5}$$

where $\hat{z}$ is the maximum profit, $\overline{a_i^*}$ is some convex combination of elements
a_{ij}^* in the ith row of the normalized cost matrix A^*, and minimizing is over the
entire set of such convex combinations.[10]

Aggregating Activities and Constraints in Linear Programming. An excellent intuitive insight into effects of aggregation on the linear programming solution can be obtained in the two-dimensional case. Using Figure 13.1, consider again the composite activity represented by $\overline{P}_{45}$. It also could be called an *aggregate activity*. Suppose that $\overline{P}_{45}$ replaces the individual points P_4 and P_5 on the diagram. The solution point to the problem is then $\tilde{P}$, instead of $\hat{P}$, and the profit is $1/\tilde{a}_1^*$ instead of $1/\hat{a}_1^*$, a lower profit, but the change is not great. Consider next the aggregate activity point $\overline{P}_{145}$, which is the centroid of the triangle $P_1P_4P_5$, and consider the effect of replacing the three points by their centroid. This aggregation is more severe. The frontier is pushed back to the dotted line connecting $\overline{P}_{145}$ with P_3; the new solution point is $\tilde{\tilde{P}}$; and the new profit is $1/\tilde{\tilde{a}}_1^*$, substantially less profit than in the two previous cases. The reason for the larger decrease in profit apparently is aggregation of points quite distant from each other.

Going back to the original points, suppose now that P_1 and P_1 and P_2 had been aggregated. The frontier is still the line connecting P_3 and P_4, and profit remains at $\hat{P}$. The reason for this aggregation having no effect is that neither point aggregated was effective (i.e., was not on the frontier and was therefore at zero level in the solution).

This analysis suggests that when convex combinations (weighted averages) of original activity points (vectors) are used as aggregate activities to replace original activities, the following effects occur: (1) the profit is either reduced or remains the same (remains the same when only ineffective activities are aggregated) and (2) profit reduction will be small when the distances between the activity points aggregated are small.[11]

Now extend the analysis to N points in M-space and extend the concept of aggregation as follows: define an *aggregation partition of activities* as a partition of the columns of the normalized cost matrix A^* into J disjoint and exhaustive subsets, where J is some integer less than N (geometrically, this groups the N activity points into J clusters); then replace the original columns of A^* by J *aggregate activities*, each aggregate activity being a column vector that is some convex combination of the original column vectors of a subset of the partition (geometrically that uses the J centroids of the clusters instead of the original points). Then it is not difficult to show that the conclusion (1) of the preceding paragraph holds; conclusion (2) would seem to hold also, but we have been unable to derive a rigorous bound on the profit bias in terms of distances.[12]

Now turn to the aggregation of constraints, or of the rows of A^*. Define an *aggregation partition of constraints* as a partition of the rows of A^* into F disjoint and exhaustive subsets, where F is some integer less then M. Define an *aggregate constraint* as a row vector that is some convex combination of the original row vectors of a subset of the partition. Geometrically, this may be conceived by inverting the roles of "points" and "coordinates" as previously defined and considering the *rows* of A^* as points in N-space. Then there are M original points and F aggregate points.

By the Duality Theorem of linear programming, if we consider the dual problem with the roles of rows and columns of A^* interchanged so that rows of A^* are *activities* and the objective function is to be *minimized,* the solution of the dual problem is precisely the profit solution of the primal problem. By applying our previous analysis of the effects of aggregating activities to the dual problem, we conclude that the criterion value of the dual is raised (or remains the same) by aggregation. Therefore, the aggregation of *constraints* in the original problem *raises* (or leaves unchanged) profit. The magnitude of the effect should be small when points defined by the rows of A^* are close together.

If the constraints in the original linear programming problem are given by nature, a decision maker cannot change them and has no option of "aggregating" them—which would lessen the limitations and hence ease the situation. The assumption that constraints are aggregated is one that may be used by an investigator to simplify an analytical problem, but one that will, in general, lead to some error in the conclusions.

Aggregating activities and constraints may be carried out independently and jointly. In the representative firm problem, both types of aggregation are carried out simultaneously, and the major questions include the method of selecting the activites and constraints to be aggregated and the weights to be used in the combinations. We must first place the representative firm problem into the framework just developed.

Representative Firms in One Large Program. The original problem posed in this chapter was expressed in terms of atomistic decision making by the separate firms or as the problem $\binom{c}{A}_b$. The industry supply response and the industry profit were regarded as a by-product of these decisions—namely, as the sum, or average, of the individual firm solutions.

The same industry solutions will be obtained, however, if the firms are regarded as branches of one large firm, with no external economies or diseconomies between branches, and if one large linear programming problem is formulated, with the number of activities and constraints equal to the respective number for each firm multiplied by the number of firms in the industry and in which the objective function is total profit.[13]

If n is the number of activities per firm, m the number of constraints per firm, and K the number of firms, data for such a problem may be displayed before normalization in tabular form (see Table 13.1). The table is of size $Km + 1$ by $Kn + 1$. A subscript in parentheses refers to a firm. Symbol b denotes a column vector; c', a row vector; and A_k, an $m \times n$ matrix for firm k. When the data of Table 13.1 are normalized, all vectors b_k and c'_k have all elements equal to unity, and matrices $A_{(k)}$ are replaced by normalized cost matrices $A^*_{(k)}$ whose typical element is

Table 13.1. Large linear programming problem with data grouped by firm

$c'_{(1)}$	$c'_{(2)}$	•	•	•	$c'_{(K)}$	
$A_{(1)}$	0	•	•	•	0	$b_{(1)}$
0	$A_{(2)}$	•	•	•	0	$b_{(2)}$
•	•		$A_{(k)}$	•	•	•
0	0	•	•	•	$A_{(K)}$	$b_{(K)}$

$$a^*_{ij(k)} = a_{ij(k)} / [b_{i(k)} \; c_{j(k)}] \tag{13.6}$$

The tabular data could be arrayed in another tabular form (see Table 13.2), of size $Km + 1$ by $Kn + 1$. Subscripts here refer to constraints or activities. The term A_{ij} is a $K \times K$ diagonal matrix for constraint i and activity j. All other notations are similar to those of Table 13.1.

Formally, the data array of Table 13.2 is identical with the form of the micro firm problem $\binom{c}{A \; b}$. For convenience in presentation we define the data of Table 13.2 as the problem $\binom{c_\ell}{A_\ell b_\ell}$, where the subscript ℓ is used to denote the large programming problem. Then the normalized data of Table 13.2 can be expressed as the problem $\binom{1}{A^*_\ell \; 1}$. Let us now regard the large programming problem as identical to the micro firm problem of the last subsection $\binom{c}{A \; b}$ but containing $M = Km$ constraints and $N = Kn$ activities. It now is possible to show the correspondence between the conventional representative firm problem and the large linear programming problem.

Representative firm problem

1. Define K firms with data in the form $\binom{c}{A \; b}$.

2. Group the K firms into G strata to construct G representative firms.

3. Within each stratum, using the data on individual firms, construct data for a representative firm by taking averages of corresponding firm data.[14]

4. Program each representative firm and take a weighted sum of firm profits to obtain industry profit.

Large linear programming problem

1. Group data of K firms each with data of form $\binom{c}{A \; b}$ in the form of Table 13.2 defined as $\binom{c_\ell}{A_\ell b_\ell}$ of size $Km + 1$ by $Kn + 1$ and normalize to $\binom{1}{A^*_\ell \; 1}$.

2. Select a partition of the Km rows of A^*_ℓ into Gm subsets of rows and a partition of the Kn columns into Gn columns, each to be done "firmwise"—i.e., when A^*_ℓ is subdivided as in Table 13.2, the partition of each A^*_{ij} is the same.

3. Simultaneously aggregate activities and constraints with respect to partitions of step 2 above using some weights, say $u_{i(k)}$ for the constraint aggregation and $v_{j(k)}$ for the activity aggregation, obtaining a reduced aggregate normalized cost matrix $\overline{A^*_\ell}$ with submatrices $\overline{a^*_{ij(g,I)}}$ whose typical elements are given by equation (13.7).[15]

$$\overline{a^*_{ij(g,I)}} = \frac{\sum\limits_{k \in g} a^*_{ij(k)} \; u_{i(k)} v_{j(k)}}{\left(\sum\limits_{k \in g} u_{i(k)}\right) \left(\sum\limits_{k \in g} v_{j(k)}\right)} \tag{13.7}$$

where I represents industry level data.

4. Solve the large programming problem with the reduced $\overline{A^*_\ell}$ matrix to get industry profit.

Table 13.2   **Large linear programming problem with data grouped by activity and constraint**

c_1'	c_2'				c_n'	
A_{11}	A_{12}	•	•	•	A_{1n}	b_1
A_{21}	A_{22}	•	•	•	A_{2n}	b_2
•	•	•	A_{ij}	•	•	•
A_{m1}	A_{m2}	•	•	•	A_{mn}	b_m

This correspondence enables us to employ the theory of the last subsection regarding aggregating of activities and constraints of a linear programming problem and to obtain guidance choosing strata. We conclude that it is desirable to minimize bias in profit resulting from the macroprogramming procedure and to select strata in such a way that corresponding cost coefficients for individual firms within the same stratum are similar in some sense—i.e., that in some sense the distances between activity points (or constraint points) within the same stratum are small. The idea is pursued, after a discussion of weights.

THE PROBLEM OF WEIGHTS. The problem of selecting weights to combine individual firm data into aggregates has already been referred to in the first section. Previous investigators have not agreed on the matter, especially in the realistic situations where cost coefficients vary among firms. It is an old, familiar problem in economics when aggregates are constructed.

Some general observations seem appropriate. First, the method of weighting used will affect the profit bias and therefore the method used to select strata, which can be verified by tracing through the two-dimensional examples presented with different systems of weights. Second, the number of possible weighting systems is infinite, and an attempt to optimize vigorously a decision on weighting would undoubtedly cost more than the savings from aggregating. Third, in view of the first two observations, a feasible approach seems to be to study a few well-known and simple weighting systems and examine their probable effects. Two systems are studied here.

The first, the one that would probably occur first to most persons, is to take simple unweighted averages of the original firm data in a stratum before normalization—i.e., of the A, b, and c matrices—to form the corresponding matrices for the representative firm. We call it the *Agg-Norm* method.[16]

The normalized cost coefficients of the representative firm resulting from this method are[17]

$$\overline{a_{ij(g,F)}^*} = \frac{\sum\limits_{k \in g} a_{ij(k)}^*}{K_g \left(\sum\limits_{k \in g} b_{i(k)} / k_g \right) \left(\sum\limits_{k \in g} c_{j(k)} / k_g \right)} = \frac{\sum\limits_{k \in g} a_{ij(k)}^* b_{i(k)} c_{j(k)}}{\left(\sum\limits_{k \in g} b_{i(k)} \right) \left(\sum\limits_{k \in g} c_{j(k)} \right)} K_g \quad (13.8)$$

(where the subscript F refers to representative firm data of g stratum); the last expression of (13.8) results from using (13.3) and expresses the result in terms of the *normalized* microcoefficients. Compare the result with (13.7). If we set the weights $u_{i(k)} = b_{i(k)}$ and $v_{j(k)} = c_{j(k)}$ in (13.7) and divide both sides of (13.8) by K_g, then (13.7) and (13.8) become equivalent. But dividing every cost coefficient given by (13.8) by K_g is equivalent to multiplying the programmed activity levels and the profit of this representative firm by K_g—that is, dividing (13.8) by this factor gives aggregate stratum profit instead of stratum profit per firm—and summing profits over strata gives the industry profit. So the equivalence of (13.8) with (13.7) after the suggested weights are used in (13.7) means that the Agg-Norm method is equivalent to solving the large programming problem with *normalized* coefficients and using the *b* and *c* vectors as weights.

It is almost, but not quite, true to say that the aggregate coefficients resulting from the Agg-Norm method are weighted averages of the individual firm normalized coefficients in (13.8). Multiply numerator and denominator of (13.8) by $\Sigma b_k c_k$ and let $\bar{a}^*_{ij(g,F)} = \bar{a}^*$.

$$\bar{a}^* = (\Sigma a^*_k b_k c_k / \Sigma b_k c_k) \frac{\Sigma b_k c_k}{(\Sigma b_k)(\Sigma c_k)/K_g} = \bar{a}^0 F \qquad (13.9)$$

where $\bar{a}^0 = \Sigma a^*_k b_k c_k / \Sigma b_k c_k$ and

$$F = \frac{\Sigma b_k c_k}{(\Sigma b_k)(\Sigma c_k)/K_g} = 1 + r_{bc} \frac{\sigma_b}{\bar{b}} \frac{\sigma_c}{\bar{c}}$$

where r_{bc} is the correlation coefficient between b_k and c_k within stratum g, and $\sigma_b/\bar{b}$ and $c/\bar{c}$ are coefficients of variation. That is, the Agg-Norm coefficient $\bar{a}^*_{ij(g,F)}$ may be represented as the product of a weighted average $\bar{a}^0$ of normalized coefficients (with the $b_k c_k$ as weights) and a "covariance factor" F, which takes a value greater than unity when there is positive covariance within the stratum between the resources b_k and net revenues c_k, and less than unity when there is negative covariance, and unity when b_k and c_k are independent.

The second system is to take simple unweighted averages of the normalized cost coefficients of the individual firms. We call it the *Norm-Agg* method. That is, "normalize, then aggregate." The normalized cost coefficients of the representative firms resulting are

$$\overline{a^*} = (1/K_g)\Sigma a^*_k \qquad (13.10)$$

This procedure—after dividing each side of (13.10) by K_g for expansion of stratum profit—is equivalent to using (13.7) with each $u_{i(k)}$ and $v_{j(k)}$ set equal to unity. The ratio of an Agg-Norm coefficient to a Norm-Agg coefficient is, from (13.9) and (13.10)

$$\bar{a}^*/\overline{a^*} = (\bar{a}^0/\overline{a^*}) F \qquad (13.11)$$

where $\bar{a}^0$ is the weighted average and F the covariance factor. In the typical production economics situations in which the representative firm method is of practical interest, the weights $b_k c_k$ used in forming the weighted average $\bar{a}^0$ should be fairly strongly inversely correlated with the normalized cost coefficients a_k^* for two reasons. First, firms that are larger and have higher net revenues will probably tend to have lower unit money costs. Second, as a result of normalizing, such firms have their cost coefficients divided by larger b and c factors, which make the cost coefficients even lower in "real" terms. Therefore, the weighted average $\bar{a}^0$ will tend to be systematically lower than the unweighted average of normalized coefficients $\overline{a^*}$ It seems probable that the covariance factor F will be slightly larger than unity. On balance, the ratio in (13.11) will probably be less than unity, which means that the Agg-Norm method will tend to give lower normalized cost coefficients to representative firms than will the Norm-Agg method. It also seems probable that, since linear programming solutions involve low-cost solutions, the Agg-Norm method will be closer to the microprogramming solution.

Another way of expressing the result is to say that the Norm-Agg method of weighting probably gives undue weight to smaller, higher-cost firms.

In the special case where the A matrices are identical for all firms within the stratum, we have

$$\bar{a}^* = K_g^2 a / [(\Sigma b_k) \ (\Sigma c_k)] = aK_g F / \Sigma b_k c_k \quad \text{(Agg-Norm)} \tag{13.12}$$

$$\bar{a}^* = a / K_g \ \Sigma \ 1 / (b_k c_k) \quad \text{(Norm-Agg)} \tag{13.13}$$

$$\frac{\bar{a}^*}{\overline{a^*}} = \frac{K_g F / \ \Sigma b_k c_k}{(1 / K_g) \ \Sigma \ [1 / (b_k c_k)]} = \frac{\text{harmonic mean of } b_k c_k}{\text{arithmetic mean of } b_k c_k} F \tag{13.14}$$

For any population the harmonic mean is equal to or lower than the arithmetic mean, the degree depending on the absolute range of the data. (For the first 10 integers the ratio of the two means is 0.63.) In other words, (13.14) tells us again, but in simpler form, that the Agg-Norm cost coefficients tend to be lower than the Norm-Agg coefficients; consequently under the Agg-Norm procedure, overall profit will tend to be higher. Of course, with successful stratification, variation within strata could be reduced; then the discrepancies would become smaller.

To summarize, both methods examined to weight individual firms within strata to form representative firms may be regarded as using particular kinds of weighted averages of the normalized cost coefficients in the large programming problem defined in the last subsection, where both rows and columns are combined (both constraints and activities are aggregated). The method of using equal weights (Norm-Agg) probably will entail a larger negative bias in total profit, compared with microprogramming, than the method of using weights proportional to elements of the b and c vectors (Agg-Norm).

A Proposed Method

Measures of Similarity of Cost Coefficients. We now return to the suggestion made above that to minimize the aggregation error in profit it would be desirable to stratify the firms so that corresponding cost coefficients within the same stratum are "similar." Geometrically such a criterion means that the activity points of Figure 13.1 (or the constraint points of the dual problem) be grouped so points in the same group are "close together." With specific reference to the representative firm problem, it is therefore desired that the nonzero elements of the diagonal submatrices A_{ij}^* in the normalized version of Table 13.2 be partitioned in a way so those assigned to the same stratum are of similar size.[18] The partitioning needs to be performed simultaneously for all of the mn submatrices while attempting to obtain "similarity" among the K diagonal elements of each one.

A familiar measure of "lack of similarity" among individuals, on which several numerical scores are available, is the sum of squared deviations from the arithmetic mean for each score. If each individual is conceived to be a point in a Euclidean space, with one dimension for each score, the measure is the sum of the squared distances of the individual points from their centroid; it is sometimes called the moment of inertia.

The measure can be applied to the normalized cost coefficients as a criterion to group the K firms into G strata. We choose the strata to minimize

$$D_a^* = \sum_{k=1}^{K} d^2(a_k^*) = \sum_{i=1}^{m} \sum_{j=1}^{n} \sum_{k=1}^{K} \left(a_{ij(k)}^* - \bar{a}_{ij(g)}^* \right)^2 \tag{13.15}$$

where $a_{(k)}^*$ is the point (or vector) for firm k, $d^2(a_k^*)$ is the squared distance of that point from the centroid for its stratum, and $\bar{a}_{ij(g)}^*$ is a coordinate of the centroid—namely, the arithmetic mean of all normalized coefficients $a_{ij(k)}^*$ that belong to firms k assigned to stratum g. We are dealing with a total of K points in a space of mn dimensions. By minimizing D_a^* we are, crudely speaking, maximizing "similarity" according to one particular measure. The method, which is applied in the numerical example of the next section, is called "stratification by cost coefficients."

One may well ask, however, Why deal with the normalized coefficients, rather than the original coefficients, and why is the particular measure chosen? Both choices admittedly are somewhat arbitrary. Squared distances may be defended because of their symmetry with respect to positive and negative errors, their mathematical convenience, and their common usage. It is probable, however, that a better measure is obtainable by using the reciprocals of the normalized coefficients rather than the coefficients themselves. The reason is this: the goal is to minimize aggregation error in profit, z. Let $\hat{z}$ represent the total profit under microprogramming, as given by formula (13.5). Let $\bar{z}$

denote the profit under macroprogramming. Let the absolute aggregation error, or bias, be $|\partial z| = |\hat{z} - \bar{z}|$. It is conjectured that an upper bound for $|\partial z|$ is

$$|\partial z| \leq \max_{\substack{i,j \\ g}} \left[\frac{1}{\min\limits_{k} \left(a^*_{ij(k)}\right)} - \frac{1}{\max\limits_{k} \left(a^*_{ij(k)}\right)} \; |k \, \epsilon \, g \right] \qquad (13.16)$$

That is, the absolute profit bias is posited to lie within the largest range of reciprocals of the smallest and largest coefficients within any one block.

For the case of the general linear programming problem where the microsolution and macrosolution involve convex combinations, say $\hat{a}$ and $\bar{a}$ of only one and the same submatrix of the partitions, the conjecture follows immediately from the relations

$$|\partial z| = |\bar{z} - \hat{z}| = |1/\bar{a} - 1/\hat{a}| \leq 1/\min(a) - 1/\max(a) \qquad (13.17)$$

where asterisks on all a are understood, and where min and max are over elements within the submatrix. The authors believe that the conjecture is true for the general case also, although they have not succeeded in proving it. The general case is needed for the representative firm problem where stratification implies partitioning A^* into a number of submatrices.

Minimizing a distance metric defined in the space of reciprocals of the cost coefficients should be more efficacious in preventing large biases than if defined in the space of the coefficients themselves. For example, for a given dispersion or variance of normalized costs, it probably is more important to consider separately firms with large reciprocals (large firms) than firms with small reciprocals (small firms).

Applying the squared distance criterion to the reciprocals, let

$$r_{ij(k)} = 1/a^*_{ij(k)} \qquad 13.18)$$

Then choose strata to minimize

$$D_r = \sum_{k=1}^{K} d^2(r_k) = \sum_{i=1}^{m} \sum_{j=1}^{n} \sum_{k=1}^{K} \left(r_{ij(k)} - \bar{r}_{ij(g)}\right)^2 \qquad (13.19)$$

where r_k is a vector of reciprocals and the other symbols have the same definitions as in (13.15), only applied to reciprocals. This method is called "stratification by reciprocals of cost coefficients."

Where the A matrices are identical for all firms within the same stratum, (13.19) becomes

$$D_r = \sum_{i=1}^{m} \sum_{j=1}^{n} \left(1/a_{ij}^2\right) \sum_{k=1}^{K} \left(b_{i(k)} c_{j(k)} - \bar{b}_i \bar{c}_j\right)^2 \qquad (13.20)$$

from using (13.3). In this case the method becomes one of stratifying by similarity of products $b_{i(k)}c_{j(k)}$. In the even more specialized case where the net revenue vectors $c_{j(k)}$ are constant for all firms within a stratum, the method becomes one of stratifying by similarity of resource availabilities $b_{i(k)}$, which is directly related to "size of firm," a criterion instinctively preferred by many investigators.[19]

In the following numerical example a rough-and-ready approximation of the first method is tried. It is called the "method of common zero resources" and is based on the presence of zero elements in certain rows of the b vector for certain firms. To apply the principles of this chapter it is necessary to add a small number to the zero elements, as suggested earlier. That avoids obtaining infinite normalized cost coefficients, but it results in coefficients of the same row as the zero element being quite large—that is, unless the original cost coefficient was also zero. The number of such zero cost coefficients varied systematically by row for all firms. It follows that firms with zero elements in the same cell or cells of the b vector (sometimes referred to as the "P_0 column") will have the same number of "large" normalized coefficients and might be expected to have $d^2(a_k^*)$ values of similar magnitude. Then, to make D_a^* in (13.15) small, one would attempt to group firms whose "zero structure" in the b vector is the same, or nearly the same, in the same stratum. The method of common zero resources attempts to do that. The numerical values of the nonzero elements of the b vector are not used for stratification, nor are any elements of the c vector or A matrix.[20] It is often possible to implement the method by visually inspecting the data.

From the foregoing discussion and the preceding section, the favored method of constructing representative firms is proposed: (1) stratify the firms according to the method of reciprocal cost coefficients; (2) within each stratum construct data for a representative firm by averaging the individual firm data by the Agg-Norm method. As alternates to (1), the two other stratification methods described may be tested (i.e., normalized cost coefficients and the method of common zeros).

A Computer Routine for Stratification. The first two methods of stratification described—involving selecting an optimal partition of firms into subsets to minimize a squared distance function—are substantial computational tasks even when m, n, and K are moderate in number. To our knowledge no computational routine is available that guarantees obtaining the true solution, except in very special cases.

A routine for finding a near optimal partition has been described by Fisher (1966). This routine proceeds stepwise, merging two firms or sets of firms in each step successively, until the desired number of strata are obtained. One may set the required number of strata a priori, or one may look at the results of the merging and then decide how many strata are wanted. At each step the value of the D function (called the r function by Fisher) is computed for all possible pairings, and the merger is effected that minimizes the increase in D. It cannot be guaranteed that the true optimal partition into a prescribed number of strata is obtained—in fact, in general it will not be—but experience with the routine indicates that the final partition obtained is quite close to the optimal, in terms of D value.

In applying the routine of the present squared-distance problem, Fisher's M matrix is here the identity matrix, and his P matrix is here the $mn \times K$ matrix of normalized cost coefficients, or their reciprocals. If mn is substantially larger than K, the matrix $P'P$, of size $K \times K$, may be used instead of P as input to the program with a minor change of procedure. As discussed in Fisher, it is possible to require a priori that certain pairs of firms not be placed in the same stratum.

That routine was used in stratifying by cost coefficients and by reciprocals of cost coefficients in the numerical example described in the next section.

A Numerical Example

Data and Procedure. Kelley and Knight (1965) developed detailed data for 49 dairy farms in the Topeka, Kansas, milkshed and solved linear programming problems involving matrices of the order of 50 × 150 for each individual farm. Their data were adapted here to provide smaller matrices of the type consistent with the positive linear programming problem. Reducing the A matrices to size 11 × 28 prior to aggregation procedures outlined here was accomplished by retaining four labor constraints, four land constraints, and restricting amount of three crops that could be grown: wheat, soybeans, and alfalfa.[21] Each of 28 activities retained for seven crops—wheat, oats, corn, barley, alfalfa, grain sorghum, and soybeans—were subclassififed according to four qualities of land to be used in producing them.

Severing those crop-producing activities from the larger set of activities, including milk production and marketing, required development of some imputed net revenues in cases where certain crops were used on the farm for livestock production as defined in the 50 × 150 matrices. Sometimes imputed elements of the b, or P_0, vector, also had to be derived. Those modifications were made to reduce the size of the problem.

When a farm produced none of a certain crop, a problem existed to define the elements of the missing activity column. For example, if the farm had no class B land, it produced no wheat on class B land. The entire column could be omitted from its individual matrix but should be included when its matrix might be averaged with others in the aggregation process. It is not correct to state that cost coefficients for the missing activity, or the net revenue (c_j element) facing it, are zero. The problem was handled by computing for the missing columns average data from other farms in the same or neighboring size-region category.[22]

Where zero elements occurred in the b vector for a farm, a relatively small number (0.1) was substituted for the zero, so the problem would be in the form of the positive problem and normalized cost coefficients could be computed.

After the normalized cost coefficients were computed, it was discovered that the four labor constraint rows and the eight activity columns pertaining to oats and barley on all 49 farms were redundant. The activity associated with a redundant column is operated at zero level. After eliminating the redundant rows and columns, the cost matrix for each farm was reduced to size 7×20, and it also happened that the resulting coefficients (before normalization) were identical for all farms, either unity or zero.[23] The pattern of the coefficients is shown in Appendix Table A-1 of Fisher and Kelley (1968).

The linear programming problem of operating at maximum profit was solved for each of the 49 individual farms. The sum of the profits divided by 49 is regarded as the microprogramming solution. The farms were then stratified by four different methods—by the three methods described above and by a conventional size-region classification that was used in Abou-el-Dahab (1965). These latter strata are defined by Appendix Table A-9 of Fisher and Kelley (1968). In each method nine strata were used.[24]

For the methods of cost coefficients and of reciprocals of cost coefficients, the progressive merger computer routine previously described was used, starting with the 49×49 symmetric matrix $P'P$, where P is a matrix of size 140 $\times$ 49, containing the normalized $a_{ij(k)}^*$, or their reciprocals.[25]

Then, for each stratification method, representative farms were constructed for each stratum by the Agg-Norm method of averaging, and the linear programming problem was solved for each representative farm.

Results. The overall average profit per farm, when computed as a weighted average of the profits of the nine representative farms for one of the methods of stratification, may be regarded as a macroprogramming solution and may be compared with the microprogramming solution, or "true" profit per farm. The macrosolution less the microsolution is the bias. When the bias is computed for each representative farm by neglecting the algebraic sign, and then averages are taken, it is called "absolute bias." For all weighted averages mentioned, the weights are the relative frequencies of farms per stratum. Summary results for each of the four stratification methods are shown in Table 13.3. More detailed results for each method—giving identification numbers of the individual farms assigned to each stratum, the programmed profit of the representative farm, the true average profit of the individual farms, and the bias caused by the macroprogramming—are shown in Appendix Tables A-5 to A-8 of Fisher and Kelley (1968).[26]

Table 13.3. Effect of stratification method on overall profit

Stratification method	Profit per farm,$		Profit bias per farm,$	
	Via strata	True	Algebraic	Absolute
Common zero resources	5816	6028	−212	224
Cost coefficients	5933	6028	− 95	339
Reciprocals of cost coefficients	5956	6028	− 72	100
Size-region	5891	6028	−137	174

Note: Weighted average of strata figures with strata frequencies as weights. True profit is unweighted average of individual microprogrammed farms.

All methods gave a negative profit bias but relatively small percentage biases—only 1.2 to 3.5 percent of true profits. Average absolute biases are higher because the algebraic signs have no opportunity to cancel each other. The method of reciprocals of cost coefficients performed the best, judged by both algebraic and absolute bias. That confirms theoretical expectations, based on the previous discussion. The method of cost coefficients was second best on the basis of algebraic bias, but the large value of the average absolute bias (largest for the four methods) suggests that canceling signs was fortunate and that repeatability is uncertain. Evidence from this example indicates no superiority of either the method of cost coefficients or that of common zero resources over the conventional size-region method. There is some evidence to support the superiority of the method of reciprocals of cost coefficients.

As expected, the method of reciprocals segregates the large farms more precisely. Three of the 4 largest farms of the 49, in terms of profit, were placed in a separate stratum. At the other end of the scale, 14 of the smaller farms were grouped together. The dispersion in farm numbers per stratum is less for other stratification methods, none of which allotted one farm alone to a stratum.

The method of common zero resources proved disappointing, for at least three possible reasons. (1) Different zero patterns with only nine strata could not be segregated completely. Compromises were made, somewhat arbitrarily, by placing different patterns of zeros in the same stratum. (2) Complete neglect of numerical information other than zeros may be too heroic an approximation. (3) The method is intended as an approximation of the method of cost coefficients, which is rather inferior to the method of reciprocals.

Conclusions. The representative firm method has been found by previous investigators to be feasible for reducing the computational cost involved in large programming studies, with reasonably small biases. That finding is confirmed here, where only small biases result from various methods of choosing nine representative firms from an original population of forty-nine firms.

Our empirical findings of negative biases controvert most previous findings of positive biases. However, most previous investigators studied response variations in only one commodity, while we studied general profit response, without attempting to study changes in prices. Further research is needed to clarify the differences in results on this point.

Our theoretical investigation of the representative firm problem as a type of two-way aggregation of a general linear programming matrix has resulted in a specific proposal: to stratify firms in such a way that within strata the reciprocals of the normalized cost coefficients are of similar size, and then to take simple averages of the nonnormalized data to construct data for the representative firms. That method performed best among four alternatives in a numerical test. It appears promising and warrants testing on further problems, including parametric programming problems.

The way of looking at the representative firm problem pursued here leads to another question beyond the scope of this chapter. If the final objective is a simplified analysis with smaller matrices and lower computation costs, ways of reducing the large programming matrix other than by aggregating firms should be considered. Aggregating over activities and/or constraints, possibly in the same firm, and eliminating redundancy appear promising. Given the size of the desired reduced matrix, other ways may attain that size with lower biases than the representative firm method gives.

Notes

1. Implications for aggregation of industry effects on factor costs and resource availabilities are omitted.

2. See literature cited in the next subsection.

3. Sometimes it is convenient to obtain the industry solutions on a "per firm" basis. Then a weighted average of the strata solutions is obtained using stratum firm numbers as weights. Numerical results of this chapter are thus presented. To obtain total industry solutions, a weighted sum (equivalent to multiplying the per firm solution by the number of firms in the industry) is obtained.

4. The investigator may be interested in results for only one commodity output (activity). With a research group, it is likely that interest will extend to more than one commodity; then the problem includes defining a scalar measure that expresses the importance of aggregation error in *all* commodity outputs. The value of the objective function itself, overall profit, might be so used. Overall profit combines outputs of all commodities in the program, the weights being net revenues. Many investigators are interested in results at alternative prices, thus wanting an industry supply curve in the classical sense. Much of the published literature on the representative firm problem is written in the context of the classical supply curve.

5. The method is used, but not completely described, by Sheehy and McAlexander (1965).

6. H.O. Hartley (1962) suggested some type of averaging; Abou-el-Dahab used weighted averages in most cases, the weights being "potential crop yields reported by producers" (1965, p. 46); Sheehy (1964) also used weighted averages with the weights determined from additional information; Miller used coefficients from modal farms within the stratum (1967, p. 111); Frick and Andrews (1965) did not specify their method of weighting. Our comments appy to the A coefficients and in some cases to elements of the c vector; there seems to be a consensus that simple averages or simple sums of elements of the b vector should be taken when they refer to the same commodity. The literature is not clear whether only one commodity is defined when two different firms have different cost coefficients for a commodity.

7. So the normalized cost coefficient a_{ij}^* states the fraction of available resource i needed to produce \$1 worth of product j.

8. The ray is the straight line through the origin making a 45° angle with every coordinate axis.

9. This can be seen as follows. The largest profit, z, that can be realized by operating any activity, original or composite, without violating constraints, is the highest activity level in terms of dollars (i.e., the largest multiplier of a unit level of $1) that is possible before the most restrictive constraint is violated. For example, the largest profit that can be realized from the activity represented by $\bar{P}_{45}$ in Figure 13.1 is the ratio $O\bar{M}/O\bar{P}_{45}$, which equals the reciprocal of the ordinate of $\bar{P}_{45}$ (since, for a larger multiplier, more of Resource 2 would be required than is available). It follows that the optimal program (the one yielding highest profit) is represented by the point whose largest coordinate is the smallest possible and is still some convex combination of the original activity points (i.e., lies in their convex hull). The point that meets such requirements in Figure 13.1 is $\hat{P}$, which lies on the frontier segment P_3P_4.

10. The result follows directly from correspondence between the positive normalized linear programming problem and the rectangular game problem. See, for example, D. Gale (1960, pp. 217–18) for proof of the correspondence.

11. When the distances are large, the decrease in profit will not necessarily be large, since the conclusion regarding profit also depends somewhat on the direction of the distances (e.g., if P_3 and P_5 are aggregated, the reduction in profit is quite moderate, even though those points are quite distant from each other. The reason for that is that the direction of line P_3P_5 is almost the same as that of the frontier P_3P_4).

12. Such a derivation will not be easy when one does not know a priori where the true frontier is.

13. This interpretation has been labeled "area programming." For purposes of aggregation, all firms are defined as having n activities and m restraints. Empirical procedures dealing with that specification are discussed later.

14. The method of taking the averages is deliberately left vague. This problem is discussed in the next subsection.

15. Equation 13.15 is derived by taking the prescribed weighted averages twice—row-wise, then column-wise (the order is immaterial)—remembering to average in the zero coefficients of the a_i^* matrix.

16. That is, "aggregate, then normalize"—meaning normalize the aggregate data. In computing the solution of a linear programming problem, it makes no difference in optimal profit whether or not data are normalized, but it is conceptually instructive to do so and often convenient computationally because of scaling attributes.

17. In part of this subsection, to avoid using subscripts, a_k is an abbreviation for $a_{ij(k)}$, b_k for $b_{i(k)}$, c_k for $c_{j(k)}$, and it is understood that the equations hold for all i and j. The summations are understood to be over all firms k that belong to stratum g, and K_g is the number of firms in the stratum.

18. The particular structure of the presentative firm problem leads us to restrict attention to the diagonal (nonzero) elements of the matrices. In a more general linear programming problem one would need to consider the nondiagonal elements also.

19. In Day's case (1963), where the A_k are constant for all firms and the b and c proportional (i.e., the A_k^* are proportional), there is no bias in profit, although neither D_a^* nor D_r are necessarily true. Once discrepancies from proportionality occur, however, discrepancies in absolute measures may be important also.

20. The same result of a certain a^* coefficient being large would result from an element of the c vector being zero; but with the usual interpretation of the c vector being net revenues, such zero elements usually would not occur. If they did, the method described should be extended to account for them.

21. Wheat and soybean restrictions resulted from government control programs and agronomic considerations. The alfalfa restriction was introduced after preliminary results indicated that the restriction would furnish more realistic solutions. The restriction is imposed either by considering a history of previous alfalfa production or by defining a ratio of total cropland allowed in alfalfa.

22. The way the missing columns are filled makes no difference in the microprogramming solution for an individual farm, since the zero (or near zero) entry in the b vector (P_0 column) makes the normalized cost coefficient in the artificial column in that row very large in any case, sufficient to cause that activity to be used at zero level. The procedure does matter, however, for the macroprogramming solutions.

23. Eleven of the twelve cases of redundancy for all farms were detected by visual inspection of the data and pencil-and-paper computations, using convex combinations of at most four parallel rows or columns. In the twelfth case (labor row 2), redundancy was assumed after inspection of the microprogramming solutions revealed that the constraint was always ineffective. The

reduction accomplished by this technique is striking (the reduced problem gives an A matrix of simpler form with fewer than half the elements in the former A matrix) and indicates that examination for redundancy is worth the cost of computing normalized coefficients. The degree of simplification accomplished is comparable to that initially hoped for by studying the aggregation problem.

24. Profits of the individual farms as microprogrammed, their size-region classification, and their structure of zeros as required by the method of common zero resources are shown in Appendix Table A-4 of Fisher and Kelley (1968).

25. Mr. E. V. Brown, Department of Mathematics, Kansas State University, gave programming and other assistance in obtaining results on the IBM 1410 computer.

26. Results for the methods of common zero resources and size-region were obtained by Letourneau (1966).

References

Abou-el-Dahab, M. G. 1965. "An Aggregation Procedure for Deriving Representative Firms in Estimating Supply Functions." Ph.D. diss. Manhattan: Kansas State University.

Day, R. H. 1963. "On Aggregating Linear Programming Models of Production." *Journal of Farm Economics* 45(November):797–813.

Dorfman, R. 1951. *Application of Linear Programming to the Theory of the Firm.* Berkeley: University of California Press.

Fisher, W. D. 1966. "Simplification of Economic Models." *Econometrica* 34(July): 663–84.

Fisher, W. D., and P. L. Kelley. 1968. "Selecting Representative Firms in Linear Programming." Technical Bulletin 159. Manhattan: Kansas Agricultural Experiment Station.

Frick, G. E., and R. A. Andrews. 1965. "Aggregation Bias and Four Methods of Summing Farm Supply Functions." *Journal of Farm Economics* 47(August):696 700.

Gale, D. 1960. *The Theory of Linear Economic Models.* New York: McGraw-Hill.

Hartley, H. O. 1962. "Total Supply Functions Estimated from Farm Surveys." Paper presented before the North Central Farm Management Research Committee.

Kelley, P. L., and D. A. Knight. 1965. "Short-run Elasticities of Supply for Milk." *Journal of Farm Economics* 47(February):93–104.

Letourneau, J. L. 1966. "Testing Methods of Aggregating Linear Programming Problems." Master's report. Manhattan: Kansas State University.

Miller, T. A. 1966. "Sufficient Conditions for Exact Aggregation in Linear Programming Models." *Agricultural Economics Research* 18(April):52–57.

———. 1967. "Aggregation Error in Representative Farm Linear Programming Supply Estimates." Ph.D. diss. Ames: Iowa State University.

Sheehy, S. J. 1964. "Selection of Representative Benchmark Farms in Synthetic Supply Estimation." Ph.D. diss. University Park: The Pennsylvania State University.

Sheehy, S. J., and R. H. McAlexander. 1965. "Selection of Representative Benchmark Farms for Supply Estimation." *Journal of Farm Economics* 47(August):681–95.

Waugh, F. V. 1951. "The Minimum-Cost Dairy Feed." *Journal of Farm Economics* 33(August):299–310.

III

On Research, Technology, and Resources

14

Economics and Agricultural Research

THEODORE W. SCHULTZ

A Preface on Methodology and Style. My prefatory remarks pertain to the importance of the thoughtful economics, the simple and appropriate analysis, the directness of the empirical evidence, and the clarity of the exposition of Geoffrey Shepherd. I will then present what I trust is in keeping with his economic style, a preliminary overview of some of the knowledge at hand and of various unsettled issues in bringing economics to bear on agricultural research.

There is much to be said in favor of the economic style of Geoffrey Shepherd. His style is revealed in his purpose as an economist, in his mode of expressing economic thought, in his appeal to basic economic principles, and in his commitment to staying close to robust evidence in investigating economic behavior. His purpose has not been to please governments. He has not been beholden to political authority. His guiding purpose has been that of an educator letting the chips fall where they may. He has not sought to be the consultant of farm organizations, labor unions, business, foundations, or of national and international agencies. He has valued highly the integrity that is essential in education.

Economic thought is first and foremost in Geoffrey Shepherd's mode of analysis, and quantitative techniques are not a substitute for economic thinking. A low priority is placed on intricate models in his work. What Bridgman, the physicist, said about physics is applicable to Geoffrey Shepherd's style, namely, economic behavior is more complex than our thoughts about it. Our economic thoughts, however, are more comprehensive than our economic language, our language is more comprehensive than standard economic theory, and standard theory is more comprehensive than mathematical economics. The neglect of thoughtful economics has become the bane of all too much of modern economics.

I turn to some of the contributions of Geoffrey Shepherd during the first years of the 1930s to exemplify his approach. The economic events associated with the Great Depression placed their imprint on the subsequent behavior of the economy and, needless to say, on the thinking of economists. The dissarray of the economy during that period induced economists at Iowa State College to defer their standard research projects in order to use their research time in an attempt to clarify the economic problems that had suddenly arisen. A series of ten economic studies were published in rapid succession by the agricultural experiment station, beginning in November 1932 and continuing on into 1933, under the general title, *The Agricultural Emergency in Iowa*. The second study in the series, "The Causes of the Emergency," was by Geoffrey Shepherd, and so was the fifth, "Control of the General Price Level," prepared jointly with Professor Wallace Wright. These two studies were examples of the style to which I refer. It is noteworthy that the demand for these economic studies turned out to be far larger than had been anticipated. Although 15,000 copies of each study were printed, they were soon exhausted. By early summer of 1933 a paperback book that contained all ten of the studies was published by the Collegiate Press, Ames, Iowa. Geoffrey Shepherd wrote the preface to this book. A reading of that preface bears strong testimony to the clarity and pertinent insights on the issues of that day to which these studies were addressed. I also refer here to his essay, "Commodity Loans and Price Floors for Farm Products," which first appeared as pamphlet #6 in the spring of 1943 in the *Wartime Farm and Food Policy Pamphlets,* Iowa State College Press. This series of pamphlets has been reprinted as a book by the Arno Press, New York Times Company. There is in my view much merit in the simple, straightforward approach and analysis that is the hallmark of Geoffrey Shepherd, as it is exemplified in that pamphlet.

The Business of Agricultural Research.[1] I now want to consider the production of agricultural research and some key unsettled issues connected with its effective development and application. I shall treat research as an economic activity because it requires scarce resources and it produces something of value. It is a specialized activity that calls for special skills and facilities that are employed to discover and develop new and presumably useful information. The resources that are allocated to various research enterprises are readily observed and measured. But the value of the new information that these enterprises produce is always hard to determine. Organized agricultural research has become an important part of the process of modernizing agriculture throughout the world. It has been increasing at a rapid rate and annual expenditures on research are in the billions of dollars.

It should be kept in mind that the future increases in food supply depend in substantial part on the achievements of agricultural research. Whether or not we succeed in doing the necessary research is of no concern to the sun or to the earth and the winds that sweep her face. Our popular doomsday activists know it will be impossible for agricultural research to save us from disaster! For them the history of the struggle of mankind to produce enough food is irrelevant.

What I plan to do is of five parts. I will begin with some estimates of the growth and magnitude of agricultural research throughout the world and with some observations on the increases in agricultural productivity from this research. I will then consider what I deem to be a very important question, namely, who should pay for agricultural research? I will then proceed to the organizational quandary. I will close with two very brief parts dealing with the harm that is done to agricultural research by the distortions in agricultural prices and with the function of research enterpreneurship.[2]

Expenditures on Research and Agricultural Productivity. Annual expenditures on agricultural research throughout the world have increased over fivefold since 1951. I view the rapid growth of this sector as a response to its success. When one adds up the costs of all the national agricultural research systems, those of industrial firms and of related university research, as Kislev and Evenson (1975) have done, which has been extended and updated by Boyce and Evenson (1975), the estimates covering the period from 1951 to 1974 in constant 1971 U.S. dollars show that the total world expenditure for this purpose increased from $769 million to $3.84 billion. I have extrapolated these estimates under very conservative assumptions. My estimate for 1979 is $4.13 billion in terms of 1971 constant dollars. In 1979 prices it would total over $7 billion for the current year. It should be noted, however, that in Latin America, compared with the other five major regions of the world, the percentage of total research expenditure relative to the value of the agricultural products of each region is less than in any other region.[3]

Returning to the total world agricultural research expenditures, this research sector is obviously no longer an infant. Many parts of it have all the earmarks of maturity. Are there signs of senility in any of these parts? In the language of economists, are there specific classes of agricultural research that are entering the diminishing returns stage? It will not do for us to be silent on this issue. To answer this question will require both the knowledge of scientists pertaining to scientific possibilities and that of economists with respect to the value of the required resources compared with the potential value of such research contributions.

Allocative decisions, however, must be made on the basis of limited information. In fact, we know a good deal. I consider actual allocative behavior as very useful information. The observed rapid growth tells me that those who have made and are making the allocative decisions do so because they deem it to be worthwhile. There are also a fairly large number of competent economic studies that show that the rates of return on investment in various specific classes of agricultural research have been much higher than the normal rates of return. It could be argued that research endeavors that have not been successful have received all too little attention. Nevertheless, the classes of agricultural research that have been analyzed are of major economic importance in agricultural production, especially so in the case of food, feed, and fiber crops.

Recent economic history provides additional useful information on the value of the contributions of agricultural research. I rate this historical information highly for the purpose at hand. The following achievements are pertinent:

1. No doubt agriculture throughout the world will find it increasingly more costly to increase the area of cropland. Agricultural research along with complementary inputs has been very successful in developing substitutes for cropland (some call this "land augmentation"). Actual increases in yield per acre have held and may well continue to hold the key to increases in crop production. For example, during my first year at Iowa State College, 1931, the U.S. yield of corn was 24 bushels per acre, a normal crop. Last year, 1978, this yield came to 101 bushels. Although the corn acreage harvested in 1978 was 39 million acres less than in 1931, total production was over 7 billion bushels compared with 2.57 billion in 1931. No wonder the estimated rates of return on corn research in the United States are exeedingly high. The achievement in the case of sorghum is even more dramatic. Taking 1929 as a normal year, the yield of sorghum grain rose from 13.9 bushels per acre to 45.3 bushels in 1978, despite the fact that the area devoted to this crop increased from 4.4 to 16.5 million acres. Total production in 1978 was 748 million bushels, which is over 15 times as much as that in 1929.

2. It is no longer true that a large per capita supply of beef can be produced only in countries with a sparse population and with much good grazing land. As corn and sorghum have become cheaper than grass in the United States, producers of beef have turned increasingly to feed grains. Here again one sees the large economic effects of corn and sorghum research along with complementary inputs on the reduction of the real costs of production and on increases in supply. The per capita consumption of beef in the United States doubled between 1940 and 1975 (retail weight in the civilian population: 43.4 lb in 1940 and 88.9 lb in 1975). The rise in real per capita income tells most of the story of this extraordinary increase in the demand for beef. The decline in the real price of feed grains as a consequence of much higher yields and lower costs in turn tells most of the story explaining the threefold increase in domestic beef slaughter and the approximately constant real-producer-beef price trend, with fluctuations, to be sure, about that trend (Schultz 1976).

3. The returns to poultry research are well known (Peterson 1966). Adding to it the effects of research on the supply of poultry feed, the result is a major improvement in the production of poultry products and a large gain for consumers. In the United States per capita consumption in terms of retail weight increased almost threefold between 1940 and 1975 (from 17.5 lb to 49.6 lb).

4. Last on my partial list of research achievements are those pertaining to wheat. The real costs of producing wheat have declined very much. As yet, the costs of producing rice have not come down as they have for wheat. Back in 1911–1915, the world price of these two primary food grains tended to be equal. During 1947–1962 wheat sold at about 60 percent of the price of rice. Between 1965 and 1970 the wheat price had declined to half that of rice. My most recent figure is from August 1978, when wheat was quoted at 35 percent of the price of rice, namely, wheat at $129 and rice at $366 per ton.[4] I leave it to others to clarify why the effects of wheat and rice research have been so different. When will the real costs of producing rice come tumbling down?

Who Should Pay for Agricultural Research? In my view this is a critical question. There is, I regret to say, a good deal of confusion on this issue. The international agricultural research centers have prospered as a successful innovation.[5] The donors who have provided the funds have been generous. Why not allow these centers to expand and do most of the necessary agricultural research? These centers, good as they are, will not suffice; they are not a substitute for national agricultural research enterprises, nor are they capable of doing more than a small part of the required basic research in this area.

Since basic research is very expensive and what may be discovered is subject to much uncertainty, why not let the rich countries do it and pay for it? Presumably, they can afford to do it. The implication of this view is that low-income countries can be "free riders" when it comes to basic research related to agriculture. This is, however, a shortsighted view because even to be a free rider requires a high level of scientific competence. To take advantage of such advances in the pertinent sciences achieved elsewhere throughout the world calls for a corps of highly skilled scientists. The unique requirements of agriculture in different countries is still another important consideration in this context.

My conclusion at this point is that it would be a serious mistake for Chile or any other major country in Latin America to assume that the international agricultural research centers and the ongoing agricultural research in high-income countries are substitutes for first-rate national agricultural research enterprises.

Who then within a country should pay for agricultural research? Economists, of course, raise their hands wanting to be heard. They will, however, modify the question and proceed to comment on who pays the bill. These are two quite different questions. What we know suggests that the answers tend to converge. Consider the activities of experiment stations and of universities related to agriculture. They do not normally sell their products; they make their findings available to the public. Nor do they provide the funds that cover the costs of doing the research in which they engage. Who benefits and who bears the costs of agricultural research requires some elaboration.

I shall begin with the agricultural research that is being done by private industrial firms, because in terms of economics it is the least difficult to present. Industrial firms, understandably, restrict their agricultural research to projects from which they expect to derive a profit. A good example has been the research of private firms pertaining to the medication of poultry feed and to the optimum mix of poultry feed ingredients at the lowest cost as the relative prices of the various feed ingredients change. Some types of research on insecticides, pesticides, animal antibiotics, drugs, location-specific seeds (e.g. hybrid corn), and various types of engineering research oriented to the requirements of agriculture are profitable for firms to undertake. In an advanced industrial economy there are many such research opportunities. About 25 percent of all expenditures on agricultural research in North America and Oceania is accounted for by the industrial sector.[6] In Latin America industrial firms account for about 5 percent of all agricultural research; note, however, that given the state of industrial development, it would not make sense for governments to attempt to mandate their industrial firms to increase their share of expenditures for this purpose. In an open market economy these firms will increase their expenditures on agricultural research when it becomes evident that it is profitable for them to do so.[7]

The same economic logic is sometimes used to argue that farmers should pay for the research from which they profit because private farms are in principle like private industrial firms undertaking profitable activities. It is true that landlords with large landholdings have engaged at various periods in something akin to agricultural research. Landlords in England in the past took much pride in developing various breeds of livestock. What they did, however, required very little scientific knowledge. I recall my impressions while in Uruguay in 1941. The large livestock farms were at best relying on the advice of individuals with a bachelor's degree in livestock, who had a modicum of knowledge about genetics, whereas at the small agricultural experiment stations in South Uruguay the plant breeding projects were designed and carried out by highly competent geneticists who had full knowledge of R. A. Fisher's experimental design.

Individual farms the world over are obviously too small to undertake scientific research on their own. Nor are commodity organizations of farmers capable of doing it. The scale of the research enterprise and the continuity required to recruit and hold competent scientists entails a capability that is beyond that of the individual farmer or that of various farm organizations.

It is necessary at this point to consider who actually benefits from agricultural research. Under the assumption that the contributions of this research reduce the real costs of producing agricultural products, the reduction in cost results in either a producer surplus or a consumer surplus or some combination of the two. Under market competition over time the benefits derived from this research accrue predominantly to consumers. It enhances their real income and welfare. Some farmers benefit during the early stages when, for example, a new high-yielding variety is being adopted. Those farmers who are among the first to adopt and who are successful at it benefit, often substantially so. Once, however, all farmers have adopted such a variety, the reduction in costs under competition results in a lower supply price, to the benefit of consumers. When such a high-yielding variety has been for a time location-specific, as in the case of Mexican wheat in the Punjab, farmers, landowners, and farm laborers profit. In general if the commodity that is produced is solely for domestic consumption, domestic consumers are the primary beneficiaries; if the commodity is solely for export, consumers abroad benefit, and farmers in other countries who produce the same commodity and sell in the world market will experience a decline in their comparative advantage.[8] Although the consumer surplus derived from the contributions of agricultural research are real and are large over time, it is not feasible for consumers here or elsewhere to organize and finance modern agricultural research enterprises. The complexity of university-related basic research raises additional issues of who can and will finance this type of research.

In summing up, the implications of my arguments on paying for agricultural research are as follows:

1. International agricultural research centers are not substitutes for national research enterprises.

2. Large agricultural research institutions in high-income countries do not serve the unique requirements of Latin American countries.

3. Industrial firms within any country will undertake only strictly applied research from which they can derive a profit. In countries where the industrial sector is small and not highly developed, their expenditures on agriculture-related research is, for good reasons, a very small part of the total agricultural research that is required.

4. It is beyond the capacity of the individual farmer to do the required research on his own; nor are farmers collectively up to organizing and financing national agricultural research.

5. Although over time most of the benefits from agricultural research accrue to consumers, it is not feasible for them to organize and finance national agricultural research enterprises.

6. Therefore, the only meaningful approach to modern agricultural

research is to conceptualize most of its contributions as *public goods*. As such they must be paid for on public account, which does not exclude private gifts to be used to produce public goods.

The Organization Quandary. Organized agricultural research has a long history. Despite the constraints and difficulties that have been encountered and the mistakes that have been made, organized agricultural research viewed historically has been a remarkable success. I featured some of its achievements at the outset. We may learn from past mistakes and we should ponder the puzzles, a list of which follows.

1. Why did many of the states in the United States establish all too many tiny, subagricultural experiment stations? Most of them were inefficient. They could not recruit competent scientists. The staff that could be had was in general isolated intellectually, having too little interaction with the principal experiment station of the state and with scientists at the land grant colleges. (Robert Evenson's comment on this paragraph has real merit. While agreeing that many of the tiny substations of the past were inefficient, he noted that most of them have been discontinued and those that remain are, in general, useful. Moreover, there is an increasing tendency on the part of the central experiment station to lose interacting contact with farmers, and he feels a strong case can be made for the remaining substations on these grounds.)

2. Agricultural laboratories established to do research on agricultural product processing, where the scientists are off by themselves far removed from university scientists, are a mistake. The puzzle is, why did the U.S. government establish four expensive regional laboratories of this type? It behooves other countries not to repeat this costly mistake.

3. There are too many examples throughout the world of important crops being neglected when it comes to agricultural research. Who is to blame? In the United States, there is a gross underinvestment in soybean research, considering the fact that the value of the annual soybean crop exceeds by a wide margin the value of the wheat and cotton crops combined. It is hard for me to believe that geneticists who are also plant breeders have no theories from which to derive research hypotheses to improve the genetic capacity of the soybean. Why this neglect of soybean research?

4. All too much of the foreign aid for agricultural development has undervalued agricultural research. When it has supported such research it has been generally short-term aid, notwithstanding the fact that the gestation period in research is a matter of years and it should for that reason be approached as a long-term investment. The commitment to quick results has been the bane of most foreign aid, not only for research but also in other program areas. It continues to be the better part of wisdom for low-income countries not to rely on foreign aid in financing their agricultural research enterprises.

5. It is difficult to understand why any of the major private foundations should assume that the necessary research results for agricultural modernization are at hand and on that assumption proceed to support agricultural extension work. The dissemination of existing knowledge and better communication featuring new approaches in extension activities has been and continues to be the announced policy of the Kellogg Foundation. The prestigious Ford Foundation made the same mistake during its early agricultural programs in India. It is to the credit of the Rockefeller Foundation that it has had the wisdom to see that research must come first, holding to that policy until recently.

6. It is still a puzzle for me why so few worthwhile agricultural research results were available throughout Latin America at the time when President Truman's Point Four program was launched. It was my responsibility during the early fifties, with ample foundation funds and with five competent colleagues, to make an assessment of the achievements of the Point Four programs. Our project and publications were labeled Technical Assistance Latin America (TALA). We roamed over all parts of Latin America and found that in the area of agriculture Point Four had accomplished very little. Agricultural extension work was prematurely emphasized. In general the Point Four–supported extension work was ineffective for lack of available agricultural research results. Funds allocated to agricultural research were used far less effectively than the funds of the Rockefeller Foundation's joint program with the Mexican government in Mexico, called International Maize and Wheat Improvement Center (CIMMYT).

7. The last item on the list reaches far back in time, serving the purpose of deflating our self-acclaimed importance in augmenting the production of food. It is a disconcerting puzzle. Neolithic women invented agriculture and developed nearly all the food crop species we have today, while our highly skilled plant breeders have produced only one new food species, triticale. Norman Borlaug (1976), our agricultural Nobel Laureate, puts it this way: "The first and greatest green revolution occurred when women decided that something had to be done about their dwindling food supply." Neolithic men hunting for meat were failing to bring home enough to eat. Ponder and try to explain the implications of the achievements then and now.

Important as it is to avoid making the mistakes that other countries have made in organizing and administering agricultural research, we must be aware of other considerations. Robert Evenson's (1978) recent essay on the organization of research is an important contribution to the allocation of research funds by commodities. By his criteria (see Evenson 1978, Table 3, p. 230), the allocation of funds for cotton or rubber research is twice as large as that for wheat or sugarcane, and that allocated for rice, corn, millet, and sorghum, or livestock and its products, is only half as large as that for wheat or sugarcane. Pulses, groundnuts, oilseeds, and roots and tubers are among the neglected crops. Evenson also deals competently with the allocation of research resources by environmental regions and with the issues pertaining to single-commodity, multiple-commodity, and discipline-oriented research.

My own experience and observations lead me to stress the following organizing decisions:

1. Having selected the commodities, the state of the market for the services of the scientists required to do the research becomes an important consideration.

2. It is all too easy to become enamored of the phrase "interdisciplinary research." What matters is the actual value realized from the complementarity between scientists with different professional skills. So-called interdisciplinary research is as a rule weak on theory and soft in quality.

3. The effects of various incentives on research workers' productivity is of major importance. The built-in incentives that characterize organized agricultural research in most low-income countries are bad. All too often agricultural scientists are worse off in this respect than high-class clerks in the bureaucracy of the government.

4. All too little attention is given to the effects of alternative accountability requirements on research efficiency. Unnecessary paperwork abounds. Those who provide the funds call the accounting rules; they are rarely aware of the sharply diminishing returns of the burdensome accounting that they call for. In my view, the international agricultural research centers are no exception.

5. The trade-off, the compromise between the loss from fragmentation and the gain from location-specific research within a country, is a choice that has to be made. The mistakes that various high-income countries have made in their organizational decisions on this issue are instructive on what not to do.

6. Each of the major Latin American countries must have its own corps of competent agricultural scientists. The long-term payoff on this investment is very high. The ever-present strong desire of those who make organizational decisions for quick results is a serious obstacle in recruiting and maintaining a corps of competent scientists. Where the main agricultural experiment station is an integral part of a university, it is possible to give due attention to basic research oriented to agriculture, provided the decisions of the government in allocating funds do not thwart such basic research.

7. Economics uses the concept of the optimum scale of an enterprise. Although it is difficult to apply this concept in determining the optimum scale of an agricultural experiment station, it is nevertheless relevant. There is a strong tendency in agricultural research to violate all scale considerations by ever more centralization of its administration.

The Harm Done to Research by Price Distortions.[9] The scarcity of agricultural resources—land relative to labor, and both relative to the stock of reproducible forms of physical capital—are major considerations in determining the forms of useful knowledge that are appropriate for an economy. The historical responses of agricultural research in various countries to resource scarcity considerations are presented by Hayami and Ruttan (1971) in their well-known book on agricultural development. (See also Binswanger et al. 1978.)

The scarcity of the factors of production is not self-evident. It requires proof, and proof calls for measurement. The price of the services of each of the factors of production in an open, competitive market is a unit of measurement of scarcity. When the market is rigged, be it by governmental intervention or by means of private monopoly pricing, the resulting prices are distorted. The price signals that are a consequence of such distortions do not reveal the true scarcity of the factors of production and for that reason are beset with misinformation. The allocation of funds for agricultural research and the use to which these funds are put are not immune to the adverse effects of such price misinformation.

The overpricing of sugar beets in Western Europe and the United States, and the associated expenditures on sugar beet research, is a case in point. The expenditures on rice research in Japan have not been immune to vast overpricing of rice in that country (Otsuka 1979). In India, pricing of rice is the other way around. There is no end to examples. The harm that is being done to agricultural research throughout the world as a consequence of the distortions in prices and in agricultural incentives is very substantial.

The Function of Research Entrepreneurship. The dynamic attributes of research are pervasive both in the domain of economic growth and in the conduct of actual research. Advances in useful knowledge are compelling dynamic forces. Such new knowledge is the mainspring of economic growth. Were it not for advances in knowledge, the economy would arrive at a stationary state and all economic activities would become essentially routine in nature. Over time new knowledge has augmented the productive capacity of land, and it has led to the development of new forms of physical capital and of new human skills. The fundamental dynamic agent of long-term economic growth is the research sector of the economy.

The concept of meaningful research conducted to enhance the stock of knowledge useful in production and consumption is inconsistent with static, unchanging, routine work on the part of scientists. The very essence of research is the fact that it is a dynamic venture into the unknown or into what is only partially known. Research, in this context, is inescapably subject to risk and uncertainty. Although funds, organization, and competent scientists are necessary, they are not sufficient. An important factor in producing knowledge is the human ability I shall define as *research entrepreneurship.* It is an ability that is scarce, it is hard to identify this talent, it is rewarded haphazardly in the not-for-profit research sector, and it is increasingly misused and impaired by the overorganization of our research enterprises. What is happening in agricultural research is on this score no exception.

Who are these research entrepreneurs? In profit-oriented business enterprises, the chief executive officers perform the entrepreneurial function; the skilled factory worker is not an entrepreneur in doing his job. In research it is otherwise; whereas administrators in charge of a research organization are entrepreneurs, much of the actual entrepreneurship is a function of the assessment by scientists of the scientific frontiers of knowledge. Their professional competence is required to determine the research hypotheses worthwhile pursuing.

Briefly and much simplified, my argument is that in the quest for appropriations and research grants, all too little attention is given to that scarce talent that is the source of research entrepreneurship. The convenient assumption is that a highly organized research institution firmly controlled by an administrator will perform this important function. But in fact, a large, tightly controlled organization is the death of creative research, regardless of whether it be the National Science Foundation, a government agency, a large private foundation, or a large research-oriented university. No research director in Washington or Santiago can know the entire array of research options that the state of scientific knowledge and its frontier afford. Nor can the managers of foundation funds know what needs to be known to perform this function. Having served as a member of a research advisory committee to a highly competent experiment station director for some years, and having observed the vast array of research talent supported by funds that we as a committee had a hand in allocating, I am convinced that most working scientists are research entrepreneurs. But it is exceedingly difficult to devise institutions to utilize this special talent efficiently. Organization is necessary. It too requires entrepreneurs. Agricultural research has benefited from experiment stations, from specialized university laboratories, and from the recently developed international agricultural research centers. But there is the ever-present danger of overorganization, of directing research from the top, of requiring working scientists to devote more and more time to preparing reports to "justify" the work they are doing, and to treat research as if it were some routine activity.

Notes

1. This essay was written for the Seminar on Socio-Economic Aspects of Agricultural Research in Developing Countries, May 7–11, 1979, Santiago, Chile. It is presented here by permission of Don Winkelmann, of the committee that organized this seminar.

2. The economics of agricultural research has long been high on the Ph.D. research agenda of graduate students at the University of Chicago. I am much indebted to them for their contributions. I shall also draw on Schultz (1978b).

3. See Table 1.5, for the year 1974, in Boyce and Evenson (1975).

4. Why there has not been more substitution of wheat for rice, inasmuch as the nutritive values of rice and wheat are virtually the same, presents a puzzle. See Schultz (1979).

5. It should be noted that the Rockefeller Foundation in cooperation with the government of Mexico was the first to launch this type of venture. Not to be overlooked is the importance of research entrepreneurship in this connection. I shall have more to say on research entrepreneurship later in this chapter.

6. This estimate and the one that follows for Latin America are for 1974, based on Table 1.1, Boyce and Evenson (1975).

7. Experience in the United States indicates there is a tendency for some agricultural experiment stations to hold on to research work that has been successful and has reached the point where private firms would continue it, such as the case of the Southern Experiment Stations holding on to the development and production of hybrid corn for seed.

8. The economics of the preceding arguments is greatly simplified. Much depends on the elasticity of the demands and on the shifts in the supply curves as a consequence of the production effects of the contributions derived from agricultural research.

9. For an extended treatment of the adverse effects of distortions in agricultural incentives, including their effects on the adoption of research results and on providing the wrong price signals to guide agricultural research, see Schultz (1978a).

References

Binswanger, H. P., V. Ruttan, et al. 1978. *Induced Innovation: Technology, Institutions, and Development.* Baltimore: Johns Hopkins University Press.

Borlaug, N. E. 1976. "The Green Revolution: Can We Make It Meet Expectations?" *Proceedings of the American Phytopathological Society,* vol. 3. St. Paul, Minn.

Boyce, J. K., and R. Evenson. 1975. *National and International Agricultural Research and Extension Programs.* New York: Agricultural Development Council.

Evenson, R. E. 1978. "The Organization of Research to Improve Crops and Animals in Low Income Countries." In *Distortions of Agricultural Incentives,* edited by Theodore Schultz. Bloomington: Indiana University Press.

Hayami, Y., and V. W. Ruttan. 1971. *Agricultural Development: An International Perspective.* Baltimore: Johns Hopkins University Press.

Kislev, Y. and R. E. Evenson. 1975. "Investment in Agricultural Research and Extension: An International Survey." *Economic Development and Cultural Change* 23:507-22.

Otsuka, K. 1979. "Public Research and Rice Production—Rice Sector in Japan, 1953-76." Ph.D. diss. University of Chicago.

Peterson, W. 1966. "Returns to Poultry Research in the United States." Ph.D. diss. University of Chicago.

Schultz, T. W. 1976. "The Politics and Economics of Beef." *Proceedings of Conference on Livestock Production in the Tropics* (Acapulco, Mexico, March 8-12). Banco de Mexico.

_____, ed. 1978a. *Distortions of Agricultural Incentives.* Bloomington: Indiana University Press.

_____. 1978b. "What Are We Doing to Research Entrepreneurship?" In *Transforming Knowledge into Food in a Worldwide Context,* edited by W. F. Hueg, Jr., and C. A. Gannon. Minneapolis: Miller Publishing, pp. 96-105.

_____. 1979. "Reckoning the Economic Achievements and Prospects of Low Income Countries." James C. Snyder Memorial Lecture, Purdue University, February 22.

15

On the International Transfer of Technology: A Case Study of the Indian Experience with Cereal Grains

R. T. S H A N D

IN DEVELOPING COUNTRIES, technology transfer has a special urgency owing to the need for a sustained rate of growth of agricultural output that can match high population growth and can provide for widely distributed increases in material living standards. This need was dramatized in the mid-1960s in India when, with two successive drought years, the country had to import huge supplies of food grains simply to sustain the population. This led to a major change in policy in India toward modernization of the sector's scientific and technological base.[1] From developed countries, the most significant response to the need was the establishment and development of nine international agricultural research centers. Two of the earliest of these, the International Maize and Wheat Improvement Center (CIMMYT) in Mexico and the International Rice Research Institute (IRRI) in the Philippines, played a crucial role in India's Green Revolution experience by providing jumping-off points for the transfer of high-yielding varieties of wheat and rice. Using data from the joint study carried out by the Programme Evaluation Organisation of the Indian Planning Commission and the Australian National University (PEO/ANU), the present paper evaluates this example of an international transfer of technology.[2]

Concern has been expressed in relation to agriculture, as with other sectors, about the appropriateness of various transferred technologies and about the socioeconomic consequences of their introduction. There have been fears that the new wheat and rice technology is labor displacing and that a differential impact exacerbates regional differences in income levels and, within regions, differences in income levels between social groups (laborers and farmers, tenants and owners, large and small farm owners).

Some authors have set forth broad generalizations relating to this concern. For example, Ruttan (1977) offered the following conclusions concerning the "initial impact of the adoption of the new varieties on production, and on the functional and personal distribution of income":

1. There was a very rapid adoption rate for high yielding varieties (HYVs) of wheat and rice where these proved technically and economically superior to local varieties
2. Adoption of the HYVs was not seriously constrained by farm size or tenure
3. Farm size and tenure did not give rise to differential rates of productivity growth
4. The new technology raised the demand for labour
5. Landowners benefited relatively more than tenants from the new varieties
6. The HYVs contributed to a widening of wage and income differentials among regions
7. They also reduced the rate of increase in consumer foodgrain prices.

My objective here is to reconsider these broad generalizations using field survey data from the PEO/ANU study. The evidence appears to support the first of these while calling into question some of the others.

The analysis of the data underlines the importance of recognizing adaptation as a two-way process: one way concerned with the modification of the varieties themselves by the inclusion of characteristics considered desirable by producers and consumers of the grains, the other with the modification of the environment to meet the requirements of the exotic and locally adopted varieties. *Environment* in this paper is defined broadly to include not only the physical conditions of crop production, but the socioeconomic setting as well, and in particular the various institutions established to provide services to the cultivator.

It is argued that policymaking and resource allocation for the new technology have to achieve the difficult balance in emphasis between two directions of adaptation: the degree to which a country should depend upon scientific research for a continuing evolution of the crop technology to better fit the existing environment and the extent to which it should concentrate resources upon measures to modify the environment in order to take fuller advantage of the potential of the existing varieties.

The paper first reviews briefly events surrounding the introduction of the new technology in India. Measures of performance and impact of the new technology are then presented as a basis for the interpretation of the nature and extent of the two-way adaptation process and its strength and weaknesses.

The New Strategy in Indian Agriculture. In 1966 the government of India took the bold step of allocating a major part of scarce foreign exchange to the purchase of dwarf, high-yielding varieties of Mexican wheat. This action effectively signaled a firm decision by the government to commit itself to raising the growth rate of Indian food grain output by scientific, technological means. It was initially to depend heavily on the research output of two international crop research organizations—CIMMYT in Mexico, and a little later, IRRI in the Philippines.

High-yielding varieties of wheat from Mexico had first been introduced to India in 1962. By 1965 they had been tested, selections had been made, and results of field trials were promising. Thus, there was in fact a scientific basis for the high expectations held for the impact of this new technology. However, owing to the urgency of the food problem it was decided not to wait for the multiplication of the new selections but to import a large volume of parent seed of the dwarf Mexican wheat varieties for direct release to farmers, without proof of the acceptability of this seed to local farmers. For paddy the situation was similar: Taiwanese varieties were imported directly in 1965–1966 and IRRI-bred varieties a year later, neither adequately tested under Indian conditions prior to their release. Local research on selection and crossbreeding programs for rice were not as advanced as for wheat.

This transfer of technology involved importation of a quantity of seed and also the technology it required. The use of this seed called for chemical fertilizers, increased and more timely water supplies, plant protection measures, increased credit for these technologies, and extension work to disseminate recommended practices for the new technology. To meet these needs the government created the High-Yielding Varieties Program (HYVP), the field program of the New Strategy. The HYVP was first introduced to a number of districts selected for their favorable resource endowments. In particular, availability of irrigation was a major criterion, given the heavy requirements for water of the new varieties, but these districts had other advantages such as a concentration of administration, extension, and input supply services.

The performance of the HYVP and the distribution of the benefits of the new technology are examined below, principally for wheat but with some observations for paddy.

High-Yielding Varieties Program: The Case of Wheat. According to the two most commonly used aggregate indicators of performance for the new technology—area coverage and the growth of total output—the HYVP for wheat has been a major success. In area terms, there has been an expansion from 4.8 million hectares in 1968–1969 to 13.56 million hectares in 1975–1976, while in 1974–1975 total wheat area (including nonirrigated areas) was 18.11 million hectares. Similarly, total output has shown a remarkable expansion, rising from 12.3 million tons in 1964–1965 to around 28 million tons in

1975-1976. Most of this can be attributed directly to the new technology for wheat. A major expansion and improvement of irrigation facilities occurred over this period, largely stimulated by the prospects of high net returns from the HYVs of wheat. There was also an expansion of area under wheat during the period, but this too followed from the introduction of HYVs and the extension of irrigation facilities and was to some extent at the expense of areas under other nonirrigated crops. The contribution of the new technology in this latter respect should be calculated less the substitution effect of wheat for other crops.

Estimated coverage by HYVs of total irrigated area under wheat shows that some districts achieved close to total HYV coverage as early as 1968-1969, only 3 years after the program commenced, such as Ludhiana in Punjab.[3] In 1969-1970, the irrigated wheat areas of 6 of the 16 survey blocks were four-fifths or more converted to HYVs. Other districts approached full coverage over the years to 1974-1975, though somewhat more slowly than the leaders, so that in that year, 12 of the 16 survey blocks had between 93 and 100 percent of irrigated area under the new varieties. *Notably though, 2 of the other 4 blocks still showed low to negligible proportions under HYVs after a full decade of the HYVP.*

In 1974-1975 there were 6 survey sample blocks in which some wheat growers still had not adopted (or had discarded) HYVs.[4] In 4 of these, nonparticipants were heavily concentrated in the smallest size groups, small or marginal farmers. In the other 2 blocks where nonparticipants were actually in the majority (Hissar and Sonepat) they were spread throughout the holding size groups.

Data from almost all survey districts showed a rapid spread of the two Mexican wheat varieties initially introduced in 1965-1966. These two were dwarfs, photoinsensitive and fertilizer responsive, bred in Mexico under conditions similar to those in India. They proved their high-yielding capacities in the field in India. However, they had the disadvantages of a reddish grain color, low cooking quality, and poor taste. For these reasons they were unpopular with consumers and brought lower prices relative to traditional varieties, but from the producers' viewpoint, the high yields compensated for the lower prices.

Research on local selections from these varieties had meanwhile been carried out in India, and scientists were able to offer a number of these to growers as alternatives within the first few years of the program. These selections retained the high-yielding characteristic and had improved appearance, cooking quality, and taste, though not to the point of equaling the traditional varieties. Their seasonal duration also fitted the local cropping patterns (paddy-wheat) better and some were more tolerant or resistant to local diseases. There were still some undesirable characteristics in these selected HYVs, particularly their susceptibility to rust disease, but the progress that had been made through selection narrowed the market price differential in favor of traditional varieties, and with high yields made conversion from local and local improved varieties highly profitable under favorable conditions of cultivation.

The spectacular rate of expansion of coverage of irrigated wheat area by HYVs took place partly because the imported varieties and local selections were suited to local agroclimatic conditions, and these conditions were found over a wide area of the northern wheat belt of India. It is also partly explained by the availability of assured supplies of irrigation water and by the rapid development of irrigation facilities during the early years of the HYVP.

It was quickly found that delivery of water from existing canal irrigation systems was inadequate for HYVs, in both timing and volume. Fortunately these systems could be supplemented by exploitation of the reserves of groundwater resources available under a large area of the Gangetic plains. Spread of HYV adoption was fastest where exploitation of groundwater by tube wells and pump sets was already taking place. In the Punjab, for example, Ludhiana was more advanced in this respect than Amritsar, and the Punjab as a whole was more advanced than Uttar Pradesh in the early years of the HYVP. This is reflected in the relative speed of HYV spread shown in the 1968–1975 period.[5]

Official policy for the HYVP was to select those districts and blocks for inclusion that were well supplied with irrigation water. This did not always occur in practice. Lack of availability of assured water largely explains the poor performance of the 2 exceptional blocks (Hissar and Sonepat) in Haryana where in 1974–1975 HYV area coverage was still low. Selected villages in these 2 blocks were located in a dry belt with restricted irrigation or none at all. Rainfall was low, canals did not serve the villages adequately, and tube wells were not feasible owing to brackish groundwater. Water supply was a problem for large and small farmers alike and the performance of these 2 blocks is a good indication of response to the HYVP in an area marginal for water supplies.

In other areas such as Gaya in Bihar small- and medium-sized cultivators depended entirely on canals and state tube wells. They were vulnerable to irregular and inadequate canal water (e.g., in Obra more than in Arwal block), especially in tail-end locations, and to unsatisfactory and high-cost services from state tube wells where these were available. Delays in energizing new tube wells affected this group of farmers most, as large farmers could install their own tube wells and diesel engines. These disadvantages help to explain the high incidence of HYVP nonparticipants among the small and marginal farmer groups.

Demand for power in the wheat belt grew rapidly with exploitation of groundwater resources, but it had to compete with the demand for irrigation water. Availability varied with the strength of the monsoon, storage volume, and the incidence of winter rainfall. In times of power shortage, smaller farmers who were dependent upon purchases from larger farmers suffered most, as the large farmers met their own needs first.

Distribution of Benefits of the New Technology. The above data clearly indicate a high level of participation among farmers and of coverage of HYVs in areas selected for their assured irrigation supplies. They also indicate the limits of the new technology where water availability is restricted. The measures used, however, are of little help in determining the distribution of benefits among participants. Direct measurement of the incidence of benefits was not a part of the PEO/ANU surveys, but data were collected on inputs applied to the HYVs during the period 1972–1975. These are used below to construct indicators, giving some insight into how benefits might be distributed.

There has in fact been much speculation and only limited empirical evidence about the distribution of benefits from the green revolution in wheat.[6] There is a strongly held view that it has served to widen the income gap between farmers both between and within regions. PEO/ANU survey data indicate that those areas correctly chosen for their suitability to the new technology have progressed beyond those without the same favorable concentration of resources, particularly irrigation. However, it should be pointed out that the new technology has also stimulated the exploitation of water resources in large areas where, without it, the investments probably would not have been made. The figures quoted above show that by 1974–1975 total wheat area under irrigation had reached the high proportion of 75 percent. Because of the availability of untapped reserves of groundwater, the benefits of the new technology have been widely extended through the wheat belt as the area under irrigation has expanded. It is only where these reserves are not available, or if available are not yet exploited, that interregional income disparities have widened.

Within those areas participating in the HYVP, particular interest has focused on the distribution of benefits among different farm size groups.[7] Ultimately this distribution pattern depends upon four sets of data relating to these size groups: the distribution pattern of participants; the distribution pattern of land ownership of irrigated wheat area planted to the HYVs; the level of inputs applied to HYVs of wheat; and input response curves of HYV wheat, especially to chemical fertilizers. We shall look at each of these in turn.

Blocks selected for the PEO/ANU surveys show wide variation in distribution patterns of HYVP participants[8] among holding size groups. There is a discernible trend for farm size to decrease from west to east geographically. In the northwestern states of Haryana and Punjab, a large majority of cultivators are found in the 2–8 hectare groups. Muzaffarnagar in western Uttar Pradesh shows larger proportions in smaller size groups, especially in Budhana block where 57 percent were in the 0–2 hectare group. Further eastward in Sitapur, Basti, and Bihar, the small and marginal farmers generally predominate to the point in Basti block where 90 percent of participants have less than 2 hectares.

The ownership pattern of land under HYVs of wheat shows a heavier concentration in the larger holding size groups (over 4 hectares). Thus, for exam-

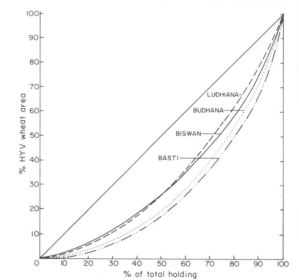

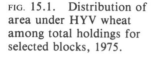

FIG. 15.1. Distribution of area under HYV wheat among total holdings for selected blocks, 1975.

ple, in selected blocks of Sonepat district in Haryana 51 and 37 percent of participants are in the farm size groups with more than 4 hectares, but they account for 82 and 63 percent of the area under the HYVs respectively. Correspondingly the 21 percent of participants in these blocks with less than 2 hectares account for only 5 and 6 percent of HYV wheat land respectively. This tendency toward concentration of HYV wheat land among large farmers is reinforced too, as shown above, in 4 of the 6 blocks with nonparticipants because the majority of these latter farmers were also in the smallest holding size groups. The varying degrees of concentration or inequities in landownership in relation to farm size groups are illustrated in Figure 15.1 with Lorenz curves. The Gini concentration ratios range from 0.19 to 0.33.

The third influence on the distribution of benefits from the new technology is the level of input application to land sown to the HYVs. The most important of these inputs is chemical fertilizer. Survey data were collected on dosages of chemical fertilizers applied by HYVP participants for three recent years, 1972–1975. The year 1972–1973 was one in which fertilizer supplies were generally quite plentiful and could be considered a "normal" year. In 1974–1975 the depressing effects on usage of a major price rise were evident following the steep increase in international oil prices.

The first striking and negative feature of the utilization patterns of chemical fertilizers was the large proportion of HYVP participants who used none at all. In 1972–1973, for example, basal nitrogenous (N) fertilizer, nonusers comprised 40 percent or more of the participants in 5 of the 16 survey blocks. In 1974–1975, with the higher prices, the number of blocks with 40 percent or more had risen to 7 and there were substantial proportions of nonusers in 4 others. Nonusers were in much higher proportions for basal phosphatic (P) and potassic (K) fertilizers than for basal N. Usage of N fertilizers for top-dressing on the other hand was more common than for basal applications.

In considering holding size groups it is clear that in 1972–1973 there was a heavy concentration of nonusers of chemical fertilizers in the smallest size groups. In that year 6 of the 13 sample blocks with participants in the 0–1 hectare group showed a majority of nonusers of basal N, and there were substantial proportions (20 percent or more) of nonusers in 9 of the 16 blocks in the 1–2 hectare size group. Some blocks showed a considerable number of nonusers in larger size groups as well, but it was noticeable in most that the proportions of nonusers declined with increasing size of holdings. By contrast there was universal usage of basal N fertilizer among sample farmers in Ludhiana district in 1972–1973 and a low incidence of nonusers in Amritsar blocks. With higher fertilizer prices in 1974–1975, there were greater proportions still of nonusers of chemical fertilizers than in 1972–1973, thus reinforcing the tendency for users to be concentrated in the larger size groups. Again, usage continued to be universal in Ludhiana district despite the price rise.

A second feature was the low absolute dosage level of each of these fertilizers (N, P, and K) applied by users relative to officially recommended dosages. In relation to basal N fertilizer, for example, the majority of users in 1972–1973 applied 50 percent or less of recommendations in 11 of the 16 blocks. High dosage rates were applied by sample farmers only in Ludhiana district and then only by a limited proportion of users.

Among users of chemical fertilizers, average dosages varied by size of holding but not in any consistent pattern according to size of holdings. For instance, in 1972–1973, for basal N fertilizer, only about 5 of the 16 blocks showed a discernible positive association between dosage level and size of holding. In 1974–1975, reductions in average use of basal N were more marked for the smallest size groups and a positive association was evident for 9 blocks.

The pattern of total fertilizer use (basal N) by holding size groups takes account of all the above features.[9] For the overall sample, the smallest size groups with less than 2 hectares applied only 9 percent of total utilization of basal N in 1972–1973 and 8 percent in 1974–1975. Those with holdings larger than 4 hectares, on the other hand, used 68 and 72 percent in these two years. Comparison with the distribution pattern for estimated HYV wheat area shows a considerably greater skewness toward the larger size groups in fertilizer use than in HYV area and thus points to a greater share of the benefits accruing to the larger farmers than is suggested by the pattern of landownership. Thus, there were 43 percent of participant farmers with less than 2 hectares in 1974–1975. They had 13 percent of the HYV wheat area in 1974–1975 but applied only 8 percent of the total basal N fertilizer used. By contrast, the 8 percent of farmers with more than 8 hectares had 24 percent of the area under HYV wheat and applied 29 percent of the total basal N used. This widened

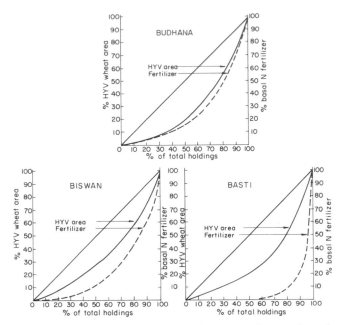

FIG. 15.2.   Distribution of area under HYV wheat and total basal N fertilizer dosages among total holdings for selected blocks, 1975.

disparity, as we discussed above, was due principally to the relatively high proportions of small and marginal cultivators in many blocks who did not apply any basal N fertilizer. This is illustrated in Figure 15.2 by a comparison, with Lorenz curves, of the aggregate use of basal N fertilizer in 1974–1975 with the distribution pattern of irrigated HYV wheat land by holding size groups for 3 blocks.[10]

Ludhiana's performance was exceptional. In these 2 blocks the distribution pattern of basal N fertilizer use, and thus, we infer, of benefits from the new technology, showed only a slightly greater skewness toward larger holdings than that of irrigated HYV wheat land. This is supported by the only slight increase in the farmers' Gini concentration ratio, to 0.25 from 0.22. This was because all participants applied basal N fertilizers, and there were no substantial differences in dosage rates between holding size groups. By contrast, other blocks showed a considerably greater concentration of fertilizer use among large farmers, compared with the HYV wheat area, and more significant increases in the Gini concentration ratios. In Budhana block in Muzaffarnagar, for example (Fig. 15.2), the 18 percent of farmers with 4 hectares or more had 41 percent of the HYV wheat area but used 48 percent of total basal N applied. The 57 percent with less than 2 hectares and with 25 percent of the HYV wheat area in 1974–1975 used only 19 percent of total fertilizer in that year. The Gini ratios rose from 0.28 for HYV area to 0.36 for basal N fertilizer use. In Biswan block (Sitapur), the 77 percent of the HYV growers with less than 2 hectares had 60 percent of the area but used only 46 percent of the total chemical fertilizers, while the Gini ratio for basal N was double that for HYV area distribution. The contrast was extreme in the 2 Basti blocks, where the 85 and 90 percent of participants with less than 2 hectares had 53 and 66 percent of HYV area but used only 30 and 29 percent of the basal N applied in 1974–1975. For this block the difference in Gini ratios was 0.83 versus 0.33.

The foregoing analysis has concentrated solely on use of chemical fertilizer. Other inputs are also important, such as plant protection and water, but quantitive data on usage and effects are very difficult to obtain for these. Qualitative survey data suggested that there was only a limited need for plant protection measures during the decade under review, partly because major outbreaks of pests and diseases of wheat were scattered and occasional and partly because the most important disease reported was rust, for which there was no effective means of field control. Where these problems were reported, treatment was very often applied too late or ineffectively. Generally, only large and medium farmers applied treatment, as small farmers frequently found the costs beyond their means.

The fourth factor affecting the distribution of benefits from the new technology referred to above, in relation to size of holdings, was the yield response curve for chemical fertilizer. Specifically, this is a question of whether, at any given level of chemical fertilizer use, there are any differences in yield response between holdings of different sizes. Direct evidence is not available on this; however, the surveys do suggest that if any relation exists, it is likely to be a positive one. PEO/ANU survey data indicated that small and marginal farmers had more difficulty than large farmers in securing adequate and timely input supplies, particularly of water; for the new technology this would work to the disadvantage of the former group. If so, this would be another factor tending to concentrate benefits in the larger holding size groups.

To review briefly, the above analysis of input use shows first that, with few exceptions, the dosage level of chemical fertilizers has been low and that much of the potential of the new technology for raising farm incomes and contributing to the growth of food-grain output has remained unexploited.[11] Second, underutilization of fertilizer is particularly evident among small and marginal farmers, to the point where, for the many who have not applied any chemical fertilizer, participation in the new technology is only nominal. This fact added to the disproportionate concentration of HYV land among medium and large farmers means that the benefits obtained have also accrued disproportionately to medium and large farmers.

The Role of Credit in Input Utilization. PEO/ANU survey data indicate that a key determinant of the level of inputs applied to the HYVs was the volume and terms of finance available to cultivators.

The introduction of the new technology through the HYVP changed the scale of production costs for wheat, with additional requirements in the short run for purchases of seed, fertilizer, and plant protection materials, and for investments in land improvement and the extension or improvement of irrigation facilities in the medium to long run. Given the limited capacity of cultivators other than those on large holdings to meet these costs themselves, there has been a heavy demand for additional short- to long-term credit, and in this the role of government credit institutions has been crucial. The extent to which these extra demands have been met has been a vital factor influencing the pattern of input use, and thus the distribution of benefits beyond the pattern set by the distribution of landownership.

At the time the HYVP was introduced, short-term credit was available through state cooperative institutions under the crop loan system with cash and kind components. State departments of agriculture also provided loans in kind as seed, fertilizer, and pesticides for nonmembers of cooperatives and nationalized banks became a third institutional service after 1969. Noninstitutional sources were big landlords, traders, private moneylenders, and relatives and friends. Medium-term credit for land development and tube well and pump set installations was provided by cooperative agencies, and long-term loans were given by land mortgage banks for agricultural machinery and tube well installation. Commercial bank loans were mainly made available for the short and medium term and principally for tube wells and machinery.

Credit for the HYVP was liberalized after 1966–1967. The sanctioned loan rate was raised, as was the maximum credit limit set for various land-use types. These were adjusted over the years as production costs rose. The tolerance limits for cooperative societies with defaults were raised and nondefaulting members of defaulting societies were made eligible.

In practice, there was expansion in the volume of institutional loans disbursed over the first 10 years, but this was highly variable between districts. Ludhiana district, for example, was markedly successful in adjusting credit supply to new needs, largely through the cooperative system. There, even at the time the HYVP commenced, about 95 percent of farmers were members of cooperatives. Efforts were made to expand membership, new branches were opened, and the volume of all types of loans expanded. There was a high recovery rate with few defaulters for medium- and long-term loans used for groundwater exploitation with tube wells and pump sets. There were weaknesses with some nonrecoveries of short-term loans, there was some ignorance of their availability in early years, and some were misutilized; but overall the ensuing expansion in loan volume led to a reduction of dependence of cultivators in this district on noninstitutional sources of credit. The performance of cooperative societies contributed greatly to the high rates of fertilizer use on HYVs as indicated above for basal N fertilizer.

The performance of cooperatives in supplying credit for the HYVP in other survey districts was much weaker. Many primary societies were defunct, many had high proportions of defaulters or were themselves defaulters to the Central Cooperative Bank and were denied credit as a result. Factionalism was often rife, leading to exclusions, favoritism, and low membership. Members complained of delays, inadequate loans, untimely disbursements, and difficulties with the terms of loans. Loans were misutilized, and there were problems with recoveries. Overall, it was generally the medium to large farmers who had access to funds in the active cooperative societies, and they often secured credit from several sources to the neglect and exclusion of small and marginal farmers. Thus in many districts, while the volume of credit rose over the years, it was still inadequate to cover the expanded needs. Typically it failed to meet the needs of small and marginal farmers in the short term to cover cash costs of cultivation, and for the medium and long term to meet necessary investment costs for land development and irrigation equipment. Their short-term needs could only be met from noninstitutional sources that were high priced and either discouraged these farmers from applying any chemical fertilizer or restricted them to low dosages. Lack of medium- and long-term financing excluded many small and marginal farmers from the benefits of more assured water. This left them dependent for their supplies either on canals or on large farmers who imposed high charges and often gave little assurance of timely supplies. Some small cultivators enjoyed access to state tube wells, but the performance of these tube wells over the period was frequently unsatisfactory, with high charges and limited distribution. Without assurance of adequate irrigation water, there was no incentive for small and marginal farmers to apply large dosages of chemical fertilizers.

Conclusions

Wheat. It is clear from the above analysis that much of the potential for output growth and income benefits has not as yet been realized from the new technology for wheat, and that while most cultivators in resource-favored areas have adopted it, participation is nominal, particularly among small and marginal farmers. The process of transfer and adaptation of this technology to the well-irrigated, high-fertility areas in India's northern wheat belt has been very rapid and successful. There has been a fast rate of adaptation of that physical environment to meet the favorable conditions demanded by the high-yielding varieties, and this has been achieved to a large degree by private initiative and capital. The real weakness is the limited degree of adaptation accomplished in the socioeconomic conditions or environment in which participant farmers operate. Among the relatively better-off farmers this has not been such a serious constraint. Some have been able to meet short- to long-term financial requirements from their own earnings and savings. This group, too, has had easiest access to credit sources, on the cheapest terms. The generally low levels of application of chemical fertilizer were indicative of a shortage of credit widespread throughout the wheat belt, affecting all but the affluent. However, it was the small and marginal farmer with no or little financial or asset backing who was most constrained.

The greatest source of disparity in the distribution of benefits from the new technology arises from the pattern of landownership. Removal of or lessening differences from this source requires land reform or tax and redistribution measures, as is widely recognized. Clearly, however, the problem of unequal distribution of benefits is exacerbated by the inadequate attention given to date to the task of institutional adaptation to enable more effective participation in the new technology by small and marginal farmers. On grounds both of tapping a further unexploited potential for growth in output and of spreading income benefits more widely, there are strong reasons for direct government intervention, focusing on this group of farmers. But it must be admitted that the task is difficult. It is tempting in this regard to cite the case of Ludhiana as one in which the process of institutional adaptation has been successfully accomplished and to suggest that the lessons learned there should be more widely applied. However, while they may well be appropriate to a degree, it should be borne in mind that this district was not typical of those in which the problems are most serious, as there were relatively few small and marginal farmers to contend with. The central problem is one of evolving policies and the institutional means for effectively ensuring the availability of inputs and credit to this large, often majority, group of farmers on reasonable terms.

The lesson of the first decade for wheat is that the interplay of the first two processes of adaptation, of both crop technology to the physical environment and vice versa, laid the basis for a fast rate of growth of output. The third process, that of the adaptation of the socioeconomic environment to the crop technology, which not only enables further growth but is the fine tuning that greatly influences the distribution of benefits, has lagged behind, to the detriment, in many areas, of the majority of cultivators.

In terms of Ruttan's (1977) generalizations mentioned earlier, the evidence corroborates the first point, that a rapid adoption rate for HYVs occurred under favorable technical and economic conditions, and the second, that farm size and tenure did not act as major constraints on the adoption of HYVs. But data on input use by size of farm, especially chemical fertilizer dosages, strongly point to differential rates of productivity growth in the majority of areas whose institutional and infastructural supports for small and marginal farmers were weak.

Rice. It is not possible in the limits of this paper to examine at length the experience of the HYVP for rice over the past decade. However, some observations are offered on the basis of PEO/ANU survey data within the analytical framework of technology transfer and adaptation used above for wheat.

It was pointed out early in the paper that the circumstances of international transfer of rice HYVs were similar in many respects to those of wheat. Initially, exotic Taiwanese varieties were introduced, soon followed by HYVs from the IRRI in the Philippines, and released to farmers under pressure of urgent food problems without adequate prerelease trials to test their suitability for local conditions. The significant difference from wheat was that local adaptive research for HYV rice had progressed little at the time the exotics were released. There was therefore a heavier and longer reliance on the imports directly released.

Experience with the exotics in the early years, in contrast to wheat, was disappointing. The Taiwanese introductions did not prove their high-yielding capacity in the field and gained little popularity. Problems included pest and disease susceptibility, threshing difficulties, and poor grain quality and taste. Their most important contribution was in the high-yielding potential subsequently used in crossbreeding with local varieties. The first IRRI variety, IR-8, performed better in the field but was also restricted by its duration, pest and disease susceptibility, and unfavorable market characteristics, so that yield performance and adoption of this variety were both limited. Again, though, this variety's high-yielding character contributed to the national varietal breeding program.

During the early years it was quickly recognized that, unlike wheat, homogeneity in rice-growing conditions does not extend far between seasons or geographically. There are two or even three growing seasons for rice in many areas, each with particular agroclimatic characteristics such as seasonal duration, water availability, and pest and disease incidence. Of these differing characteristics, the southwest monsoon season is the most important, and in that season conditions are highly variable across the country. Hopes that a single HYV or even a few could achieve the same rapid and widespread grower acceptance as for wheat were soon disappointed.

This was recognized early both internationally and nationally, and varietal breeding programs broadened in scope in an endeavor to develop new HYVs with characteristics to match the wide range of field conditions—for short and long seasonal duration, to incorporate pest and disease resistance, to withstand particular moisture conditions, and to improve the quality of grain by attending to consumer preferences in terms of taste, appearance, and cooking characteristics. In crossbreeding, use was made of local and local improved varieties while retaining the high-yielding characteristic. The well-known succession of IR varieties marked the international effort. The All India Coordinated Rice Improvement Project (AICRIP) became the national focus in India. This latter project has tested and released a considerable number of new varieties bred for a range of conditions. Some of these replaced IR varieties; others extended HYV area coverge into new areas.

Despite the considerable number of internationally and nationally bred HYVs of rice released in India, PEO/ANU surveys showed even in 1975 that grower participation and paddy area coverage with HYVs were still low in most areas. Survey districts, as for wheat, were from among those expected officially to participate actively because of their favorable resource endowment. Out of 27 blocks in that year, estimated HYV area coverage exceeded 33 percent of total paddy area in only 8 and it was below 20 percent in 12. HYV area coverage was much greater in the winter (rabi) season than summer monsoon (kharif) season but total paddy area in rabi is much less than in kharif. There were, however, a few areas in which HYV area coverage was notably high, such as Amritsar in Punjab, the 2 survey districts in Tamil Nadu, and West Godavari in Andhra Pradesh.

Application levels of chemical fertilizer were generally low in 1974–1973 for N fertilizers and even lower for P and K fertilizers. The price rise in 1974 subsequently caused a further reduction in these application levels. In all 3 years from 1972 to 1975 there were very large proportions of cultivators who used no chemical fertilizers at all, and these proportions rose in 1974–1975 after the price rise in 1974.

Nonparticipants in the new technology were heavily concentrated in the smallest holding size group (of 1 hectare or less) in most blocks, and a clear inverse relation existed between nonparticipation and holding size. Among participants, high proportions of those in the smallest holding size groups used no chemical fertilizers at all. Exceptions to these above patterns were few but included the 2 Tamil Nadu districts, especially Coimbatore and Amritsar in Punjab and West Godavari, where most or all cultivators in sample villages were participants. In Coimbatore, too, almost all participants regardless of size group used chemical fertilizers and at high-dosage levels.

Experience with the new technology for rice has shown the complexity of the process of adapting HYVs to local conditions in India. The most promising results have come most recently from decentralized varietal breeding work that takes account of seasonal and local combinations of agroclimatic and biological conditions for rice growing. However, even by 1975 there were few areas in which HYVs satisfied all the important environmental requirements.[12] Even with an expanded decentralized varietal crossbreeding program the process of developing suitable HYVs for the array of growing conditions in India will clearly be lengthy.

The primary constraint on the new technology for rice is in the area of adaptive research. In areas where this has been lifted with well-adapted HYVs, it has been succeeded by an environmental one, typically the inadequacies of the existing irrigation systems in meeting the greater demands of the HYVs. Availability of a controllable supply of water removed a major constraint on cultivation of HYV wheat in the relatively dry conditions of the northern Indian winter season. Similar conditions are not nearly so widespread in rice-growing areas. Water control is lacking in areas influenced by the southwest monsoon season. Large areas experience problems of flooding, deep standing water, and waterlogging. Many areas with a weak and uncertain monsoon influence, and where winter rice is grown, lack groundwater reserves to supplement rainfall. Also, as mentioned above, existing surface water storage systems have been found inadequate for the heavier demands of the HYVs.

The slow progress in developing suitable HYVs and the constraints of the physical environment explain the limited adoption of the new technology for rice by 1975. These factors serve notice that the task of achieving a consistently higher growth rate in rice output is more difficult than for wheat. Plant breeders may in time evolve HYVs that do not have the high demands for water of those currently released, but in their absence policymakers will have to strike a balance between reliance on adaptive research to evolve HYVs better adapted to local conditions in areas well endowed with resources and high-cost investments to expand the areas suited to these varieties.

The restricted area spread of the HYVs of rice has meant that only limited additional demands have been placed on institutional sources of inputs required for the new technology. But even so, survey evidence suggests that institutional capacity to serve the needs of the small and marginal rice farmer is weak, as it is for wheat, and thus the distribution of benefits from the new technology again favors the medium and large farmer. Therefore policy must also include institutional initiatives to take direct account of the needs of the disadvantaged farmers if further progress is to be made with the new technology in a distributional sense.

Notes

1. The politics of, and reorganization for, this change have been recently documented by its principal architect, C. Subramaniam (1979).

2. This paper is largely an extension of the analysis given in PEO/ANU (1976). However, the author alone is responsible for the interpretations given here.

3. See PEO/ANU (1976, Part II, p. 92).

4. Ibid., p. 100.

5. See ibid., p. 92, Table.

6. See, for example, Singh (1973).

7. The PEO/ANU surveys did not consider the impact of the new technology on the landless laborers as a group. However, the surveys did explore the impact of tenancy arrangements on the progress of the new technology. Since tenants were typically landless laborers and marginal farmers, one aspect of this important question was in fact explored. Survey evidence for three key districts indicated there was no negative influence of various contractual arrangements either on HYV adoption or on input levels applied to HYVs.

8. They are also the distribution patterns for all cultivators, except in 4 of the 6 blocks with nonparticipants who are concentrated in lower size groups.

9. This was calculated by multiplying the total HYV wheat area for each holding size group

by the proportion of participants who used fertilizer to obtain an estimate total of HYV area to which fertilizer was applied. This was then multiplied by the average dosage used by holding size groups. Percentage use by each group was then calculated.

10. Aggregated chemical fertilizer use (N, P, and K) showed a pattern of utilization by holding size groups for 1974–1975 that was almost identical with that shown for basal N fertilizer. The latter was used for ease of illustration.

11. Exactly how much would need to be calculated with reference to the wide range of agronomic and economic conditions encountered. The gap between actual and recommended dosages, for instance, is not an accurate guide.

12. In a recently completed study Kalirajan examined the outstanding success record of Coimbatore district in Tamil Nadu. He found that local adaptive plant breeding research had evolved location-specific HYVs for one of the two rice-growing seasons and that agroecological, institutional, and market conditions placed virtually no constraints and minimal risk upon producers. Under these conditions, the differences in HYVP performance between small and large farmers were insignificant, as claimed in Ruttan's third generalization. (See Kalirajan 1979.)

References

Kalirajan, K. 1979. *An Analysis of the Performance of the High Yielding Varieties Programme in Coimbatore District, Tamil Nadu.* Ph.D. diss. Canberra: Australian National University.

Programme Evaluation Organisation and the Australian National University. 1976. *The High Yielding Varieties Programme in India (1970–75), Part II.* New Delhi, India: Indian Planning Commission.

Ruttan, V. W. 1977. "The Green Revolution: Seven Generalizations." *International Development* 4:16–23.

Singh, K. 1973. "The Impact of New Agricultural Technology on Farm Income Distribution in the Aligarh District of Uttar Pradesh." *Indian Journal of Agricultural Economics* 28:1–11.

Subramaniam, C. 1979. *The New Strategy in Indian Agriculture.* Edited by R. T. Shand. New Delhi, India: Vikas Publishing House.

16

A Product-Characteristics Approach to Technical Change: With Application to Animal Breeding

G E O R G E   W.   L A D D

IN THIS CHAPTER the product-characteristics approach (Lancaster 1971; Ladd and Zober 1977; Ladd 1978) is applied to production inputs to study technical change. The area of technical change is a natural one for the application of the product-characteristics approach because technical change is often ascribed to improvements in quality of production inputs (Nadiri 1970; Kennedy and Thirlwall 1972; Peterson and Hayami 1977) and quality can be represented by measures of characteristics of the inputs. A consideration of problems facing plant and animal breeders will show that the production function, appropriately formulated and analyzed, provides a way of predicting effects of technical changes before they are made. These predictions provide a way of helping to determine which technical changes should be made.

Some Animal Breeding Concepts

Basic Population Genetics. This section presents just enough basics of population genetics to allow the reader to make sense of the later economic analysis. For a complete discussion, see Falconer (1960).

The work reported here was done in cooperation with P. J. Berger, A. E. Freeman, R. L. Willham, and L. L. Christian of the Iowa State University Animal Science Department. I am grateful to these men for the education, encouragement, and help they provided. The usual caveat is in order: These people are not responsible for the things they taught that I did not learn or learned incorrectly. I am also grateful to W. Huffman for checking the accuracy of my economic argument.

Financial support for this research was provided by the Iowa Agriculture and Home Economics Experiment Station through Project Nos. 1906 and 2369.

The many hereditary units (or genes) that determine the heredity of each living thing and influence its characteristics occur in pairs, one gene of each pair having come from the individual's mother and the other from the father. A parent passes to each offspring half of his (or her) genes, one gene at random from each pair. This chance division and recombination of many pairs of genes at each generation makes each individual unique. If both genes of a pair are the same for all individuals in a population, the population has no genetic variation in the trait affected by this pair. Only pairs of unlike genes contribute to genetic variation, which is a prerequisite to breeding programs. An individual's hereditary constitution is his (or her) genotype. The visible (or observable) characteristics are the individual's phenotypes, which result from genetic effects and environmental effects. Consider the pair of genes S (say for straight hair) and s (for curly or wavy hair). This pair of genes can result in three genotypes (SS, Ss or sS, and ss): the first letter in each pair identifies the gene from the father, the second, the gene from the mother. Commonly, but not universally, one gene of a pair (say S) is dominant and the other recessive. Then individuals having the pairs sS or Ss display the same phenotype as individuals having the pair SS. The genetic variation in a population results from differences in genotypes and the frequency of the three genotypes. The problem in breeding is that genes affect phenotypes in pairs but are transmitted singly from parent to offspring, and the single gene transmitted from each parent is randomly selected.

The forces that affect gene frequency are mutation, migration, selection, and chance division and recombination. Mutation or the sudden change of a gene provides new genetic variation and the material for evolution. Migration involves the introduction of genetically different individuals into a population. Selection, or the choice of parents in a breeding program, is the common element of all breeding programs because it is the primary directional force that breeders can use. In selection, superior individuals produce more offspring than inferior individuals. The basis of selection is the resemblance between parent and offspring. This resemblance results because each offspring receives half its genes from each parent and makes phenotypic expressions of traits predictable. When resemblance is high, selection of superior parents results in above-average offspring. The degree of resemblance for a trait is determined by the relative importance of gene effects and environmental effects in determining phenotypic variation and is referred to as heritability of the trait.

The questions, What's a better animal (or plant) worth? What makes an individual (animal or plant) worth more? What individuals should be used in a plant (or animal) improvement program? What traits should be improved? are faced regularly by plant and animal breeders. Answering these questions is complicated by some realities of genetics:

(1) Some pairs of traits have negative genetic correlations. Efforts to improve one desirable trait may degrade another desirable trait.

(2) An individual that is superior in some desirable traits may be inferior

in other desirable traits. An individual can even carry undesirable traits in its genes but give no sign of this, especially if the trait is inherited in a recessive manner.

(3) Breeders are concerned with effects of heredity. But effects of heredity are not observable. What is observed is the result of heredity and environment. (Breeders use the term "environment" to include all relevant factors other than heredity. Thus for animals it includes weather, buildings, rations, veterinary care, inter alia.)

(4) Some traits are more easily changed by breeding than other traits.

Consider point (3) first. An individual's characteristics are the result of heredity and environment. It is usually assumed that their effects are additive, and this can be expressed

$$p_{ij} = g_{ij} + e_{ij} \tag{16.1}$$

where p_{ij} = phenotypic (observable) value of trait i for animal j = value of phenotype i, g_{ij} = genotypic (unobservable) value of trait i for animal j = value of genotype j, and e_{ij} = environmental effect on trait i of animal j. Genotypic effect and environment are usually assumed to be independently distributed in the population of inference, and in this chapter we shall assume them to be independent. Thus, among other things,

$$\xi(g_{ij}e_{hk}) = 0 \quad \text{for all } i, j, h, k \tag{16.2}$$

and the mean of e_{ij} over all animals is zero

$$\xi(e_{ij}) = 0 \tag{16.3}$$

where ξ denotes expectation operator. Thus, for example, an animal's birth weight (p_{ij}) is the sum of the effects of heredity (g_{ij}) and of environment (e_{ij}), such as the mother's diet before and during pregnancy, shelter if any, and veterinary care provided during pregnancy.

Define $P, G,$ and E as $K \times n$ matrices of n phenotypes, genotypes, and environmental effects on K individuals. From equation (16.1), $P = G + E$ and the matrix of phenotypic variances and covariances is

$$P'P = (G + E)'(G + E) = G'G + E'E + 2E'G \tag{16.4}$$

To accomplish anything in breeding programs, breeders need to be able to partition the total phenotypic (observed) variance into its components. Assumption (16.2) is used to accomplish this for the population. Taking expectations of both sides of (16.4) yields

$$\xi(P'P) = \xi(G'G) + \xi(E'E) + 2\xi(E'G)$$

From (16.2) this can be written $\xi(P'P) = \xi(G'G) + \xi(E'E)$. The population's phenotypic variances and covariances are the sum of the population's genetic variances and covariances and environmental variances and covariances.

Obviously this is of limited practical use unless we have populations of data to work with. One thing that has struck me in working with animal breeders is that they are much more familiar with experimental designs than economists are. The reason derives partly from the importance of assumption (16.2) in their work. One of the objectives of their experimental designs is to achieve independence of E and G in each set of experimental data. Assuming they are successful, then

$$E'G = 0 \tag{16.5}$$

and (16.4) can be expressed

$$P'P = G'G + E'E \tag{16.6}$$

Thus experimental phenotypic variances and covariances are the sum of experimental genetic and environmental variances and covariances.

From phenotypic and genetic variances and covariances it is possible to compute phenotypic and genetic correlations. Phenotypic correlations are observed correlations among traits: correlations of phenotypes. Genetic correlations are correlations among genotypes.

Point (4)—some traits are more easily changed by breeding than others—is reflected in the breeders' use of heritabilities. The heritability of trait i, symbolized as h_i^2, is the portion of the trait's phenotypic variance in a population that is due to heredity

$$h_i^2 = \sigma_{g_i}^2 / \sigma_{p_i}^2 = \sigma_{g_i}^2 / \left(\sigma_{g_i}^2 + \sigma_{e_i}^2\right) \tag{16.7}$$

where $\sigma_{g_i}^2$, $\sigma_{p_i}^2$, and $\sigma_{e_i}^2$ are the genetic, phenotypic, and environmental components of variance of trait i. The term $1 - h_i^2$ is the proportion of a population's phenotypic variance that is due to environment.

Another basic concept is an individual's breeding value. For a single trait, the individual's breeding value can be defined as twice the difference between the average phenotype of the trait for a large number of the individual's progeny and the population average phenotype. The members of the other sex to whom the individual is mated must be a random sample of the population.

Genetic change is sometimes measured as genetic change per year, expressed as

$$\text{response}/\text{year} = \frac{\text{male response}/\text{generation} + \text{female response}/\text{generation}}{\text{male generation interval} + \text{female generation interval}}$$

Response per generation is the product of accuracy, intensity, and variation.

Accuracy is the correlation between the true and estimated breeding values of an individual. Accuracy depends upon heritability and upon the number of relatives (including progeny) used to estimate breeding value. Intensity is measured as the number of standard deviations that an individual's phenotype differs from the mean phenotype of the population. More intense selection means fewer animals saved or selected as parents. Variation is the genotypic standard deviation. If any one of accuracy, intensity, or variation is zero, response is zero. The generation interval is the age in years of the parents when the offspring destined to replace them are born. Accuracy and generation interval are antagonistic. Increasing accuracy by increasing the number of progeny tested lengthens the generation interval.

Selection Indexes. To select individuals to use in breed improvement programs, breeders need some basis for comparison of different individuals so that superior individuals can be selected. Genotypes, and not phenotypes, determine what an individual will pass on to its offspring. Animals have many traits. And it is more important to affect some traits than others. These three considerations—genotypes, multiplicity, and importance—are all incorporated into aggregate genotype or aggregate breeding value. Let v_j be the aggregate genotype for animal j. The definition of the animal's aggregate genotype is

$$v_j = \sum_{i=1}^{n} a_i g_{ij} \tag{16.8}$$

where a_i is the economic value (or weight) of trait i. A later section of this chapter concerns measurement of the a_i. For now, let us assume, as breeders do, that the a_i are known. Because the g_{ij} are unobservable, the value of v_j is unobservable. Thus the aggregate genotype, though an important concept, is not an operational one. The value of v_j can be estimated by use of a selection index. Smith (1936–1937) introduced the selection index into plant breeding as a measure for selecting plants for seed improvement programs. Hazel (1943) introduced it into animal breeding.

I will briefly summarize the classical approach of Hazel. The best single reference on selection indexes is Henderson (1963). Arboleda et al. (1976) provide a convenient summary and an application. The value of the selection index for animal j is I_j:

$$I_j = \sum_{i=1}^{n} b_i p_{ij} \tag{16.9}$$

where b_i is a weight whose value is to be determined. After values of b_i are determined, the value of I_j can be computed because the P_{ij} are observable. The individuals with the highest values of I_j can then be identified for use in breed improvement programs.

Assume we have data on K different animals and write their aggregate genotypes and selection indexes in vector-matrix form as

$$V = GA, \qquad I = P\beta \tag{16.10}$$

where $V = v_j$, a K-element column vector, and $I = I_j$, a K-element column vector. Assume temporarily that $m = n$. Then $G = g_{ij}$, a $K \times n$ matrix, $P = p_{ij}$, a $K \times n$ matrix, $A = a_i$, an n-element column vector, and $\beta = b_i$, an n-element column vector. It is desired that I be a good estimator or predictor of V. Write

$$V = I + \mu \tag{16.11}$$

where μ is a vector of errors. From (16.10) and (16.11),

$$GA = P\beta + \mu \tag{16.12}$$

where β is to be estimated. Write the estimated version of (16.12) as

$$GA = P\hat{\beta} + u \tag{16.13}$$

A plausible criterion for obtaining $\hat{\beta}$ is minimization of

$$u'u = \hat{\beta}'P'P\hat{\beta} - 2\hat{\beta}'P'GA + A'G'GA$$

The first-order condition for minimizing $u'u$ with respect to $\hat{\beta}$ is

$$(\partial u'/\partial \beta)u = 0 = 2P'P\hat{\beta} - 2P'GA \tag{16.14}$$

The second-order partials are $(\partial^2 u/\partial \beta^2)u = 2P'P$, where $P'P$ is an $n \times n$ matrix of phenotypic variances and covariances. It must, therefore, be at least positive semidefinite. It is usually positive definite, and will be assumed so here. The estimated value of β is, from (16.14), $\hat{\beta} = (P'P)^{-1}P'GA$. From (16.1), this can be written $\hat{\beta} = (P'P)^{-1}(G' + E')GA$. From (16.5), this yields

$$\hat{\beta} = (P'P)^{-1}G'GA \tag{16.15}$$

Thus, the estimated weights in the selection index are functions of phenotypic variances and covariances, genotypic variances and covariances, and economic values. As expression (16.7) shows, the ith diagonal element of $G'G$ equals the product of the ith trait's heritability and its phenotypic variance. The weights are, therefore, also affected by heritabilities.

It may be that $m < n$, as, for example, if few traits are included in aggregate breeding value and the additional traits that are correlated with the traits in the aggregate breeding value are included in the selection index. It may be that $m > n$, as, for example, if aggregate breeding value is affected by a large number of traits but only a few of these are included in the index. Assume $m = n + \alpha$ ($\alpha > 0$), and write $G = (G_n, G_\alpha)$ and $P = P_n$. Then,

$$\hat{\beta} = (P_n'P_n)^{-1} (G_n'G_n, G_n'G_\alpha) \begin{bmatrix} A_n \\ A_\alpha \end{bmatrix} \tag{16.16}$$

The difference between (16.15) and (16.16) is that in (16.15), $G'G$ is square but in (16.16), $G'G$ is not square.

Suppose G and P contain two traits that are phenotypically and genotypically uncorrelated. Let $\sigma_{p_i}^2$ and $\sigma_{g_i}^2$ be phenotypic and genotypic variances. Then

$$\begin{bmatrix} b_1 \\ b_2 \end{bmatrix} = \begin{bmatrix} \sigma_{p_1}^2 & 0 \\ 0 & \sigma_{p_2}^2 \end{bmatrix}^{-1} \begin{bmatrix} \sigma_{g_1}^2 & 0 \\ 0 & \sigma_{g_2}^2 \end{bmatrix} \begin{bmatrix} a_1 \\ a_2 \end{bmatrix} = \begin{bmatrix} h_1^2 a_1 \\ h_2^2 a_2 \end{bmatrix}$$

Heritabilities and economic values have equal importance in determining the weights in the selection index. If a_1 and $a_2 = 1$, b_1 and b_2 equal the heritabilities. If $h_1^2 = h_2^2$, the ratio of b_1 to b_2 equals the ratio of economic values.

Economic Values of Traits

Definition. To compute a selection index, a breeder needs measures of economic values of traits. The economic value of a trait has been defined as "the amount by which net profit may be expected to increase for each unit of improvement in that trait" (Hazel 1943). It must be said that the economic value for a trait should reflect the net profit expected to accrue to the livestock enterprise as the result of one unit of change in that trait alone. It should not include any net profit that will accrue to the livestock enterprise as the result of a change in correlated traits that may change as the initial trait changes, thereby causing net profits to accrue to the livestock enterprise indirectly (Hazel 1956).

Although breeders have been measuring and using economic values of traits for some 35–40 years, they have yet to receive help from economists in developing methods for measurement. (The reason may be that they have not asked for help.) This chapter presents one procedure for measuring economic values and presents an application of the procedure. The definition of economic value to be used is: the amount by which maximum profit per animal may be expected to increase for each unit of improvement in that trait in each animal. This definition suggests what needs to be done: determine maximum profit and then determine the effect on maximum profit of change in a trait. In determining this effect, no input price is allowed to change. (This is not the definition commonly used by animal breeders; it is, among other things, more precise.)

Derivation of Measure. This chapter measures economic value for a producer of slaughter animals. The firm's profit is expressed in a customary way as

$$\pi = p_0 q_0 - \sum_{i=1}^{n} p_i q_i - F$$

where p_0 and q_0 are price and quantity of output, p_i and q_i are price and quantity of ith variable input, and F is fixed costs. The production function might be termed an "interdisciplinary production function" because it contains the standard economic variables (quantities of inputs) and also contains items that economists usually treat as parameters, but breeders treat as variables: measures of traits of livestock. Let T_h be the measured value of the hth trait. Then

$$q_0 = f(q_1, q_2, \ldots, q_n, T_1, T_2, \ldots, T_m)$$

The purpose of measuring economic value is to determine the effect on profit of an improved livestock—livestock that is an improvement over livestock currently available. The values of T_h are, therefore, parameters to the firm. They represent characteristics of animals on hand or of animals available to the firm. (The values of T_h are, however, variables to breeders.) Now

$$\pi = P_0 f(q_1, q_2, \ldots, q_n, T_1, T_2, \ldots, T_m) - \sum_i p_i q_i - F \qquad (16.17)$$

Abbreviating the production function as f and letting $f_i = \partial f / \partial q_i$, the first-order conditions for maximum profit are

$$\partial \pi / \partial q_e = 0 = p_0 f_e - p_e \qquad (e = 1, 2, \ldots, n) \qquad (16.18)$$

The second-order condition is that the Hessian, H, be at least negative semi-definite, where

$$H = p_0 \begin{bmatrix} f_{11} & f_{12} & \cdots & f_{1n} \\ f_{21} & f_{22} & \cdots & f_{2n} \\ & & \vdots & \\ f_{n1} & f_{n2} & & f_{nn} \end{bmatrix} \qquad (16.19)$$

and $f_{ij} = (\partial^2 f / \partial q_i) \partial q_j$. The production function is assumed continuous so that H is symmetric. In the sequel, H is assumed to be negative definite.

Because the second-order conditions for a unique profit maximum are satisfied, equations in (16.18) have a solution for $q_1, q_2, \ldots, q_n$. These values can be substituted into (16.17) and the maximum level of profit can be thereby obtained. To obtain economic value of trait h, we must find, What happens to the levels of inputs, output, and maximum profit as the value of T_h is changed? Assume all prices and all traits but h remain constant, but T_h varies. To obtain the effect of variation in T_h, differentiate (16.18) with respect to T_h. Let $f_{eT_h} = \partial f_e / \partial T_h$. The result is

$$P_0 \sum_{j=1}^{n} f_{ej}(\partial q_j/\partial T_h) + p_0 f_{eT_h} = 0 \qquad (e = 1, 2, \ldots, n) \qquad (16.20)$$

Define dQ/dT_h and F_h as

$$dQ/dT_h = (\partial q_1/\partial T_h, \partial q_2/\partial T_h, \ldots, \partial q_n/\partial T_h)'$$
$$F_h = P_0(f_{1T_h}, f_{2T_h}, \ldots, f_{nT_h})'$$

The n expressions in (16.20) can be written as

$$H(dQ/dT_h) = -F_h \qquad (16.21)$$

Because H is negative definite, H^{-1} exists and

$$dQ/dT_h = -H^{-1}F_h \qquad (16.22)$$

This expression shows how the profit-maximizing levels of the various inputs change as T_h changes. The optimum level of output also changes. Its change is determined by the values of $\partial q_j/\partial T_h$ and by the nature of the production function,

$$\partial q_0/\partial T_h = \sum_{j=1}^{n} f_j(\partial q_j/\partial T_h) + \partial f/\partial T_h$$

Let $F = (f_1, f_2, \ldots, f_n)'$ and $f_{T_h} = \partial f/\partial T_h$; F is a vector of marginal physical products of inputs and f_{T_h} is the marginal physical product of trait h. Then $\partial q_0/\partial T_h = F'(dQ/dT_h) + f_{T_h}$. Finally, the effect on maximum profit of varying T_h is

$$\partial \pi/\partial T_h = p_0(\partial q_0/\partial T_h) - \sum_{i=1}^{n} p_i(\partial q_i/\partial T_h)$$

Define $P' = (p_1, p_2, \ldots, p_n)$; then

$$\partial \pi/\partial T_h = p_0 F'(dQ/dT_h) + p_0 f_{T_h} - P'(dQ/dT_h)$$

Because $P' = p_0 F'$ from (16.18),

$$\partial \pi/\partial T_h = p_0 f_{T_h} \qquad (16.23)$$

Thus, the analysis leads to a fairly simple result. If the firm is maximizing profit with existing levels of traits, and one trait changes and the firm adopts the improved variety of input and continues to maximize profit, the change in profit equals output price multiplied by the marginal physical product of the changed trait: the change in profit equals the value of the marginal product of the hth trait. I see a useful analogy between (16.18) and (16.23). In (16.18), value of the marginal product of the eth input equals price of the eth input: a parameter. In (16.23), value of the marginal product of the hth trait equals the change in profit from varying the hth trait: a variable. The change in profit in (16.23) is not quite economic value. Economic value reflects number of animals raised. Economic value, a_h, is obtained as

$$a_h = (\partial \pi / \partial T_h)/n_h \qquad (16.24)$$

where n_h is number of animals that are produced that undergo a change in trait h.

Up to this point it has been assumed that $\partial p_0 / \partial T_h = 0$, that is, varying trait h does not affect product price. But some traits do affect product price; backfat in swine is one. Suppose that variation in the hth trait affects the quality of the firm's product and hence affects p_0; therefore $\partial p_0 / \partial T_h \neq 0$. To obtain (16.22), values of q_j ($j \geq 1$) were allowed to vary in response to variation in T_h. Now, values of q_j and p_0 are allowed to vary. Define the vector F'_{h0} as

$$F'_{h0} = [p_0 f_{1T_h} + f_1(\partial p_0 / \partial T_h), \ldots, p_0 f_{nT_h} + f_n(\partial p_0 / \partial T_h)]$$

The results of taking the total differentials can now be expressed as

$$H(dQ/dT_h) = -F'_{h0} \qquad (16.25)$$

The solution for dQ/dT_h is (16.26) instead of (16.22):

$$dQ/dT_h = -H^{-1}F_{h0} \qquad (16.26)$$

The effect of dT_h on optimum level of output is

$$\partial q_0 / \partial T_h = F'(dQ/dT_h) + f_{T_h}$$

where dQ/dT_h comes from (16.26). The effect of varying T_h on the maximum level of profit is now

$$\partial \pi / \partial T_h = p_0 f_{T_h} + q_0(\partial p_0 / \partial T_h) \qquad (16.27)$$

Compare this with (16.23). For a given level of initial prices, if increasing T_h results in a higher-priced output, economic value is increased.

Effects of Parameter Changes. Variations in product and input prices affect economic values of traits. Let

$$dQ/dp_j = (\partial q_1/\partial p_j, \partial q_2/\partial p_j, \ldots, \partial q_n/\partial p_j)'$$
$$dQ/dp_0 = (\partial q_1/\partial p_0, \partial q_2/\partial p_0, \ldots, \partial q_n/\partial p_0)'$$

The effects of changes in p_j and p_0 on levels of inputs and output are

$$dQ/dp_j = H^{-1}e_j = H^j = j\text{th column of } H^{-1}, \qquad dQ/dp_0 = -H^{-1}F$$

and the effects of changes in p_j and p_0 on level of output are

$$\partial q_0/\partial p_j = F'(dQ/dp_j) = F'H^j, \qquad \partial q_0/\partial p_0 = F'(dQ/dp_0) = -F'H^{-1}F$$

To determine effect of a product price change on economic value, evaluate $\partial(\partial\pi/\partial T_h)/\partial p_0$. From (16.23), this can be written $\partial(\partial\pi/\partial T_h)/\partial p_0 = p_0(\partial f_{T_h}/\partial p_0) + f_{T_h}$. And

$$p_0\partial f_{T_h}/\partial p_0 = p_0 \sum_j (\partial f_{T_h}/\partial q_j)(\partial q_j/\partial p_0) = F_h'(dQ/dp_0) = -F_h'H^{-1}F$$

$$\partial(\partial\pi/\partial T_h)/\partial p_0 = -F_h'H^{-1}F + f_{T_h} \gtreqless 0 \tag{16.28}$$

An increase in product price may increase or reduce economic value of a trait. This is not so surprising as it may look at first.

A heuristic explanation is that economic value is a first derivative of the maximum profit function. The effect of a price change on economic value is obtained from the differential of this derivative of the profit function. The effect of variation in p_j is

$$\partial(\partial\pi/\partial T_h)/\partial p_j = F_h'(dQ/dp_j) = F_h'H^j \gtreqless 0 \tag{16.29}$$

An increase in an input price may increase or reduce economic value of a trait. Finally, the effect of variation in trait r upon the economic value of trait h is simply

$$\partial(\partial\pi/\partial T_h)/\partial T_r = -F_h'H^{-1}F_r \gtreqless 0 \tag{16.30}$$

Setting $r = h$ in (16.30) yields

$$\partial(\partial\pi/\partial T_h)/\partial T_h = -F_h'H^{-1}F_h > 0 \tag{16.31}$$

which gives the unexpected (at least unexpected to me) result that increases in the level of one trait raise the economic value of that trait.

Application of Measure. Equation (16.23) is here applied to a production function estimated by Melton et al. (1979). The data used to estimate the production function were obtained from steers in a crossbreeding experiment. Let q_0 = kg of retail product from one animal, q_1 = number of days on feed, T_1 = kg of average daily gain, and T_2 = kg of weaning weight. The production function is

$$q_0 = f(q_1, T_1, T_2) = -14.515 - 19.558T_1 + 0.486T_2 + 0.108q_1 + 20.909T_1^2$$
$$- 0.000224T_2^2 \; 0.00141q_1^2 + 0.279q_1T_1 - 0.000095q_1T_2 - 0.111T_1T_2$$

Let p_0 = \$2/kg, p_1 = \$0.50/day, T_1 = 0.785 kg, and T_2 = 193.8 kg.

$$\partial q_0/\partial q_1 = f_1 = 0.108 - 0.000282q_1 + 0.279(0.785) - 0.000095(193.8)$$
$$\partial \pi/\partial q_1 = 2 f_1 - 0.5$$
$$0.000564q_1 = 2(0.108 + 0.219015 - 0.018411) - 0.5$$
$$q_1 = 0.117208/0.000564 = 207.8 \text{ days} = 208 \text{ days}$$

In $f(q_1, T_1, T_2)$, set T_1 = 0.785, T_2 = 193.8, and q_1 = 208.

$\partial f/\partial T_1 = -19.558 + 41.818(0.785) + 0.279(208) - 0.111(193.8) = 49.78933$
$2(49.78933) = \$99.57 = \partial \pi/\partial T_1 =$ value of 1 kg average daily gain
$\partial f/\partial T_2 = 0.486 - 0.000448(193.8) - 0.000095(208) - 0.111(0.785) = 0.292283$
$\partial \pi/\partial T_2 = 2(0.292283) = \$0.58 =$ value of 1 kg weaning weight

Appropriate Measure of Traits. In my derivation, T_h was defined as size of the hth trait. But each trait has two measures: its phenotypic value and its genotypic value. My definition, purposely, avoided specifying which value is used. The reason was that the standard definition of economic value also fails to specify the measure of a trait. The definition simply concerns effect of variation in a trait.

The concept of economic value was introduced in the definition of aggregate genotype: equation (16.8). In this equation, the economic values are parameters; they are weights of the variables—genotypes. This suggests that T_h be the genotype of hth trait. Consider the total differential of (16.8),

$$dv_j = \sum_i a_i dg_{ij}$$

The question is: Should a_i equal $\partial \pi/\partial p_{ij}$ or $\partial \pi/\partial g_{ij}$? In the first case and second case, respectively,

$$dv_j = \sum_i (\partial \pi/\partial p_{ij})dg_{ij}, \qquad dv_j = \sum_i (\partial \pi/\partial g_{ij})dg_{ij}$$

The last expression for dv_j seems more reasonable than the preceding one. This argument leads to the conclusion that a_i should be derived from the partial derivation of maximum profit with respect to genotypes of trait i.

The use of genotypes for the T_h also seems correct on other grounds. Certainly, for a producer of slaughter animals, q_0 should be measured as a phenotype, e.g., total carcass weight or total liveweight. The production function then describes how the phenotype of total production is affected by traits and by levels of inputs used. Animals' responses to ration, shelter, veterinary care, implants, and other variable inputs are determined more by genotypes than by phenotypes. But genotypes are not observed. Only phenotypes are. This has implications for statistical estimation of the production function. What is desired is an estimate of $q_0 = f(q_1, q_2, \ldots, q_n, G_1, G_2, \ldots, G_m)$, but what is observed is not values of G_h (genotypes) but values of P_h (phenotypes). What is observed is not G_h, but G_h + environmental effects. An errors-in-variables model is appropriate for estimation of f. The environmental variances and covariances are the variances and covariances of the errors of measurement. Thus, it is appropriate to use an errors-in-variables model in which measurement-error variances and covariances are known. One such procedure was published by Warren et al. (1974).

Suppose T_h is the genotype of trait h, G_h. The effect on maximum profit of varying G_h by the amount dG_h is

$$d\pi = (\partial\pi/\partial G_h)dG_h = p_0 f_{G_h} dG_h$$

The effect on maximum profit of simultaneous variation in more than one trait is

$$d\pi = \sum_h (\partial\pi/\partial G_h)dG_h = p_0 \sum_h f_{G_h} dG_h$$

By analogy with (16.8) this might be termed differential aggregate breeding value.

Choosing to estimate the production function as $q_0 - f(q_1, q_2, \ldots, q_n, G_1, G_2, \ldots, G_m)$ raises two other issues. How useful is this estimated production function for a livestock-feeding enterprise? The genotypes of animals cannot be known to a manager of a livestock enterprise. Although breeders use appropriate experimental designs and assume E and G are distributed independently, and thereby justify taking a mean phenotype as an estimate of the mean genotype, it is likely that E and G will not be distributed independently in each herd or lot or litter of livestock and mean G will not equal mean P. Is it necessary to estimate $q_0 = f(q_1, q_2, \ldots, q_n, G_1, G_2, \ldots, G_m)$ by an errors-in-variables model to obtain economic values, and to estimate $q_0 = f'(q_1, q_2, \ldots, q_n, P_1, P_2, \ldots, P_m)$ by another procedure to obtain results to be used in managing a livestock-feeding enterprise?

The phenotype of total liveweight or total carcass weight is a less appropriate measure of output for a producer of breeding stock than some other measures, at least if the producer wants to stay in business. Breeders' customers will judge their products by reproductive performance and the performance of the offspring, which are determined by genotypes. A more appropriate measure of output for the breeder might be aggregate breeding value.

Applications

Prior Evaluation of Technological Effects. The thing that I find most exciting about the breeders' concept of economic values is their ex ante spirit: they are used to *predict* effects of various changes that can be, but have not yet been, made. They are used to construct selection indexes to identify the individuals that will be used in future breed improvement programs and to determine what genetic changes will be made in future programs to improve plants and livestock available to farmers. Economists have made many ex post analyses of historical technical changes. See Binswanger and Ruttan (1978) for recent studies and Peterson and Hayami (1977) for a long list of previous studies. Perhaps, by working with breeders, we economists can do more than simply try to understand the past; perhaps we can contribute to the future by helping breeders to become more effective. Johnston (1977) cites studies done at the IRRI showing that some yield-increasing innovations are frequently not profitable. They are, therefore, not adopted. Ex ante use of economic values may help to avoid misallocation of research resources to the development of innovations that will not be adopted.

The concept of economic value has other ex ante applications in addition to those in breeding. Economic values can be computed to predict microeconomic effects of any technical change that affects a characteristic of an input or of an output. Such predictions could be used in determining which machines, fertilizers, pesticides, or feeds to develop in the future. For example, Taylor et al. (1968) used parametric linear programming to determine the value of dehydrated alfalfa meal (dehy) in poultry feeds. They report that "parametric linear programming can help scientists evaluate the potentials of other research such as investigations of methods of altering the content of an ingredient."

The use of the procedures presented here is not limited to agriculture. If quantity of a firm's output depends upon number of hours some factory machine is used and upon characteristics of the machine, then hours of use and machine characteristics can be included in the production function. Economic values of machine characteristics can be used to measure effect upon profit of adopting a machine having a different combination of characteristics. This information can be used by machinery manufacturers to determine what modifications to make in machinery and can be used by buyers of the machinery to determine the maximum price they can afford to pay for a modified machine.

Three recent studies deal with the economics of technical adoption. Rhee and Westphal (1977) found that technical characteristics of looms affected the choice of new looms purchased by the Korean textile industry. Vaughan and Russell (1976) use a linear programming model of integrated iron and steel production to compare the economics of the basic oxygen furnace and open hearth capacity. Their purpose was to examine the rate of adoption of the basic oxygen furnace in order to test the accusation that the U.S. iron and steel industry had lagged in its adoption of basic oxygen furnaces. These two studies were ex post to development and ex post to adoption. They do suggest possibilities for studies that are ex ante to development and/or to adoption. Buck et al. (1978) write, "Potential users of new technology need to appraise composite economic effects in terms of investment and return cash flow streams with new technology compared to their current operations. Manufacturers of new technology must appraise their potential markets among these users for long range production planning, future research and development efforts and sales strategies. An economic evaluation of this type is described . . . for a new[ly available] technology in processing tomatoes." They use simulation to study effects of adoption of the new technology in various model plants.

Choosing among Existing Traits. The procedures presented previously for determining economic value of a trait are consistent with Hazel's definition. The measures presented are also appropriate for determining what price a firm can afford to pay for genetically improved animals.

Another question a firm may consider is, What quality of input should I use when I have several qualities available and their prices are related to their qualities? The difference between this problem and the problem formulated in measuring economic values is that now input traits are instruments along with input quantities. Suppose $T_1, T_2, \ldots, T_m$ are traits of input 1 and $\partial p_1/\partial T_h \neq 0$. The first-order conditions for profit maximization are (16.18) and (16.32)

$$\partial \pi/\partial T_h = 0 = p_0 f_{T_h} - q_1(\partial p_1/\partial T_h) \quad (h = 1, 2, \ldots, m) \quad (16.32)$$

The term $\partial p_1 \partial T_h$ is the hedonic (implicit) price of trait h; it is the marginal expenditure per animal on trait h. From (16.18), $p_0 f_e = p_e$: the value of the marginal product of input e equals the price of e. From (16.32), $p_0 f_{T_h} = q_1 (\partial p_1/\partial T_h)$: the value of the marginal product of trait h equals the marginal cost of trait h in all animals. Also, from (16.18) and (16.32), $f_e/f_j = p_e/p_j$ and $f_{T_h}/f_{T_j} = (\partial p_1/\partial T_h)/(\partial p_1/\partial T_j)$. At the profit-maximizing point, the ratio of marginal physical products of two inputs equals the ratio of their prices, and the ratio of marginal physical products of two traits equals the ratio of their implicit prices. Essentially the same conditions apply for the level of each trait as for the quantity of each input.

Effect of Input Price Change. The literature on technical change has contained some debate on the effect of changes in relative input prices on profitability of different innovations. We may cast some light on this by using previous results on effects of price changes on economic values. Suppose input 1 is livestock (say feeder cattle or pigs), input 2 is a ration, trait 1 is a livestock trait, and trait 2 is a ration characteristic, and variation in T_1 and T_2 have no effect on p_0. From (16.29), we have

$$\partial(\partial\pi/\partial T_1)/\partial p_1 = F_1'H^1 \gtrless 0$$
$$\partial(\partial\pi/T_2)/\partial p_1 = F_2'H^1 \gtrless 0$$

An increase in the price of a livestock input may raise or lower the profitability of a genetic change in livestock and increase or decrease the profitability of a technical innovation in a ration.

Macroeconomic Interpretation. The topic of this chapter is the microeconomics of technical change. But the derivation of economic value also has a macroeconomic interpretation if f is an industry production function and product price received depends upon amount produced. Suppose that $\partial p_0/\partial q_0 < 0$ but $\partial p_0/\partial T_h = 0$. The first-order conditions for profit maximization are now

$$\partial\pi/\partial q_e = 0 = p_0 + f(\partial p_0/\partial q_0)f_e - p_e$$

In expression (16.21), the element in row e and column j of H is

$$[p_0 + f(\partial p_0/\partial q_0)]f_{ej} + 2f_e f_j(\partial p_0/\partial q_0)$$

and the eth element of F_h is $[p_0 + f(\partial p_0/\partial q_0)]f_{eT_h} + 2f_e f_{T_h}(\partial p_0/\partial q_0)$. Now (16.23) is replaced by

$$\partial\pi/\partial T_h = [p_0 + q_0(\partial p_0/\partial q_0)]f_{T_h}, \qquad \partial\pi/\partial T_h = p_0(1 + 1/\eta) f_{T_h}$$

where η is price elasticity of demand.

Assume $f_{T_h} > 0$. Then, if $-1 < \eta < 0$, $\partial\pi/\partial T_h < 0$; if $\eta < -1$, $\partial\pi/\partial T_h > 0$. If the marginal physical product of trait h is positive, and demand is price inelastic, improvement in trait h, ceteris paribus, results in a reduction in profit. This, of course, is what people have been saying about agriculture for years: Because demand for farm products is price-inelastic, technical change in farming reduces net farm income.

Could a stochastic version of this be used to study rate of diffusion? If one had a frequency distribution of values of f_{T_h} over all firms and a demand function for the product, one could compute a frequency distribution of values of $\partial \pi / \partial T_h$. By relating profitability of adoption to rate of adoption it might be possible to determine rate of adoption. This could be used to determine effect of adoption on value of q_0. The demand function would show the resulting change in p_0, which could be used to compute a new frequency distribution of values of $\partial \pi / \partial T_h$ for the firms that had not yet adopted the innovation. In performing such an analysis one should probably incorporate the finding from a number of hedonic price studies that input prices are related to input characteristics, i.e., $\partial p_1 / \partial T_h \neq 0$.

Because the procedure developed previously provides measures of effect of variation in a trait on use of inputs—$\partial q_i / \partial T_h$—it may also provide a framework for studying effects of technical adoption on labor employment and income levels.

Optimal Breeding Program. An unspoken slogan of much of economics seems to be "Anything worth analyzing is worth optimizing." Suppose we accept that and we believe our economic values are correct and we want to develop an optimum breeding program. One possible objective is to maximize $\Sigma_h \, p_0 f_{T_h} dT_h - C = B$ where C is cost of a breeding program. Write existing values of traits as $\overline{T}_h$. Then

$$B = p_0 \sum_h f_{T_h}(T_h - \overline{T}_h) - C = p_0 \sum_h f_{T_h} T_h - C - K \qquad (16.33)$$

where constant $K = p_0 \Sigma_h f_{T_h} T_h$. Obviously we can, at least formally, manipulate the partial derivatives of B with respect to T_h to find first-order and second-order conditions for maximization. It seems to me that, without some constraints on the nature of the production function, this is not likely to be anything more than a formal exercise. The first-order conditions will contain the second-order partial derivatives $\partial^2 f / (\partial T_h \, \partial T_i)$. The second-order conditions will contain the third-order partials $\partial^3 f / (\partial T_h \partial T_h \partial T_i)$. The profit function approach to measurement of economic values would be useful here. (See Fuss and McFadden 1978, for a discussion of profit functions.) The first- and second-order conditions for maximization of B would involve the first- and second-order partial derivatives of the profit function.

Needed Extensions. Several relevant issues are not addressed in this chapter. One is variability (risk or uncertainty or both). Hazel's (1943) definition of economic value concerns "the amount by which net profit may be *expected* to increase" (italics added). One can reasonably argue that to be consistent with this definition, the correct measure of economic value should be the expected value of $\partial\pi/\partial T_h$ rather than $\partial\pi/T_h$ from (16.23). The previous discussion of appropriate measures of traits argued that genotypes of traits should be included in the production function. But genotypes are not known. At most we know their means and variances. A firm that is trying to determine the amount it can afford to pay for improved livestock or is trying to determine which breeder animals or lot of feeder animals to buy may want to consider variability. The expected value of $\partial\pi/\partial T_h$ and its variance are both relevant measures.

Carlson (1979) has used market price data to study the effect of variability. He used multiple regression to relate prices of semen of dairy sires to expected milk gain, an index of type, repeatability of milk gain, and repeatability of type. His measure of repeatability is a measure of the degree of uncertainty in the transmission of traits to offspring.

The economic value procedure presented here does not account for the cumulative effects that result if superior animals are purchased for breeding purposes. Their contribution to profit is different from the contribution made by superior animals used strictly for feeding. The breeding animals' contributions to profit come from their genetic contribution to future generations of animals, some of which will be marketed as slaughter animals and some will be retained for breeding.

Another issue is the kind of firm that should be studied in measuring economic values. Publicly supported animal breeders want their economic values to be average or typical or representative of a large number of firms.

The levels of some traits in some species can only be changed slowly because of low heritability, or long generation interval, or low genetic variation. Thus, a thorough evaluation of a breeding program must include provisions for discounting the future flow of earnings from improved animals and for discounting the future cost stream. Related to the discounting issue is the question of what prices to use. Certainly the relevant prices for improved animals produced in future years are input and output prices in those future years. A breeder cannot change the objectives of the breeding program every time prices change.

References

Arboleda, C. R., D. L. Harris, and A. W. Nordskog. 1976. "Efficiency of Selection in Layer-type Chickens by Using Supplementary Information on Feed Consumption. I. Selection Index Theory." *Theoretical and Applied Genetics* 48:67–73.

––––––. 1976. "Efficiency of Selection in Layer-type Chickens by Using Supplementary Information on Feed Consumption. II. Application to Net Income." *Theoretical and Applied Genetics* 48:75–83.

Binswanger, H. P., and V. W. Ruttan. 1978. *Induced Innovation: Technology, Institutions, and Development*. Baltimore: Johns Hopkins University Press.

Buck, J. R., G. H. Sullivan, and P. E. Nelson. 1978. "Operational Impacts and Economic Benefits of a New Processing Technology." *Engineering Economist* 23:71–92.

Carlson, G. A. 1979. "Variability and Market Indicators of Breeding Values." In *Applications of Economics in Plant and Animal Breeding,* Proceedings of symposium held at annual meeting of American Agricultural Economics Association, Pullman, Washington, July 29–August 1, 1979. Ames: Iowa State University, Department of Economics, Staff Paper no. 98.

Falconer, D. S. 1960. *Introduction to Quantitative Genetics.* New York: Ronald Press.

Fuss, M., and D. McFadden. 1978. *Production Economics: A Dual Approach to Theory and Applications,* vols. 1 and 2. Amsterdam: North-Holland.

Hazel, L. N. 1943. "Genetic Basis for Selection Indexes." *Genetics* 28:476–90.

_____. 1956. "Selection Indexes." Mimeographed. Ames: Iowa State University, Department of Animal Science.

Henderson, C. R. 1963. *Selection Index and Expected Genetic Advance.* Washington, D.C.: National Academy of Sciences, National Research Council Publication 982.

Johnston, B. F. 1977. "Food, Health, and Population in Development." *Journal of Economic Literature* 15:894.

Kennedy, C., and A. P. Thirlwall. 1972. "Surveys in Applied Economics: Technical Progress." *Economic Journal* 82:11–72.

Ladd, G. W. 1978. "Research on Product Characteristics: Models, Applications, and Measures." Ames: Iowa State University, Agriculture and Home Economics Experiment Station Research Bulletin 584.

Ladd, G. W., and M. Zober. 1977. "Model of Consumer Reaction to Product Characteristics." *Journal of Consumer Research* 14:89–101.

Lancaster, K. 1971. *Consumer Demand: A New Approach.* New York: Columbia University Press.

Melton, B. E., E. O. Heady, and R. A. Willham. 1979. "Estimation of Economic Values for Selection Indexes." *Animal Production* 28:279–86.

Nadiri, M. I. 1970. "Some Approaches to the Theory and Measurement of Total Factor Productivity: A Survey." *Journal of Economic Literature* 8:1137–77.

Peterson, W., and Y. Hayami. 1977. "Technical Change in Agriculture." In *A Survey of Agricultural Economics Literature,* vol. 1, edited by L. R. Martin. Minneapolis: University of Minnesota Press.

Rhee, Y. W., and L. E. Westphal. 1977. "A Micro, Econometric Investigation of Choice of Technology." *Journal of Development Economics* 4:205–37.

Smith, H. F. 1936–1937. "A Discriminant Function for Plant Selection." *Annals of Eugenics* 7:240–50.

Taylor, R. D., G. O. Kohler, K. H. Maddy, and R. V. Enochian. 1968. *Alfalfa Meal in Poultry Feeds . . . An Economic Evaluation Using Parametric Linear Programming.* Washington, D.C.: U.S.D.A. Economic Research Service, Agriculture Economics Report 130.

Vaughan, W. J., and C. S. Russell. 1976. "An Analysis of the Historical Choice among Technologies in the U.S. Steel Industry: Contributions from a Linear Programming Model." *Engineering Economist* 22:1–26.

Warren, R. D., J. K. White, and W. A. Fuller. 1974. "An Errors-in-Variables Analysis of Managerial Role Performance." *Journal of the American Statistical Association* 69:886–93.

17

The Economics of Gasohol

ROBERT N. WISNER

NEARLY FIFTY YEARS AGO, Geoffrey Shepherd and his co-workers at Iowa State College began an intensive research program on the use of grain alcohol as a motor fuel. Interest in this subject was generated by the depression, low grain prices, and a desire to develop new markets for surplus agricultural products. In addition, known U.S. petroleum reserves at that time were equivalent to only 12 to 14 years' utilization. Limited reserves created a strong interest in developing alternative fuels.

Interest in alcohol fuels in the 1930s resulted in efforts in several states and at the federal level to pass legislation encouraging its use. Additionally, a subsidized plant was constructed at Atchison, Kansas, to produce alcohol for motor fuel, although economic difficulties eventually forced alcohol production to be halted at that location (Shepherd et al. 1940b).

Shepherd's Findings. Important conclusions that emerged from the work of Shepherd and his colleagues included: (1) gasoline-alcohol blends are technically feasible as a motor fuel, (2) such blends would cost up to 2 or 3 cents more per gallon than regular gasoline under normal market conditions for petroleum products, corn, and protein feeds in the 1930s, (3) while large supplies of distillers' grains (a high-protein feed) would be generated with a fuel-alcohol program, rapid growth in U.S. protein markets should absorb such supplies without serious disruption, (4) alcohol could be viewed more as an antiknock agent than as a gasoline extender, (5) in a fuel-alcohol program, some means of ensuring stable corn supplies and prices to alcohol plants would be important, and (6) a 10 percent blend of alcohol with all U.S. gasoline would raise corn prices about 24 cents per bushel (from a base price of 50 cents per bushel). In a 1940 article, Shepherd and others noted the trend toward higher compression automobile engines and the need for antiknock compounds in gasoline to meet the requirements of such engines. Considering this trend, they concluded, "Subsidy or not, gasoline-alcohol blends promise to be coming over the motor fuel horizon before long" (Shepherd et al. 1940a). But heavy wartime demand for grain and low-cost production of tetraethyllead delayed this development.

Rebirth of Interest in Alcohol Fuels. Four decades later, after a Middle East petroleum export embargo, an unprecedented leap in world petroleum prices, declining U.S. oil output, and a political crisis in Iran, interest in fuel-alcohol programs has reached new heights. The product is being referred to as "gasohol" and is often presented to consumers as a way of reducing dependence on the OPEC cartel, while at the same time lessening the drain on the nation's balance of payments. Secondary benefits are said to include the production of a premium quality motor fuel with less tendency to cause engine knock and a reduction in certain types of exhaust emissions. Gasohol appeals to grain farmers as a way of developing new markets for their products and as a means of bringing farming closer to the self-sufficiency it once enjoyed.

Trade sources indicate gasohol, a blend of 10 percent ethyl alcohol and 90 percent gasoline, was being marketed in at least 36 states in mid-1980. The most extensive use appeared to be in Iowa, the nation's leading corn-producing state, where some reports indicate alcohol had replaced up to 1.3 percent of the gasoline sold at the retail level. As an incentive to produce gasohol, U.S. regulations have recently exempted gasoline-alcohol blends from the 4-cent-per-gallon federal motor fuel tax. The Crude Oil Windfall Profits Tax Act of 1980 provides for this exemption to remain in effect through December 31, 1992. Other incentives for the production of gasohol include federal loans and loan guarantees, investment tax credits of up to 20 percent, "entitlement" benefits for domestic energy production, and tax credits for blending of fuel-alcohol mixtures (Gross and Stoppelman 1980). In early 1980, sixteen states also were providing partial exemptions of state taxes on gasohol, with exemptions either on motor fuel or sales taxes. These exemptions ranged from 1.0 to 9.5 cents per gallon. States with such exemptions covered an area ranging fron New England to Arkansas to Montana (Notari et al. 1980).

Additionally, several other countries have become interested in gasohol, including Brazil, South Africa, Australia, Zimbabwe, and Austria. The most extensive program is in Brazil, where government policies are encouraging rapidly expanded gasohol production in an effort to completely eliminate petroleum imports. Brazil's program utilizes sugar rather than grain for alcohol production. The energy balance reportedly is more favorable when sugar is used as raw material for alcohol production than when corn is used as the feed stock. Additionally, world sugar supplies have exceeded consumption in recent years and Brazilian sugar prices are sharply below those in U.S. markets. These conditions provide substantially different economics for gasohol production in Brazil than in the United States. Brazil's 1979–1980 fuel-alcohol production is placed at 0.9 billion gallons, equivalent to 0.8 percent of recent U.S. gasoline consumption.[1]

Beyond the emotion of the gasohol issue lie several important economic facts and areas where further research is needed if rational U.S. policy decisions are to be made. Scores of publications on gasohol have appeared in the past five years, dealing with both technical and economic aspects of its production and use. The economic studies from most land grant universities confirm one of Geoffrey Shepherd's original conclusions: ethyl alcohol manufactured from grain is a more expensive fuel than gasoline even at mid-1980 petroleum prices (see Kendrick and Murray 1978; Klosterman et al. 1978; Litterman et al. 1978; and Schruben 1978). A key area where additional research is needed if gasohol is to become a realistic alternative fuel is the net energy balance—the Btus of energy obtained from alcohol relative to the Btus required to produce it. Even with major improvement in this area, there is a still more important question of whether future world grain supplies will be large enough to support a grain-based gasohol industry without substantial adjustments in U.S. and foreign food consumption patterns.

Costs of Gasohol Production. The cost of producing ethyl alcohol depends on the raw material used, the level of raw material prices, the size and type of processing plant, energy costs, and prices for the resulting by-products. Ethyl alcohol can be produced from grains, potatoes, molasses, crop residues, sugar beets, forest by-products, sugarcane, and sweet sorghum. Potential costs under mid-1980 conditions are shown in Tables 17.1 and 17.2 for large-scale

Table17.1. Estimated cost of alcohol production, mid-1980

Cost component	$/Gallon
Corn (at $2.50/bu)	$0.926
Variable processing cost, 1978 and early 1979 estimates[a]	.444
Adjustment for rise in fuel costs in late 1978 to mid-1980[b]	.289
Fixed costs[c]	.146
Total costs	$1.805
Less by-product feed credit ($150/ton)	− .510
Net alcohol costs (excluding transportation and distribution expenses)	$1.295

[a] Based on average of cost estimates from M. Litterman et al., *Economics of Gasohol,* Economic Report ER 78-10, Department of Agricultural and Applied Economics, University of Minnesota (St. Paul, Minn.), December 1978; W. E. Tyner and M. R. Okos, "Alcohol Production from Agricultural Products: Facts and Issues," *CES Paper 29,* Purdue University (West Lafayette, Ind.), January 1978; and Chemapec, Inc., *Industrial Alcohol by Continuous Fermentation and Vacuum Distillation with Low Energy Consumption—Chemapec T.E.R. Process* (Woodbury, N.Y.), March 1979, as cited in J. C. Converse et al., *Ethanol Production from Biomass with Emphasis on Corn,* University of Wisconsin (Madison, Wis.), September 1979.
[b] Based on energy requirements shown in M. Litterman et al.
[c] Average of median fixed costs reported by J. C. Converse et al.

Table 17.2.   Estimated cost of Iowa gasohol, mid-1980

Cost component	$/Gallon
$0.90/gal gasoline (before retail markup and 14¢/gal tax) × 90%	$0.810
$1.295/gal alcohol × 10%	.130
Total	$0.940
Plus assumed 15¢/gal for transportation and retail margin and 3% Iowa sales tax	.183
Approximate total cost/gal	$1.123

commercial fermentation plants using corn as a raw material and producing 200 proof ethyl alcohol. Corn is used here in cost calculations since most other U.S. crops would not be available in large enough supplies to support a nation-wide gasohol program.

Cost estimates in Table 17.1 are based on an alcohol yield of 2.7 gallons per bushel of corn[2] and 6.8 pounds of distillers' dried grains and solubles (DDGS) per gallon of alcohol or 18.4 pounds per bushel of corn. DDGS would be the main by-product in a large-scale fermentation plant; other less impor-tant by-products would be available although trade sources indicate their value would be quite low at quantities produced under a nationwide gasohol pro-gram (Trevis 1979).

With the corn and DDGS prices prevailing in mid-1980, these estimates indicated alcohol could be produced in large-scale plants at approximately 39 cents per gallon more than unleaded gasoline. Reported wholesale prices for ethyl alcohol at that time were approximately double those of gasoline as a result of marketing margins, strong demand for alcohol, and limited alcohol manufacturing capacity.

Table 17.2 illustrates estimated costs for gasohol in Iowa and other states with similar tax policies in mid-1980, after taking into account retail margins and the sales tax as well as the absence of state and federal motor fuel taxes. These cost components add up to an indicated retail cost of about $1.12 cents per gallon, 6 to 8 cents less than mid-1980 unleaded gasoline prices. The lower estimated cost for gasohol is due entirely to the absence of the 14-cent motor fuel tax included in retail gasoline prices. In actual practice, Iowa retail gasohol prices in mid-1980 tended to be at or slightly above unleaded gasoline. Thus, marketing margins probably have been greater for gasohol than for gasoline. From these calculations, it can be seen that future motor fuel tax policies will be a key influence on gasohol's competitiveness and the will-ingness of the motor fuel industry to utilize it.

How Volume of Alcohol Output Affects Costs. A large-scale, national gasohol program with corn as the main raw material would have two impor-tant effects on the cost of alcohol production. First, it almost certainly would cause a large increase in corn prices. Second, supplies of DDGS would rise very sharply above recent levels, thus tending to reduce DDGS prices and lower the by-product credit in alcohol production. Table 17.3 shows estimates

Table 17.3.   **Estimated alcohol production cost with $4.25 per bushel corn and $110 per ton DDGS**

Cost component[a]	$/Gallon
Corn (at $4.25/bu)	$1.574
Variable processing cost, 1978 and early 1979 estimates	.444
Adjustment for rise in fuel costs, late 1978 to mid-1980	.289
Fixed costs	.146
Total costs	$2.453
Less by-product feed credit ($110/ton)	−.374
Net alcohol costs (excluding transportation and distribution expenses)	$2.079

[a] Based on the same sources of fixed and variable costs indicated in Table 17.1.

of alcohol production costs if corn were priced at $4.25 per bushel and DDGS at $110 per ton. Prices such as these would be quite possible with a large-scale, national gasohol program. Under these market conditions and assuming no change in world petroleum prices, net alcohol production costs are estimated at approximately $2.08 per gallon.

In this case, alcohol costs are estimated at more than 2.3 times recent wholesale gasoline prices. However, with a continued absence of motor fuel taxes on gasohol, the product could be marketed at retail at approximately the same price as unleaded gasoline. Without tax breaks, gasohol would be priced moderately above unleaded gasoline and probably would not be competitive as a motor fuel.

Even in years of normal crop yields, a large-scale, national gasohol program would hold corn prices sharply above recent levels. That would likely cause a substantial decrease in domestic livestock feeding, with U.S. food prices tending to run considerably above late 1979 levels. In years of short crops, domestic livestock and poultry producers could face severe adjustments to reduced feed supplies with additional upward pressure on food prices.

Rising energy prices would alter the competitive position of gasohol only slightly since corn production expenses and fuel costs for distillation plants would increase as petroleum prices rise. For example, if wholesale gasoline prices were three times the level prevailing in mid-1980 and with the corn and by-product prices shown in Table 17.3, retail gasoline prices would be only about 3 cents per gallon above estimated gasohol costs—assuming current Iowa and U.S. motor fuel tax policies remain in effect. If motor fuel taxes were reinstated on gasohol, its estimated cost would be modestly above gasoline prices. Thus, current grain alcohol production cost estimates raise serious questions about the ability of gasohol to be fully competitive with gasoline in the foreseeable future without a subsidy.

These cost estimates are based on commercial plants producing 20 to 34 million gallons of 200 proof alcohol per year. Comparable estimates of production costs in small, on-farm distillation units are not available at this writing. However, if combined with a sizable livestock feeding operation, such units would provide an opportunity to feed distillers' grains without drying and with a resulting saving in cost and energy. In addition, some engineers believe on-farm production costs could be reduced by utilizing crop residues such as corn stalks and straw as energy sources for the distillation plant. Whether or not these aspects of on-farm alcohol production would more than offset potential economies of scale in commercial plants is uncertain.

Volume of Grain Needed for U.S. Gasohol Program. Approximately 110 billion gallons of gasoline were used in the United States in 1978. A nationwide gasohol program to replace 10 percent of all U.S. gasoline with grain alcohol would require 11 billion gallons of alcohol. If corn were the only feedstock used, annual corn requirements would be about 4.1 billion bushels or approximately 54 percent of the record 1979 crop. Alternatively, if 25 percent of the U.S. wheat, oat, barley, and grain sorghum crops (at 1979 production levels) were used for alcohol production, 3.23 billion bushels of corn or 43 percent of 1979 production would be required for a nationwide program. Table 17.4 shows estimated volume of various grains needed, assumed 200 proof alcohol yields per bushel, and billions of gallons of alcohol that would be produced under such a program. At late 1979 price levels, raw material costs of alcohol production from oats, barley, and wheat would be 56 cents, 21 cents, and 67 cents per gallon higher than corn, respectively. Raw material costs for producing alcohol from grain sorghum would be about 5 cents per gallon less than from corn.

As an indication of the potential impact on grain prices from a U.S. gasohol program of this size, the historical price elasticity of demand for corn would be expected to produce a doubling of corn prices. Such a price response is based on the assumption that other demands for corn and supplies of competing products remain constant. A doubling of corn prices would push the

Table 17.4. Estimated grain requirements and alcohol production under a U.S. gasohol program utilizing 25 percent of the U.S. wheat, barley, oat, and grain sorghum production, with remaining alcohol requirements produced from corn

Grain	Million bu required	Alcohol yield gal/bu[b]	Billion gal alcohol produced
Wheat	528.5	2.6	1.374
Grain sorghum	206.3	2.7	.577
Oats	132.8	1.05	.139
Barley	91.0	2.05	.187
Corn	3,230.0	2.7	8.723
Total	4,188.6		11.000

[a] Calculations are based on preliminary 1979 crop estimates from ESCS, USDA, *Crop Production* (Washington, D.C.), November 9, 1979, assuming all gasoline used in the United States is replaced with a blend of 10 percent ethyl alcohol–90 percent gasoline.

[b] Sources: Miller, D. C., *Fermentation Ethyl Alcohol*, USDA, Northern Regional Research Center (Peoria, Ill.), 1976; USDA, *Motor Fuels from Farm Products*, Miscellaneous Publication No. 327 (Washington, D.C.), December 1938.

U.S. average price received by farmers up to $4.70 per bushel, sharply above the 1976–1978 average of $2.12 per bushel.

Potential investors in gasohol plants and policymakers should also consider the growth in demand for corn experienced during the 1970s. This growth rate suggests a large-scale, corn-based, U.S. gasohol program would place severe pressures on the world livestock economy, with possible political implications. For example, U.S. domestic corn utilization and exports in the 1970–1971 marketing year totaled 4.5 billion bushels. Projections for 1979–1980 indicated total corn utilization would set a new record of 7.4 billion bushels, 64 percent higher than at the beginning of the decade (Economics, Statistics, and Cooperatives Services 1976, 1980).

With the phaseout of acreage setaside programs, most readily available U.S. cropland now is in production. Additionally, it should be noted that record grain utilization in the late 1970s has been sustained only through favorable weather and record U.S. corn yields. Most projections indicate the export demand for U.S. feed grains will continue to grow in the decade ahead, thus raising serious questions about the availability of large grain supplies for use in alcohol production.

Impact on Protein Feed Markets. After fermentation of corn in distillation plants, about one-third of the original weight is retained as DDGS. This by-product feed is a medium protein ingredient best suited for use in feeding of cattle and other ruminant animals. With a large-scale gasohol program, DDGS would likely become a substitute for soybean meal, urea, cottonseed meal, and other current sources of protein in livestock feeding. If produced under a large-scale, national gasohol program, supplies of DDGS would greatly exceed protein needs for U.S. ruminant feeding and would likely be used in hog and poultry production. Since high fiber content, limited digestibility, and amino acid composition are limiting factors in DDGS use for hog and poultry feeding, downward pressure on DDGS prices would almost certainly result.[3] Large exports of DDGS also would be expected to develop, with a tendency for such exports to replace soybean meal in foreign livestock rations.

With a national gasohol program, DDGS production could boost U.S. high-protein feed supplies by up to 95 percent from recent levels. Such an increase would place downward pressure on soybean and soybean meal prices in the short run, producing a moderate shift of midwest cropland from soybean to corn production. Acreage adjustments would temper but probably by no means completely remove upward pressure on corn prices.

An Alternative Alcohol Production Process. These conclusions assume most alcohol production would be in plants that ferment whole corn.

However, an alternative production process separates corn into starch, corn oil, corn gluten feed, and corn gluten meal. In this case, the starch is converted into alcohol and the main by-products are corn oil, corn gluten feed, and gluten meal. The process involves larger investment costs than whole-corn fermentation plants and appears to be unsuitable for small, on-farm production units. Commercial plants using this process would have greater flexibility than conventional fermentation plants, although estimates of differences in alcohol production costs are not available. With this technology, corn oil production under a nationwide gasohol program would increase total U.S. fat and vegetable oil output by up to 50 percent from recent levels. Protein meal production in soybean meal equivalent would be increased by 95 percent from 1978–1979 levels. Thus, downward pressure on both soybean oil and meal prices would likely result in the short run if this process is widely used.

Energy Balance in Alcohol Production. In addition to being aware of production costs and impacts on world grain and oilseed markets, government policymakers should note the energy balance in production of alcohol from grain. Published studies indicate energy requirements for producing alcohol from corn range from 1.54 to 2.44 times the Btus of energy obtained from alcohol itself (see Kendrick and Murray 1978; Klosterman et al. 1978; Litterman et al. 1978). If corncobs, stalks, and husks are utilized as a fuel source for fermentation plants and the energy value of the DDGS is included, the net energy balance in alcohol production may become slightly positive (Scheller and Mohr 1976). However, it is questionable whether the energy value of the DDGS should be used in such comparisons, since the by-product is not actually used to replace petroleum fuels. These data indicate that the use of petroleum or natural gas as an energy source in alcohol production would actually increase U.S. dependence on imported petroleum. If coal were used as the primary energy source, alcohol production could be viewed as a means of converting coal to a motor fuel. From an economic viewpoint, however, one should ask whether the conversion can be done at a lower cost by other means such as coal gasification or production of methyl alcohol from coal. Recent research indicates such alternatives may be more economical than production of grain alcohol (Anderson 1977). In addition, alcohol production from wood wastes and cellulose in crop residues, which is expected to become technically feasible soon, would not compete directly with food uses and might offer a lower-cost source of gasohol than grain (Miller 1979).

Potential Impact of Gasohol on U.S. Petroleum Imports. If the main purpose of a gasohol program is to reduce dependence on foreign petroleum, it is appropriate to examine the potential impact of such a program on crude oil imports. A U.S. Department of Agriculture analysis indicated gross savings of crude oil would have been 8.2 percent of the average daily U.S. imports during January–July 1978 if a 10 percent blend of alcohol had been used nationwide in all gasoline. If one-fourth of the U.S. gasoline consumption had involved such a blend, gross savings would have been equivalent to about 2.1 percent of average daily imports at the first half 1978 rate.[4] Net savings would have been substantially less and could have been negative if petroleum or natural gas had been used as the main fuel in distillation plants.

Recent research indicates energy requirements in corn production with conventional cropping methods would equal 26 percent of the energy available from the alcohol (Litterman et al. 1978, p. 29). Energy used in corn production and drying is largely derived from petroleum or petroleum substitutes and is utilized in herbicides, insecticides, fertilizer, and fuel. Using this estimate and assuming all fuels for distillation plants are from nonpetroleum sources, a grain-based gasohol program for one-fourth of the nation's gasoline would reduce U.S. petroleum imports by 1.55 percent if conventional corn production methods were utilized. A mandatory gasohol program for all U.S. gasoline would be expected to reduce imports by a maximum of 6.07 percent under these assumptions.[5]

Conclusions and Unanswered Questions. Ethyl alcohol currently is a more expensive motor fuel in the United States than gasoline. With a large-scale, national gasohol program utilizing grain as the primary raw material, production costs would increase further because of upward pressure on corn prices and downward pressure on prices of the main by-product, DDGS. Sharp increases in petroleum prices also would raise the cost of producing alcohol by increasing the expenditures for energy in fermentation plants and corn production. With these sources of upward pressure on alcohol production costs, it is questionable whether gasohol can be competitive with gasoline in the years immediately ahead without a continuing subsidy.

Even more important from a public policy standpoint is the question of whether large surplus grain supplies will be available over the next fifteen to twenty-five years for conversion into motor fuel. The rapid growth of world grain demand during the 1970s, world population trends, and continued concern over world food security should not be taken lightly in policy decisions about gasohol. It should be recognized that commercial alcohol production plants have a potential operating life of at least twenty to twenty-five years with few alternative uses. If large investments are made in U.S. grain alcohol production facilities, major adjustments in the U.S. and world livestock industries almost certainly will follow. Additional severe pressures on U.S. livestock producers would likely develop in years of short crops. Such adjustments would be expected to generate upward pressure on food prices beyond increases from the general rate of inflation. With chronic food short-ages already present in parts of the world, a large-scale U.S. gasohol program also could contribute to increased political instability in developing nations.

Unanswered questions about gasohol include (1) the potential for an im-proved energy balance in alcohol production through new technology, (2) the costs and energy requirements for grain alcohol production in small, on-farm facilities, (3) the costs of producing alcohol from cellulose in crop and forest product residues, and (4) the quantity of forest product wastes and crop residues realistically available for alcohol production. With a growing world demand for grain, gasohol production from crop residues and other waste materials appears to offer greater potential than grain alcohol in meeting U.S. energy needs.

Notes

1. Based on a Reuters news wire report, May 5, 1980, quoting Brazilian government statistics.
2. An alcohol yield of 2.7 gallons per bushel is commonly used in published literature although some sources indicate actual yields of 200 proof alcohol may be 2.5 to 2.6 gallons per bushel.
3. Potential effects on DDGS prices are examined in Wisner and Gidel (1977).
4. Statement by Secretary Bob Bergland before the Committee on Science and Technology, Subcommittee on Energy Development and Applications, U.S. House of Representatives, "Production on Fuel-Grade Ethanol from Grain," Washington, D.C., May 4, 1979, p. 1.
5. Trade officials indicate a gasohol program could reduce petroleum imports slightly more than shown here by blending low-octane with alcohol, thus using the alcohol as a means of upgrading the final product to an acceptable octane rating. Production of low-octane gasoline would reduce energy requirements in the petroleum-refining industry slightly below current levels.

References

Anderson, C. J. 1977. *Biosolar Synfuels for Transportation*. Berkeley, Calif.: Univer-sity of California Laurence Livermore Laboratory.
Economics, Statistics and Cooperatives Services. 1976, 1980. *Feed Situation*. November 1976 and May 1980. Washington, D.C.: USDA.
Gross, E., and J. S. Stoppelman. 1980. "Gasohol: Loans, Guarantees and Tax Incen-tives." *Feedstuffs*. June 9. Minneapolis: Miller.
Kendrick, J. G., and P. J. Murray. 1978. *Grain Alcohol in Motor Fuels, An Evalua-tion*. Lincoln, Nebr.: University of Nebraska Department of Agricultural Economics, Agricultural Experiment Station Report No. 81.
Klosterman, H. J., et al. 1978. *Production and Use of Grain Alcohol as a Motor Fuel: An Evaluation*. Bismarck, N.D.: Report on the 44th North Dakota Legislative Assembly's Senate Concurrent Resolution No. 4035.
Litterman, M., V. Eidman, and H. Jensen. 1978. *Economics of Gasohol*. St. Paul, Minn.: Department of Agriculture and Applied Economics Economic Report ER 78-10.
Miller, D. L. 1979. "Energy from the Farm." *1980 Agricultural Outlook, Papers Presented at the U.S. Department of Agriculture, National Outlook Conference*, Washington, D.C., November 5-8. Committee Print, 96th Congress, 1st session, Washington, D.C., December 23, 1979, pp. 123-29.

Notari, P., et al. 1980. *Fuel from Farms: A Guide to Small Scale Ethanol Production.* Golden, Colo.: Solar Energy Research Institute, SERI/SP-451-519, UC-61, P.A.-7.

Scheller, W. A., and B. J. Mohr. 1976. "Net Energy Analysis of Ethanol Production." Paper presented at 171st National Meeting of the American Chemical Society, Division of Fuel Chemistry, New York, April 7.

Schruben, L. W. 1978. "Evaluation of Kansas Senate Bills 591 and 592 as Relates to Agricultural Ethyl Alcohol as a Motor Fuel." Manhattan: Kansas State University.

Shepherd, G., W. K. McPherson, L. T. Brown, and R. M. Hixon. 1940a. "Alcohol Gasoline." *Iowa Farm Economist,* February, pp. 7–10.

_____. 1940b. "Power Alcohol from Farm Products: Its Chemistry, Engineering and Economics." *Contributions from Iowa Corn Research Institute* 1:283–375. Ames: Iowa Agricultural Experiment Station.

Trevis, J. 1979. "Gasohol May Offer Energy Relief, Corn Crop Problems." *Feedstuffs.* November 12. Minneapolis: Miller.

Wisner, R. N., and J. O. Gidel. 1977. "Economic Aspects of Gasoline-Alcohol Fuel Blends, with Emphasis on By-Product Feed Markets." Ames: Iowa State University Department of Economics Economic Report Series No. 9.

18

The Quality of Water: Problems, Identification and Improvement

JOHN F. TIMMONS

WITHIN THE NEXT two or three decades, water problems in the United States, particularly in the Western Region, may well constitute a greater crisis than does energy today.[1] The major difference between water and energy crises is there are no known physical substitutes for water in satisfying direct needs of people, but there are many known substitutes for petroleum in producing energy. This probably means we must learn how to live with our current water supply endowments through managing water in terms of its use, development, and conservation.

Similarities between the present energy crisis and the expected water crisis emphasize increasing scarcities and increasing costs. Water is a necessity of life and constitutes an essential resource in most economic activities. Thus, increasing costs and scarcities of water are likely to bring profound effects upon economic progress affecting production, employment, income distribution, investment, and debt retirement in affected regions.

Since approximately three-fourths of the world's area is covered with water, augmented by moisture fall and aquifers on and under the remaining one-fourth of the earth's surface, what is the basis for future concerns about water?

This paper was presented at the symposium "Western Water Resources: Coming Problem and Policy Alternatives," Denver, Colorado. This symposium was sponsored by the Federal Reserve Bank of Kansas City and was held on September 27, 1969. Research results cited in this paper were developed in Iowa Agriculture and Home Economics Experiment Station project 2247 and Iowa State Water Resources Research Institute Project 425-40-03-09-2247.

My colleagues in Economics and Civil Engineering, particularly Neil Harl, John Miranowski, and Ronald Rossmiller, have contributed much toward the development of ideas and clarity of communication within the paper. However, I alone must assume full responsibility for all that is said and all that is left unsaid in the paper.

One answer was implied in the words of Coleridge's Ancient Mariner who, while dying from thirst, lamented, "Water, water, everywhere, nor any drop to drink." This answer concerns water quality. The Ancient Mariner was served well by the transportation service of the ocean water that carried his ship, but the same water did not possess the quality to quench his thirst.

Irving Fox reminds us, "In the minds of many people, the existing and potential degradation of water quality is our foremost water problem" (see Anderson et al. 1977, p. 32). This problem is magnified by the many and increasing uses for water and their vastly different water quality requirements. The solution to water quality problems rests with water quality management. This solution provides the opportunity for avoiding the expected water crisis in the future.

Limited to discussion of water quality, this paper strives to describe the nature of water quality problems, to investigate possible means for identifying water quality requirements for uses of water, and to consider how water supplies may be managed in meeting future water quality demand requirements.

Origins and Nature of Water Quality Problems. Traditionally, water (as well as air and soil) has been used to assimilate, dilute, and recycle the residual wastes of human activity. But there are limits to the capacity of water to assimilate, dilute, and recycle all of our garbage. Currently, these limits are being violated by technologies and practices associated with production, fabrication, distribution, and consumption of materials.

Presently, our use of technology affecting water quality is exceeding our ability to manage the quality of water. As an example, an estimated 30,000 chemical compounds are in use today, with an estimated 1,000 new chemical substances created each year (*Minnesota Volunteer* 1979, p. 9). Most of these substances have been developed and put into use without adequate provision for their effects upon water quality. These are only examples of some of the substances and materials that may affect water quality.

Historically, natural resource scarcity has been interpreted in measures of quantities of resources, such as gallons of water, depth of soil, or barrels of oil. Increasingly, however, we are realizing that scarcity of water and other resources is largely a function of quality. This realization is part of a much larger syndrome developing in our culture that holds qualities are, within limits, more important than mere quantities.

The total quantity of water, for example, may be abundant or even superfluous, but we may not have available sufficient water of a particular quality to satisfy a particular use-demand. The water may be too salty—as was the case with the Ancient Mariner—or too hot or too toxic for a particular use. As a consequence, a use process may be made more costly, a use may be diminished, or a use may be precluded entirely because requisite quality is lacking, even though there is an abundant quantity of water in the aggregate.

As state and national governments proceed to take action in water quality management, costs of quality improvement are likely to meet resistance from many of the same people who previously supported quality enhancement efforts. As costs of pollution controls press on producers, as prices of products reflecting pollution control costs press on consumers, as pollution control taxes press on taxpayers, and as pollution control measures restrict individual freedom in resource use, voluntary support and enthusiasm for water quality improvement may well diminish.

Such resistance may thwart quality improvement unless facts are ascertained and made available to people regarding (1) proposed water quality standards, (2) costs of achieving these standards, (3) benefits from quality improvements, (4) incidences of costs and benefits in terms of who pays them and who receives them in both short and long terms, and (5) the nature and effects of antipollution regulations and controls upon individual freedom and choice (U.S. Environmental Protection Agency 1978).

These issues will be and are being decided in legislative, executive, and judicial processes of government. However, under our form of government, support for and enforcement of these decisions rest with the general citizenry. Their support and compliance in turn depend upon how well citizens are informed regarding these very important yet very complicated issues. How well people are informed, in turn, depends upon availability of relevant information and how well this knowledge is made available to citizens.

As a citizen, I am deeply concerned about the deterioration of our water quality. At the same time, I am optimistic concerning our ability to produce the facts and analyses needed in developing remedial policies and programs. Such policies and programs should seek to improve the quality of our water and, concomitantly, to engender widespread understanding and acceptance by diversely affected groups of people. This is not an easy task.

In our attempt to comprehend and interpret water quality as a major public policy goal, in relation to other public goals, three difficult but strategic questions arise and demand answers.

First, what are the measures of water quality that can serve as policy and program goals and at the same time engender widespread and continuing public understanding and support? Here I am thinking about the general nature of standards and targets for water similar to those needed in defining and achieving such goals as economic growth, full employment, income distribution, and inflation control.

Second, what are the costs, both monetized and nonmonetized, of achieving and failing to achieve specified standards of water quality?

Third, who pays the costs, and who receives the benefits, with and without achievement of standards of water quality?

Answers to these questions are difficult, but I believe they are essential in developing policy and programs in water quality management. In pursuing answers to these questions, it becomes apparent that the nature and level of standards are directly related to the nature and magnitude of costs. The nature of costs, in turn, determines their incidence, that is, on whom the costs will fall. The nature, magnitude, and incidence of costs affect the determination of quality standards and their achievement. In answering these questions, possible trade-offs and side effects with respect to other national goals, including production, full employment, inflation control, and income distribution, will be revealed (Committee on Science and Technology and Committee on Agriculture 1979).

Water Quality Variability. The quantity theory of water emphasized in and perpetuated through the various doctrines of water rights, with few exceptions,[2] has tended to ignore variations in water quality and to treat all water alike. However, instead of being homogeneous, water is extremely heterogeneous in terms of its properties, its technologically permitted uses, and its economically demanded uses.

It becomes helpful, at least from an economic viewpoint, to regard water as differentiated in kinds and grades, determined by its quality (Ackerman and Lof 1959). Thus, supply and demand functions of water are each regarded as consisting of numerous quality-oriented segments, each segment characterized by relatively homogeneous quality.

Quality Variations in Water Supplies. Water occurs in three distinct forms: solid, liquid, and gas. Most substances contract when frozen, but water expands. Water possesses a very high heat capacity and surface tension. It dissolves many compounds, which thereafter remain in solution. Thus, water has been called the "universal solvent."

The character of water has been further complicated by the discovery of three isotopes for both hydrogen and oxygen that form thirty-three different substances.

In addition to its indigenous characteristics, water serves as a vehicle of transport for many exogenous materials that become introduced into water through natural as well as human actions. Suspended silt from soil erosion is one of these materials that through adsorption and absorption serves as a transport agent for numerous residues from fertilizers, pesticides, and other compounds.

Thus, various water sources and supply segments possess different properties that must be analyzed in terms of the uses to be made from the water.

Quality Variations in Water Demands. Various demands for water require different water properties and vary in their tolerance of particular properties. For example, living cells may require the presence of certain minerals in water, whereas battery cells may not tolerate the same minerals. Even organisms vary in their mineral requirements and toleration of minerals. Quality of water must necessarily be viewed in terms of a particular use if quality is to be manageable. Different qualities are required (or tolerated) for animal consumption, navigation, power, irrigation, food processing, air conditioning, recreation, manufacturing, and other uses of water. Even within each of these major categories, demands are specialized. Within manufacturing, for example, beer, aluminum, paper, and synthetic fiber production each possesses important quality differentiations.

Water quality suited for one use may be absolutely unsuited for another use. Thus, it appears there is little, if any, relevancy for a universal water quality standard. Instead, quality standards should be developed in relation to specific uses to be made of particular water supplies at particular points or periods of time in the process of satisfying specific human wants. Such differentiations will likely extend to segments of the same water source, be it a stream, lake, or aquifer. In other words, the quality mix of a particular water supply must be analyzed in terms of uses to which it is put (Timmons 1974).

Projections for water demands are basic and necessary in providing essential elements of a normative and predictive framework for planning and carrying out water policy. However, these projections should not be considered as aggregates. On the contrary, they must be disaggregated into segmented quality differentiations derived from relevant use-demand requirements (Ackerman and Lof 1959).

Included as demand by uses are qualities by amounts of water demanded. Also included are the spatial and temporal occurrences of quality-linked supplies available for serving quality-linked amounts to the estimated demands. Finally, the cost dimension is involved in terms of least-cost alternatives for gearing (bringing or keeping) supply qualities to demand qualities.

Identification of Water Quality Demand Requirements. Qualities of water may be affected by human use or they may be produced in the natural state. One set of qualities within a natural supply of water may satisfy a particular use but may preclude another use. Furthermore, one use of water may leave a residue or effluent within the water it has used, diminishing or precluding another use, which increases the cost of subsequent use of the same water.

This would constitute water pollution, which is a supply related concept. In economic terms, water pollution means a change in a characteristic(s) of a particular water supply such that additional costs, either monetized or nonmonetized, must be borne by the next use and the next user, either through diminishing or precluding the next use or through forcing the next use to absorb more costs in cleaning up the residue left by the initial use or to develop a new source of water supply.

Externalities and Water Quality. One user of water may be in a position to retain the benefits from use while shifting costs to other users by lowering water quality. If that user had to bear the shifted costs, the motivation would be to use the water in a manner consistent with quality demanded by other users.

On the other hand, a user of water may be in such a position that if an outlay is made to maintain or improve water quality, the benefits from the outlay that shift to other users could not be captured by the user. If such benefits could be captured, the user would be motivated to make outlays that would maintain or improve the quality of the water after it leaves that use. Such terms as "side effects," "spillovers," "fallout," or "free-rider" have been applied to such shifts of costs and benefits.

For example, a nuclear reactor in power generation uses water to disperse heat. If the increase in temperature adversely affects another use, say fish reproduction and growth, this effect is an externality of the power plant—in this case, an external diseconomy. We call it thermal pollution. On the other hand, if the effect of heat dispersion by the power plant is to warm up the water so that the water is more useful for swimming, another externality would be created constituting an external economy since the next use would be favorably affected.

Although the situation of external economies is important, the problem of external diseconomies appears far more important in water quality management. For example, wastes from manufacturing or from chemical fertilizers, pesticides, and livestock moving into streams, lakes, or aquifers may foreclose other uses entirely or make other uses more expensive to undertake. Or they may endanger the life and health of human beings.

Kneese concludes that "a society that allows waste dischargers to neglect the offsite costs of waste disposal will not only devote too few resources to the treatment of waste but will also produce too much waste in view of the damage it causes" (Kneese 1964, p. 43).

Water Quality Criteria. What does this reasoning have to do with developing quality standards for water? It suggests two necessary criteria: the next use test and the test of reversibility.

The first criterion, the next use test, holds that undesirable quality changes (or pollution) occur when the effluent or effect of an initial use adversely affects the next use to which the water may be put in meeting needs of people, i.e., quenching thirst, swimming, fabricating aluminum, etc. If there are no adverse effects on any next use(s), then there is no cause for concern and no particular need for setting a quality standard. There are no costs shifted to another use.

On the other hand, if the initial use creates adverse effects (external diseconomies), monetized or nonmonetized, on the next use(s), then the quality standard should reflect the costs, monetized or nonmonetized, for the next use as well as benefits gained in the initial use.

This approach constitutes the basis for the "next use" model for deriving and testing environmental quality standards and has been applied in several of our recent Iowa studies on water quality. (See Seay 1970; Jacobs 1972; Jacobs and Timmons 1974; and Webb 1977.)

The second criterion, that of reversibility, means that a use of water should not result in an irreversible state of quality.[3] This criterion appears desirable in formulating quality standards in order to retain options for water use that may not be apparent at the moment but that may become viable through future technological developments and increases in demand. If irreversibility of water quality is permitted, certain future use options may become foreclosed.

Through application of these two criteria, two deductions may be made that possess important implications for policy and programs.

First, only irreversible criteria may be used as the basis for universal water quality standards.

Second, the next use criterion means that quality standards will vary from area to area, from time to time, and from use to use, depending upon the actual and potential existence and requirements of other (next) uses. The latter deduction appears most likely to constitute a major concern for developing water quality standards for policy and programs.

Application of Water Quality Criteria. To illustrate application of the next use model to developing and costing environmental quality standards, let us take an example from a study in the Nishnabotna River basin of Western Iowa (see Seay 1970).

Present use of resources for agricultural production in this basin delivers an estimated 10,600 milligrams of suspended sediment per liter of water annually to the river channel.[4]

Next, let us introduce additional uses of water in the stream in the form of municipal demands for potable water, a warm water fish habitat, and contact recreation (i.e., skiing and swimming), which would tolerate only an estimated 150, 75, and 37.5 mg/L of suspended sediment, respectively.

Let us first assume that the two previously stated criteria, when applied in this basin, reveal that soil and water resources used by agriculture are kept within reversible limits and that no other (next) use of the water is adversely affected by agricultural use. It would follow, then, that the optimum use of the basin resources for agricultural purposes is also optimum for the area, state, and nation insofar as the suspended sediment load of the watercourse is concerned. In other words, there are no external diseconomies generated by agricultural use.

Through application of parametric linear programming to the quality constraint of suspended sediment per liter, the annual direct costs to agriculture within the basin in meeting the quality standards for the three specified next uses were estimated (in 1970 dollars) at $9.59, $9.66, and $9.74 million, respectively. This would translate into an average annual cost of around $2,400 per farm operating unit in the watershed.

In another study, effects on net farm income caused by direct outlays and reduced income (opportunity costs) from complying with these specific water quality standards ranged from estimates of $1,200 to $14,000 (in 1977 dollars) per farm per year, depending upon factor costs including energy costs, product prices, technologies applied, delivery ratios, and other variables (Webb 1977).

Since the watercourse also serves as a possible transport agent for residues from the pesticides, fertilizers, and feedlots that are found in the basin, the above method could be used to generate quality standards with their associated costs for each type or combination of types of pollutants found in the water and in or on suspended silt in relation to quality demands for next uses.

Similarly, this method of analysis could be extended to analyze air quality standards within an airshed where silt by itself, or other pollutants for which silt serves as a transport agent, are found. If additional quality standards were established for these other pollutants in air and water other than the suspended silt actually used in the above studies, the pollution control costs to farm operating units would be increased proportionately.

This method demonstrates a procedure for developing quality standards, along with the costs of achieving the standards. Furthermore, the analysis helps test water quality standards for next uses as to whether or not pollution control measures are worth the costs. In the process, "trade-offs" between uses and levels of pollution control could be developed.

Let us now turn our attention to possible answers to the question, Who pays the costs and who receives the benefits, with and without achievement of standards of water quality?

Continuing with our river basin analysis, let us examine who might be expected to pay the costs if the next use were contact recreation, carrying the most stringent quality requirement (37.5 mg/L sediment), which would cost the watershed's agriculture an estimated $9.74 million annually (in 1970 dollars), averaging about $2,400 per farm operating unit annually (Seay 1970).

There are several possible groups on whom these costs might fall, including initial use (farm operating units), next uses (contact recreation, fishing propagation, municipal water supply), consumers of products and/or services produced by initial use and/or next uses, taxpayers, and combinations of groups.

Frequently, the assertion is made that the polluter—in this case the initial use, agriculture—should bear all the costs of farm operations, including any externally imposed costs on other uses. However, if there were not other (next) uses and if the soil and water resources remained within the reversible range, there would be no costs assignable against the initial use (or any other use) since no water quality standards would be violated. In this instance, the watercourse with its 10,500 mg/L suspended silt load might be performing a beneficial use in diluting, disintegrating, and recycling residues of the initial use.

Also, it is usually assumed that increased costs to a firm resulting from pollution abatement would be passed to consumers in the form of higher prices for the products.[5] However, for the agricultural entrepreneur, this option is not available since farm firms tend to be price takers, not price makers, operating as they do in the most nearly perfectly competitive of all real world markets.

Ultimately, however, higher costs of production caused by pollution control measures unaccompanied by product price increases would tend to force farmers, presumably marginal farmers, out of farming. Eventually, production would tend to decrease, which would in turn tend to be accompanied by increases in product prices indirectly reflecting pollution control costs.

If pollution control measures result in reductions in the use of pesticides, fertilizers, and other production-increasing technologies, yields per acre and yields per labor hour would presumably decrease, causing increasing per unit output costs that would most likely be reflected in reduced production followed by increased prices to consumers.

Such consequences of setting and enforcing pollution control measures could be expected to result in reverberations beyond agriculture and the consumer. For example, industries providing technological inputs in the form of fertilizers and pesticides would be affected. Also, agricultural exports from the United States could be reduced, affecting the terms of trade between the United States and other nations.

It should be noted that if one state legislated pollution control costs on its producers of a product that was also produced in other states wherein producers were not encumbered with such costs, the state with the legislation would discriminate against its own producers and tend to benefit producers in other states in terms of net income.

Quality Measurement Problems. Along with externalities, measurement is a crucial problem in water quality management. Traditionally, water has not been allocated through the market system as have most other factors, products, and services. Certainly, water quality is not reflected in market values to an appreciable extent. Judging from the changing size of national, state, municipal, and other governmental budgets, an increasing share of the nation's resources is allocated through institutional rather than through pricing processes. This creates problems in resource management but these problems are not unfamiliar to the resource economist and are not outside the science of economics.

Professor Gaffney has expressed relevant views on this problem:

> Economics, contrary to common usage, begins with the postulate that
> man is the measure of all things. Direct damage to human health and hap-
> piness is more directly "economic" therefore, than damage to property,
> which is simply an intermediate means to health and happiness . . . money
> is but one of many means to ends, as well as a useful measure of value.
> . . . "Economic damage" therefore includes damage to human functions
> and pleasures. The economist tries to weigh these direct effects of people
> in the same balance with other costs and benefits [Gaffney 1962].

There exist four major alternatives for dealing with the measurement
problems in water quality management: to expand and create market
mechanisms for differential water pricing by qualities or grades; to develop institutional pricing through synthesized market prices and costs as weights
assignable to water grades or qualities; legal action through legislation and/or
executive order with a public welfare basis; and combinations of these three
alternatives.

**Achieving Water Quality Supplies to Satisfy Demand Quality Require-
ments.** According to Irving Fox, "The institutional structure bearing upon
water quality preservation and enhancement, although varying somewhat
from State to State, may be briefly characterized as follows . . ." (Fox 1970),
and I will paraphrase his characterizations.

First, persons damaged by water pollution may seek redress in the courts
under common-law procedures. Second, states may establish waste discharge
regulations either through effluent standards or stream standards, with federal
government approval of standards for interstate waterways. (In addition, actions by state departments of environmental quality and the federal Environmental Protection Agency and other governmental pollution control agencies
may set and enforce water quality standards.) Third, tax incentives may be
provided by state and federal governments to encourage reduction in waste
discharges. Fourth, grants and loans from federal and state agencies may aid
in construction of waste treatment facilities. Fifth, organized groups representing a wide array of interests may influence formal decision makers.

A decade ago, Fox concluded from his examination of the institutional
structure for water quality management "it would appear that a basic deficiency in the institutional structure for water quality management is that it fails to
illuminate (a) the technical opportunities for improving quality in the most
economical fashion and (b) the alternative arrangements for distributing costs
and returns so that a basis for agreeing upon an appropriate pattern will be
available for consideration. In addition it seems questionable, at least, that the
decision-making machinery operates with dispatch and efficiency; the im-

plementing arrangements, for the most part, are incapable of operating integrated regional plans, and feedback mechanisms are of limited effectiveness" (Fox 1970, p. 34).

More recently, Anderson et al. have attacked regulatory forms of quality determination and enforcement.

> Direct regulation, relying heavily upon centralized standard setting and enforcement, is vulnerable to inefficiency, enforcement difficulties and unpenalized delay. As Ward Elliott has remarked, "direct regulation is geared to the pace of the slowest and the strength of the weakest." The shortsightedness of current programs suggests beginning a search for programs which emphasize more than end-of-pipe controls, capital-intensive solutions brought about by massive subsidies, and technical standard setting for a variety of sources of environmental harm by large federal and state bureaucracies [Anderson et al. 1977, p. 9].

Looking to the future, there exist several approaches to managing water quality supplies in satisfying water demand quality requirements. Returning to the reasoning developed in discussing the next use concept, there are five options implicit in the concept as follows:

First, the polluter (first user) assumes full cost of external diseconomies generated, thus motivating the polluter to reduce pollution.

Second, the polluter (first user) shifts water use to other sources (or other technologies) from which external diseconomies causing pollution do not arise.

Third, the next user assumes costs of the polluter's external diseconomies and proceeds to clean up the water quality to the level required by the use demand.

Fourth, the next user shifts water use to another source that remains unpolluted (or to other technologies) in terms of the next user's quality demand requirement.

Fifth, the polluter (first user) and the next user(s) join efforts and share costs in improving the water quality to the level required by the next user's demand quality.

Traditionally, the third option has been followed, that is, the next user of water assumes the costs of the polluter's external diseconomies and proceeds to clean up the water to the quality level satisfying the next user's quality demand. This has meant that the polluter (first user) has used water uneconomically, all users considered, since the polluter did not pay the full cost for water pollution. It has also meant that the next user had to pay an additional cost increment that was probably passed to consumers of the product, depending upon market conditions.

From an economic viewpoint, the first option possesses certain advantages—that is, the first user, the polluter, might bear full cost for use of the water in maintaining a level of quality that meets the needs of the next user. Economists have been giving this option attention for many years. For more than a decade, Kneese and others have been concerned with effluent charges geared to the achievement of water incentives (see Kneese 1964).

Recently, economists have teamed up with lawyers to develop means for environmental quality management relying heavily upon economic incentives.

According to Anderson et al. (1977, p. 2), "In this strategy, a legislature authorizes a money charge on environmentally harmful conduct; by raising the costs of continuing that conduct, the charge helps persuade the entity causing the harm to adopt less costly, more environmentally acceptable means of achieving its goals. Charges could be used in this way to combat a great variety of environmental problems."

These charges provide economic disincentives to pollute. The authors point out that charges in pollution control have long been associated with water quality enhancement proposals and action in European countries and the United States. Applied specifically to water, these charges fall into the following categories: "effluent charges intended to cause sources to reduce their discharges enough so that legislatively set water quality goals would be achieved," "use of charge revenues to finance quality standards or other goals," and "charges in conjunction with effluent standards" (Anderson et al. 1977, p. 1).

Although the charges approach to water quality achievement have been used in Czechoslovakia, the Ruhr valley in West Germany, East Germany, Hungary, and other countries throughout the past decade, the United States remains in the proposal stage. Under two recent proposals, known as Meta System and Bower-Kneese, the Federal Water Pollution Control Act's 1983 standards would be replaced with effluent charges (Anderson et al. 1977, p. 66). The Meta System is designed to achieve the same level of ambient quality as would the 1983 standards, but using a charge mechanism. The latter system (Bower-Kneese) is intended to establish the principle of polluters paying for their use of public resources and to provide incentives to enhance abatement levels after achievement of the 1977 standards (Anderson et al. 1977, pp. 66–67).

Summary. In managing quality-linked supplies of water, three important questions arise. These pertain to measures of water quality consistent with water quality demands and with other goals of the economy, costs of achieving and failing to achieve specified levels of water quality, and who pays the costs and who receives the benefits of water quality enhancement.

Historically, polluters have been able to shift the cost of pollution to other, subsequent users of water. This behavior has resulted in serious deterioration of water quality and misallocation of resources. Current water quality enhancement policies and programs have concentrated on the establishment and enforcement of quality standards. These procedures have brought only limited success.

Current proposals would create economic incentives to improve water quality and economic disincentives to pollute water through a system of charges levied on polluters commensurate with the costs of water quality enhancement. These approaches have been used successfully in several European countries and they warrant testing in the United States.

Notes

1. As the senior federal administrator charged with responsibility in the area of resource management, then Secretary of the Interior Cecil Andrus expected this water crisis to occur. See *Minnesota Volunteer* (1979, p. 4).

2. Under the riparian doctrine of water rights, the flow of water past the premises of the riparian continues unchanged in quality as well as undiminished or unaugmented in quantity.

3. Irreversible state of quality refers to the economic, not necessarily to the physical, condition of water.

4. Of course, the annual amount and density of suspended sediment does not represent the amount and density at any particular time. The actual amount at any particular time may be more or less than the level tolerated by environmental standards. However, in the absence of available data refined to time application, the annual estimate was used throughout the study as a proxy for more refined data. As more refined data become available, they may be substituted for these proxies.

5. This assumption depends upon supply and demand conditions for particular products in terms of price elasticity of product demand.

References

Ackerman, E., and G. Lof. 1959. *Technology in American Water Development.* Baltimore: Johns Hopkins University Press.

Anderson, F. R., A. U. Kneese, P. D. Reed, S. Taylor, and R. B. Stevenson. 1977. *Environmental Improvement through Economic Incentives.* Resources for the Future. Baltimore: Johns Hopkins University Press.

Committee on Science and Technology and Committee on Agriculture. 1979. "Agricultural Environmental Relationships: Issues and Priorities." U.S. House of Representatives, 96th Congress, 1st Session. Washington, D.C.: U.S. Government Printing Office.

Fox, I. K. 1970. "Promising Areas for Research on Institutional Design for Water Resources Management." In *Implementation of Regional Research in Water-Related Problems,* edited by Dean T. Massey. Madison: University of Wisconsin, Department of Law, University Extension.

Gaffney, M. 1962. "Comparison of Market Pricing and Other Means of Allocating Water Resources." In *Water Law and Policy in the Southeast.* Athens: University of Georgia, Institute of Law and Government.

Jacobs, J. J. 1972. "Economics of Water Quality Management: Exemplified by Specific Pollutants in Agricultural Runoff." Ph.D. diss. Ames: Iowa State University.

Jacobs, J. J., and J. F. Timmons. 1974. "An Economic Analysis of Land Use Practices to Control Water Quality." *American Journal of Agricultural Economics* 56:791-98.

Kneese, A. V. 1964. *The Economics of Regional Water Quality Management.* Baltimore: Johns Hopkins University Press.

Minnesota Volunteer. 1979. "Water Awareness 1979." St. Paul: State of Minnesota Department of Natural Resources.

Seay, E. E., Jr. 1970. "Minimizing Abatement Costs of Water Pollutants: A Parametric Linear Programming Approach." Ph.D. diss. Ames: Iowa State University.

Timmons, J. F. 1974. "Identification and Achievement of Environmental Quality Levels in Managing the Use of Natural Resources." In *Economics and Decision Making for Environmental Quality,* Chapter 10, edited by Richard Conner and Edna Loehman. Gainesville: Florida University Press.

Timmons, J. F. and M. D. Dougal. 1968. "Economics of Water Quality Management." *Proceedings of the International Conference on Water for Peace,* vol. 6. Washington, D.C.: U.S. Government Printing Office.

U.S. Environmental Protection Agency. 1978. "Alternative Policies for Controlling Nonpoint Agricultural Sources of Water Pollution." Athens, Ga.: Environmental Research Laboratory, Socioeconomic Environmental Studies Series.

Webb, D. K. 1977. "Energy, Environment and Agricultural Production Interrelationships: A Parametric Linear Programming Case Study in the Nishnabotna River Basin." M.S. thesis. Ames: Iowa State University.

IV

Markets and Economic Development

19

Crises and Structural Change in the Developing Agroindustrial Complex

RICHARD H. DAY

THE DEVELOPMENT of world agriculture involves among other things increasing productivity of labor and land, displacement of farm workers, a shift in the production of farm inputs to the industrial sector, a decline in the economic viability of traditional sources of livelihood, and migration of rural workers to urban areas. These developments lead to a host of adjustment problems in both rural and urban areas, such as unemployment, lagging development of infrastructure in the urbanizing parts of the economy, and low income with poor nutrition, and in extreme cases starvation, on a substantial scale. How is this massive transformation to be understood and how are the concomitant problems to be solved?

Economists often analyze such issues using the well-developed apparatus of neoclassical economics based on ideas of individual optimality, supply-demand equilibrium, and social (Pareto) efficiency. In this paper the complementary approach, called adaptive or behavioral economics, is considered, which looks at precisely those aspects of real world experience from which the standard economic theory abstracts, namely, limitations in human cognition, supply-demand disequilibrium, and social or Pareto inefficiencies and disimprovements.

From the vantage point of this alternative approach, agriculture is seen as a dynamic process that endogenously generates irregular fluctuations and switches in technosocial regimes or phases. In extreme cases phase switches stimulate creative morphogenesis—the invention of new technologies and

This paper was originally presented to the International Agricultural Economics Association Meeting, September 1979, and published in G. L. Johnson (ed.), *Rural Change: The Challenge for Agricultural Economists,* Westmead: Gower Publishing Co., 1981. It was written at the Institute for Advanced Study, Princeton, when the author was a member for the 1978–79 academic year. It has been revised for this publication.

economic organizations that can restore viability and mediate disequilibrium transactions under newly evolving circumstances.

These ideas suggest a new perspective on the emerging worldwide agroindustrial complex. A growing crisis is seen in the current trends in population, energy utilization, and food production—a crisis whose magnitude, duration, and inception cannot be predicted but whose inevitability and significance can now, on the basis of recent experience, be safely assumed. Averting of extreme dislocation will require energetic technical and socioeconomic innovation.

Agricultural Development: The Agroindustrial Complex. For millenia after the emergence of agriculture the connection between agriculture and population was direct. Most people dwelled on farms or in farming villages, producing food primarily for their own consumption. A crucial surplus did make possible the emergence of a few urban centers. As civilization advanced, cities of considerable size emerged. Technology gradually improved, and agriculture expanded so that the surplus could continue to support the increasing nonagricultural population. Still, it is only in the last few centuries that development has accelerated to such an extent that some parts of the world are now primarily urban and industrial. In our own time, indeed during the last two decades, those parts of the world still dominated by agriculture have just commenced this great transformation. As a result cities teem with hundreds of thousands of rural immigrants where only backward villages stood a few years ago.

All of this means that much of what is produced by the people who remain in agriculture is sent away from the countryside. The connection between food production, processing, and consumption is no longer direct.

The improvements in agriculture that underlie the urban transformation have, in part, been indigenous. Improved plant and animal breeds and more effective rotations provide examples of such indigenous technological changes. Many improvements, however, have required investments in capital that can only come from the industrial sector. The use of internal combustion engines to replace humans, bullocks, and horses provides one prime example. This substitution released land for human food production on the one hand; it drastically reduced farm labor requirements on the other hand. Tractorization therefore stimulated the rural-urban flow and augmented the supply of food to feed the expanding urban masses.

Another example of the substitution of industrially produced goods for farm-produced inputs is the use of synthesized nutrients. This has made possible the productive use of land that is otherwise infertile and has augmented still more the productivity of already fertile land.

Such developments amount to an *indirect industrialization of agriculture,* that is, the production of inputs by the nonfarm economy to be used for the production of food on farms. It contrasts sharply with the direct industrialization of the production of food, which, though already begun and growing in importance, is not yet having the impact its indirect counterpart has had or is having.

This indirect industrialization not only involves increasing farm productivity and rural-urban migration, but also involves an additional critical characteristic, namely, the substitution of fossil fuel for solar energy in food production. This is partly because petroleum and its derivatives are used for the commercial production of both fuel and fertilizer. It is also because industrial production of machinery and of other nonfarm inputs makes heavy demands on nonsolar forms of energy. As a consequence, the Green Revolution has created an agroindustrial complex, with a corollary the dependence of the nutritional well-being of the world's population on the supply of petroleum and other exhaustible resources.

The progress of this development, when viewed from an astronomical time scale, is explosive. Along a time axis stretching from the origin of the earth to the solar heat death, trends in population, output, productivity, and fossil fuel consumption appear as spikes. From a historical perspective, however, looking back let us say to the origins of civilization, the trends appear as geometrically growing curves.

As we focus our attention on the contemporary scene, however, the epochal transition becomes less apparent. It tends to recede within a variegated pattern of differential response. In some countries where the process has scarcely begun, agriculture is seemingly stuck in ancient patterns. In others where it is under way, some regions proceed at a faster pace than others. Elsewhere the transformation is more or less complete.

In mature and fully modernized economies the dramatic changes seem to be like the classic "cobweb" phenomenon: rising and falling prices, falling and rising supplies, recurrent problems of income and employment. But in underdeveloped areas widespread famines break out from time to time on such a scale as to exhaust world resources for disaster relief, bringing human suffering to catastrophic levels. In the former setting of classic price, income, and trade policy, economists often urge the movement of resources out of the surplus-producing, unstable regions. In contrast, in the latter setting the effort is to move resources *into* agriculture so as to expand the production of food, thereby raising per capita nutritional levels and providing an increase in the well-being of rural dwellers.

The Neoclassical Interpretation. Our picture of the growing and fluctuating agroindustrial complex is a dynamic one. It is one of uneven, unbalanced growth, of rapid technological change, of the transformation of ways of life, and of periods of fluctuating fortunes for the producers and consumers of food. This is not the place to survey all the methods of economic analysis that can be brought to bear on understanding this complex picture. But to illustrate why a new perspective is needed I must discuss briefly the core feature of basic economic analysis concepts.

First of all, economic individuals are defined as those who have stationary preferences. Second, firms are defined that have stationary technologies. Third, individuals and firms are assumed to maximize preferences and profits, respectively, given prices. Fourth, economic equilibrium is defined for transactions among individuals and firms; thus the demand for commodities must not exceed the supply. Therefore, although economic exchanges are decentralized, they must be perfectly coordinated by the price system. Fifth, social equilibrium is said to prevail when, at equilibrium prices, each individual and each firm maximizes its goal, and no individual or firm can improve its situation without diminishing the situation of at least one other. Two problems are then analyzed within this framework: the existence of equilibria and the way such equilibria change when parameters of the system change. The latter type of comparative statics lies at the heart of much, if not most, policy analysis.

To have a useful correspondence with the real world such an approach to policy evaluation must rest on two critical assumptions. First, the *real* disequilibrium system must work in such a way as to bring equilibrium about. Second, the transition period of disequilibrium must not be so long and so full of problems as to matter in any significant way. If these two assumptions are fulfilled, then it is not necessary to understand the nature of disequilibrium nor is it necessary to design particular policies to cope with its implications.

Are the basic assumptions of neoclassical economics a good approximation of economic reality? According to casual observation and careful scientific experimentation as well, the answer is, probably not. We know of course—and the point has been emphasized throughout this volume—that standard economic theory nonetheless possesses great explanatory and analytical power, as if, to paraphrase Friedman, economic agents obeyed the neoclassical laws and the market mechanism worked efficaciously more or less as Adam Smith thought it should, again as if guided by an unseen hand. But for reasons that are explored in the remainder of this paper these basic assumptions do not provide an adequate basis for understanding actual development or for anticipating the consequences of alternative policies. Additional perspectives are needed. One such perspective is that of adaptive economics, whose basic feature I shall briefly review.

Adaptive Economics and Economic Development. It is belaboring the obvious to observe that human decision makers possess cognitive limitations, that they are imperfectly coordinated, and that they vary absolutely and relatively in the rewards and punishments they receive as a result of action. In contrast to orthodox economic theory, adaptive economics explicitly incorporates these basic facts of life. I will discuss them briefly in turn.

Cognitive limitations include imperfections in perception, memory, reasoning, and computational power. We may also include in this category difficulties in formulating consistent preferences on which to base rational decisions. These facts mean that rationality is "bounded," to use Herbert Simon's apt phrase, and that it involves learning. One exercises the best judgment one can—given what one knows at the time—observes the results, and attempts with more or less energy and skill to acquire more knowledge. One than plans anew and carries out the implied actions in response to circumstances as they unfold. In conducting these cognition-behaving sequences one resorts to imitation, rules of thumb, habit, inertia, and even thoughtless impulse as well as to rational planning.

Economic models that incorporate these aspects of economizing activity include the rule-of-thumb, behavioral economic models of Cyert and March (1963); the goal adaptive, adjustment behavior of March and Simon (1958) and Forrester (1964); the recursive programming approach of Day (1963), Day and Singh (1977), and Day and Cigno (1978); the X-efficiency concepts of Leibenstein (1966, 1976); and the satisficing, evolutionary selection analyses of Winter (1964, 1971) and Nelson and Winter (1978).

Within complex, interactive settings, typical of economic experience, individuals must reach decisions and behave without the benefit of a complete knowledge of what other participants in the process are doing. Therefore they cannot know in advance whether or not effective coordination can occur and whether or not supplies and demands for commodities will equate. Evidently, behavior must be possible and viability must be maintained by special disequilibrium mechanisms. For example, firms may maintain inventories. In addition specialized institutions may exist whose function it is to regulate exchange. Such institutions, which include stores and banks, constitute the marketing and financial systems. These systems must be viewed as the instruments for mediating economic transactions among individual decision makers and economic organizations that function out of equilibrium.

A proliferation of such mechanisms cannot always guarantee existence, however. Bankruptcies of farms, industrial firms, and banks in the United States run in the thousands every month. Such events signal the demise of individual enterprises, and the transfer of their resources to other enterprises in the system. During periods of economic breakdown that occur in hyperflations or depressions, human life itself may be in jeopardy, even in wealthy countries.

It should be noted in passing that socialist economies are not immune from the problems of disequilibrium that we are observing. They are in fact archetypical examples of the larger, hierarchically managed economic organizations whose constituent members have all the characteristics of adaptive

man and which must therefore display lack of perfect coordination. Therefore, they too must possess mechanisms much like those in capitalist countries for mediating disequilibrium transactions within and among individual
enterprises.

Bankruptcy provisions allow for a reallocation of resources controlled by
a person or organization without facing the demise of the person or persons in
the organization. Other mechanisms for maintaining viability of individuals
and groups who are made disastrously worse off in the ongoing process of
change include insurance, private and public agencies for disaster relief, and
philanthropic organizations of many kinds. These, like market and financial
intermediaries, are mechanisms for mediating the transfer of resources so as to
maintain individual and system viability.

How do such disequilibrium systems evolve and what is the character of
their historical trajectories? Careful computer simulation and theoretical
analysis all point to the possibility that model systems of the character we are
discussing need not and often will not converge to economic equilibria even
when the latter can be shown to exist. Two striking characteristics of system
behavior emerge instead. First, many variables display irregular oscillations of
more or less unpredictable complexity (see Day 1980). This suggests that
policies of control based on observed system performance may be exceedingly
unreliable. Second, the system as a whole is characterized by multiple phases
and corollary shifts in structure. Each phase represents a given configuration
of economic activity, scarcity and surplus, and associated values. Within this
configuration some activities grow more or less explosively, as economic advantage is successfully exploited by some organizations within the system.
These growing activities replace uneconomic, obsolescent, or otherwise unsuccessful pursuits, which are seen to diminish in importance. A counterpoint of
economic growth and decay occurs. Eventually, the prevailing structure gives
way as certain components are eliminated altogether or certain activities are
abandoned in favor of new ones designed to cope more effectively with current
opportunities and scarcities. A characteristic feature of this point-
counterpoint of development is that economic activity takes place in overlapping waves involving commodities, technologies, and corollary ways of life.

A more extreme feature is the occasional breakdown of the system
altogether. These disruptive times provide a focus for the synthetic faculty of
mind. New organizations and activities are created that temporarily resolve the
internal contradictions that have emerged and that set the system off on a new
trajectory of evolution.

To summarize the adaptive economics perspective in a nutshell, economic
change involves unpredictable fluctuations, overlapping waves of growth and
demise, periodic breakdowns, and organizational morphogenesis. This brings
us back to a reconsideration of agriculture. For in what other sector of the
economy are these characteristics more evident?

The Disequilibrium Dynamics of Agriculture. The exasperating unpredictability of farm production is so well known and so universally experienced as not to require comment, except to mention that such unpredictability can now be shown to emerge under some conditions from the internal working of the system without assuming the imposition of random stocks. This would mean that many of agriculture's problems might remain, even if the weather were much more uniform and predictable than it is (Day 1980).

Overlapping waves of development are apparent everywhere we look at the farm scene. New practices, new machines, new cropping patterns, new consumption activities replace the old with astonishing speed in the modern world. One or two decades is enough to bring about a transition in an entire way of life.

In the developed world where this counterpoint has already been repeated several times it has come to be expected, so that its disruptive effects are no longer so directly experienced. In newly developing areas, however, the changes are disrupting ancient patterns and forcing changes so fundamental as to involve the demise of basic cultural ways of life and to force the mass relocation of whole peoples. Indeed, in some parts of the world we are seeing the final destruction of paleolithic and neolithic life as the last vestages of preagricultural techology are literally plowed under by the agricultural-industrial frontier.

Somewhat less cataclysmic, but of fundamental significance, is the growing network of linkages between the industrial and agricultural sectors and, because of the uneven distribution of resources and peoples around the world, the growing web of interdependencies between the world's various regions, nations, and cultures.

Indeed everyone now knows of the petroleum crisis that has emerged as new constraints have been reached and new interactions evolved. The potential and actual instabilities are already apparent, and a new generation of policymaking is just getting under way that may be expected to lead to new national and international institutions for managing resource scarcity and for distributing world food and energy supplies.

The information, decision, and production delays that induce instabilities and fluctuations are lengthened and elaborated as the structure of interfirm, intersectoral, interregional, and international linkages grows more intricate. Ironically, the elaboration of new institutions and new marketing and monetary mechanisms to overcome system constraints and provide for enhanced viability adds to the complexity of the system. New decision variables and new decision makers are added along with corollary information, decisions, and production delays. The dynamic "order" of the system increases and with it the potential complexity of the patterns of historical behavior. Thus, the "solution" of each emerging policy problem in terms of elaborated institutional structure contains at its inception the seeds of a new order of socioeconomic difficulty. When it arrives it will demand in its turn a new solution in terms of new technical, social, or economic organization.

In the rapidly developing African continent we see this interplay unwinding with alarming speed. Savannahs that once teemed with all manner of primeval life are giving way to modern agricultural technology. The result is an urbanization that rivals in speed the expansion of Los Angeles and other such urban explosions, which, on a historical time scale, seems to have emerged suddenly, as it were, "out of nowhere." The result has additionally been the transformation of preagricultural peoples into urban dwellers, skipping the agricultural revolution itself—a jump from paleolithic to the agroindustrial age.

And this is occurring just at the time exhaustible resources such as petroleum are no longer growing in supply—the irresistible force of economic development is seemingly meeting head-on the immovable constraints of land and fossil fuels.

A Policy Perspective. Agricultural economists have long been interested in what they have rightly regarded as "adjustment problems." Their goals have often been couched in terms of helping farmers adjust. They have intended to help them deal effectively with changing economic opportunities, either by more quickly modifying their mix of agricultural activities or by pursuing opportunities outside of farming altogether. In so doing, agricultural economists have in part been pushing for policies of change in the face of the most rapid development in the world's history, when migrations from one way of life to another are taking place all over the world at speeds unprecedented in the annals of human history.

Moreover, they have advocated such changes under the assumption (sometimes implicit) that the purpose of policy is to speed up the generation of the new equilibrium inevitably following the eradication of irrational barriers to economic change.

If, however, the forces for change are disrupting what are merely temporary accommodations to fundamental disequilibrium conditions, if those forces will lead eventually to new instabilities and threats of breakdown, then the role of centralized economic policy may better lie in new directions. First, policies for *moderating* ongoing adjustments should always be considered. Second, policies focused on *preserving* exhaustible resources should receive greater attention. Third, policies for *augmenting* renewable resources should be emphasized at all times. Fourth, *emergency supplies* for meeting inevitable but unpredictable economic and natural disasters with appropriate distribution mechanisms should be put in place on a wider scale than is now done. Fifth, resources devoted to the *free play of the intellect* should be enhanced, for it is out of such free play that creative morphogenesis emerges, which I have argued in this paper is what overcomes the inevitable but unpredictable crises that threaten stability and survival even while planting seeds for the next challenge to human ingenuity.

Now this last point presents us with a paradox. For I have advocated a conservative and conservationist approach, while at the same time arguing for fostering the intellectual climate in which new ideas for changing socio-economic structure may flourish. That paradox can never be wholly resolved. It will surely continue to involve an increasing struggle between the forces that wish to preserve and those that wish to create. But if, as I think is the case, the forces of preservation, however important as moderating influences, cannot overcome inherent instabilites and inevitable crises, then society must have within itself at all times a dedicated cadre of socioeconomic inventors, innovators, and engineers. For it is from this cadre that must come the new organizations and mechanisms to overcome the crises leading to cultural and possibly demographic destruction.

The possibility of such destruction must be taken seriously by any student of history and prehistory. The artifacts of wondrous past civilizations warn us of this truth. Thus, while a call for greater resources for the intellectual community is self-serving, it is also a call to social service. For if I am correct, then every scientific paper we write, every thoughtful speech we utter, every discussion, debate, or argument intelligently pursued plays its role in the dialectic process by which the human mind seeks to understand and to enhance its own evolution.

References

Cyert, R., and J. March. 1963. *The Behavioral Theory of the Firm*. Englewood Cliffs, N.J.: Prentice Hall.

Day, R. 1963. *Recursive Programming and Production Response*. Amsterdam: North-Holland.

———. 1979. "Technology, Population and the Agro-Industrial Complex: A Global View." In *Economic Issues of the Eighties*, Chapter 10, edited by N. Kamray and R. Day. Baltimore: Johns Hopkins University Press.

———. 1980. "The Emergence of Chaos from Classical Economic Growth." University of Southern California, Modelling Research Group Working Paper No. 8014.

Day, R., and A. Cigno. 1978. *Modelling Economic Change: The Recursive Programming Approach*. Amsterdam: North-Holland.

Day, R., and T. Groves. 1975. *Adaptive Economic Models*. New York: Academic Press.

Day, R., and I. Singh. 1977. *Economic Development as an Adaptive Process: A Green Revolution Case Study*. New York: Cambridge University Press.

Forrester, J. W. 1964. *Industrial Dynamics*. Cambridge: Massachussets Institute of Technology Press.

Leibenstein, H. 1966. "Allocative Efficiency versus X-Efficiency." *American Economic Review* 56:392–415.

———. 1976. *Beyond Economic Man*. Cambridge: Harvard University Press.

March, J., and H. Simon. 1958. *Organizations*. New York: John Wiley and Sons.

Nelson, R., and S. Winter. 1978. "Forces Generating and Limiting Concentration under Schumpeterian Competition." *Bell Journal of Economics* 9:524-48.

Winter, S. 1964. "Economic 'Natural Selection' and the Theory of the Firm." *Yale Economic Essays* 4:225-72.

_____. 1971. "Satisficing, Selection and the Innovating Remnant." *Quarterly Journal of Economics* 85:237-61.

20

Capital Markets, International Interdependence, and Commodity Markets

G. E D W A R D S C H U H

THAT U.S. AGRICULTURE is part of an international commodity market is now widely recognized. Similarly, it is being increasingly recognized that domestic agricultural policy has to be formulated with a careful view to its implications for our trade in agricultural products. It is generally recognized, for example, that price supports (as determined by loan levels) can price us out of international markets. And although the direct budget costs of deficiency payments to make up the difference between market prices and politically determined target prices can be quite sizable, the alternative is similar large payments in the form of direct export subsidies. The advantage of the deficiency payment system is that it enables the international markets to work without the often arbitrary and more discretionary use of export subsidies, which are commonly perceived as going to middlemen and traders.

Less often is the importance of international capital markets considered a factor influencing our trade and ultimately a factor that could and perhaps should influence our domestic policies. Trade policy ultimately has an influence on capital flows among countries. These capital flows are an important component of the overall balance of payments and also a factor influencing the rate of development of individual countries. In a parallel fashion, exogenous capital flows can influence trade patterns through their effect on the exchange rate and through their effect on domestic and trade policies of other countries as those countries attempt to deal with balance of payment problems.

The petroleum crisis caused by the OPEC cartel has helped to focus attention on the international capital markets. In the first instance payments to the oil exporters caused them to accumulate a disproportionate share of international currency reserves (Japan being an exception, of course, due to its under-valued currency), creating the problem of how and where to invest them. At the same time, countries unwilling to change their trade and foreign exchange policies have faced serious balance of payments problems. Such countries have gone into international capital markets to finance their balance of payment deficits. In addition, special credit facilities have been created by international lending institutions such as the World Bank to provide further financing for the deficits.

The purpose of this paper is to examine in a rather broad way the implica-tions for U.S. agricultural policy and commodity markets of an emerging in-ternational capital market. We will draw on evidence that suggests that this market is now reasonably efficient despite the many interventions by in-dividual countries. Given that it is, the question arises as to the implications of this market for our commodity markets, for our trade policy, and for our domestic agricultural policy.

The paper is divided into four main parts. The first part provides some historical perspectives on trade and development policies in the post–World War II period. The second attempts to establish some dimensions of the inter-national capital market in order to gain some perspective on its relative impor-tance. The third part discusses the conundrums about what future policies rele-vant to the international economy will be, with the objective here being to develop a basis for drawing policy implications. The fourth part will attempt to draw the major implications of an increasingly integrated capital market for our agricultural and trade policies. At the end will be some concluding com-ments.

A number of important premises guide the analysis. The first is that an in-crease in exports over time is vital to the health of the U.S. economy. Export earnings are needed for this nation to import raw materials such as petroleum and consumer and producer goods produced more efficiently elsewhere. The second premise is that the continued development of the world economy is in the best interests of the United States. The third is that the strengthening of world agriculture is an important aspect of strengthening the world economy. And the fourth and final premise is that in general the United States would prefer to have resources and commodities allocated on the world scene by relatively free international markets than by arbitrary decisions of interna-tional bureaucracies.

Some Historical Perspectives. The aftermath of the Great Depression of the 1930s and World War II left both international trade and international capital markets in considerable disarray. In addition, the severing of colonial relations in the immediate post–World War II period provided an impetus to change trading relationships among countries. Moreover, there was a tendency for many low-income countries to turn inward and pursue autarchic development policies, with import-substituting industrialization the keynote of these policies.

The cold war rivalry that followed World War II also influenced the relationships among countries. In the competition of economic systems, the United States attempted to provide development assistance to many low-income countries, in part on the premise that more rapid growth in these countries would keep them from emulating the socialist bloc and in part to gain direct political influence. Development thought at this time was heavily influenced by Keynesian economics. Consequently, assistance to the developing countries was provided largely in the form of balance of payments assistance, complemented by technical assistance to help these countries implement their development programs.[1]

It was here that an important relationship evolved between U.S. domestic agricultural policy and our relations with the rest of the world. U.S. agriculture faced severe adjustment problems during the 1950s and 1960s. Rather than addressing this adjustment problem directly, income was transferred to the agricultural sector through the product market, with prices for important agricultural products set above market clearing levels, given the prevailing exchange rate among international currencies. To sustain these prices the government acquired huge stocks of selected agricultural commodities. These stocks were eventually used as an important component of our foreign aid and were disposed of abroad on concessional terms.

These developments had a number of important implications for world agriculture and for trade in agricultural products. First, the specific form of the autarchic development policies of the low-income countries caused them to neglect their agricultural sectors. This tendency was reinforced by the availability of agricultural products on concessional terms, which enabled these countries to deal with whatever short-term problems did arise. Equally as important, the protectionist measures used to promote import-substituting industrialization, plus the ready availability of balance of payments assistance, encouraged the development of productive structures that largely ignored considerations of comparative advantage.

Trading relations among nations were largely governed by rules worked out at the Bretton Woods Conference in 1944. These rules established a system of fixed exchange rates among national currencies and certain standards attempting to regulate how countries could compete with each other.

This system served the advanced countries reasonably well. Trade among countries grew at a more rapid rate than did the gross world product, and a growing economic integration among countries evolved throughout the post–World War II period. The low-income countries did not share in a proportionate manner in this expanding trade, however, in part because of their persistence in autarchic policies.

By the early 1960s there was widespread disillusionment among the less-developed countries (LDCs), both with the efficacy of their own development policies and with the benefits of foreign aid and the growing political intervention in domestic economic policies resulting from this aid. This dissatisfaction culminated in the first United Nations Conference on Trade and Development, held in 1964. Since that date, there has been a gradual turning away from demands for foreign aid by low-income countries and a growing clamor for access to the markets of the advanced countries on preferential terms. This has led to the so-called North-South dialogue between advanced and low-income countries, demands for a new international economic order, and an emerging political cohesiveness among the low-income countries as they politically confront the advanced countries. This movement culminated in agreement among the low-income countries on a charter, The Economic Rights of Nations, and in the Integrated Commodities Program, which is designed to obtain resource transfers and a redistribution of wealth from the advanced countries to the low-income countries through trade.[2]

Episodic events in the 1970s have served to change trading relations among countries and to give impetus to the pleas of the low-income countries for economic assistance through trade. The first was the successive devaluations of the U.S. dollar in 1971 and 1973, the closing of the gold window by the United States, and the shift to a semblance of floating exchange rates among the advanced countries. With these developments, the trading system established at Bretton Woods essentially came to an end. The system has since evolved with no clear-cut charter or ideology, but rather with a high degree of pragmatism as periodic international conferences are called to deal with particular crises.

The second event was the OPEC-induced increase in oil prices at the end of 1973, an event that imposed serious balance of payments problems on low-income and advanced countries alike. This event was followed by, and in a sense coincided with, an international boom in commodity prices attributable in part to a shortfall in world agricultural output. While benefiting some countries, this rise in commodity prices did further damage to those countries who had become increasingly dependent on imports of agricultural commodities, and especially to those who had been lulled into complacency by the availability of concessional food aid.

The commodity boom was followed by a severe recession in economic activity among the developed countries—the most serious contraction since the Great Depression of the 1930s. The economies of the industrialized countries recovered from this recession only to enter a period of unprecedented inflation. The ability to revitalize a more stable economic growth on a world scale will largely determine what kinds of economic and trade relations emerge in the future.

Dimensions of the International Capital Markets. At least four features of the international markets for capital in the post–World War II period merit attention as background for the following analysis. The first is the rapidly growing importance of capital flows among countries, a logical consequence of the growth of the world economy and of world trade. The second is the gradual shift from a dependence on national governments and international banking institutions as a source of international capital to a growing role for private markets and private credit institutions. The third feature is the crisis of 1974 to the present and the way the world economy has responded to this crisis. The fourth is the growing interdependence among countries, which has evolved through the capital markets—an interdependence that is as important (in a perhaps more subtle way) to economic policy as is the interdependence through trade per se.

Importance of Capital Flows. The growing importance of capital flows in the period since 1960 is documented in Table 20.1. Columns (1) and (2) show the rapid growth in merchandise trade in this period, with part of the acceleration in growth after 1970 due to an increase in the rate of inflation in this

TABLE 20.1. Selected U.S. international transactions, 1960–1975

Year	Mer-chandise exports (1)	Mer-chandise imports (2)	Total mer-chandise trade[a] (3)	Private net income[b] (4)	U.S. assets abroad net[c] (5)	U.S. private assets (6)	Foreign assets in the U.S., net[d] (7)	Non-official foreign assets, net (8)	Total capital trans-actions[e] (9)
					(*$ billion*)				
1960	19.6	−14.8	34.4	2.3	−2.8	−3.9	2.1	0.6	4.9
1961	20.1	−14.5	34.6	2.8	−4.5	−4.2	2.5	1.7	7.0
1962	20.8	−16.3	37.1	3.2	−3.0	−3.4	1.7	0.4	4.7
1963	22.3	−17.0	39.3	3.2	−5.8	−4.5	3.0	1.0	8.8
1964	25.5	−18.0	43.5	3.9	−8.1	−6.6	3.3	1.6	11.4
1965	26.5	−21.5	48.0	4.1	−4.2	−3.8	0.3	0.2	4.5
1966	29.3	−25.5	54.8	3.5	−5.5	−4.5	3.3	4.0	8.8
1967	30.7	−26.9	57.6	3.9	−8.0	−5.6	6.9	3.5	14.9
1968	33.6	−33.0	66.6	3.9	−8.6	−5.4	9.4	10.2	18.0
1969	36.4	−35.8	72.2	3.5	−8.8	−5.4	12.3	13.6	21.1
1970	42.5[f]	−39.9[f]	82.4	3.6	−6.0	−6.9	5.9	−1.0	11.9
1971	43.3	−45.6	88.9	5.7	−9.6	−10.1	22.4	−4.4	32.0
1972	49.4	−55.8	105.2	6.2	−10.2	−8.7	21.1	10.4	31.3
1973	71.4	−70.5	141.9	8.2	−16.4	−14.0	18.5	12.2	34.9
1974	98.3	−103.7	202.0	13.5	−33.4	−32.3	32.4	21.4	65.8
1975	107.0	−98.0	205.0	9.4	−31.6	−27.5	15.3	8.4	46.9

Source: Council of Economic Advisors, *Economic Report of the President, 1977*, Table B-95.
[a] Sum of columns (1) and (2), sign ignored.
[b] Fees and royalties from U.S. direct investments abroad or from foreign direct investments in the United States are exluded.
[c] Increase/capital outflow (−).
[d] Increase/capital inflow (+).
[e] Sum of columns (5) and (7), sign ignored.
[f] Data beginning 1970 not strictly comparable with earlier data.

period. Columns (5) and (7) show the net change in U.S. assets abroad and in foreign assets in the United States, respectively, in the same period.

The changes in these series over the period considered are what interest us. Total merchandise trade—exports and imports: column (3)—increased 5.9 times from 1960 to 1975. Total capital transactions—column (9)—on the other hand, increased by a factor of 9.6. Hence, we see that capital transfers grew at a substantially higher rate than did total merchandise trade. If three-year averages are considered at the beginning and end of the period to remove the importance of short-run instability, total merchandise trade is found to increase 5.2 times over the period, while total capital transactions increased by a factor of 8.9. Averaging lowers the numbers—in part because the centroids are closer together—but the relative changes are altered only slightly. Clearly, capital transactions have become increasingly important in our trade account during this period.

This trend continued in 1976 and 1977.[3] In 1976, for example, U.S. banks increased their claims on foreigners (i.e., loaned abroad) by $21 billion, while private foreign claims in U.S. banks grew by $14 billion. On balance, $7 billion of private short-term funds flowed out of the country.

Increased Importance of the Private Market. During the 1950s and 1960s, an important share of capital flows among countries was on government account. The United States first provided major assistance to Western Europe (the Marshall Plan) and Japan and then turned to assisting the LDCs with grants and loans. In recent years private banks, and especially consortia of private banks, have become increasingly important in mobilizing savings from Western Europe and the United States and transferring them to the low-income countries. In fact, the private banks of Western Europe and the United States have played a major role in intermediating the surpluses the oil-exporting countries have accumulated and the deficits incurred by the oil-importing countries.

One perspective on this increasing importance of private capital flows can be seen in Table 20.2. Total official financial resources flowing from countries belonging to the Development Assistance Committee to developing countries and multilateral institutions roughly doubled between 1970 and 1975. Total private funds from the same countries to developing countries and multilateral institutions, on the other hand, roughly tripled. By 1975 the flow of private funds was substantially larger than the flow of official funds.

Table 20.2. The flow of financial resources for DAC countries to developing countries and multilateral institutions: 1970–1975

Resources	1970	1971	1972	1973	1974	1975
			($ billions)			
Total, official and private	15.66	17.85	19.69	24.66	27.98	38.83
Total official	7.93	8.95	10.08	11.85	13.50	16.27
Total private	7.73	8.90	9.61	12.81	14.48	22.57

These data do not reflect the large private flows of capital among the advanced countries, which are a measure of the large Eurocurrency market. This market, which is largely outside the control of national governments and international agencies, is a major source of funds both for private ventures and for governments attempting to deal with balance of payments problems. The total credit outstanding from this market is now estimated at roughly $700 billion.

Finally, there is the growing role of the private sector in supplying capital to Eastern Europe and the Soviet Union. These countries increased their debt to the West by $8.3 billion at the end of 1970 to an estimated $45.3 billion at the end of 1976. Portes (1977) estimates that the Eastern European bloc financed 57 percent of their balance of payments deficits in the 1974–1976 period by borrowing from the commercial banking system. Again, these were primarily funds raised in the Eurocurrency market.

The Crisis of 1974 to the Present. Much concern has been expressed recently about what is viewed as an excessive indebtedness on the part of the LDCs. The fear is that these countries will default on their debts, and by so doing, bring the international monetary system crashing down around us. This fear is predicated in part on the role of private banks in financing the rapid increase in indebtedness.

Three events have imposed an unusual burden on the LDCs in recent years. The first was the quadrupling of petroleum prices in late 1973. The second was the commodity boom of 1973–1975. This boom favored those countries that were exporters; for those who were importers the increase in prices was of the same order of magnitude as for petroleum prices, with the added shock that the United States, which had been selling its surplus agricultural products on concessional terms, reduced such sales to virtually zero and sold its exports for the most part at commercial rates. Finally, there was the sharp economic recession of 1974–1975 in the advanced countries, followed by a slow recovery, which seriously weakened the markets for the exports from the low-income countries. These problems were further exacerbated by the renewed resurgence in petroleum prices in 1979 as a result of the crisis in Iran.

Efficiency of the Capital Markets. An important question concerning interdependence through international capital markets is how efficiently they perform their allocatory function. If the interdependency is extensive and the markets are performing well, the rate of return to capital at the margin will be approximately equal. This would suggest a high degree of mobility for capital, with important policy implications. If, on the other hand, capital markets are highly segmented, there would be substantial differences in the rate of return at the margin among countries. This would suggest that there are barriers to the mobility of capital, with policy implications in their own right.

Harberger (1977), in a remarkable paper, finds rather strong evidence that the international capital market is quite efficient, despite the barriers that some countries erect to stop or impede the flow of capital. His results suggest that the international capital market tends to equalize rates of return to capital across countries in much the same manner as a national capital market tends to equalize rates of return across activities and regions. His sample, it is important to note, included advanced countries such as the United States and Germany, as well as low-income countries such as Jamaica and Panama.

Some Conundrums. In attempting to develop the issues that derive from an international capital market and its implications for U.S. agriculture and commodity markets, there are a number of conundrums as we look to the future. How these conundrums are resolved in the coming years will have a great deal to do with the impact that international capital markets will have on U.S. agriculture.

The Exchange Rate Regime. With the second devaluation of the U.S. dollar in February 1973, the advanced countries of the world moved to a system of essentially floating exchange rates. Interventions in foreign exchange markets have still been sizable, of course, and in some cases such as Japan for relatively long periods of time. But for the most part market forces have been permitted to work themselves out in determining the value of national currencies.

This shift from fixed exchange rates was a marked break with the system that was established at Bretton Woods. There are two issues with respect to the exchange rate system. The first is whether even the advanced countries will retain this system. The second is whether the low-income countries of the world will release their exchange rates, so that we move to a generalized system of floating, or whether they will retain the present system with the result of retaining a dual system.

This is not the place to discuss the merits of a fixed or floating exchange rate system. The floating system served the advanced countries unusually well during the oil price crisis, since it provided an additional means by which resources were reallocated between the traded and nontraded goods sectors. Balance of payments problems would undoubtedly have been more severe in recent years had it not been for the float, as would the problem of handling the petrodollar gorge.

On the other hand, the transactions costs of international trade are undoubtedly higher with a system of floating exchange rates. Trading companies have to undertake parallel transactions in future markets in international currencies if they are to protect themselves from currency fluctuations, or devise other means of dealing with the risk and uncertainty. The impact of these added transactions costs on the total volume of trade is still an unanswered question. It could be substantial.

Whether countries do in fact gain the autonomy in economic policy that floating exchange rates are expected to bring is also an open question. The consultations and meetings of national leaders to coordinate economic policy have been quite numerous since the beginning of generalized floating and probably more common than they had been under the regime of fixed exchange rates. The key question here, of course, is the importance of the international capital markets and how well they work.

The important point from our perspective is that the exchange rate regime has an important influence on how domestic monetary and fiscal policy affects agriculture and is important in more general ways in shaping the impact that international capital markets have on agriculture. We will discuss these issues below.

The Economic Policies of Low-Income Countries. As noted above, many low-income countries are facing rather serious balance of payments problems due to the oil crisis and the slowdown in growth rates among the advanced countries. In addition, many of them have incurred rather large foreign indebtedness in the period since 1974 as they attempted to put off the needed economic adjustment in their own economies, or to spread the adjustment over a larger period of time.

On the assumption that the problem of higher prices for petroleum will be with us for some time, adjustments in trade and domestic economic policies are in the cards for many low-income countries. The direction these adjustments take will have an important influence on the nature of the world market for agricultural products, and in turn the interactions between the international capital markets and our own agriculture.

Policymakers in these countries have a number of alternatives. One is to release their own pegged exchange rates and take the shift in terms of trade that the rise in oil prices has inevitably imposed upon them. This is the most politically difficult route, for it almost surely involves a slower growth rate through a transitional period, higher rates of inflation for some years, and redistributions of income within the economy. It is also the route that will probably lead to the highest growth rates in the longer run.

This response on the part of the low-income countries could have a substantial impact on the market for U.S. farm commodities. In the first place, it would mean that domestic prices of imported agricultural products in the devaluing country would be higher, thereby causing the quantity demanded to be lower, other things being equal. In fact, this is one means by which the exchange rate would help to reestablish equilibrium in the external sector.

Equally as important, however, is that the devaluation that a shift to floating exchange rates would imply for many low-income countries would involve the removal of an implicit export tax on the agriculture of many countries. The removal of this tax would provide strong price incentives to the farmers in these countries and, if complemented by appropriate corollary policies such as investment in agricultural research and a supply of modern inputs, could lead to sizable increases in agricultural output. This would further reduce their demand for agricultural imports. Moverover, in some cases the country could shift from being a net importer to being a net exporter of agricultural products. If their fundamental comparative advantage is with agricultural products, the shift to a system of floating exchange rates, or at least a devaluation, could enable them to capitalize on that comparative advantage. In the short run, at least, this would mean stronger competition for U.S. markets.

An alternative response, of course, is to redouble the import-substituting drives of the 1950s and early 1960s and to return to autarchic development policies. This is the route that Brazil appears to be taking (Schuh 1978). The impact such policies would have on the international capital market and on our market for agricultural products would depend on the particular direction that import substitution took. In the case of Brazil, the import-substitution drive now has three thrusts. One is along traditional lines and is designed to build a domestic capital goods industry to reduce this important component of imports. The second is designed to reduce imports of oil directly and involves a retreat from a long-held nationalistic oil policy to permit the entry of foreign capital for exploration purposes. The third is to produce petroleum substitutes by developing alcohol as a fuel for automobiles.

If Brazil is successful along these lines it will be able to reestablish equilibrium in its foreign accounts without making changes in its foreign exchange policy and without taking the interim reduction in income such a policy would bring with it. The consequence may be a slower rate of growth in the long term, however, although that will depend on a number of other factors. Perhaps the most important point from our perspective is that with policy along these lines Brazil may not become the strong competitor in international markets for agricultural products that it is capable of becoming.

To conclude, Brazil represents in many respects the unknowns we face on the world scene. The commercial banking system and the special facilities or "windows" provided by international institutions have helped to cushion the shock of the increase in oil prices by providing an important intermediation function: transferring the surpluses accumulated by the OPEC countries to the LDCs (and advanced countries) to finance balance of payments deficits. In the process, however, many countries have incurred large external debts that will require accommodative changes in economic policy.

The route these countries take in devising new policies will be an important factor shaping our markets for agricultural products. If they go to export promotion by appropriate changes in trade and exchange rate policies, we may find our markets reduced, especially if the change in trade policy is coupled with strong efforts to develop their agriculture. Alternatively, many countries that now import agricultural products may turn to self-sufficiency. This also could have a deleterious effect on our exports. And finally, those countries may turn to import substitution of other products, such as Brazil is doing. This may be the better situation for our agricultural exports in the short term, although the efficiency losses from such policies may not augur well for longer-term growth patterns in the world economy.

Trade Policies of the Advanced Countries. The post–World War II period has seen a general lowering of barriers to trade. The Kennedy Round of multilateral trade negotiations gave special impetus to these reductions, especially among the advanced industrial countries, but reductions both preceded and succeeded that important example of international cooperation.

Recent years have seen a resurgence of protectionism, however, that does not augur well for the future. There are a number of factors behind these pleas to reduce the competitive pressures from international markets. In the first place, there has been a growing competitive potential from semiindustrialized countries such as South Korea, Taiwan, and Brazil as these countries not only turned away from autarchic development policies in the mid-1960s but also adopted and adapted international technology in their export sectors. Second, the realignment of currency values in the early 1970s altered the comparative advantage of many countries. The suddenness of these realignments imposed rather sizable shocks to prevailing trade patterns. Third, the balance of payments problems during the period of 1974 to the present, with their focus on petroleum imports, have reduced the degrees of freedom of policymakers in many countries. This problem has been compounded by the economic recession and the accompanying generalized problem of unemployment.

Finally, some countries such as Japan have pursued policies of undervaluing their exchange rate. Just as an overvalued exchange rate is an implicit tax on exports and a subsidy to imports, so is an undervalued exchange rate an implicit subsidy to exports and a tax on imports.

In the case of Japan, the implicit subsidy has at times been substantial, as evidenced by the rather large rise in the value of the yen when it was finally floated. It is little wonder that the Japanese accumulated such large trade surpluses or that they put such severe stress on the television and other industries in the United States. More important, however, is that the deluge of imports from that country has rekindled all the old protectionist fires, while at the same time causing the United States to doubt its ability to compete in international markets.

History has shown that protectionism engenders more protectionism. Unfortunately, it is a poor way to deal with either trade problems or problems of the international capital market. The goal of policy should be to negotiate changes in exchange rates when governments intervene in foreign exchange markets and to reduce other barriers to trade, either explicit or implicit. The advanced countries, moreover, should demonstrate a greater willingness to accept labor-intensive imports from the LDCs, for that is the key to solving the balance of payments problem and in turn to sustaining a viable international capital market. It is also the key to the advanced countries maintaining strong foreign markets for both their agricultural products and their high-technology manufactured products.

Needless to say, maintaining the present degree of trade liberalization—or even extending it—will require political leadership of a high order, especially in light of the stress in the balance of payments and the accumulation of foreign debt that has occurred in recent years. It will also require ample use of trade adjustment programs to facilitate the necessary reallocation of resources in the respective domestic economies.

An important issue here, of course, is the linkage between trade and the international capital markets. We cannot be both internationalists in finance and protectionists in trade, accommodating the borrowing needs of the LDCs but denying them the means to earn their way out of debt by providing us with goods and services. Put somewhat differently, and perhaps somewhat more positively, our banks—by lending to the LDCs—have tied our futures together in a way that will be difficult to break. In effect, they can no more turn away from us than we can turn away from them, unless we are willing to release them from their debt.

The International Capital Markets and U.S. Agricultural Policy. In discussing the issues in this last section, I will assume an optimistic scenario vis-à-vis the conundrums discussed above. That is, we will assume that we retain a system of generalized floating exchange rates about as we now have it,[4] that the international capital market thrives and becomes increasingly well integrated, and that, although we may not make substantial progress in further reducing trade barriers, we won't take major steps backward to a more protectionist system.

The discussion will focus on three issues: floating exchange rates and the international capital market and domestic economic policy; the international capital market and the development of world agriculture; and the international capital market and U.S. agriculture.

The International Capital Market and Domestic Economic Policy.[5] The shift to floating exchange rates, especially in the presence of a reasonably efficient international capital market, has more implications for domestic monetary policy and how it affects the economy than seems to be generally recognized. More specifically, with a regime of flexible exchange rates and an integrated capital market, agriculture bears more of the burden of changes in monetary policy than it has in the past.

With fixed exchange rates, U.S. agriculture was reasonably immune from changes in monetary policy, except insofar as the latter affected the level of unemployment. Monetary policy under such a regime acted by influencing the level of aggregate demand. Since the demand for agricultural products is relatively insensitive to changes in aggregate demand, monetary policy had very little effect on the demand side. However, since the outmigration from agriculture is sensitive to the aggregate level of unemployment, and since there has been a need to transfer labor out of agriculture, monetary policy has had an effect through the supply side. Stimulative monetary policies have promoted outmigration, while tight monetary policies have restricted it. This in turn has been reflected in income levels in agriculture.

With floating exchange rates and an efficient international capital market, on the other hand, agriculture—as an export sector—has to bear an important share of the burden of adjustment to changes in monetary policy. Moreover, this adjustment is induced by changes in demand, with the driving force coming from changes in foreign demand.

The basis for this difference in response can be seen in the following way. With an integrated and sizable international capital market, the Federal Reserve has only limited control over the rate of interest. If it tries to lower the rate of interest in domestic capital markets by pursuing a stimulative monetary policy, money will flow to other countries where the rate of return is higher. Similarly, if it attempts to pursue a tight monetary policy and to raise interest rates, money will flow in from other countries.

This is not to say, of course, that the Central Bank cannot influence aggregate economic policy by the use of monetary policy. The point is that it influences it in a very particular way. For example, the consequence of money leaving the country in response to a stimulative monetary policy is that the dollar will decline on foreign exchange markets, other things being equal. This will raise the price of imports and provide a stimulus to import-competing industries. Similarly, it will provide a stimulus to the export sectors, such as agriculture. Hence, the burden of adjustment is borne by the export sector and the import-competing sector.

The same kind of an adjustment takes place in response to a tight monetary policy. The inflow of money will cause the dollar to rise in foreign exchange markets, and this will lower the price of imports, thereby making them more competitive and reducing the competitive potential of exports. The domestic economy is dampened, but again primarily through the trade sectors.

Hence, the consequence of a well-developed international capital market in a regime of floating exchange rates is that agriculture receives more shocks due to monetary policy than it has in the past. These shocks are transmitted in large part through shifts in foreign demand. To the extent that the mobility of resources between the farm and nonfarm sector is low, agriculture can be expected to suffer rather wide fluctuations in income due to changes in monetary policy as well as to greater fluctuations in prices.

These changed conditions cast buffer stocks in a new light, of course. Their value as a stabilizer of domestic farm prices and incomes is probably greater. By the same token, however, they will act to attenuate the effect of monetary policy if they are managed in a rational fashion and may force a greater burden of the adjustment onto other sectors.

The Development of Third World Agriculture. Largely as a result of the world food crisis of 1973–1975, the United States has renewed its commitment to assist in the development of agriculture in the low-income countries. A vital international capital market can play an important role in that effort.

An important issue here is that the United States has committed itself to help develop new production technology for world agriculture. This is reflected in Title XII of the 1975 Foreign Assistance Act, as well as in our continued support of the growing network of International Agricultural Centers. If this effort to develop the new technology is successful, the capital markets will become increasingly important. To date, there has been little incentive for private capital to go into Third World agriculture. Because of the lack of new technology, the investment opportunities have not been attractive. Consequently, much of the international capital for the development of agriculture in these countries has been provided through bilateral assistance or through international lending agencies on concessional terms.

The availability of a more productive technology should raise the rate of return to capital in the agricultural sectors of these countries. This in turn should make agriculture a more attractive investment for the private international capital markets. To the extent that governments are willing to permit entrepreneurial talent to provide capital, there may be more private direct investment in the agricultures of such countries. If, on the other hand, governments take a negative view of such investments, it still may be possible to raise sectoral loans through public institutions, much as balance of payments support has been raised by governments working with private consortia.

The strengthening of world agriculture through the production of new technology and the mobilization of capital through international capital markets may pose some hard policy choices for the United States. This improvement in world agriculture may reduce our foreign markets in individual instances. Hence, it may cause us to reduce our commitment to strengthening Third World agriculture, or it may lead to pressures for export subsidies or protectionist measures.

The key here is to recognize that the strengthening of agriculture in these countries is an important means of obtaining higher growth rates for them. The increase in per capita incomes resulting from higher growth rates will be the source of expanded markets of our products.

The Development of U.S. Agriculture. International capital markets can also have more direct effects on U.S. agriculture. On the one hand, there could be major flows of foreign capital into U.S. agriculture, thereby creating a fear that our vital food sector and land resources might be taken over by foreigners. Alternatively, capital could flow into the agriculture of the low-income countries, making them stronger competitors of the United States in international markets. Which of these happens will depend on political developments here and abroad and on the relative rates of technical change in U.S. agriculture and in the agriculture of the LDCs.

There has been very little direct investment of foreign capital in U.S. agriculture in the post–World War II period. This has probably been because the United States as a nation has been a major exporter of capital rather than an importer. This situation may be changing.[6] The conservative investment policies of the Arab countries may cause them to invest their surpluses in agricultural land, although so far they have been rather reluctant to undertake such commercial ventures.

Private foreign capital has also failed to flow into the agriculture of low-income countries, with the exception of Brazil in recent years. This is in marked contrast to the tendency of foreign capital to move into the industrial sector of these countries.

There are a number of reasons for this difference in response of the international capital markets. First, economic policy in the LDCs has tended to discriminate rather strongly against the agricultural sector. This in itself has made world agriculture a rather unattractive investment alternative. At the same time, the strong protection of the industrial sector in these countries has caused this sector to attract foreign capital. Both of these influences are reinforced by the lack of technical progress in the agriculture of the LDCs. The absence of such new production technology is a further factor reducing the attractiveness of investment alternatives in these sectors.

These conditions may be changing. The severity of the agricultural squeeze in the 1973–1975 period appears to have caused many countries to reduce their discrimination against agriculture. Similarly, international investments in agricultural research, together with stronger bilateral commitments from such countries as the United States, hold out the promise of new production technology for low-income countries. If that technology should be forthcoming, there could be a sizable flow of investment funds from the international capital markets to exploit it.

In the aggregate there has probably been a substantial underinvestment in world agriculture in the post–World War II period. We may be at a point in history where that imbalance will be redressed. If this should be in response to more favorable economic policies toward agriculture in these countries and to the increased availability of new production technology, we could face rather severe pressure in international commodity markets. Efficient international commodity markets could, in effect, cause an income squeeze on U.S. farmers.

Some Concluding Comments. Customarily, American economic analysis as well as economic policymaking have virtually ignored foreign influences upon the health of the U.S. economy. That no longer seems realistic. The nations of the world are increasingly tied together through trade and through an international capital market that has grown rapidly and at the same time become more efficient.

Recent developments help to put these changes in perspective. For example, the world's largest free trade area formally became a reality on July 1, 1977, when the final removal of tariff barriers on most industrial goods was implemented among the nine members of the expanded European Common Market (EC), and among Common Market and European Free Trade Association (EFTA) members.[7] The 16-nation trade area, with a population of nearly 300 million, accounted for 39 percent of world trade in 1976 and had an estimated gross domestic product of $1.7 trillion.[8]

Similarly, sales by majority-owned foreign affiliates of U.S. companies totaled $458 billion in 1975.[9] Some 66 percent of these sales were destined for markets in countries where the companies were located and 27 percent for non-U.S. foreign markets. Only about 7 percent of the total production of U.S. foreign affiliates was shipped to the U.S. market. But this total represented 32 percent of the total of U.S. merchandise imports in 1975.

In a somewhat different context, the commodity boom of 1973–1975, the increase in oil prices in late 1973, the world recession of 1974 and 1975, and the successive devaluations of the dollar and the shift to floating exchange rates have constituted sizable external shocks to U.S. agriculture and to the economy as a whole. However, some of the stresses and strains of recent years are a logical consequence of rather large realignments of currencies and an increasingly well-integrated capital market. As the market works there are reallocations of resources among sectors within individual countries, and with it reallocations among countries. If these markets are to successfully perform their equilibrating function, it is inevitable that some groups in society will benefit while others suffer losses.

Many low-income countries are making concerted efforts to pull themselves up by their bootstraps. The international capital markets are becoming an attractive source of funds for these activities. If capital flows out of this country, there may well be a loss of jobs and a slower growth rate. The alternative is to accept more labor-intensive imports, but that also can threaten particular groups in the society.

In light of the sizable stresses and strains that are a logical consequence of this growing economic integration, political leadership of a high order will be required if we are not to slip back to protectionism and to beggar the neighbor economic policies. But in this difficult transition to greater economic interdependence, it behooves us to remember that a more efficient use of the world's resources implies higher growth rates in the aggregate and with that an expanding market for our agricultural output. Slipping back into autarchic development policies means sacrificing potential output and growth in income in our own country, while at the same time limiting the development possibilities of the poor and disadvantaged of the world. To do this is to retreat from the policy stance we have taken in international fora throughout the post–World War II period.

Notes

1. For a penetrating discussion of these policies, see Johnson (1967).

2. For an excellent discussion of the Integrated Commodity Program and its potential implications for North American agriculture, see Warley (1977).

3. The following data are from Manufacturers Hanover Trust, *Economic Report,* New York, N.Y., October 1977.

4. It is not likely, nor is it perhaps necessary, that the LDCs join the floating system. More flexibility, with a closer proximity to equilibrium rates, would obviously be desirable, however.

5. A more detailed discussion of the issues in this section can be found in Schuh (1977).

6. It is worth noting that this country has been able to avoid borrowing to pay for its current account deficits in recent years because of the large inflow of funds for investment purposes. Some of these funds have gone into U.S. treasury securities, but reportedly much of them have been invested in real estate and in buying control of American companies. A decline in the value of the dollar, of course, means that our assets can be purchased more cheaply.

7. Despite the significance of this event, it was practically unnoticed in the U.S. press.

8. These data are taken from *International Letter,* Federal Reserve Bank of Chicago, no. 336, July 22, 1977.

9. Data in this paragraph were taken from *International Letter,* Federal Reserve Bank of Chicago, no. 327, May 20, 1977.

References

Harberger, A. 1977. "Perspectives on Capital and Technology in Less-Developed Countries." Mimeographed. Chicago: University of Chicago.

Johnson, H. G. 1967. *Economic Policies toward Less-Developed Countries.* Washington, D.C.: The Brookings Institution.

Portes, R. 1977. "East Europe's Debt to the West: Interdependence is a Two-Way Street." *Foreign Affairs* 55:751 892.

Schuh, G. E. 1977. "Income and Stability Implications of Monetary, Fiscal, Trade, and Economic Control Policies." Presented at Farm and Food Policy Symposium, Kansas City, Missouri, February 22–24. Great Plains Agricultural Council Publication No. 84.

_____. 1978. "The Case of Brazil: Import Substitution Revisited." *Journal of Comparative Economics* 2:97–110.

Warley, T. K. 1977. *Agriculture in an Interdependent World: United States and Canadian Perspectives.* Montreal and Washington, D.C.: C. D. Howe Research Institute and National Planning Institute.

21

The Position of Agriculture in the Social Market System

ARTHUR HANAU

IN THE SOCIAL MARKET ECONOMY we see an economic order that makes possible a particularly effective unfolding of production facilities. Production and consumption are primarily governed by a free adjustment of prices and not by government regulation. The planning and execution of economic undertakings are left to business firms and households. In this way production is controlled according to the priorities set by consumer needs based on the relative scarcity of supply.

In such an economy, competition, which should force enterprise toward greater production efficiency and rationality, is secured by inhibitions or measures against restrictions on competition. Such measures are not alone, however, in differentiating this sytem from the "free" enterprise system. The former does not simply leave business trends to the mercy of economic self-regulation. An active economic policy to insure economic growth, with a stable purchasing power of money, is just as much a part of its significant economic tasks.

The term "social" emphasizes two different but similarly directed tendencies with respect to social aims. First, consumer freedom of choice and the consequent competition-oriented price adjustment, as a rule, guarantee an op-

This contribution is a slightly simplified, but not revised, translation of an article, "Die Stellung der Landwirtschaft in der Sozialen Marktwirtschaft," published in the monthly *Agrarwirtschaft,* vol. 7, 1958, pp. 1-15. Some footnotes to the original version have been omitted to save room.

The article was written before the common market was enacted, in a time of heated debates on the advantages or disadvantages of an extensive migration of peasants and their family members out of agriculture. At the same time, modern knowledge of the reasons and consequences of this kind of migration was not yet widespread.

The author and certainly many other German agricultural economists owe very much to Professor Shepherd for his advice during his visit to Germany at the aftermath of World War II and from his excellent books in the field of agricultural economics.

timal coverage of consumer needs. Second, the term "social" indicates that under certain circumstances we deviate from a purely economic principle for the benefit of a better social arrangement. Indeed, herein lie the greater difficulties and problems of practical economic policy, because differing opinions can always arise as to where, when, and to what extent these "deviations" are justifiable.

To what degree can the fundamentals of the social market system be applied to the field of agricultural economics? That is a question that is quite controversial in discussions of economic policy. But the practice of economic policy in most countries has become oriented toward a special treatment of agriculture. In reality, one is nowadays more concerned with the target and degree of government intervention than with the principle of intervention itself.

According to Constantin von Dietze (1942, 1946), who worked out the salient aspects of "Agriculture and Competitive Order," and to Niehaus (1956), who subsequently advocated the realization of a competitive order in the agricultural sector, agriculture was not to have a special status; global aid in the form of price relief and subventions, for example, were unjustified. This point of view was shared by many economists through this period. Niehaus did recommend promotional measures directed at improving the agricultural structure and at raising the level of education. In addition he proposed a stronger economic penetration of rural areas with commercial economic undertakings. But agricultural market and price policy should be formed in keeping with the market situation. The weak market position of agriculture should be balanced by increased resistance to restrictions on competition rather than by market intervention for the benefit of the agricultural sector.

In contrast, Strisch and Weippert (1956) emphasized the special characteristics of the agricultural sector. They concluded that its unique disadvantages should be balanced out or diminished by global measures for its benefit. In addition, the disadvantages peculiar only to certain types or regions of farming should be alleviated by specifically directed measures.

It is not my intention to repeat the contents of this literature regarding the position of agriculture within a competitive order. Instead, I want to focus on certain special aspects of the sector and its development that appear important to me. My intention is to offer considerations that may contribute to the further development of scientific conceptions of the position of agriculture in the social market system, a position that, as we shall see, compels special policy considerations.

Production in Chains. Production enterprises are constantly concerned with adjusting to the flow of economic and technological development by changing and recombining production factors. However, these possibilities are, to a great extent, dependent on the mobility of production factors (land, capital, and labor) as well as on "geistige Techniken" (know-how), to use an appropriate expression coined by Niehaus (1956). In this respect, particular difficulties and restrictions exist in agriculture that can only be overcome after a considerable time lag.

Only Limited Mechanization Possible. In industry the most important means used in achieving an increase in productivity, the source of increased real income, are mechanization or advanced technology. Increased mechanization in agriculture, in contrast to its application in industry, leads primarily to a reduction of human labor and of animal-driven systems under our present conditions; here, increased production arises only as a secondary effect. This effect can be realized most directly when increased technology is employed hand in hand with an enlargement of individual farms or with utilization of new land.

The possibilities for increased mechanization depend to a great extent on the size of the operation, that is, on the attainable degree of production, on the availability of cooperative sharing of machinery, on the skills and experience of farm managers and farm labor in the application of machines, and on financing. Here it is always a matter of covering additional costs through savings and possible increased returns. Moreover, if reliable methods of cooperative sharing are unavailable or infeasible, small farms cannot attain a higher level of mechanization. As long as such conditions prevail, these farms continue to apply extensive manpower that remains inadequately compensated. Even when the farm management is optimal, these "too small" farms remain a problem for agricultural and social policy. For economic forces—in the face of wage increases and the comparatively reduced cost of, and ever-increasing perfection of, technology—press for increasing acreage and increasing output per head. With higher wage increases that tendency will become even more apparent, with the smaller farms with insufficient access to mechanization falling farther behind.

The investments in the German agricultural sector are much less directed toward expansion than those of the industrial sector. Agricultural investments are directed more toward economizing on human labor and animal power. This would explain the cutbacks in human labor capacity and working time and the decreased application of animal-driven systems following the rapidly expanding use of versatile tractors. Consequently, increasingly widespread use can be found among those technological aids that relieve and replace the labor of continuing tasks in farming, animal husbandry, and housework.

Pressure toward Increased Sales of Animal Products. It is generally recognized that not only mechanization but also the expansion of animal husbandry lead to an increase in individual income and in net production per man (with an unchanged or decreasing number of workers). In the first half of the twentieth century the expansion of animal production in Western Europe had a greater effect on income than the mechanization of agricultural operations. As Folke Dovring (1956) aptly pointed out in his work, the West European farming and agricultural structure, with its limited size of operations and its relatively low level of mechanization, was able to maintain itself through the first half of the century only because, in the wake of increased demand, animal production could be extensively expanded.

In animal production, invested capital is operative day and night, on workdays and holidays. In "industrialized" meat and egg production, particularly in its commercial form in which the fodder is purchased rather than domestically produced, an even faster turnover in capital is possible. This would also explain why these high-capital-investment-using enterprises have become so widespread in the United States, and why this trend is apparent in other countries as soon as market conditions allow it. Small, family-run farms of European structure can also increase their level of more efficient methods of animal production in order to utilize available working capacity better in an attempt to increase income per head.

Now the more all this is recognized and the more rational production methods based on optimal use of feed and manual labor are adopted, the more the price ratio of feed to animal products shrinks. For example, the price ratios between feed and hogs in Germany continually declined from 1:7.5 before World War I to 1:7.0 in 1928, to 1:6.5 in the 1930s, to perhaps 1:6.0 or less at present or in the near future. This leads to a constant pressure toward increased turnover. If the profit per produced unit declines, more units must be produced in order to maintain or increase the level of income and management profit. Herein lies the structural weakness of agriculture: each individual farm must increase its turnover in order to raise income per head. However, the agricultural sector as a whole encounters, as we shall soon see, obvious limits imposed by the market.

Inhibited Consumption. The limits imposed on the supply of agricultural products by nature and by the agricultural structure would encourage rather than impair higher earnings in agriculture if it were not for the diminishing rate of increase in the consumption of food in the development of the national economy. First, the population growth of West Europe has slowed down considerably. In addition, Engel's Law becomes increasingly valid. According to this law, household expenditures for food do not keep pace with household income, so that with increasing consumer income the portion spent on food relative to total expenditures decreases.

When the German statistician Engel derived this law from laborers' family budgets over a century ago, food processing and service costs did not yet play a significant role. Nowadays we have to divide up consumer spending into one fraction from which the agricultural sector benefits and a remainder that flows into other economic areas, namely, into the food-processing industry, food distribution and trade, and the restaurant business. The share of the market allotted to agricultural products decreases faster than the total portion spent on food. The agricultural sector benefits only from sales of its primary products and its own consumption.

Income Parity through More Animal Production? Again and again the idea arises as to whether small farms could attain the desired increased sales and income by lowering feed grain prices on the one hand and expanding the volume of production on the other. Such an adjustment in price policy would probably be counterproductive. At lower feed grain prices, hog feeding would be increased beyond present levels until the consequent price drop for hogs reestablished the average hog-to-feed-grain price ratio of 6:1. Thus, the savings gained in fodder purchases would be lost in diminished hog prices. The volume of marketable production could be expanded because lower pork prices would increase consumption, but this increase would probably be proportionately half as important as the drop in pork prices. The consumption increase would only be half as important because the price cut in feed grain is only weakly passed on to pork due to the wide price margin.

In addition, a price elasticity in demand of less than one has to be considered. Ceteris paribus, price reductions diminish production returns (volume times price) when the quantitative price elasticity is less than one, as is the case for animal products. The less elastic the demand, the less favorable are the economic effects of lower prices for the producer. In the marketing of industrial products the returns are, as a rule, more favorable because the elasticity of demand for these goods is greater than one. Under these conditions sales and production returns increase with falling prices. The marketing problems of agriculture and industry are fundamentally different and therefore cannot be mastered with a market and price policy formed from the same mold.

If West German agriculture continues to disregard these effects by accelerating the pace of production of animal products, increases in supply will eventually surpass increases in demand. The consequence would be dropping prices and a disappearance of import needs, not increased income for agriculture nor a more extensive division of labor with agricultural export countries. In most discussions these points are usually overlooked.

Higher sales and income per head can be achieved for the animal production industry only under the following conditions:

1. Growing demand with increasing consumer income.

2. Expansion of feed production by improved production techniques (which would not exclude the use of imports of high-grade nutritional supplements for increased output).

3. Increasing output of animal products per kilogram of fodder intake.

4. Increased efficiency per worker. This holds true only for increased efficiency gains in excess of expenditure for engineering aids and capital investment.

5. The increased productivity achieved is not absorbed by price reductions of the finished product.

Migration from Agriculture Inevitable. Continuing technological advances and progressive wage increases have brought about a migration of the labor force away from agriculture. We have already seen that mechanization in agriculture serves to economize on manual labor and animal power rather than to increase production. Accordingly, the percentage of the population engaged in agriculture has declined as follows:

Territory of the Reich	Federal Republic of Germany
1882—39.9	1939—17.9
1907—27.0	1950—14.7
1925—22.8	1957—approximately 12.0
1933—20.8	
1939—17.7	

Also, the absolute figures have decreased slowly but steadily. This decline must be viewed in contrast to the increasing nonagricultural population. The nonagricultural population absorbs not only the newcomers, but also the excess in birth of the rural population, their own birth rate excess, and foreign immigrants.

These facts are often viewed by the agricultural side as proof of negligence of agriculture within the framework of economic policy or as a consequence of a free enterprise system that favors the commercial economy over, or at the expense of, agriculture. Such an interpretation is untenable. It can lead ad absurdum to the observation that the structural shrinkage of the agrarian share has come about under the most diverse economic systems, and continues to do so throughout the world. In Germany from 1933 to 1939 the migration away from agriculture even rose sharply during a time when self-sufficiency and production increase were among the top priorities of agricultural policy. Even then the agricultural economy was disadvantaged by a considerable income disparity; in those days it was called "Unterbewertung der Landarbeit" (underpayment of labor in agriculture). These observations are puzzling and should compel us to search for deep-seated causes.

Over 25 years ago, Quante, the well-known German agricultural statistician, is accredited with having worked out the true causes of the so-called rural exodus.

> Owing to the demand limit on the one hand and the technological improvement in agriculture on the other hand, the working capacity of the agricultural sector has become so restricted that even with an overall population increase with its concomitantly expanded demand for food, part or all of the farming population's offspring, and possibly those presently employed in agriculture, will have to abandon their occupations and, as a rule, leave the countryside as well, as their location of employment [Quante 1933, p. 357].

As another reason for the migration away from agriculture, a certain "draining of functions" from agricultural production and households can be cited. This refers to an economic process involving a removal of certain activities from agriculture that are taken over by industry and trade.

At another point Quante arrives at the following observation: "Consequently, coming generations will not have the 'freedom of choice' to decide between farming and some other occupation; rather the opportunity to become a farmer is absolutely limited by the level of technology in connection with the total population increase" (Quante 1933, pp. 336–37). An increase in productivity that helps to raise the income of, and is thus pursued by, the farmers leads to an income increase per worker in the whole agricultural industry only as long as demand keeps pace with rising supplies and greater price drops are avoided. As a consequence of the limit of demand, such a result can only be reached when the superfluous labor force fraction leaves the agricultural sector, i.e., when at the same time the labor force in agriculture is being reduced (particularly through mechanization).

Quante (1933, p. 332) recognized this correlation as follows: "In every economic society regardless of whether growing or static, the degree of rural exodus (urbanization) is greater, the more effectively agricultural production takes shape." This is the general rule to which exceptions can exist, for example, when the import and export of foodstuffs in a country are of great importance and undergo great changes. Accordingly, in a system of free trade the agricultural migration away from agriculture could exceed technologically induced labor force reductions, thereby confining growth of agricultural production.

The classic example of this was Great Britain, whose free trade policies up to the 1930s resulted in a reduction of the agricultural population to only 5 to 6 percent of the total population and in a decrease in self-sufficiency to about 30 percent of the national consumption. Great Britain intentionally tolerated this development in order to boost industrialization of the mother country and to look for ways of securing division of labor and inexpensive sources of foodstuffs, particularly from the Commonwealth, Argentina, and certain neighboring European countries dealing in agricultural exports (Ireland, Denmark, and the Netherlands). These countries were thus offered a welcome expanded market in the British mother country. However, two world wars and their repercussions brought about a switch toward protection of agriculture. The strong increase in production apparent since the 1930s, which rose to cover 50 to 60 percent of the national consumption, was remarkably achieved with the help of an extraordinary reinforcement of technological aids, yet without expanding the agricultural labor force.

But there are also cases involving minimal migration that are equated with disguised unemployment and insufficient utilization of working potential in agriculture. We have seen it in former times in East Europe with agricultural overpopulation, and we can still see it in today's densely populated countries just at the initial stage of industrialization, as in the Far East and elsewhere. Here it is primarily a lack of capital that prevents a more rapid development. All over the world economic development characterized by industrialization, accumulation of capital, increased output, increased supply of goods, and a raised real income per head is necessarily coupled with a migration of established and potential laborers away from agriculture toward industry and later toward the service sector. Without such shifts in the employment structure there is, as a rule, neither strong economic development nor a lasting increase in per head income in agriculture.

The increase in agricultural production per head of labor force in agriculture compared with prewar levels is considerable: it is reported to be 30 to 80 percent in West European countries, 100 percent in the United States, and 130 percent in Canada. For West Germany the figure is roughly 40 percent; here an increase in production of at least 20 percent arose with a reduction in the labor force of about 10 to 15 percent. The West European countries showing top figures of increased output per head compared with prewar statistics are Denmark, the Netherlands, Belgium, France, Great Britain, and Sweden. The most prominent influence operating here for Great Britain and the Netherlands was an increase in production; for Sweden, Belgium, and France the most influential factor was the reduction in labor, whereas in Denmark a production increase of 30 percent was matched by a comparable reduction in labor.

The effects of migration from agriculture are different from one farm to another. On overstaffed farms (often the case with small-scale farms) the per head income of farm labor increases directly when family members pursue employment opportunities outside agriculture. Yet where the number of laborers is in line with actual operational needs, the missing workers frequently, at least temporarily, leave behind a shortage of labor that often can only be compensated for with great difficulty through application of machinery, work-saving reorganization, or additional work by the remaining crew. Should a saving of labor be successfully carried out, an increase in per head income results since fewer workers achieve the same, or an increased, level of output. This holds true, of course, only when the additional costs of investments and technological aids do not exceed the savings acquired through a reduced payload. In this light, a reduction in the farm labor force can be seen as an inevitable consequence of efforts directed toward increased productivity and cost reduction.

The economic incentives stemming from the income disparity draw underpaid workers away from agriculture into other sectors of the economy and other professions. Industry and the service sector provide alternatives, particularly in times of prosperity, whereas during periods of economic stagnation no new jobs are created; and when unemployment levels are high, a population return to rural communities can occur. A universal phenomenon, income disparity influences the distribution of the labor force, thereby influencing trends in production of the agricultural sector in the long run.

During the postwar period from 1945 to 1952, when gaps in the supply of food also existed in the western industrialized nations, it was sometimes feared that the developing countries heavily involved in international agricultural export would neglect their agricultural production because of forced industrialization. At that time it was expected that longer-lasting difficulties and higher costs would arise in covering the import needs of West Europe. There were also concerns that the developing countries would not even be able to cover their own growing needs for food, enlarged by increased industrialization and income.

Indeed, in many agricultural export countries past and present, a tendency toward export limitation exists, occasionally even to the point of requiring compensatory imports, not to mention certain densely populated and underdeveloped countries in the Far East characterized by chronic undernourishment. Indications for this tendency are also found in the communist East Block countries where industrialization is known to be intensely encouraged. Nevertheless, we do not observe or expect an undersupplied international market at present or in the foreseeable future, provided that a peacetime economy with a stable currency can be maintained. The reason for this is that, above all, the United States has been able to increase its agricultural production and exports in spite of its considerably reduced farm population, and at the same time lower its import needs (particularly of vegetable oils). The same applies to other countries that have greatly increased agricultural exports or have reduced their import needs as did Great Britain, the largest import country.

Thus, the migration away from the agricultural sector is an inevitable part of this overall economic development, so that the remaining labor force in agriculture can share in the increased per head income brought about within the national economy.

However, we cannot simply leave it at that. Rather, we must take into consideration the great difficulties and structural disadvantages that are automatically coupled with this long-term process in agriculture, such as migration of mobile labor, education for the young in unfamiliar occupations, removal of capital due to inheritance, and depopulation of rural communities. I wish to particularly emphasize here the fact that a branch of industry restricted by a limited unfolding of its potential does not have the opportunity to automatically adapt itself to the latest technological advances through new investments in buildings, machinery, and other engineering aids, as is possible in other lines of business with more favorable production and demand conditions. A branch of industry with a shrinking labor force also lacks the otherwise available opportunity to attract and hire experts and specialists for managerial positions.

Indeed, these difficulties and disadvantages, only rarely found in commercial business branches—except among shrinking industries—justify a special status for agriculture. They are especially important in connection with price formations, which in periods of abundant supply (relative to demand) are disadvantageous to agriculture and contribute to its income disparity.

Considerations Regarding Price Formation of Food Commodities. Within this framework I cannot deal exclusively with all the problems of price formation. I wish to limit myself here to those aspects significant to the context of our topic.

With free adjustment of prices, the market prices reflect prices of equilibrium that balance out supply against demand. Only in the long run can average prices assume a more or less close correlation to the elusive, actual costs. We want to attempt to determine here whether differences exist between agriculture and industry with respect to cost recovery, vague as this concept might be.

With respect to market supply, the following differences exist between agriculture and industry.

Short-Term Considerations. Industrial firms can regulate the degree of production, through a shutdown if necessary. The discharged employees can then either join other manufacturing establishments or get by with unemployment benefits.

Since the demand for industrial goods is usually elastic, or at least not exceedingly inelastic, price reductions and increased income lead to an increase in quantitative demand that absorbs any temporary excess of supply. Prerequisites for this are, first, maintenance of steady growth of "overall demand" and, second, the output not encountering an inelastic or declining demand. Of course, this does not mean that restrictions in industrial production do not result in losses; in fact, the higher the capital intensity and fixed costs, the greater the losses. Moreover, the decline in income suffered by the unemployed represents a very perceptible, serious disadvantage. The full-employment policy of recent times is aimed at preventing such unfavorable developments whenever possible.

In agriculture this situation is quite different. Short-time work and shut-down of business firms in order to reduce supply in agriculture are out of the question. Stockpiling is restricted by the perishability of farm products, the great expense that such stockpiling would entail, and the improbability of such actions. Due to a more or less inelastic demand with respect to price, accumulated stocks as well as oversupplies of farm products can be absorbed neither by price reductions nor by increases in consumer income in a relatively short time as in the case of industrial products.

Long-Term Considerations. The growth of industrial production is contingent worldwide on commercialized and intensive manufacturing processes as well as permanent investment of capital. Buildings, installations, and machinery, and additional technicians, specialists, and skilled and unskilled labor are required. The amounts of capital input and productivity differ considerably here, but wages are, as a rule, closely correlated with productivity. At a low level of productivity, wages are correspondingly low; with higher and growing productivity, wages increase concomitantly. The different levels of wages in the industrial sector of various countries balance out the differences in productivity. In contrast, industrial merchandise on the international markets are offered at the same price, in spite of having been manufactured in countries with very different wage levels, such as the United States in contrast with Italy. Where an adequate balance between wage level and productivity is unattainable, as in labor-intensive industries, countries with high wage levels do not remain competitive. They either have to leave the production (for both export and domestic markets) to their more efficient competitors or to retreat to their own domestic markets, if it is more or less protected from the competition of cheaper imports by duties, import quotas, transport costs, and other conditions.

The possibilities and capabilities of achieving rises in productivity through reducing labor input (increased net production per worker) are extremely different from one branch of industry to another, and also from one industry to another. The chemical and manufacturing industries take the lead in achieving such increased productivity, whereas the progress in efficiency in coal mining and agriculture lag behind. Trade, especially retail trade, and other service industries are characterized by their limited ability to make use of technological progress. The very complex situation in the handicraft trade cannot be dealt with here.

At a given rate of growth in the net added value per head of goods and services, with a parallel increase in real wages, three different groups can be defined:

1. Branches of industry and firms with above-average rises in productivity: They can lower the prices for their goods accordingly, and will do just that when forced by competition.

2. Branches of industry and firms with average rises in productivity: By substitution of labor for capital they can balance out wage increases and maintain stable prices.

3. Branches of industry and firms with below-average rises in productivity: They fall under pressure from rising costs that can be passed on to product prices only to the extent allowed by market conditions. Those branches of industry that cannot pass on rising costs to product prices are forced by the market to forego parts of wages, managerial profits, rents, and full returns on investments; they end up in a so-called "income disparity." Coal mining over the last few years has been able to pass rising costs on in price increases. The producer price index in coal mining in July 1957 reached a level of 370% of the price in 1938 and 179% of the price in 1950. Up until now market conditions have allowed this upward price adjustment since import prices for coal were even higher. In October 1957 an additional price increase in coal followed in order to cope with previous wage and cost increases. The service industry also passes on the increased wages to the consumer, provided they cannot be balanced out by rises in productivity. Examples include the increase in transportation fares, repair costs, and raised prices (and service charges) in restaurants and hotels; and the list goes on.

In manufacturing and service industries, it has obviously remained possible over the last few years for cost increases, which have their impact on an industrial branch as a whole, to be passed on in prices of goods and services because the "overall demand" has developed favorably and because worldwide inflationary trends prevented price cutting by foreign competitors.

All these conditions lead to the fact that industrial supply exhibits a relatively close dependence on the price cost relationship. "No increase in production without the prospect of covering of costs" is the rule here. In no way is this rule contradicted by the fact that costs are not at all rigid, but remain in a dynamic flow due to the influences excited by competition and technological progress. Revolutionary cost reductions occur above all with "new" goods (e.g., automobiles, radios, television sets, and refrigerators); price reductions in these newer goods open up mass consumption as a prerequisite for large-scale production at low cost.

In price formation of agricultural goods other conditions are involved from the start, since agricultural production in the world is not bound to commercialized manufacturing processes in the same way that industry is. On the contrary, there are production and exports that exist side by side that are the outcome of extremely different modes of production. For this reason, the level of agricultural supply, above all in the world economy but also on a national level, does not exhibit the direct and relatively close dependence on the price-cost relationship found in nonagricultural trade. Land and the rural working population represent, so to speak, production factors offered by nature. They are leaving agriculture and yield a greater remuneration only if alternatives arise, such as when farmers or other farm laborers migrate to other economic sectors. Thus, a downward price tendency exists in agricultural production until supply excess is removed by increasing demand, and a situation of supply shortages may arise thereby boosting prices. Should demand take the lead over supply, the improved price-cost relationship (or terms of trade) strengthens production efforts, either through exploitation of new land or through intensifying production. More and more industrially manufactured inputs are used. A wide variety of technological progress enhances the efficiency of all input, e.g., the productive capacity of land and the productivity of labor. In the process of mechanization, labor and animal draft power can be substituted for by capital investments.

The application of technological advancement and the intensification of production through increased use of inputs are influenced by the price-cost relationship and the expectation of profits in agriculture as well. Favorable terms of trade encourage production. However, a distinctive characteristic of total agricultural supply is its downward rigidity, that is, a resistance to reductions of total production in the case of falling prices, when those are caused by supply excess or diminishing demand. The reason for this is well known: at price conditions prevalent throughout the market, the situation for an individual farm is that, due to high fixed costs, lower levels of production are as a rule more expensive per unit than previous or even increased levels. The deeper cause of this phenomenon lies in the rigidity of production factors— acreage, livestock, invested capital, and the labor capacity of the farming family.

Of course, these factors are not completely inflexible. However, they react little to price and income reductions and are occasionally even "anticyclic" (more supply at lower prices), usually with a considerable time lag in response. This means that under price pressure the agricultural supply remains relatively greater and the prices lower than with "normal" price-cost response. Conditions were and are more favorable for agriculture when a high population growth rate and a high elasticity of demand for animal products result in fast-rising consumption of food measured in primary calories.

Many general economists do not consider the downward rigidity of supply to be a significant weakness in the market position of agriculture, perhaps because the total agricultural supply is also seen as being relatively rigid with respect to rising prices. In this case, relatively favorable agricultural prices for the producers could indeed arise in times of supply shortages. In reality, however, things look somewhat different. First of all, the total supply is, in spite of the law of diminishing returns, much more elastic in an upward direction, given the possibility of further intensification of production. Moreover, supply shortages have never occurred during times of peace since 1913 in western industrialized countries, because population growth has slowed while the rate of growth of production has accelerated. In addition, with increased satisfaction of demand for food we approach saturation limits, which is why the income elasticity of demand for primary calories of agricultural products (measured in grain equivalents) dwindles. In the present phase of development in the western industrialized world, actual supply shortages occur only when production imports and supply are hindered during wartime and postwar periods, during times of international political crises, or during runaway inflation. But during such times in Germany the "political" food prices were regulated in the interest of consumers, and agricultural producers were unable to enjoy prices adequately elevated by shortages. In some other countries, however, agriculture was able to initiate extensive investments during or after such periods. These special circumstances have, in some countries, contributed much to raising the level of technology in agriculture.

Thus, we come to the conclusion that for the most part the prices for industrial goods are more strongly dependent on production costs, whereas prices of agricultural products are more oriented toward the given supply-and-demand situation, that is, toward the situation of the market. In addition, dumping of agricultural products on the international market is quite customary. There are also specific reasons for this with respect to agriculture: since agricultural output is difficult to restrict and domestic consumption does not react elastically to price cuts, it suggests that exports at reduced prices be used as an outlet. Such practices were particularly stimulated by both world wars. In time of war, agricultural production is forced in those countries where conditions allow for it. After a normalization of conditions ensues, a supply excess occurs that is difficult to eliminate. In this respect also, the food sector assumes a special position because it belongs to those branches that turn out the same products in times of war as in times of peace. Moreover, financially weak countries lack foreign currency, including especially those developing nations that rely heavily on agricultural exports and must sell them at any price; indeed, this also holds true where dumping is not practiced.

Marketing and Processing Margins. Of all the considerations of agricultural price policy and its influence on the costs of food, the growing processing and marketing margins have to receive increasing attention.

Up until now these margins have been considered primarily from the aspect of whether they have been raised excessively and whether a compression of margins would result in an increase in producer prices or a decrease in consumer prices. As always, the task at hand is to carry out the marketing and processing functions as efficiently and inexpensively as possible in the interest of producers of agricultural goods as well as in the interest of the food consumers. Moreover, overall economic interests are also involved here, since the size and composition of the national product and especially the possibilities for production and consumption of goods are, next to service, influenced most by the efficiency of the distributive sector.

But recently we have been viewing the system of marketing and processing margins from still other aspects. We had to recognize that the process of price formation for marketing services is quite independent of the price formation for agricultural goods on the producer level. This leads to a phenomenon that, up until now, has not always been well understood, namely, short- or long-term discrepancies of producer prices on the one hand and margins on the other. Without going into great detail here, I would like to enumerate some important problems and tendencies resulting from the different changes in producer prices and margins.

1. Under free market conditions on the producer level, producer prices show greater fluctuations than prices on the consumer level. The price elasticity of demand is, thus, less pronounced on the producer level than on the consumer level. The wider and more rigid the margins, the greater the differences in price elasticities.

2. A low degree of flexibility of consumer prices renders difficult the balancing out of supply and demand through price changes.

3. From the viewpoint of market structure and performance, which must be seen in connection with the perishability of produce and with storage costs (including a possible reduction in quality), the marketing sector is in a much stronger, more favorable position in periods of rapidly increasing supply, when compared with the agricultural sector. The reverse situation appears during periods of supply shortages. It follows that due to the specific market position there is a tendency toward the widening of margins in periods of oversupply and a tendency toward the reduction of margins in periods of shortages. This observation does not contradict the fact that, over medium and long periods of time—when the market has adjusted to a prolonged increase or decrease in sales volume—a growing sales volume lowers the marketing costs per unit, and a reduced one increases them.

4. There exists, in the long run, a tendency toward increased marketing costs per unit. This tendency is based on two completely different factors. First, we are dealing with the growing consumer demand for better food quality, processing, packaging, and service. With an increasing income, consumers can afford more, and they are making greater demands for improved processing and packaging of food to make kitchen work easier and less time consuming. Second, the increase in wages and salaries in food handling and trade induced by higher wages in industrial manufacturing cannot be compensated for fully at this time by cutting back labor inputs, i.e., through economizing. When viewed in the long run, both factors effect an increase in the marketing and processing margins per unit and a reduction in the share of consumer expenditures flowing into agriculture for remuneration of productive factors.

Farmers are most interested in seeing competition in marketing, in the processing and distribution of food, remain strong. If competition is weak it must be encouraged. Just as an effective competitive order is beneficial in price formation of industrial inputs for agriculture, it is also beneficial to agriculture.

The increasing consumer demand for higher quality, packaging, processing, and services must, however, give rise to increased markups per unit, even when strong competition predominates in distribution and processing. Consequently, there is little hope that a detectable narrowing in processing and marketing margins might occur, yielding a higher share of consumer expenditures for the agricultural producers.

Necessity of Curbing Price Fluctuations on Agricultural Markets. In a system of free price formation, agriculture would have a manifestly weak market position, limited by the perishability of produce and by the fact that this market performance based on perfect competition would, in its truly unrestricted form, only strictly apply to agricultural goods.

In addition, a low elasticity of supply and demand combined with a free price formation would bring about a tendency toward intense price fluctuations, thus creating a disadvantageous situation for producers during times of oversupply, an advantageous one during supply shortages. Considerable fluctuation in agricultural supply inevitably occurs with seasonal influences and weather changes from year to year.

Decisive differences exist between industry and agriculture in the steering of market supplies. Furthermore, the demand for industrial goods in general reacts much more elastically with respect to prices and income than with the demand for food products. Consequently, with free price formation the prices for industrial merchandise show less fluctuation than prices for agricultural produce. Although a system of free price formation is the cornerstone of a market economy when applied to goods subject to elastic demand, in particular to industrial wares, free price formation does more harm than benefit when applied to products characterized by an inelastic demand such as agricultural produce. A systematic market and price policy in the social market economy is imperative here, though it must remain flexible under political pressure.

Results and Conclusions. In the discussion of the position of agriculture in the market economy, mainly the conditions of production deviating from those of industry are placed in the foreground: bound to the land, bioorganic production is dependent on fluctuations in weather conditions and seasonal growth factors, low mobility of production factors, the law of diminishing returns, limited possibilities for mechanization, and so forth. In addition, institutional and social restrictions also keep agricultural production in chains: the size structure of farms; an inadequate rural educational system; family farms; and the functional connection between manager, operator, and laborer, without sufficient selection and specialization in these positions according to qualification and training. These factors certainly are significant. But the difficulties and disadvantages stemming from them are exaggerated, particularly when they are viewed only statistically, and when possible improvements and adaptations are underestimated.

The possibilities for increases in productivity in agriculture are greater than often assumed. This is borne out by experience and relevant statistical data in West Germany, West Europe, North America, and elsewhere. Though the effort toward an increase in the physical productivity per worker in agriculture encounters obstacles in a number of countries, increased productivity in agriculture has kept pace with industry over long periods of time. In contrast, there are only a few countries in which agricultural income per head approaches that found in the nonagricultural economy.

The income disparity of agriculture is first caused by the coincidence of factors that inhibit production and productivity on the one side and two other significant factors on the other side—diminishing increase of food consumption with economic growth and a price formation of agricultural goods that, except during periods of supply shortages, could not completely compensate for the lag in growth of productivity under conditions of free pricing. These causes are based on the compound effect of the competitive market, which is fully realized only for agricultural supply, in combination

—with the perishability of agricultural products,

—with a tendency toward surpluses resulting from a slow rise in consumption and an accelerated output (caused by expanded technological progress and national price supports),

—with an inelastic demand, leading to an overproportional price fall when supply grows faster than demand, under conditions of free pricing,

—with agricultural production showing an inelasticity with respect to lowering prices because of production factors resistant to change—in particular the rural workers who can only migrate slowly and who cannot simply leave their jobs in agriculture due to income disparity—and because individual farms with greater output and supply are, as a rule, better off than those operating under a restricted output in view of the high fixed costs of production; during times of supply shortages the situation is fundamentally different because, with a free formation of prices, relatively high agricultural prices have a favorable effect on agricultural income. However, since 1913 extended periods of supply shortages have not been encountered in western industrialized nations during times of peace.

The real income per capita in any branch of the economy is determined by the development of physical productivity (net production per laborer), as well as by the changes in producer prices (in relation to other prices). Consequently, various combinations of changes in physical productivity, producer prices, and real income in the economy are possible; an accelerated rise in physical productivity can lead to a favorable or less advantageous change in income, depending on whether an increasing production results in favorable or unfavorable market prices.

When considered worldwide, agriculture finds itself in a phase of abundant supply (in comparison with the effective demand), with income disparity and with pressure on market prices. Although West German agriculture is extensively isolated from the world market by enacted market policies and price subsidies, it still cannot offer a level of income equal to that of comparable jobs in other sectors of the economy, as noted by the "green reports." The situation in the last few years has been aggravated by the somewhat inflationary accelerated economic boom and forced wage increases in industries profiting from recent economic developments, whose indirect effects on agriculture have been particularly distressing. The situation in the lagging sectors, particularly agricultural, becomes intolerable when the leading economic sectors, with their increased productivity and income gains, transform production returns solely into increased wages, taxes, and profits, rather than into some form of price reduction that could benefit the other sectors subject to less favorable economic conditions. *These developments are certainly not in line with the principles of a competitive economic order.*

The profit base and per capita income within agriculture are quite varied, depending on factors such as the size of the farm, fragmentation of land, soil quality, water supply, topography, direction of production, invested capital, and possibilities of earnings outside farming. Also important are the great differences in the quality of management, affected by many factors including the age, initiative, education, and experience of farmers. Technological and economic developments are continually placing greater and more diverse demands on management and the labor force, for which they are unprepared, making adaptation difficult.

With the agricultural law (*Landwirtschaftsgesetz*) enacted September 5, 1955, the Federal Republic of Germany set the legislative groundwork for the strengthening of agriculture, following similar efforts already undertaken in other countries. The objective of this law is formulated in the first paragraph as follows:

> In order to allow agriculture to share in the progressive development of the German national economy, and in order to secure the best possible provision of food for the people, agriculture is to be placed in a position, by means of agricultural and economic policy, in particular by tax, credit, and price policies, to compensate for inherent natural and economic disadvantages compared with other economic sectors, and to increase agricul-

tural productivity. With these measures, the social position of those people being occupied in agriculture is to be adjusted to that of comparable occupational groups.

Here we are confronted with the great and difficult task of finding the appropriate starting point for, and the right degree of measures to promote agriculture. The agricultural professional organization places the greatest importance on global measures in the form of price increases and cost reductions. However, in order to deal fairly with the actual state of affairs, agricultural policy must take into account the diverse set of conditions existing within agriculture. Effective promotional measures directed at increasing the productivity of those working in agriculture are therefore indispensable. Often mentioned, urgent tasks, which cannot be dealt with here, include an improvement of the agricultural structure; raising the level of education; the enlargement of the advisory service; the encouragement of different forms of cooperative sharing of machinery; the arrangement of easier and less expensive financing; and improved road construction, electric power supply, water supply, and regional culture.

Another conclusion that becomes obvious is that political-economic interventions should not preferentially benefit those branches of the economy already ahead of the agricultural sector.

A detailed treatment of agricultural market and price policy and, in particular, of the complex issue of foreign trade policy within the framework of the social market economy must be withheld for another occasion. I will limit myself here to the observation that a systematic market and price policy for the agriculture market is imperative. However, it must remain flexible and must not stagnate under political pressure. The present market order could be organized more purposefully, with more freedom of movement, and more economically without generally reducing the protection of agriculture.

However, the demands of farmers' unions on market and price policy have expanded from stabilization efforts alone to demands for higher prices and income. Having confirmed, in our examination of the problem, the structural disadvantages of agriculture imposed on income acquisition, the objectives outlined in the agricultural law are indeed justifiable. This, however, says nothing about the degree to which income could be redistributed to benefit agriculture without destroying the market economy.

An exaggerated egalitarian approach to income distribution contradicts the principles of free enterprise. Redistribution of income is primarily thought of as a tool for social policy. The progressive income tax system already provides for widespread corrections in income distribution. If egalitarianism is taken too far, the limit is soon reached where overall progress is slowed or even completely stifled. The question is then raised, To what extent is it reasonable to place increased burdens on the happily thriving economic sectors and business in order to compensate the economically less successful sectors?

Maintaining strong advances might more efficiently benefit the needy sectors directly and indirectly than could an intensified global redistribution of income. By demanding a total leveling of income among economic sectors, one fails to recognize the great preference for an independent existence; and one could bring on a demand for income redistribution within agriculture, thus drifting toward an economic order characterized by a dubious contradiction of the principles of our economic order, based on individual responsibility, private property, and economic progress.

Global aid in the form of price supports or fertilizer price subsidies is considerably more beneficial to the larger, relatively favored farms with high output. A solution to this dilemma is exemplified by Swedish agricultural policy, which pursues an agricultural price level at which the costs of rationally managed farms with 10 to 20 hectares of land surface are covered. In addition, a program aimed at the improvement of agricultural structure is carried out for the smaller farms. Agricultural policy should take into account the true state of affairs.

I share the opinion of Gasser (1957) that, in economic theory and economic policy, the special attributes of agriculture deserve closer examination and evaluation. This holds true, in particular, for a truly sensible integration of the agricultural economy into the market economy. In view of the unique nature of agriculture, an effective "economic policy from one mold" does not exist. There are no pat solutions to the income problems of agriculture.

References
Dovring, F. 1956. *Land and Labor in Europe, 1900–1950; A Comparative Survey of Recent Agrarian History.* The Hague: M. Nijhoff.
Gasser, W. 1957. "Die Eingliederung der Landwirtschaft in die Gesamtwirtschaft eines Industriestates, betrachtetvom Standpunkt der Landwirtschaft aus." In *Schriftenreihe der Landwirtschaftlichen Fakultat der Universitat Kiel,* no. 16 (papers read at the 1956 conference).
Niehaus, H. 1956. "Das Bauerntum in Wirtschaft und Gesellschaft." In *Agrarpolitik in der Sozialen Marktwirtschaft* (Fifth conference of the Aktionsgemeinschaft Soziale Marktwirtschaft, March).
Quante, P. 1933. *Die Flucht aus der Landwirtschaft.* Berlin-Grunewald: K. Vowinckel.
Strisch, H., and Weippert, G. 1956. "Die Eingliederung der Landwirtschaft in die Marktwirtschaft." *Berichte uber Landwirtschaft* 34:369–92.
Von Dietze, C. 1942. "Landwirtschaft und Wettbewerbsordnung." *Schmollers Jahrbuch fur Gesetzgebung, Verwaltung und Volleswirtschaft im Deutschen Reich* 66:124–57.
———. 1946. "Bauernwirtschaft und Kollektiv." *Schweizerische Zeitschrift fur Volkswirtschaft und Statistik* 82:230–59.

22

The Market Economy in Western European Integration: Agricultural Policy

G. BODDEZ

THE COMMON AGRICULTURAL POLICY is rooted in the measures that had already been worked out at national level in the member states. Market expansion within the European Economic Community (EEC) framework without providing the agricultural sector with its own machinery would therefore have brought about a sizable reduction in farm income.

Whereas simply pulling down tariff walls and abolishing quotas is more or less enough to create a common market in industrial goods, much more is needed for trade in farm products. There are many ways of intervening in agricultural markets: through fixed prices, market control, limitation of harvests, monopolizing imports, compulsory mixing of home-produced grain in flour and bread, seasonal bans on imports of certain products, bilateral agreements permitting imports from specified countries only, and so on. In short, customs duties and quotas are accompanied by a number of other barriers to free trade in farm products that in fact boil down to various forms of market regulation introduced to accommodate the special social structure of agriculture with special conditions of production and to defend the interests of the consumer.

The determination of the member states to retain agricultural support led inevitably to the formulation of a common agricultural policy, since it was out

This paper first appeared in the Proceedings of the Seventh Flemish Economic Congress, Louvain, May 8-9, 1965. Participants in the discussion that led to the present paper were A. G. Baptist, chairman; G. Boddez, rapporteur; F. A. Derwael, secretary; and C. Boon, Th. Dams, A. DeLeeuw, A. De Taverneir, R. Grooten, R. Kinget, W. Laevaert, G. Pevenage, M. Stuyck, L. Tindemans, J. Van Lierde, W. Van Merhaege, W. Van Slobbe, A. Verkinderen, and R. Verschaeken.

of the question to exclude agriculture from the Common Market just because it was impossible to set up an absolutely free market for farm products.

A number of other factors argued for the extension of European integration to agriculture. For instance, it would have been impracticable to expose industry to greater competition while wages and costs still showed considerable divergences as a result of the different levels of prices for farm products. This is why express provision was made for a common agricultural policy in the Treaty of Rome.

Objectives of Farm Policy. According to economic theorists such as Professor Hartog (1964, p. 5), the aims of farm policy are to keep or make agriculture economically sound, which means that agriculture: (1) must be able to provide the factors of production involved from proceeds on the market with the income they could obtain from the same or similar productive activities in other sectors of the economy; and (2) must be able to cope with normal outside competition (excluding dumping) in commodities adapted to the home soil and in the home climate.

Apart from theoretical economic considerations, Hartog leaves little room for noneconomic motives. In his view, the argument of food supplies in case of armed conflict can at most be used to justify some restriction of the minimum volume of production but not of the minimum active farm population. Within this framework, the problem of the optimum production structure and productivity of agriculture does remain an economic datum.

Professor Hartog maintains further that while social considerations are perhaps worthy of attention where the optimum conditions in which the adjustment processes should take place are at issue, they must not excuse the retention of economically unhealthy situations at the root of social problems.

It may be mentioned in passing that numerous government measures have been enforced in each of the EEC countries because of the special circumstances of agriculture (dependence on the weather, social significance, particular economic features) and in most cases to cope with crises. A point that is perhaps too often overlooked is that some government interventions subsequently became a contributory factor in the difficult position in which agriculture is currently placed—uneasy balances between production and sales of some farm products, and farmworkers' incomes lagging behind those of other groups such as industrial workers. This will be dealt with in detail later.

Objectives Set Out in the EEC Treaty. Article 39 of the treaty specifies that the objectives of the common agricultural policy shall be:
1. to increase agricultural productivity by promoting technical progress

and by ensuring the rational development of agricultural production and the optimum utilization of the factors of production, in particular labor;

2. thus to ensure a fair standard of living for the agricultural community, particularly by increasing the individual earnings of persons engaged in agriculture;

3. to stabilize markets;

4. to guarantee supplies;

5. to ensure the delivery of supplies to consumers at reasonable prices.

Here too, then, greater productivity in agriculture and the consequent rise in per capita income are major considerations. Another point to be noted is that where a theorist such as Professor Hartog stresses the operation of the market without any form of protection (other than antidumping regulations), the EEC objectives underline the need to adjust free price formation so as to increase stability with a view to safeguarding the interests of producers and consumers. This difference in emphasis suggests a difference in the weight given to, on the one hand, market and price policy (from which protection in any form is not explicitly excluded) and, on the other, structural policy.

A proper appreciation of these rather important distinctions also presupposes a knowledge of the basic problems of agricultural economics to which the objectives are attuned. The usual distinction between the short and the long run is also in evidence in this field.

Basic Problems

In the Short Run: Stability of Prices and Incomes. The price inelasticity of demand for and supply of a number of farm products results in slight swings in these curves, causing relatively big fluctuations in prices. The thing that matters now is that such swings are anything but exceptional.

Regarding demand, it was mainly the general economic situation in the past that produced considerable fluctuations. An example of this is the crisis in the 1930s. The influence of business conditions has perhaps declined since the war, but political disturbances have continued to play a definite role (the Korea boom, the Cuba crisis and its repercussions on the world sugar market, Russian grain imports, etc.)

Fluctuations in supply have their origin in the inherent nature of agricultural production and are fortuitous, seasonal, or cyclical. The importance of climatic and seasonal influences on agricultural production is so well known that there is no need to go into the matter here. Suffice it to say that geographical expansion resulting from European integration may well have a stablilizing effect.

Cyclical factors are more conspicuous in agriculture than in any other market. They derive from the combination of a biologically determined production period and the reaction of the producer to current prices, and an expansion of the market will not help to eliminate fluctuations but only to ensure that they occur at the same time throughout the community. The beef and pork cycles are examples of this phenomenon; unlike the general business cycle, they are characterized by antagonistic changes in prices and supplies.

As these variations in supply and demand are not correlated, and given the price inelasticity of supply and demand in the case of a number of farm products, disproportionate instability of prices results in the short run.

This variability of prices impairs the value of the price mechanism as an indicator of production to the extent that the tendency toward equilibrium behind these short-run price fluctuations is blurred. It also affects the stability of the cost of living, which is difficult to reconcile with the interests of the consumer, who wants assured supplies of food, particularly basic commodities, at reasonable prices. As a matter of fact, the problem takes on a general economic significance through the familiar machinery of wages being adjusted to the cost of living.

For the producer, increased production leads to a more than proportionate fall in prices (for products with price-inelastic demand) and so to a drop in income, threatening the livelihood of the farmers. Furthermore, severe price fluctuations are not conducive to winning and keeping foreign markets.

The immediate and obvious conclusion is that a great deal of market and price policy is concerned with this short-run instability of agricultural markets; no real protection is involved, though regulation of the market and correction of the free play of the market are required. In view of the perfect competition that is typical of agricultural production, this task can only be performed by public authorities, not by individual producers. Government intervention of this kind in the member states is now leading to a nonprotectionist element in EEC market and price policy. We shall have an opportunity later to show the connection between built-in price instability and the extent to which the market was rejected as a regulating factor for the various farm products at the EEC level.

These basic short-run problems largely explain, therefore, the significance of the EEC's objectives of market stabilization and supplying food at reasonable prices. Whether this is of empirical origin or is consciously based on economic deduction is not important.

It has just been pointed out that market and price policy has been left considerable freedom of action without suggesting protectionism. It is, however, also true that prices seldom are stabilized at the long-run equilibrium level— that "upward" stabilization is strived for—and that market and price policy lends itself fully toward both goals. It is doubtless for these reasons that the attention of some economists is held by the evil of agricultural protection. Clearly, to emphasize structure policy at the expense of market and price policy is only a short step further. This brings us directly into the sphere of the long term—that of economic development.

In the Long Run: Agriculture and Economic Development

GENERAL DISCUSSION. At the moment, the center of the population explosion is in the developing countries, where the problem is how long food production will be able to keep pace. Stepping up food production is a more complex problem that will take much longer to solve than the drop in the mortality rate achieved by introduction of relatively cheap medical techniques. This might lead the countries that are giving more and more technical assistance to the "third world" to pay more attention to world food supplies in general and to the relief of hunger by means of farm surpluses in particular.

In view of the nature and volume of technical assistance as we now know it, and in view of the insufficient demand (in terms of purchasing power) from the developing countries, the economic field in which our farms operate is still largely confined to the developed countries.

In this part of the world there is a mechanism at work that causes the expansion of supply to exceed that of demand in the case of a number of major agricultural products.

Technological progress entails increased productivity, and in general this is accompanied by an appreciable rise in output. And the possibility of cutting back production in order to restore the market equilibrium runs up against a system of complete competition that prevents the numerous individual small farms from influencing the market.

In contrast to this expansion of supply, demand for many farm products is expanding relatively little as a result of the growth of population because of the rather moderate income elasticity of demand for food. As is only too well known, the proportion spent on food in the total consumers' expenditures declines as the standard of living rises. The price inelasticity of overall demand for agricultural produce also ensures that no fall in agricultural prices can result from a marked increase in overall consumption of farm produce. In short, overall demand for farm products is not very expansionary, because of the inelasticity of the human stomach, although there is a specific, more or less sizable expansion of demand for individual products.

The withdrawal of factors of production from agriculture in order to restore the balance between supply and demand is concentrated on the labor factor since technological innovations are generally capital-using or labor-saving in character. The rather widespread practice of interest subsidization naturally speeds up the process of substituting capital for labor and consequently the release of manpower. What is more, technological progress raises the optimum plot and farm area and thus brings problems of scale with regard to the rather widespread small plot and farm. This phenomenon is likely to concentrate the required withdrawal of factors of production from agriculture still more to that of labor rather than of land.

The supply of farm products expanding more rapidly than demand for them ultimately results in a drastic reduction in the numbers employed in agriculture. First of all, the imbalance between supply and demand causes the equilibrium price of a number of farm products to shift the price-inelastic demand curve downward, i.e., downward pressure on the terms of trade. This pressure on relative farm prices further affects farm incomes and therefore the numbers of farms and the active population. Professor G. S. Shepherd (1964, p. 283), referring to American conditions, consequently speaks of imbalance between supply of and demand for "farmers" rather than farm products as the cause of the relatively low per capita incomes in agriculture.

So there is clearly a negative correlation between the percentage of the total active population working in agriculture and average per capita income, which we use here as an indicator of the level of economic development in various economic-geographical regions. On the average, a 1 percent reduction in the active farm population is accompanied by a rise of about 0.54 percent in per capita income (Zimmerman 1960, p. 52). Over a period of one hundred years, then, a downward trend in the percentage of the active population working in the primary sector can be discerned in the prosperous countries. This trend has assumed major proportions in recent decades particularly. However, this does not preclude the average income in the nonfarm sector from being higher in general than that in agriculture: about 1953, for instance, output per worker in the primary sector in North America and northwestern Europe was less than two-thirds of that in the secondary and tertiary sectors. A closer analysis of the disparity of farm incomes is therefore imperative, especially as increasing the individual earnings of persons engaged in agriculture is expressly stated to be one of the aims of the common agricultural policy.

HOW INCOME DISPARITY ARISES. It was shown above that the process of economic development presupposes a certain intensity of migration of labor from the agricultural sector to other sectors of the economy. This requirement is intensified by the relatively higher birth rate in rural areas and by interest subsidization.

Under conditions of perfect mobility of labor, the total migration required would not give rise to a disparity in income per head between agriculture and the nonfarm sector. If there is a disparity, then equilibrium is set up between migration, resistance, and income disparity, resistance tending to brake and income disparity to accelerate the former. This rather sketchy train of thought has many points of similarity with the electricity formula $I = E/R$, where E = potential difference (income disparity); I = current (intensity of migration); and R = resistance (lack of mobility).

This perhaps oversimple presentation of a complex economic phenomenon nevertheless has the advantage, in our view, of grouping a great number of relevant factors logically and synthetically around this formula. Alignment of incomes, for instance, may be kept back because of lack of mobility due to job preferences or other noneconomic considerations. In that case equilibrium will be established where income disparity exactly offsets the advantages deriving from the factors mentioned.

Further, the high degree of competition in the farm sector will perhaps help to keep more factors of production on the land than would be the case with a more monopolistic structure such as we have in industry.

Not only the existence of a large number of farms in the sector, but the mere fact that they are family businesses, has a damping effect on migration from agriculture. Indeed this renders the marginal calculus inadequate, since farmhands are not paid on the basis of the marginal productivity principle but on that of the average productivity of all the family labor present on the farm. Farmhands whose marginal productivity may be well below their wage (possibly deferred) can resist a move as a result of their disproportionate pay. In bigger industrial firms, on the other hand, marginal equilibrium is attained much more easily.

Another very important consideration is that resistance to moving is greatly weakened by alternative local employment offered outside agriculture. This shows how the farming economy must be seen in conjunction with the economy as a whole and how regional disparities in farm structure can be fitted into the context of regional economic policy.

Lastly, great importance must be attached to mental attitudes, to the type and amount of guidance, to the level of transfer costs, and to the risks inherent in any form of professional changeover.

The purpose of this exposition was to give a clear picture of the most significant types of resistance to occupational mobility and of how they affect the income of the farm population. Given a certain required intensity of movement away from the land, the disparity in incomes will grow proportionately wider as there is more resistance to be overcome. Conversely, given the resistance to be overcome, a wider disparity in incomes will stimulate the exodus from agriculture.

It is now all too plain that measures of support may retard the permanent redistribution of the active population over the various sectors of the economy that is being made inevitable by economic development. Here again we may quote Professor Shepherd on similar problems confronting the United States: ''What is needed is to reconstruct farm policy so that it will deal less with farm products and farm land and more directly with farm people. This needs to be done, not by supporting prices for farm products or increasing incomes to existing farmers—leaving the underlying causes of the problem still at work—but by dealing directly with the supply and demand for farmers'' (1964, p. 283).

However, the final result will depend on the relative strength of all relevant factors. Support for Belgian farming, for instance, has not prevented the proportion of farm population to total active population from dropping fairly low in comparison with many other developed countries. The distribution of the active population over the different sectors of economic life, then, is in line with a high standard of living. Alternative employment in industry has perhaps had an important compensating effect here. It is in the nature of things that in a small country such as Belgium industries are set up close to agriculture.

In our view, what we have said above clearly shows that the workings of the free market are inadequate not only for the problems of short-run equilibrium but also in respect to long-run equilibrium. This time, however, the solution is not to be found in market and price policy alone, though this may perhaps be held responsible for an attendant disturbance of equilibrium. Putting pressure on agricultural prices and incomes does not seem to be the best way of bringing about the necessary adjustments, both for social reasons and because it would be in conflict with the very aims of the EEC. The answer will have to be sought in an efficient structure policy in the broad sense to supplement the market and price policy studied above.

Let us now look more closely at how well the common agricultural policy, especially the EEC's market, price, and structure policy, meets these fundamental problems.

Main Features of the Common Agricultural Policy

Freedom of Movement for Farm Products within the Common Market. The essential feature of the EEC agricultural policy is the system of variable internal levies (and refunds) worked out for the important sectors of agricultural commodities.

The levy is charged by importing countries to offset the difference between the import price of a product and its price on the home market. And in the case of livestock products the levy also neutralizes price differences in relation to the primary commodities. This system replaces all kinds of protective measures previously applied by individual member states (quotas, temporary import regulations, minimum prices, etc.) and has therefore simplified matters on the whole.

This system makes it possible to ensure free circulation of farm products despite the differences in prices among the member countries. And it converts the effects of national policy measures into "internal" levies as a result of internal price differences. Thus clarified, intracommunity protection can be relinquished as the size of the levies is reduced through the gradual alignment of national prices. This is how the technique of "internal" levies makes the transition to a single market much easier. In this final stage the effect of comparative productivity will lead to specialization and productivity boosts. Consequently, extreme importance is attached to the EEC Council's decision that common grain prices—which more or less govern all the others—will come into force in July 1967.

Protection for European Agriculture at the Frontier. Here, too, a system of variable levies (and refunds) has been elaborated for the major farm sectors as a substitute for national protective measures. These external levies are higher than the internal ones, which ensures preference for Community countries at the outset. Unlike the intra-Community levies, which are gradually reduced, the external levies remain as they are, so that in the unified market they will represent manifest Community preference or protection from outside.

The levies, which in the beginning offset the difference between the world price and the price in the importing country, will be fixed in light of the Community price level at the unified-market stage. The level of Community prices in relation to world prices will therefore determine how great a role is played by comparative cost and specialization between the EEC and the rest of the world. Since dumping has an adverse effect on the price of farm products on the world market, only that component in the levies on imports that is not concerned with preventing dumping should really be regarded as protection.

The EEC Council decision on common grain prices mentioned earlier is of enormous significance in this connection. For if price alignment as such is decisive for the elimination of internal agricultural protection, then the level at which Community prices are fixed in relation to prices outside the Community will determine how protectionist the common agricultural policy will remain.

Returning to the EEC objectives, we note that they hold out no explicit prospect of a sound agriculture in the sense that it "must be able to cope with normal outside competition (excluding dumping) in commodities adapted to the home soil and climate"—as required by the objectives for farm policy put forward by Professor Hartog, for example.

At any rate, it would seem that cost comparison will only be fully carried through internally, while the degree of competition with the outside world will be governed by (1) the highest common denominator among the forces on which the member states' farm protection policies were based already, including the political if not the economic limitations of those policies; and (2) the pressure that can be exerted by interested countries outside the Community, mainly the United States.

Community Market, Price and Commercial Policy. It has already been pointed out and illustrated that market and price policy has protectionist consequences when it gives rise to upward price stabilization. We now give rather more attention to the role of market and price policy—apart from any protectionist aims—in relation to short-term price and income instability.

Economic Grounds for the Choice between Regulation and Freedom. About 85 percent of agricultural production comes under European market organizations. And still more products can be expected to be incorporated into the system—partly because of pressure from the professional organizations.

Extending market regulations to the majority of farm products does not mean that the market is ceasing altogether to be a regulating factor in this sector. It is conceded, however, that the market in the sense of completely free price formation will presumably continue as the most important regulating factor only for "inedible horticultural products" (plus leguminous plants and seeds), which of course are unaffected by the inelasticity of the human stomach.

In this sector, then, the absence of a regulated market is connected with the relative price- and income-elasticity of demand and with the fact that these are not primary commodities for the agricultural or food economy.

All this is likely to prevent the aims of farm policy affecting producers' and consumers' interests from suffering.

Things are quite different in the case of basic products of the agricultural and food sectors—wheat, for example. Here the market organization is of such proportions that it becomes the most important regulating factor. The explanation for this is the slight price elasticity and (possibly negative) income elasticity of demand, coupled with a comparatively unfavorable land/man ratio compared with other countries, particularly those in the New World. There is far-reaching stabilization of the markets, especially of short-run price and income fluctuations, and considerable Community preference or protection against nonmember countries.

Between these extremes lie the other agricultural and horticultural products, for which the importance of the market as a regulating factor is curtailed—though not as much as in the case of wheat.

The livestock undertakings that are not tied to the land (pigs, eggs, chickens) have such a high elasticity of supply that free price formation on the internal market had to be retained as an essential regulator of production, even though this solution is much less satisfactory in the short term in view of cyclical price instability. This explains why these sectors are further to the right along the scale between regulation and freedom than is a product such as beef, which is still endowed with quite considerable price- and income-elasticity of demand but whose production process is as yet tied to the soil and slowed down by biological factors.

Groups of Instruments and the "Regulation-Freedom Scale." The position of the various farm products on the scale can also be assessed in light of the instruments used to determine the framework within which the market is retained as a regulating factor. Three groups can be distinguished:

Group I: Products for which there are measures at the external frontier (in the form of levies) and on the internal market. These are products such as grain, sugar beets, milk, and beef.

For these products there are *target* or *guide* prices and intervention prices. The fact that the market still has a certain part to play is apparent if we note that no real fixed prices are laid down but only a narrow price margin, and that this may be reviewed annually, in which case experience with the prices existing on the market is also taken into account.

Group II: Products for which there are measures (in the form of levies) at the external frontier only. The internal market prices will be formed by the free play of supply and demand. This group includes pork, eggs, and poultry.

Group III: Products for which the sole measures specified (in the form of a customs tariff) are applied at the external frontier. Internal market prices are formed by the free play of supply and demand. This is the case for fruit and vegetables. The commission has now proposed measures of intervention. If the proposal is adopted, this will rob the free market of some of its importance.

Table 22.1.   Operating measures for major farm products or foodstuffs

	Internal market			Measures at the frontier				
	Price intervention					Sluice-gate price or equivalent		
Products by group	Target price	Inter-vention prices	Free price	Threshold price	Levies + refunds	Internal	External	Customs duties
Group I								
Grain	*	*		*	*			
Sugar (proposed)	*	*		*	* (a)			
Dairy produce	* (b)	* (c)		* (d)	* (d)	*	*	* (e)
Beef (f)		(g)			*			*
Group II								
Pork		(h)	*		*	* (i)	*	
Eggs			*		*		*	
Poultry			*		*		*	
Group III								
Fruit and vegetables (j)								*
Group IV								
Inedible horticultural products (+ legu- minous plants and seeds)			*					* (k)

(a) Possibly negative.
(b) For fresh milk.
(c) For butter.
(d) For condensed milk, butter, and types of cheese on which the duties are not bound in GATT; there is also a reference price for these products.
(e) For certain types of cheese on which the duties are bound in GATT.
(f) Guide price.
(g) Intervention possible for grown animals.
(h) Intervention possible.
(i) Until common grain prices come into force on July 1, 1967.
(j) Reference price.
(k) Customs duties not imposed within a market organization.

Machinery of Measures Operating along the "Regulating-Freedom Scale." It is impracticable to go into the machinery of all the measures introduced for these products. Table 22.1 gives an outline of the most important measures provided for a number of major farm products of foodstuffs; now we will take a closer look at how they work.

The target price (for grain, for instance) is the price obtained over a given period in the marketing center with the greatest deficit for a product of well-defined standard quality. The threshold price is equal to the target price less freight and selling costs from the frontier to the region with the greatest deficit. The levy (see Groups I and II) represents, as noted above, the difference between the prices in the importing and the exporting country and is thus a kind of variable customs duty.

Where an international agricultural market is in surplus (which is the case on the world grain market, for example), the levy system prevents prices from rising above the target price, and this ensures short-run stability of the markets with reference to consumers' interests (see the EEC objectives above). However, this only applies if the conditions we have just mentioned are fulfilled, except on the sugar market where there is the possibility of negative levies. Refunds must, mutatis mutandis, be taken into account for exports.

The intervention price is the price at which products may at any time be bought up by the intervention agencies of the member states. The price guaranteed to grain producers, for instance, is 5 to 10 percent below the target price (limits of the price margin). Intervention on the internal market thus stabilizes the markets with reference to producers' interests (see the EEC objectives above).

Finally, the sluice-gate price corresponds to what is regarded as the normal minimum offer price free-to-frontier, account being taken of the evolution of feed grain prices on the world market and of a feed conversion rate that is representative for exporting countries. A type of antidumping effect is obtained by leveling the offer price up to the sluice-gate price by means of an extra levy.

The diagonal distribution of the asterisks on both the left (internal market) and the right (measures at the frontier) of Table 22.1 indicates that the products are more or less arranged according to the degree to which government intervention is used as a regulating factor, since the machinery is as far as possible set out from left to right in descending order of intervention. This more detailed analysis confirms the grouping suggested earlier on the regulation-freedom scale: at the top left of the table we find both curtailment of short-run price instability and Community preference (protection vis-à-vis nonmember countries); at the bottom right there is no price stabilization on the internal market and only customs duties as protection.

It would be wrong, however, to think that the EEC's agricultural policy is concerned only with market and price policy, including long-term leveling-up of prices, giving no further attention to basic equilibrium in the long run. This would be simply overlooking the EEC's action on farm structure policy.

Agricultural Structure Policy. One of the aims of the common agricultural policy is to ensure a reasonable income to those fully employed on well-run and economically viable farms, together with a fair return on capital invested. This can apply both to family farms and to farms employing paid labor. What is a fair income should be assessed in the light of what can be earned in comparable nonfarm occupations.

Price and market policy alone—as has already been pointed out in the analysis of the basic long-run problems—cannot bring about this result. It must be backed up by structure policy and by social policy in agriculture.

The ratio between the labor force and the basis of its income is expressive of the structural situation in agriculture. Because agriculture is becoming increasingly capital intensive, as a result of the substitution of capital for labor and of technological progress in agriculture, the classical man/land ratio no longer holds good: it must be replaced by a man/capital ratio or, better still, by a man/income ratio. Measures of structure policy should therefore be aimed at improving or removing existing structural deficiencies and pushing the process of agricultural development in the right direction by exerting influence on one or both of the factors of this relationship. Here again, readers are referred to the analysis of basic long-run problems.

Structure policy in agriculture should, however, be considered in close conjunction with the problems of market equilibrium (long run) and of the development of the economy at regional levels. Regarding this last point, the migration of labor away from farms, for instance, which is often so essential, cannot be obtained within the narrow limits of agriculture alone: it depends to a considerable extent on the existence or creation of alternative nonfarm jobs.

So it is within this structure-market-region triangle that the measures of structural improvement should be appraised economically.

Within the framework of the common agricultural policy, the member states' structure policies are coordinated, i.e., attuned to each other so that they will help to realize the aims of the common agricultural policy. In this field, unlike that of market and price policy, the member states retain responsibility for implementing the policy.

In order to give strength to structure policy and to lead it in the direction best suited to the needs created by the institution of a common market for farm products, by the introduction of a common agricultural policy, and, last but not least, by the need to realize the aims of this policy, Community financial assistance is granted to promote and guide to fruition certain schemes for structural improvement. These schemes fall under the following four categories: (1) adaptation and improvement of conditions of production; (2) adaptation and guidance of production; (3) adaptation and improvement of marketing of farm products; and (4) improvement of sales of farm products (expansion of sales of certain commodities).

The financial assistance extended by the Community for given structural improvement schemes in the member states is provided through the guidance section of the European Agricultural Guidance and Guarantee Fund (EAGGF).

The funds provided for structural improvement in agriculture amount to one-third of the total sum appropriated by the Community via the guarantee section of the EAGGF to finance market and price policy (intervention, refunds, etc.). This ensures that financial action by the Community itself in structure policy is not neglected in favor of action in the field of market and price policy. The resources of the fund are currently drawn from contributions by the member states. Once the common market in farm products comes into force—probably on July 1, 1967—EAGGF expenditures will be met chiefly if not exclusively from the yield of levies on imports from outside the Community.

The financial consequences of Community decisions on farm policy will thus be borne by Community financing.

Any possibility there may be of obtaining a common agricultural policy with less protection than we now have will depend largely on the results of this policy of structural reform. The various measures involved are expensive and will sometimes come up against opposition. But they constitute the only possible way of realizing the aims of the common farm policy, which include improving the competitive position of European agriculture. It is perhaps not superfluous to point out that short-run problems are discussed elsewhere in this study and that it can therefore be regarded as no great failing on the part of structure policy if progress happens to be slow in this field. Where we have been too slow is in making structural adjustments to the structurally optimum conditions, which are constantly shifting. It is in fact the consequences of such past failings that are now being brought home to us.

Summary, Conclusions, and Suggestions. 1. Nothing like a complete and scientifically responsible analysis and synthesis of the common agricultural policy would be possible—nor was this intended—within the bounds of this modest contribution. What we have attempted is to illustrate and sum up this complex set of problems from the angle of market economy suggested by the general theme of the Seventh Flemish Economic Congress; this placed a welcome restriction on our task and concentrated our attention on a fundamental approach rather than a description of the common agricultural policy as it stands. And the latter is after all derived from the earlier policy measures elaborated by the member states.

2. The impossibility of making the market in farm products entirely liberal could not be used as a pretext for excluding the farm sector from the Common Market because of the interdependence of economic phenomena. The determination of the member states to retain some form of farm policy led inevitably to the elaboration of a common agricultural policy.

3. The rather different emphasis in the EEC objectives vis-à-vis those laid down by theoretical economists (such as Professor Hartog) suggests that different weight is given to market and price policy—in which all forms of protection are not explicitly prohibited—than to structure policy. Before we can properly understand this, at first sight, relatively great interest of the Community in market and price policy, we must have some insight into the basic problems of agricultural economics to which the objectives are attuned. Here too we have the usual distinction between the short and the long term.

4. Much of market and price policy is concerned with the short-run instability of agricultural markets; this does not really involve protection, but it does mean regulation of the markets—adjustment of the free play of supply and demand so as to better regulate production, processing, marketing, and food supply in the interests of producer and consumer and thus of the economy as a whole. Government intervention of this kind at national levels, the justification for which was usually centered too exclusively on the nature of agricultural production itself and not enough on the defense of producers' interests, has now led to the EEC's market and price policy. The connection between the degree of built-in price instability and the extent to which the market was rejected as a regulating factor for the various farm products at EEC level is shown in detail. Whether this rejection is based on empirical processes or on conscious economic deduction is unimportant.

5. Although considerable room has been left for a protection-free market and price policy, this policy as it stands is nevertheless achieving, at national and Community levels, a far from negligible "upward" price stabilization and consequently contains an important protectionist element. Perhaps this explains why theoretical economists have reservations about this policy and are so interested in structure policy. This is a long-term problem, which means that it concerns farm policy in the context of economic development.

6. The supply of farm produce is expanding more rapidly than demand, and this results—through pressure on the terms of trade and per capita farm income—in a reduction in the number of farms and finally in the active farm population. It seems that the free-market mechanism is inadequate not only to produce short-run equilibrium but also to solve long-run problems.

Exerting pressure on the farm sector through prices and incomes does not seem to be the best way of bringing about the necessary adjustments, particularly increased mobility of the factors of production, chiefly labor. There are social objections to such action, and it would in fact be incompatible with the aims of the EEC's agricultural policy. The solution must therefore be sought in a more efficient structure policy and in appropriate social measures to supplement market and price policy. Great importance is also attached to the availability of alternative employment outside agriculture and consequently to general and regional economic policy.

7. The main feature of the common market and price policy is the introduction of free movements of farm produce within the Community. At the single-market stage, the free play of comparative productivity will bring with it specialization and increased productivity. The Council decision on common grain prices (which more or less govern all the rest) coming into force in July 1967 is thus of exceptional significance.

8. Another feature of the common agricultural market and price policy (and commercial policy) is that it introduces protection at the external frontier as a substitute for the various national protection measures.

The agreement reached on common grain prices is most important here too. For where approximation of prices is the decisive factor for the removal of internal farm protection, the relative *level* at which the common prices are to be fixed is the determining factor in protection from nonmember countries (including antidumping arrangements). It looks as if cost comparison will only be fully carried out inside the Community, while the degree of competition vis-à-vis the outside world will be controlled by the highest common denominator among the forces at the basis of the member states' national protection policies and the pressure that can be exerted by nonmember countries concerned, the United States in particular.

It would therefore be incorrect to assert that agriculture is now much more protected than it was on the average in the individual EEC countries.

9. The old machinery of the farm policies of the member states has been replaced by new, Community-level mechanisms that have so far operated without much difficulty. The essential feature is a system of variable levies (price differences) that replace a whole range of divergent measures, and this implies a simplification. On the whole, it seems that the farm sector is no less *organized* (in the sense of short-term price stabilization) than it was in the member states.

However, about 85 percent of agricultural production now comes under a European market organization. And we may expect that pressure from trade circles will help to ensure that still more products are included in the system.

10. The fact that most farm products have been brought under market organizations does not mean that in this sector the market is no longer a regulating factor at all. On the contrary, the various farm products are spread out along the regulation-freedom scale, with grain and inedible horticultural products at the extremes. But even in the case of grain there is no question of fixed prices; what we find is a narrow price zone with an upper limit constituted by the target price in the interest of the consumer and on general economic grounds, this price operating through a system of levies. To ensure,

among other things, that the producer stays in business, the lower limit is formed by intervention prices guaranteed by purchases on the domestic market. As the fixed prices may be reviewed annually on the basis of experience gained with prices obtained on the market, the market is, to some extent, reintroduced as an indirect regulator.

11. Whether these market organizations are the result of mainly empirical processes or of deductive economic thinking, the fact remains that the position of the various farm products on the regulation-freedom scale can be logically explained by a number of specific economic characteristics and commercial-policy practices, especially by price and income inelasticities in relation to the inelasticity of the human stomach, or the fact that this inelasticity does not apply (inedible horticultural products); supply elasticity in general, and in particular whether or not the crop is tied to the soil; whether or not the product is a basic agricultural or food commodity, insofar as this is not already reflected in the above-mentioned elasticities; and the unfavorable man/land ratio (important for the extension of the protectionist element in market, price, and commercial policy) and dumping practices on the world market.

12. The market organizations for the pork, egg, and poultry sectors by no means offset the short-run instability caused by cyclical supply fluctuations in view of the danger involved in stable prices in sectors whose production is not tied to the soil, i.e., those with considerable elasticity of supply. Nor will market expansion result in the elimination of these cycles, since they are psychological in origin. The risks inherent in growing specialization brought about by technical progress and keener competition are therefore not removed. European unification might speed up vertical integration (covering of risks) and in some cases convert the production unit of the farm into a pork, egg, or poultry factory and the farmer into a wage earner in an industrial and commercial complex. This explains the necessity of promoting the formation of producers' associations. And it also explains the importance of a Community policy of anticyclical information, anticyclical variation of the slaughter tax (for example), and so on, since fixed prices—and here we are in agreement with the EEC Commission—are injurious in this case.

13. In a more general view, the danger of strengthening asymmetrical economic relationships at the expense of the farm sector is not imaginary. The effect of a concentrated wholesale trade and food industry is the increasing domination of isolated agricultural producers, which justifies the formation of a stronger *countervailing* power for the farm sector. This presupposes more cohesion through organization of the profession or specialized branches of it.

14. The EEC's farm policy is not restricted to market and price policy and the long-run leveling up of prices: it is also concerned with fundamental equilibrium in the long term. This is why provision is made for the coordination at Community level of member states' structure policies within the com-

mon agricultural policy. For there can be no lasting improvement in farm incomes through the operation of market and price policy alone.

15. Apart from the coordination of the member countries' farm structure policies, the Community also grants conditional financial assistance to certain structural improvement projects in these countries. By this means the Community intends to prevent its action in the field of structure policy from falling behind its action in the market and price sector.

Whatever possibility there may be of obtaining a common agricultural policy with less protection (not antidumping) than we have now will largely depend on the results of this policy of structural reform.

16. Where medium-term planning for the economy as a whole is proposed in the EEC, agriculture—as an integral part of the economy— cannot be left out, especially as the common organization of markets and the central fixing of unified prices make it essential to employ both forecasts and/or targets for production and consumption.

17. Finally, it may be noted that Belgian farm prices, except for butter, generally reflect an average of prices in the member states, so Belgian agriculture may well be able to hold its own in the face of keener competition. Too often, we seem to lose sight of the fact that a number of adjustment problems are always raised by the ever more rapid pace of economic development, irrespective of any question of integration. European integration will undoubtedly raise additional adjustment problems, but basically what is putting strain on agriculture are the effects produced by economic development. In the past these have been tackled with insufficient energy or perhaps altogether wrongly. All this means that organized agriculture and the authorities will have a more important task to carry out than was previously realized.

The rapidity with which the conversion projects clamoring for attention are finished will have a significant influence on our relative competitiveness. And much will depend on another kind of fundamental adaptability—that of our mental attitudes and institutions. Experience on this score justifies only moderate optimism.

References

Hartog, F. 1964. "Economische Aspecten van de Nederlandse Landbouwprotectie." *De Economist* 112:1–17.

Shepherd, G. S. 1964. *Farm Policy: New Directions*. Ames: Iowa State University Press.

Zimmerman, L. J. 1960. *Arme en rijke landen*. The Hague: Albani.

23

In Search of Appropriate Marketing Technology for the Third World

FRANK MEISSNER

> The ultimate purpose of development is to provide increasing op-
> portunities to all people for a better life.[1]
>
> *The General Assembly of the United Nations:*
>   1. *Urges* the developing countries to incorporate the Basic Services
>   concept and approach into their national development plans and
>   strategy;
>
>   .   .   .
>
>   3. *Urges* the international community to recognize its responsibility
>   for increased cooperative action to promote social and economic
>   development through its support of Basic Services at the interna-
>   tional and the country programming level.[2]

IN THE PREFACE to the third edition of his classic volume *Marketing Farm
Products* (1955, p. vii), Geoffrey S. Shepherd simply and masterfully described the dynamics of marketing as "continually churning over and changing. As fast as one problem is solved, another arises; nothing stays put."

Dr. Shepherd was referring to the U.S. marketing scene. In the quarter
century since then he has spent a great deal of time exploring the marketing
scene in Third World countries. He served with distinction as consultant to the
Agency for International Development in such places as Indonesia and Peru,
and he worked on projects on the Inter-American Development Bank in
Venezuela and Paraguay. This volume contains an "output" of Geoff's consultancy with the Iowa Universities Mission to Peru (see Chapter 24); it provides an example of clarity, simplicity, and practicality for which his contributions to marketing have become known around the world.

The author is solely responsible for this paper. The views expressed do not necessarily represent policies of the Inter-American Development Bank or any other institutions or agencies referred to.

In this essay I aim to contribute to the ongoing dialogue about relationships between appropriate marketing technology and basic needs strategies for developing countries, a topic close to Dr. Shepherd's heart.

Objectives and Scope. The triple purposes of this paper are (1) to explain why Western capital-intensive mass marketing technology, even a stripped down model of it, is ill suited to serve low- and middle-income consumers in the Third World; (2) to sketch out elements of intermediate marketing technologies that better fit the implementation of basic needs strategies, which will increasingly dominate approaches to development during the decade of the 1980s; and (3) to suggest elements of a guideline for marketing decision makers in the developing world as well as in agencies providing technical and financial assistance to such countries.

The essay is introduced by a series of definitions of marketing, appropriate technology, and basic needs. It then proceeds directly to a presentation of a development banker's highly preliminary ideas about the pragmatic guide to technologies, which appear appropriate to different parts of marketing channels for consumer staples in urban areas of developing countries. The main purpose of that guide is to provoke constructive dialogue.

The presentation is colored by my experience in Latin America and the Caribbean. This is simply because, since the early 1960s, my professional work focused on that region.

Definitions

Marketing. Depending on the eye and purpose of the beholder, marketing can and has been defined thus: a business activity; a frame of mind; a group of institutions aimed at facilitating exchange of ownership as well as physical transfer of products and services; a process of physical concentration; the processing and dispersion of goods; a creator of time, place, form, and possession utilities; a set of devices for adjusting forces of supply and demand; etc.

This paper deals with marketing as a tool of socioeconomic development of Third World countries. For that purpose marketing can therefore be considered the design, organization, and implementation of socioeconomic action programs and projects aimed at effectively creating time, place, form, and ownership utilities related to satisfaction of basic needs. In addition to physical distribution of goods and services over space and time, marketing thus includes policy-oriented research; product selection, planning, and design; pricing; and communication aimed at making the market "transparent," thus facilitating open interplay of forces of supply and demand.

Being a behavioral discipline, marketing must not only deal with trading institutions and the flows of goods and services, but also with people and in-formation flows. It not only deals with public acceptance of new products but also with public acceptance of new ideas. It strives for tangible improvement of the standard of living as well as for creation of a better overall quality of life. And so, for purposes of this essay, we define the main activities of marketing as follows: the identification of unmet basic needs, the development of products and services to meet these unmet basic needs, pricing, the search for channels of distribution to the target markets, and communication to potential consumers about availability of products and services capable to satisfactorily meet specific unmet basic needs.[3]

Technology. Technology is knowledge systematically applied to practical tasks. Marketing technology, appropriate for use in developing countries, should "neither be so primitive that it offers no escape from low production and low income, nor so highly sophisticated as being out of reach for people and therefore ultimately uneconomic."[4]

Third World. The term Third World apparently originated in France, a country that used to govern many far-off places. *Tiers Monde* was used to describe the relationship of colonies to Mother France just as *Tiers Etat* (third estate) was previously used to describe the relationship of commoners to the monarchy. During the 1940s the French extended the use of *Tiers Monde* to embrace developing areas of the world. In the 1950s and 1960s the term was applied to politically nonaligned nations that formed part of neither the Western alliance (First World) nor the Soviet bloc and China (Second World). In the 1970s the phrase has increasingly come to refer to the world's economic "have not" countries. Even within what is generally accepted as the Third World, there is enormous disparity in income levels. The term embraces Venezuela, where in 1977 annual per capita income was $2,570, as well as Bangladesh, where it was $110. In this paper we simply follow the World Bank listing of Third World developing countries, subdivided into five income groups: higher; upper middle; middle; lower; and capital-surplus, oil-exporting countries (see below).

Basic Needs. The aim of "basic needs" strategy is to increase and redistribute production so as to eradicate deprivations that arise from lack of basic goods and services.

The basic needs are food and nutrition, drinking water, health, shelter, and education (Howell Jones 1980).

AN ADEQUATE BASIC DIET. This is the daily intake of sufficient protein, car-bohydrates, fats, vitamins, and minerals to allow human beings to conduct in good health required physical and mental activites. The average daily per capita calorie requirement for such survival is about 2,350 for an adult male (Meissner 1979); presently close to 1 billion people take in less than this requirement.

THE BASIC NEED FOR DRINKING WATER. This is defined as reasonable access to water that does not contain any substances harming consumer health or making the water unacceptable for use. Reasonable access is defined as availability of public hydrants within 200 m in urban areas. In rural areas, the source of water should be sufficiently close so that no disproportionate part of the day is spent fetching it. The world population without clean drinking water is estimated at roughly 1.2 billion.

HEALTH SERVICES. Health services are the public and private measures needed to prevent and cure the most common avoidable and curable diseases and other forms of bodily harm. They include maternal and child care, public instruction in elementary sanitation and nutrition, and family planning. The number of people in the world presently deprived of these public health services is estimated to be at least 0.8 billion.

THE BASIC NEED FOR HOUSING. Housing can be sufficiently satisfied by permanent shelter protecting individuals, families, or other social groups from harmful climatic influences and other dangerous factors in the natural environment. Basic housing would present the minimum socially acceptable dwelling standards among the poor. In the world there are at least 0.8 billion persons deprived of basic housing.

BASIC EDUCATION. Basic education is intended to provide functional, flexible, and low-cost instruction for those whom the formal system cannot yet reach or has already passed by. The target groups may vary according to age (children, youths, adults) and socioeconomic characteristics. About 1.1 billion persons are deprived of basic education, including 0.3 billion out-of-school children and 0.8 billion illiterates.

Empirical work is under way at the World Bank and in different United Nations agencies aimed at defining the national and global basic needs, determining feasible standards, measuring shortfalls, and quantifying resource requirements for remedial action.

Streeten and Burki (1978) estimate that capital costs would be close to $400 billion in order to finance global basic needs programs in less-developed countries over the next decades.

Selective Appropriateness of Western Mass Marketing Technology. Over the past quarter century Western literature on marketing consumer staples within developing countries often recommended transfer of relatively capital-intensive mass marketing technology as a solution to Third World problems related to the distribution of consumer staples. The horizontally and vertically integrated systems surrounding institutions known as supermarkets were hailed as generators of substantial benefits due to economies of scale, self-service, and shortening of the distribution channel. Supermarkets supposedly help bypass the public wholesale markets; replace the crowded, old-fashioned, noisy, disorderly, and picturesque but dirty food stands in municipal retail bazaars; do away with pesky street vendors who cause permanent health and safety hazards in busy downtown areas; etc.

In short, the small, limited-line retailer of consumer staples—plus the long, labor-intensive, haphazardly coordinated distribution chain, were arrogantly brushed aside as inadequate, inefficient, and irrelevant.[5]

Sounds logical does it not? The trouble is that, from some 25 years of hindsight plus evidence of many bankrupt supermarkets in Third World countries, the above counsel turned out to be largely wrong. In short, Western marketing technology is too big and too expensive for Third World countries. It does not create the jobs needed to absorb the rapidly expanding labor force, and it is not appropriate for the very small farm and business enterprises that make up the bulk of economic activities in developing countries.[6]

As we enter the 1980s the development profession is humbly returning to square one. Gradually we are starting to appreciate variations of the traditional, labor-intensive food retailers as, by and large, an appropriate technology suitable for marketing staples to the bulk of the world's population—neither so primitive as to offer no escape from low production and low income nor so highly sophisticated as to be out of reach for poor people and therefore ultimately politically and economically unacceptable. Within this context it becomes evident that "the supermarket, even in its more rudimentary version, is ill-equipped to service the low- and middle-[income]consumers in developing . . . countries;. . . if gains in distribution are to be obtained, they must be secured through improvement in domestic or intermediate technologies" (Bucklin 1977, p. 114).

Inappropriate supermarket mass marketing technology is by no means an affliction confined to developing countries only. Thus the mid-1979 "decision by Safeway Stores to close its supermarket in central Anacostia [a district of Washington, D.C.]—which threatens to leave an estimated 10,000 black, low income residents nothing but small, high priced food markets is a national trend. The number of supermarkets in cities has declined by about 50% during the last 10 years; in the District of Columbia, the number has dropped from 91 to 40. From a pure business point of view supermarkets are failing in the face of limited space, high labor costs, shoplifting, vandalism, and employee turn-over'' (Asher 1979, p. A13).

As a result the high-cost corner mom-and-pop grocery stores, likely to be owned by recent, hard-working immigrants—entrepreneurs from such developing countries as South Korea and Vietnam—are thriving. Their traditional technology of grocery marketing is apparently far more suitable for poor Americans than is the supermarket.[7]

And so supermarkets, an institution as American as McDonald's hamburgers, have not as yet penetrated Third World countries. The main reason is that supermarkets are primarily merchandisers of processed foods, which few poor people can afford to buy. Also, the lack of a sustained supply of uniform-quality produce, typical in Third World countries, makes it difficult for supermarkets to organize efficient field procurement; as a result they have to go through central wholesale markets, just like their "traditional" colleagues. Consequently, even in the relatively few unprocessed foods they sell, mostly fresh fish and vegetables, capital-intensive supermarkets can hardly ever compete with the low prices charged by traditional labor-intensive huckster-higgler type retailers or ambulatory street vendors with little overhead.

Consequently, supermarkets tend to be found in high-income areas of Third World cities, bringing the benefits of western type mass marketing to those who can best afford to pay for them.

The First and Second Worlds—in which supermarkets are flourishing—nowadays represent 30 percent of the global population. Projections of current population trends show that by the year 2000 their share is likely to be down to about 20 percent, and to a miniscule 10 percent by the year 2050. This seems to indicate that the current type of supermarket mass marketing technology is unsuitable for a growing proportion of the world population, a fact seldom explicitly recognized by the Western marketing establishment.

Search for Appropriate Marketing Techologies. Multinational financial and technical assistance agencies—such as the Asian Development Bank (ADB), the Inter-American Development Bank (IDB), and the World Bank—seem to have understood instinctively that the technology of the Western supermarket is not well suited to serving the needs of low-income food buyers. They have therefore been searching for more appropriate technologies.

Thus, in IDB the bulk of food-marketing projects are aimed at improving *traditional* rural assembly centers, municipal retail markets, and wholesale producers, plus strengthening the corresponding software infrastructure such as establishment of grades and standards, mobilization of working capital for traders, in-service training of food retailers and wholesalers, and market news services.

From its very inception in 1961, IDB thus recognized the importance of distribution as a crucial supplement to its production-oriented agricultural projects such as irrigation, crop and livestock credit, land settlement, and rural development.

As of January 1, 1981, the Bank approved 29 loans for marketing and agroindustries, totaling $711.3 million. IDB loans amounted to $298.6 million, or 41.9 percent of the total. Three major types of facilities form more than half of the marketing portfolio: agroindustries, grain storage, and public markets.

IDB tends to assign high priority to marketing and agroindustry projects that satisfy at least four major requirements: to provide effective incentives for farmers to increase production; to improve facilities at different stages of the marketing channel to assure urban and rural consumers timely and sustained supplies of reasonably priced basic foods and other staples; to help distribute equitably benefits from improved marketing among producers, intermediaries, and consumers; and to use relatively labor-intensive technology.

IDB provides a substantial technical assistance aimed at facilitating effective organization of small farmers for purposes of jointly selling their produce and for procuring production inputs; at helping band together small intermediaries for purposes of mobilizing reasonably priced working capital resources; and at improving the management practices of individual assembly, processing, wholesale, and retail firms. This type of "software" often represents up to as much as 10 percent of the project cost.

In contrast, capital-intensive, mass-marketing, "supermarket" technology, which primarily tends to serve middle- and high-income consumers in Latin American countries, is considered to be a suitable area for private financing.

It often takes a great deal of courage to swim against the stream of benign neglect, and/or counteract "facts that ain't so." IDB's participation in financing public wholesale food markets is a case in point. This is because urban planners often fear that mass-marketing technology will make public wholesale markets obsolete, hearing so much about private supermarkets "integrating backward" by buying directly from producers and performing the wholesaling function themselves in their own central warehouses.

In reality, even in the highly developed industrialized countries of Western Europe where supermarket chains are rapidly becoming a crucial distribution channel for consumer staples, the volume of fruits and vegetables moving through central wholesale markets remains stable or tends to increase as years go by, amounting in most cases to over 70 percent of total consumption.

Furthermore, in North America the newer central markets are actually broadening their functions. When adequate land is available, agroindustrial parks tend to become integral parts of the complex. The brand new, publicly financed, and highly profitable Maryland Wholesale Food Center in Jessup (near the Friendship International Airport of Baltimore) is an outstanding illustration. Indeed, the private Giant supermarket chain has constructed its central warehouse—considered the most modern in the world—next to the public wholesale produce market, a perfect example of symbiotic public-private agribusiness that is evidently opening up many opportunities for creative complementary relationships between the private and public sector agribusinesses.

In spite of floods of literature on marketing in developing countries (see Table 23.1), no systematic policy-oriented study has so far been made of the growing body of experience with appropriate marketing technology of multinational and bilateral development agencies.[8]

Indeed, in the more than a quarter century I have worked on development activities one truism was valid, is valid, and will continue to be valid in years to come: a "drought" of potentially bankable projects is the greatest challenge of multinational development agencies trying to improve agricultural marketing systems in developing countries. In short, money can usually be found for a good project (Meissner 1981). The intensive search of Organization of Petroleum Exporting Countries (OPEC) members for suitable outlets for their huge funds available for investment is a case in point.

In fact, adaptation of marketing systems for effective use by urban and rural poor, including the small farmers, is a relatively new field of endeavor. It is so new a subject that the conventional marketing profession tends to consider it somewhat "far out."

Policy Implications. When Mohammed does not go to the mountain the mountain has to go to Mohammed. Academic marketing researchers have so far not been overly helpful in guiding development bankers in the identification, selection, preevaluation, preparation, analysis, and implementation of marketing projects. Let us sketch a few possibilities based on the observations presented so far.

In the Third World consumption of processed and packaged consumer staples is evidently limited by low incomes. The supermarket tends to serve only a relatively small section of the middle- and upper-income urban residents. As a rule it therefore appears that within an overall development strategy aimed at satisfying the basic needs of the bulk of rural and urban populations, governments should (1) strive to use public funds for improving marketing of food and nonfood consumer staples by upgrading and developing existing traditional institutions such as wholesale produce markets and municipal retail bazaars and by regulating street vending in large cities as well as the periodic fairs in rural areas and in small cities; and (2) let the private sector take care of investment in mass-marketing supermarkets, which tend primarily to serve the higher-income populations.

For this upgrading to be effective, substantial investment is needed in the

Table 23.1. Income levels in GNP/capita/year[1]

Factors	Low (under $280)	Lower and inter-mediate middle ($281–$1,135)	Upper middle ($1,135–$2,500)	High (over $2,500)
Number of developing countries[1]				
Latin America and Caribbean	1	16	8	3
Asia	12	10	5	8
Africa	22	19	3	1
Total: 108	35	45	16	12
Food expenditures as % of disposable income[2]	over 60%	45–60%	35–45%	under 35%
Share of perishable products (fresh or processed fruit, vegetables, meat and fish) in cost of popular diets[2]	under 30%	30–40%	40–45%	45–50%
Labor cost or minimum wages ($/day)	under $2.00	$2.00–$3.75	$3.75–$6.00	over $6.00
Access to private motorized transport and refrigeration	Practically nonexistent	Rare	Rapidly increasing	Common
Assembly of Agricultural products at point of first sale[2]	Occasional surpluses in small lots of ungraded product brought to market either by farmer (on foot, cart, public bus) or picked up at farm by intermediary. Quantities marketed fluctuate greatly.	Large lots informally graded by buyer-trucker at farm or assembly market. Truck transport common where adequate farm-to-market roads exist.	Commercial producers specialize in production of food crops that reflect demand specifications. Intermediaries bring produce to wholesale markets or farmers form marketing groups. As area of outreach broadens, supply tends to stabilize, grading and standards being accepted by trade.	Increasing quantities of produce bought directly from farmers by retail organizations. Government standards established. Production contract becoming common. Supply sustained.
Wholesale:[2] Assortments	Wholesale-retail combined in individual enterprises that specialize in a few products.	Specialized wholesalers develop, concentrating individual enterprises on a few commodities	Wholesale food distribution centers located in suburbs or adjacent open country, with sections	As local agribusiness grows, assortment broadens into processed and packaged goods, in addition to

Category	(Stage I)	(Stage II)	(Stage III)	(Stage IV)
(continued from previous page)	located close to traditional downtown of major cities. Stalls average roughly 10-20 square meters.	from central city areas. Stalls average about 40-80 square meters.	retail trade are being added to wholesale centers, which provide stalls averaging over 80 square meters.	which—in addition to highly specialized wholesalers—central warehouses of chain stores as well as agroindustries, public warehouses, etc., also tend to locate.
Retail:[2]				
Public markets, bazaars, and periodic fairs	Stall tenants supply most of consumer staples bought by low- and middle-income families.	As cities grow, traditional public markets become more and more crowded. Inadequate facilities drive trade into other channels.	Satellite public markets and periodic fairs being built, old central facilities renewed. Stall sizes increase; refrigeration more frequently available.	Specialization in perishables increasing. Processed and packaged goods tend to bypass public retail markets.
Itinerant vendors	Numerous street vendors handling tiny quantities of merchandise constitute bulk of the "informal sector."	Itinerant vendors grow in importance, selling in streets surrounding the public markets as well as delivering to households in residential neighborhoods.		Relative importance of itinerants depends largely on degree of employment. The more unemployment, the more feasible and attractive is this sort of retailing, which is easy to enter.
Neighborhood grocery stores	Small, family-owned, fixed-location stores in houses of residential neighborhoods. Carry less than 100 items, annual gross turnover of under $5,000	Larger in size (20-40 square meters), tendency to specialize in fruits and vegetables, meat, fish, bread, etc. Annual turnover of over $10,000.	Retailers from public markets "graduate" to neighborhood stores in newer, low-income areas.	Increasing specialization and service, including home delivery.
Self-service superettes and supermarkets	Individually owned, small stores primarily located in upper-middle- and high-income neighborhoods. Large proportion of packaged and processed foods imported and high priced. Few local perishables carried.	In middle-income neighborhoods, clerk and self-service superettes appear. Supermarkets broaden assortment, including fresh fruits and vegetables. Local food processors start substituting some imported goods.	Neighborhood stores "graduate" into superettes and independent supermarket operations.	Stores tend to band together in voluntary, cooperative, or corporate chains. Local agroindustries provide increasing share of processed and packaged goods. Increasing share of products bypass independent wholesalers.
Facilitating public infrastructure:				
Grades and standards	Transactions based on inspection of individual lots.	Informal grading practiced by traders.		

329

Table 23.1. (Continued)

Factors	Low (under $280)	Lower and intermediate middle ($281–$1,135)	Upper middle ($1,135–$2,500)	High (over $2,500)
Marketing information system	Word of mouth.	Rudimentary market news services being set up in public markets.		
Education, training, and extension	Occasional consultancies by expatriate experts, scholarships for local personnel.	Gradually increasing as outreach of local pilot facilities broadens.	Within framework of national development planning, provisions being made for drawing up systematic marketing improvement programs and their gradual implementation. Substantial technical cooperation from multinational or bilateral agencies frequently required.	
Policy-oriented research	Rarely done due to lack of data, qualified professionals, and awareness of need for systematic analysis of alternatives.	Getting to be more frequent as data base increases; more professionals become available; and multinational, bilateral, and local agencies demand better quantitative guidance for better decision making.		
Mobilization of sources of capital:				
Fixed	Local public agencies tend to seek concessionary funds from multinational or bilateral assistance agencies.		Increased capability of public sector to mobilize local government funds makes possible supplementation of foreign funds at ordinary capital rates.	
Working	Inadequate at all levels, resulting in high interest and short-term lending.	Wholesalers tend to dominate "backward" finance of producers and "forward" financing of retailers.	Increasing ability of farmers and retailers to obtain funds from commercial public or private banks tends to diminish domination of marketing channel by wholesalers.	

1. *World Atlas of the Child*, Washington, D.C.: World Bank, 1979, p. 3.
2. Adapted and updated from: *Food Marketing in 13 Asian Cities*, Bangkok: Food and Agricultural Organization of the United Nations, 1975, pp. 10–11.
3. Adapted from: *Market Place Trade: Periodic Markets, Hawkers and Traders in Africa, Asia, and Latin America*, edited by H. T. Smith, Vancouver, B.C.: University of British Columbia, 1979. The 17 essays in the book relate to Ecuador, Sabah, Ethiopia, Madagascar, Iran, Papua, Hong Kong, Mexico City, Puebla Mexico, Singapore, Nigeria, Colombia, Tanzania, Liberia, and Kenya.

improvement of facilitating marketing functions, i.e., the "software" (consultancy, training, and institutional strengthening) that makes it possible for the "hardware" (storage, transport, processing, access roads, public markets, etc.) to be operated reasonably efficiently.[9]

Experience indicates that in "marketing development packages" investment in fixed capital would frequently represent roughly 50–80 percent of the total cost; working capital, needed for procurement of the goods and financing of their movements through the marketing channel, would require in the neighborhood of 15–30 percent; while technical assistance would range all the way from a relatively "normal" 1–5 percent to as high as 20 percent of total investment.

Under traditional practice it is easy for multinational development agencies (ADB, IDB, International Bank for Reconstruction and Development, etc.) to justify financing the foreign exchange content of fixed capital investment. As it so happens capital-intensive supermarket technology requires much more foreign exchange than investments in labor-intensive bazaar technology, which primarily consists of local costs. In order to assist in financing this sort of appropriate technology, multinational development agencies have to be flexible enough to help finance substantial parts of local cost components whenever required. Likewise, there needs to be a readiness to assist with provision of the often substantial "software" of technical cooperation, without which the hardware cannot operate satisfactorily.

Multinational development banks—drawing on specialized United Nations organizations (Food and Agricultural Organization, United Nations Industrial Development Organization, Organization of American States, and Organization for Economic Cooperation and Development) and/or the numerous bilateral assistance agencies—are nowadays well equipped to provide all sorts of technical cooperation software as well as capital for customary hardware. Selected references, cited at the end of this paper, indicate that some multinational and bilateral agencies have attempted to revitalize existing public markets and fairs through modernization and provision of entrepreneurial services to traditional wholesalers and retailers, who are primarily serving low-income rural and urban populations. Yet, the "marketing profession" in North America and Western Europe has not shown much interest in this type of public-marketing reform. Lest I be accused of antiestablishment bias let me quote an appraisal of the situation made by Professor Louis P. Bucklin (1977, p. 21), University of California-Berkeley, a distinguished member in good standing within the American Marketing Association:

> The research that has been conducted upon the feasibility of such policies is regretfully minimal. There has been no known cost-benefit analysis, no evaluation of improvement of facility appearance upon patronage, no examination of the sociology of the market vendors to accept direction and change and no examination of incentives necessary for introduction of

private enterprise, through market builders or stimulating their vigor to improve existing facilities.

In short, capital-intensive mass-marketing technology, which requires a high degree of vertical integration along the marketing channel, seems likely to be of dubious value for the low-income populations during the foreseeable future. Alternative marketing development options—including revitalization of existing public markets through modernization, provision of entrepreneurial services, and in-service training of wholesalers and retailers—appear more promising. Evidence is gradually being accumulated showing that from such traditional institutions, when well managed, vigorous competition can emerge.

Notes

1. Resolution of the General Assembly, 2626, XXV International Development Strategy for the Second United Nations Development Decade, paragraph 18, adopted October 24, 1970.

2. United Nations Resolution adopted December 21, 1976.

3. Freely adapted from Hughes (1978, p. 3).

4. Proposal for a program in "Appropriate Technology," U.S. Congress, House Committee on International Relations, 1978, pp. 1–2.

5. For an early manifestation of this approach see Galbraith and Holten (1955). Subsequently, Professor Galbraith intellectually more than redeemed himself. Some of the relevant insights, gained since then, are revealed in Galbraith (1979).

6. See introduction to Meissner (1978), which had the provocative title "A New Ethnocentric Myopia? Rise of Third World Demands Marketing Be Stood on Its Head." The provocation worked wonders. This paper is therefore to serve as "mass response" and acknowledgement of the valuable comments and criticisms received. Special thanks are extended to Professor Louis P. Bucklin (University of California-Berkeley), Ronald Stucky (Santa Clara University), Tannira R. Rao (University of Wisconsin-Milwaukee), Victor E. Childers (Indiana University), Eleanor Branttley-Schwartz (Cleveland State University), Edward W. Smykay (Michigan State University), Hans Mittendorf (United Nations Food and Agriculture Organization in Rome), and Klaus Moll (United Nations Industrial Development Organization in Vienna).

7. No wonder that in a limerick on the "Extra Cost of Being Poor" the USDA's *Farm Index* of May 1970 (p. 15) launched the following definition:

Poor is:

—paying more for many of the necessities of life than others do;

—trying to balance spending and income with no savings to cushion emergencies;

—buying in amounts you can afford, not being able to take advantage of twofers and threefers;

—buying whatever quality shoes and trousers you can manage on your time payments;

—buying more interest on credit terms because it takes longer to pay.

8. I myself plead guilty as coeditor (with Don Izraeli and Dafna N. Izraeli) of *Marketing Systems for Developing Countries* (1976). The two volumes contain papers presented at the First International Conference on Marketing Systems in Developing Countries, held in Israel, January 6–12, 1974. The meeting was cosponsored by the International Marketing Federation and Tel Aviv University. Volume I deals with marketing systems for products and services in individual countries. Volume II focuses on institutions and infrastructures for agricultural marketing.

9. For a "menu" of available software see Dam et al., eds. (1978). Proceedings of a conference cosponsored by the German Foundation for International Development and the Food and Agricultural Organization of the United Nations, held in Berlin, August 1978.

References

Asher, R. L. 1979. "How Others Save Supermarkets." *Washington Post,* August 4, A13.

Bucklin, L. P. 1977. "Improving Food Retailing in Developing Asian Countries." *Food Policy 2:114–22.*

Dam, Th., G. Lorenzl, H. J. Mittendorf, and H. Schmidt-Burr, eds. 1978. *Marketing—A Dynamic Force for Rural Development.* Berlin (FRG): German Foundation for International Development.

Galbraith, J. K. 1979. *The Nature of Mass Poverty.* Cambridge, Mass.: Harvard University Press.

Galbraith, J. K., and R. H. Holten. 1955. *Marketing Efficiency in Puerto Rico.* Cambridge, Mass.: Harvard University Press.

Howell Jones, D., ed. 1980. *Meeting Basic Needs: An Overview.* Washington, D.C.: World Bank.

Hughes, G. D. 1978. *Marketing Management: A Planning Approach.* Reading, Mass.: Edison-Wesley.

Izreali, D., D. N. Izraeli, and F. Meissner, eds. 1976. *Marketing Systems for Developing Countries.* New York: Wiley.

Meissner, F. 1978. "A New Ethnocentric Myopia? Rise of Third World Demands Marketing Be Stood on Its Head." *Marketing News,* International Marketing issue, October 6.

_____. 1981. *Managing Preinvestment for Agricultural and Rural Development Projects.* Atlanta, Ga.: Institute for Food Technology.

_____, ed. 1979. *Nutrition as a Tool of Socio-Economic Development of Latin America.* Washington, D.C.: Inter-American Development Bank.

Shepherd, G. S. 1955. *Marketing Farm Products—An Economic Analysis.* 3d ed. Ames: Iowa State University Press.

Streeten, P., and Burke, S. J. 1978. "Basic Needs: Some Issues." *World Development.* Washington, D.C.: World Bank.

24

Marketing and Price Policy for Agricultural Development: A Tour of Duty in Peru

GEOFFREY S. SHEPHERD

AN ECONOMIC ADVISOR in a foreign country is like a doctor called in to treat the patient's troubles. And he works much like a doctor. The patient can tell the doctor his symptoms; but the doctor's first act is to diagnose the disease that is causing the symptoms. Only then can he begin to cure the disease.

An economic advisor can play a useful role verbally in individual and group conferences, as well as by writing reports. This is indeed the principal role that many advisors play. But the impact of advising is enhanced by inter-action with participants in the policy process. My most valuable work of this sort has been done with Ing Luiz Paz, originally manager of CONAP and now director of planning in the Ministry of Agriculture in Peru.

In playing out my advisory role I was given complete freedom to determine for myself what the chief marketing diseases were. So I started, as any marketing man would, with the question, What do the customers want? This is a sufficient question for commercial purposes. But a government is also interested in what its people *need*. So I looked into that, too.

The next step was to examine one of the prime suspects in the search for causes of marketing difficulties, namely, excessive marketing margins. The case turned out to be very much different from what was popularly thought. It

The responsibility for the contents of this report is the author's. The views and opinions expressed herein do not necessarily reflect policies of either the US/AID, Oficina de Comercialización Agraria (ONCA), or the Iowa Universities Mission to Peru (IUMP). [This paper incorporates material from two reports prepared in 1968 and 1969 by the author, later edited by Dr. Frank Meissner of the Inter-American Development Bank, Washington, D.C., which I have abridged and integrated into the present chapter. Ed.]

was then time to take a look at basic price policy in the development context and to consider the proper role of government as a provider or a facilitator of marketing developments.

Since marketing and price problems in Peru differ from product to product, a series of individual studies is needed to deal with these different problems, commodity by commodity. One example of such a specialized undertaking follows the general policy discussion. It involves the case of beef in Peru.

Basic Needs: Protein. I soon found, from Peruvian and UN Food and Agriculture Organization Statistics, that the foodstuff most needed in Peru was protein. Peru does not have immense pampas like Argentina for range livestock production. Nor does it have great fertile areas like the Middle West in the United States. It does have a long coastline, but most of the fish off the coast are anchovies, used for livestock feed rather than for human food. And more than half of Peru's citizens live in the highlands (*sierra*) and in the jungle (*selva*), far from the ocean. So it is difficult to get fresh fish to them.

Peru ranks near the bottom of the nations in the world in average per capita protein consumption—only about 51 grams per day. Furthermore, the distribution of income is very uneven. Most protein is expensive, and poor people cannot afford to buy much of it; therefore, they consume much less protein than the "average."

Many Peruvians diagnose this situation correctly, and then proceed to prescribe the wrong cure: more meat, fish, eggs, and milk. These are good protein foods, but expensive, especially in Peru. And in the parts of Peru where these foods are most needed, conditions are not favorable for producing them. As a result, the more meat, fish, eggs, and milk would not go to the poor people who need it most; they could not afford it. What they need is properly selected, low-cost vegetable proteins from local grains and low-cost fish flour for direct human consumption. Nutritionists have found that either one of these can meet the needs for protein at one-fifth to one-tenth the cost of expensive "conventional" animal proteins.

Why then have these "new" proteins not caught on? The answer is simple; these foods are unfamiliar, particularly to poor people, who do not have much nutritional education. Well-to-do people want more animal proteins, but this is chiefly because they like the taste. The nutritional challenge ahead is not to provide more expensive animal proteins but rather to add good taste to the new inexpensive vegetable and fish flour proteins, get them on the market, publicize and advertise them, and demonstrate them in hospitals and schools. These then are the elements of the remedy that will cure the disease of low-protein consumption by low-income people (Shepherd 1966).

Marketing Margins. "Everybody knows that marketing margins in Peru—differences between prices in the successive links in the marketing chain—are too wide." But almost nobody bothers to measure the margins to show whether in fact they are too wide; and those who do so speak of the margins as if they were all *profit,* neglecting the fact that most of the margins are needed to cover marketing *costs.*

So we measured these marketing margins to determine whether they really were too wide. We did this for several of the most important fruits and vegetables and found that the margins actually were not too wide. They were about the same as in the United States, where marketing is efficient. Furthermore, they were about in line with the costs in Peru, so far as we could ascertain them. Apparently, the usual diagnosis is incorrect. The main disease is *not* high marketing profits, but *high marketing costs* (Shepherd 1967a, 1967b).

This situation demands quite different remedies from those that would be needed to deal with high profits. It does not call for government setting of prices and margins, nor for laws castigating speculation and belaboring middlemen for their supposed high profits. But it does call for active steps *to sharpen competition and reduce marketing costs.* This reduction in costs requires:

1. detailed current market news to keep farmers better informed about consumers' needs and competitors' bids;

2. improved roads to get the production to market;

3. better packing to reduce waste;

4. development of grade specifications to make the market reports accurate and to reduce the expense of laborious purchase by inspection;

5. action to eliminate fraud and remove impediments to competition;

6. cleaning up of congested, inefficient, and unsanitary markets, and designing of new ones.

Progress is being made with introduction of some of these remedies, but there is a considerable amount of confusion about some aspects of the problem. Let us look at some of the more important issues associated with marketing margins.

Market News. The first bit of progress is creation of a current market news system for Peruvian agriculture. Market reports are now being telephoned into Lima from Chiclayo and Arequipa. Other points are projected to be added: Huancayo, Piura, Tacna, and a little later, Iquitos and Cajamarca. A teletype machine is to be installed soon.

Crop Reports and Harvest Outlook. Crop reporting and outlook work is developing slowly. So are grading and standardization of weights and measures. These programs have the highest priority after current market news, in terms of need; but they do not have much political sex appeal, and progress is slow. They seem to have only two speeds: slow and stop.

Mass Procurement and Retailing Chains. There is a need for restructuring the whole marketing system along the lines already undertaken by corporate supermarket chains. In North America and Western Europe, competition for more efficient chains, which buy direct from the country, has forced most single-unit retailers to group themselves into voluntary chains. These voluntary procurement and wholesale chains have adopted efficient methods of corporate chains. Together they are revolutionizing the whole mass-marketing system in these countries.

In Peru, Venezuela, Argentina, Brazil, Chile, and most of the other Latin American countries, the same changes are beginning to appear. The way needs to be opened for more drastic and rapid change in the future. And plans for new facilities, such as the wholesale market in Lima, need to adapt to these impending evolutionary changes.

Cornering the Market—"Acaparamiento." A related problem in many farmers' and consumers' minds is *acaparamiento* (cornering the market). They believe that speculators frequently buy up many farm products when their prices are low, and then hold them off the market to make prices rise. Then the speculators can sell the products at these high prices and pocket their profits. This belief is so popular that the chief—almost the only—marketing legislation on the books in Peru is a law prohibiting *especulación y acaparamiento*.

The naiveté of this belief is obvious. If supplies and prices were stable, then buying at one time would raise prices above the stable level. The speculators would lose money and soon lose their enthusiasm for speculating. In contrast, if supplies were large at harvest time and prices were low, buying surplus products and putting them into storage would raise prices at that time toward the stable level. To put products into storage, until supplies were low and prices high, would lower the prices toward stable levels. This would partly stabilize supplies and prices and therefore would benefit farmers and consumers. It would benefit speculators, too, provided they could keep their operations small enough to let prices rise sufficiently to cover their storage costs. This kind of storage, from a time of surplus to a time of shortage, would, in fact, benefit everybody. The belief that speculation and *acaparamiento* can harm producers and consumers is fallacious. If it benefits speculators, it benefits producers and consumers.

The "Mafia" Syndrome. In the popular mind, wide marketing margins are attributed to the "mafia" in the marketplace. This blanket charge is actually only a coverup for the lack of knowledge that exists on the subject. No conclusive factual proof has been shown of whether a "mafia" with monopolistic powers exists at all; it may be only the product of vivid imagination.

Direct quantitative evidence on this subject is of course hard to come by. Yet, some collateral evidence has recently come to light. In 1963, a small number of firms controlled the food processing industry: one firm accounted for 57.5 percent of the total value of yeast production; two firms for practically all production of balanced annual feeds; six firms for 92.8 percent of canning and preservation of fruits and vegetables (Instituto Nacional de Planificación 1966). This indicates monopolistic conditions.

In 1963, in contrast, there were some 2,182 large firms in each of the nineteen associations of wholesalers in the Lima produce market. The size of these associations ranged in membership all the way from 15 up to 277 firms.[1] These large numbers imply competitive conditions, not a monopolistic "mafia."

Storage Facilities. Farmers often demand more storage capacity for their products. They observe low prices at some times of the year and high prices at other times. These variations in prices are caused chiefly by variations in market supplies. So what could be simpler? Build more storage capacity, put excess products in storage when prices are low, and then draw them out of storage later when prices are high. This indeed sounds simple. But is it practical?

The first step in answering this question is to measure how much the price rises from the low point to the high. The second step is to determine how regular or irregular the price behavior is from year to year. It is easy to look back at charts of prices and show when it would have paid to partially store different farm products. But it is a totally different matter to look *ahead* to any point in time and try to *forecast* whether prices will rise more than enough to cover the storage costs—when to buy products and put them into storage and when to take products out and sell them.

Available preliminary research shows that storage would be a losing proposition for most farm products in Peru. The development of a sophisticated "outlook" program would make this a less-hazardous undertaking. Before any storage warehouse construction is undertaken, more thorough research needs to be conducted, product by product, to show what the chances are that prices would rise more than costs of storage. In 1972, the U.S. government's price support and storage program ran about $4 billion. In terms of Peruvian population and monetary units, this would be about 13 billion soles. Even a program one-tenth this size would be difficult for the Peruvian government to bear (Shepherd et al. 1969).

Cooperative Marketing. Cooperation is a fine thing where is is needed. But in developing countries, farmers are frequently exhorted to "eliminate the middleman" and market their products cooperatively. This happens even before studies are made to determine whether a cooperative would be any more efficient than the existing middleman. Often the farmers have had no business marketing experience, and they do not work well together. For these reasons, many cooperative ventures have failed.

Much education and business training needs to be provided, and research needs to be conducted to see whether a cooperative would be likely to succeed before specific marketing cooperatives are set up. Many farmers tend to believe that a cooperative is a handy tool for pushing the middleman out of business and grabbing his margin, which seems to them mostly profit rather than cost. The farmers have to be taught that the primary purpose of efficient cooperative marketing institutions is to produce and package superior products while reducing marketing costs.

Price Policy

Price Control under Monopoly. In Peru, the population is small and half lives outside the economic system. This is because most large industries are more efficient than small ones and therefore operate at a lower cost per unit of output. The output of a large-scale, efficient plant may be as large as the total demand for the product in the country. Monopolies are, therefore, more prevalent than in countries with large populations. The inefficient small producers cannot survive, and production settles into the hands of a few large firms, or only one. The Instituto Nacional de Planificación (1966) study indicates that the food processing industry is small. The U.S. Department of Justice considers that if four or fewer firms in an industry do 80 percent or more of the total business, it implies monopoly or oligopoly. Thus, the situation in food processing in Peru is free enterprise, but not free competition; it is monopoly or oligopoly. It does not lead to free prices, but to controlled prices—controlled by private enterprise. This can result in exorbitant profits.

There are at least five ways for the government to deal with monopolies or oligopolies of this sort:

1. Breaking them up, a method that may result in numerous, small, inefficient, high-cost, and high-price companies, leaving the country worse off than before.

2. "Riding herd" on them, i.e., letting monopolies exist, but giving government access to their books and keeping a close watch on them. When an industry is not operating in the public interest, the government can force it to change its ways.

3. Bringing the government in as a competitor.

4. Declaring the industry a "public utility" and setting its prices or rates.

5. Nationalizing the industry.

Different methods are required for different industries. The choice of a specific method and its application needs to be worked out separately for each case. None of the methods work smoothly or easily.

Price Control under Competition. Small- and medium-sized farmers, because of their size and large numbers, operate under conditions of perfect competition. No one is large enough to substantially affect the price. The chief reason why governments try to control the prices of some farm products is that these prices are unstable. Stabilizing these prices gives farmers a firmer foundation for their production and marketing plans. Controlling prices under free competition requires controlling the supply of the product, or the demand, or both. Setting prices simply by decree is likely to be disastrous. The prices of durable crops can be controlled if, when large supplies are depressing prices, the government purchases the excess (over average supplies) and holds it to a later year when supplies are below average. But this is an expensive and hazardous business.

Forward Pricing. Farmers often urge governments to set price floors (*precio de refugio*) at "the" cost of production of the product. They do not realize that there is no such thing; there are hundreds of different costs of production, differing from farm to farm. No one of these costs of production is a sensible basis for a *precio de refugio*. Neither is the average cost, any more than the average depth of a river is a safe basis for deciding whether or not to cross it. Instead, the economic basis is to base the *precio de refugio* on the estimated open-market price that will exist after harvest when the product reaches the market. The government can reduce price risks for farmers, minimize losses to the government, and maximize consumption by setting *precios de refugio* 10 or 15 percent below the estimated open-market price for the product. This price has the most effect if it is announced before planting time, so that farmers can base their production plans on it; that is what is known as forward pricing.

Price Control on Imported Farm Products. The preceding section refers to the estimated open-market price for the product as the basis for setting prices. This means open-market prices internationally as well as domestically, a subject of thorny economic and political controversy. The domestic producers naturally want the price of their product to be set above the international level—above the level of "cheap imports of beef from Argentina and Colombia" or of apples from Chile. How can Peruvian agriculture be developed, they ask, if Peru lets the prices of different imported farm products descend to the low level of world prices, while the prices of fertilizer, farm machinery, and other inputs are raised by Peruvian tariffs above world levels to foster Peruvian industrial development?

They have a point. But if the Peruvian government accedes to their request by giving them tariffs aimed at prompting "import substitution," the end result is tariff walls all around the country. These not only reduce imports from efficient producers abroad but also raise the costs of efficient domestic

Peruvian producers and reduce their export opportunities. This configuration of circumstances is the direct opposite of progress.

The economic solution, of course, is to reduce tariffs all around, so that production will locate in the most efficient hands in the most efficient (low-cost) areas, whether they be in Peru, other countries of Latin America, or anywhere in the world. This gets into broader problems of economics and politics than an economist alone is able to resolve (Shepherd 1967c, 1969).

Individual Commodity Studies. The marketing and price problems in Peru differ from product to product. A series of individual studies is needed to deal with these different problems, commodity by commodity (Shepherd 1968a, 1968b, 1968c). As an example I will take a detailed look at the beef industry. Before turning to that subject, though, I want to make some general remarks on the role of government.

The Role of Government. After advising governments for many years on how to help agriculture, I see more and more clearly what kind of help is most effective. It is not direct government *participation* or *operation* in production and marketing—the government building warehouses, storing products, making fertilizer, or supporting or depressing prices. Rather, it is the government *facilitating, helping private enterprises to do these things.*

The economic laws of supply and demand in an *ambiente* (environment) of free competition will do the job. But they will do it only if the producers, marketers, and consumers are well informed and the competition is really free. The government can therefore help agriculture by providing a constant stream of relevant information:

—current market news

—crop and livestock production reports and "outlook" work

—grade specifications

—knowledge of the response to fertilizers and the economic quantities and kinds needed in each area

—information about new insecticides, fungicides, and herbicides, their costs, and the dosages required

—information about new equipment and machinery

—reports and demonstrations of new seeds and cultivation practices

—data on sources of credit

This type of farming intelligence is what has produced agricultural abundance in the United States and other developed countries. In contrast, most direct government operations have been counterproductive and wasteful. Along with this, the government's job is to provide for enforcement of free competition, including the supervision of grades, weights, measures, and trade practices. Where firms are large in size and small in number, effective government regulation may also be required. All this, of course, requires extensive research and extension, plus enough opportunities for general education and technical training for the farmers so that they can understand and use the information, while those who need to leave farming can qualify for urban jobs.

Thus, the government provides the rules of the game, while umpires enforce them. It does not need to provide the players. Paraphrasing Gilbert and Sullivan, one may say:

> For while the government withholds its operative hand,
> Though bureaucratic fingers itch
> To interfere in matters which
> They do not understand,
> So long will agriculture glow,
> And help the GNP to grow.

This general view is effectively illustrated by the case of beef marketing policy in Peru.

A Framework for Price Policy: The Case of Beef

Background. In 1964, per capita consumption of meat in Peru was 12 kilograms. Only Guatemala ranked lower in the Western Hemisphere. Uruguay ranked at the top in per capita meat consumption, followed by Argentina, the United States, and Canada. The ranking in per capita beef consumption is similar.

These differences in meat and in beef consumption in various countries reflect chiefly different physical resources of individual countries. Some, like Argentina, have vast pampas, well adapted to beef production. Peru is well endowed with some natural resources, but not with those that produce beef. Peru buys much of the beef it wants from other countries better endowed with beef-producing resources and pays for it with exports of other products more easily produced in Peru.

There has been a growing gap between domestic production and consumption. This gap has been filled by imports, which have been influenced by the variations in price policy and production conditions. In 1960 imports of meat were only about 4 percent of the value of domestic production. By 1963, they had risen year by year to about 20 percent; but by 1964, they declined to about 10 percent. Then in 1965, they rose to about 16 percent. Up to July 1959, beef prices were strictly controlled and imports at times subsidized. Thereafter a period of free trade followed. Starting toward the end of 1963 and in the beginning of 1964, Argentina raised its beef prices mainly because of increased world demand. Lima retail beef prices, on the other hand, were kept down all through 1964. Importers found it unprofitable to import beef and as a result beef was scarce in Lima during the latter part of 1964 and the early part of 1965. To some extent consumption was rationed during this period. During 1965, however, retail prices were allowed to increase, to the point that it again became possible to import. In 1966, prices were kept relatively constant, with imports up substantially.

Effect of Price Controls. What effect did this low-price policy have on Peruvian beef production, consumption, and imports?

In the period 1950–1966, annual average retail prices for beef in Lima and Callao rose 4.5 times. The cost of living index rose from 47.1 to 116.8, that is, 3.5 times. The real price of beef, therefore, rose 28 percent. This means that the policy of trying to keep beef prices low was not able to keep the real prices from rising. Other things were happening in addition to price controls: increases in demand, fluctuations in production, devaluation in Argentina, etc. A close look at the data clearly shows that the power of price controls is limited and minor compared with the economic forces of supply and demand. In two periods in the past, 1953 and 1957–1959, beef prices had to be allowed to increase because of changes in supply and demand. The same thing happened after the devaluation of the sol in 1967. Beef prices had to be raised substantially, in line with the devaluation. The prices of meat cannot be controlled or set, in the direct price sense, very far from supply and demand levels in an open market.

One of the forces of supply and demand affecting beef prices is drought, which sometimes drastically reduces the supply of cattle. This happened in Peru in 1963. A great increase in imports was needed in 1963 to keep beef prices from rising. Another force is occasional devaluation of the sol in relation to the currency of Argentina, which supplies more than two-thirds of Peru's beef imports. These devaluations happened several times prior to 1968, when this report was written.

In 1962, for example, Argentina devalued its currency 61 percent, from 83 pesos to 134 pesos to the dollar. This made Argentina beef relatively cheap in Peru; imports increased greatly and beef prices in Peru declined. Then in 1967, the opposite happened. Peru devalued the sol from 26.80 to 40 to the dollar, thus making imports 50 percent more expensive in soles. Beef imports declined drastically, and beef prices at wholesale rose from S/.26.80 to S/.35.0. This was a rise of 31 percent, nearly as much as the direct effect of the devaluation. Under the free import policy adopted in December 1967, beef cattle imports in the first quarter of 1968 were about 25 percent smaller than the year before; beef (meat) imports, however, were about 35 percent larger.

Import Policy. Many basic food products, including beef, enter Peru virtually duty free.[2] The purpose of this is clearly to keep internal prices down near world price levels by permitting supplies from abroad to come in to add to the inadequate supplies produced domestically. What effect does this free import policy have on domestic consumption and production? Clearly, by keeping prices low it increases domestic consumption; and clearly, it gives domestic producers less incentive to increase their production.

Would the country be better off to keep beef at world price levels by continuing free importation of beef, and to increase domestic consumption? Or would it do better to raise beef prices by reducing imports, to give domestic producers more incentive to increase their production? Economic theory provides a good basis for answering this question.

A man gets his highest income when he concentrates on producing what he is good at producing and sells it to buy things that other men are good at producing. He produces more and consumes more and has a higher standard of living than if he tried to produce all the different things he needed himself. The same thing is true of countries. It is most productive for a country to produce what it is good at producing and sell it abroad to buy what it is not good at producing itself. It makes good economic sense for Canada to develop its wheat production, not its banana production—in that cold country! And it makes good sense for Peru to develop its fishmeal industry and its mines and exchange those products for other goods it cannot produce so well.

Is beef production an industry that Peru is good at? That is a question that is not so easy to answer. Agriculture is not a monolithic single industry like one big factory. It consists rather of thousands of small or medium farms in thousands of different situations. Some are located in rich irrigated valleys. Some are located in the hills and mountains, and some in the *selva*. Some of them are efficient, some are not. Some are using modern technology and making good profits, some are not. In the late 1960s, Casa Grande estates were feeding cattle sugarcane tops and supplements, at a cost of about S/.10 per kilo of weight gain. The finished animals sold at about S/.20 per kilo. This operation was good business. Yet, less efficient operators claim that they were losing money.

Arguments could run on for years about whether an industry is efficient, or what parts of agriculture are efficient. A simple way to settle the argument is to let world prices be the guide. Then if the inefficient part of a domestic industry claims that it cannot meet foreign competition, the answer is not to raise prices by reducing the imports of that product by import tariff or direct quantitative controls, but to let the foreign products in. The way to help the domestic producers is to help them to reduce their costs, not to try to jack up their prices.

Inefficient industries need help to overcome their inefficiency. But raising prices and protecting them from foreign competition will do the opposite. It will perpetuate their inefficiency. If the thing that makes costs high is the lack of applying modern production and marketing technology, that calls for research and education and extension work to bring the new technology to the producers. This requires not only programs of the conventional type, dealing with the problems of existing beef producers where they are now, but imaginative new programs in new areas such as the *selva*. The pioneering work of Le Tourneau at Tournavista, where they say they are making a profit, and of the experiment station work in the Pucallpa area might show how to open up the vast potentialities of that large sector of Peru (Shepherd 1967d).

But if the things that make costs high are basic physical limitations—no large pampas, not enough irrigated land, insufficient or erratic rainfall—then beef production will recede to the smaller areas where physical conditions are good. The men and money in poor (submarginal) beef areas could then be employed in more efficient industries, where their products could be sold to pay for beef produced more efficiently elsewhere. This may require developing retraining facilities in the submarginal areas. This process is nothing new or strange. It has been going on for years, as general education in overpopulated rural areas around the globe increases mobility and productivity.

A free import policy would not by itself cause a significant drain on foreign exchange. Beef imports into Peru in the past few years have amounted to only about 2.5 percent of the total imports. Increasing this to 3 percent or 3.5 percent would be minor compared with most of the other changes that would be taking place, both plus and minus. In any case, a "drain on foreign exchange" simply signifies that a currency is being held at an unrealistically high exchange rate. More goods and services are being imported than exported. One way to correct this is to license importers to reduce imports. Another way is to increase exports by subsidies, dumping, etc. Both ways are difficult, costly, and artificial. The simplest way to accomplish this is by devaluation; this is the natural and healthy way. If the government does not do it when it is needed, the international gold and banking fraternity will soon do it for them.

In effect the recent devaluation of the sol has erected a 50 percent protective tariff against imports of all products, including beef. Those who request tariff protection against imports of beef now have it for several years. This will give the inefficient producers more income and time to apply new technology to meet world competition as it gradually returns over the next few years. If the inefficient producers cannot meet foreign competition by then, it will indicate that the problem is not a lag in the application of technology, but physical handicaps such as poor soil or climate, distant location, etc., that cannot be overcome by technology. In that case, it would be a waste of money to work that "dry hole" any more than a few years; experimentally, it would be better to invest those research and extension activities in other, more efficiently producible products.

Free Market and Price Controls. For several years, beef prices in Lima have been controlled by CONAP at the wholesale level and by municipal authorities at the retail level.

Before the devaluation of the sol in August 1967, CONAP controlled beef prices at the wholesale level by controlling the quantity of imports. At times, it imported live beef cattle itself. But after the devaluation (and the appointment of a new Minister for Agriculture), Decree 219-A of December 29, 1967, reestablished free importation of beef. Wholesale beef prices in Lima practically reached world price levels, except for a nominal tax per head and a variable levy equal to 75 percent of any decline below Argentine and Colombian beef prices in January 1968. The purpose was not to raise or lower prices but to stabilize them and to permit the importers to regulate the competition among themselves. The Lima municipal officials then simply supervised the markup from wholesale to retail prices.

Out at smaller cities in the country, the municipal authorities consciously kept wholesale prices low, to benefit their consumers. They tried to keep these prices below the price in Lima minus freight to Lima by refusing to let livestock shipments through. They forced the truckers to sell the cattle in their city; they kept the wholesale prices low by keeping the supply artificially high. In October 1967 the Garita de Control de Viru at Trujillo ordered that 15 percent of the cattle that passed through there be retained. Truck drivers who did not comply were heavily fined.[3] Similar things happened in Arequipa. This was contrary to Article 48 of Law 16727, which established free transit for all kinds of agricultural produce in Peru and exonerated them from taxes.

It is difficult to control prices efficiently or accurately at the retail levels. A beef carcass is cut up into dozens of retail cuts, all with different values, and all selling at different prices. It is difficult enough for a large supermarket or chain of supermarkets to set the retail prices for these different cuts at the levels that will keep them all moving at the right speed—avoiding gluts or scarcities—and come out with the right average price to cover its costs. How in the world can a small *puesto* (meat stand or market) operator do this job accurately, with practically no records and only a market inspector looking over his shoulder? How can he charge the right prices for *lomo* (backbone), chuck, tails, etc., so that the weighted average price will cover his costs and the price he paid for the carcass? And how can the market inspector check up on him?

The system is inefficient and out of date. The consumer and the retailers would be better served by a free market that permitted efficient retailers to develop their business and narrow their marketing margins. In developed countries, these margins have been reduced from 25 percent or more 15 years ago to 18 percent or less now; yet they still provide normal profits, on an increasing volume of business. And the Peruvian retail markets could greatly reduce the cost of their present system of inspectors all over the place. This would reduce marketing margins further, to the benefit of both producers and consumers.

Notes

1. This information is from Corporación Nacional de Abastecimiento, Lima, Peru.
2. Imported beef cattle for years have paid a small tax of S/.2.50 per head to support San Marcos University. There is also a municipal tax of S/.2.60 per head.
3. This information is from *La Prensa,* Lima, Peru, November 1 and 2, 1967.

References

Instituto Nacional de Planificación. 1966. "Diagnostico del Sector Industrial." Lima, Peru.

Shepherd, G. S. 1966. "Low-Income People in Peru Need More Protein: Here Is How They Can Get It." Lima, Peru: Iowa Universities Mission to Peru.

_____. 1967a. "Are the Marketing Margins for Fruits and Vegetables Too Wide?" Lima, Peru: Iowa Universities Mission to Peru.

_____. 1976b. "Market News for Farm Products in Peru." Lima, Peru: Iowa Universities Mission to Peru.

_____. 1967c. "The Economics and Legal Aspects of Price Controls in Peruvian Agriculture." Lima, Peru: Iowa Universities Mission to Peru.

_____. 1967d. "Report of Field Trip to the Selva." Lima, Peru: Iowa Universities Mission to Peru.

_____. 1968a. "Price Policy for Milk in Peru." Lima, Peru: Iowa Universities Mission to Peru.

_____. 1968b. "Price Policy for Beef in Peru." Lima, Peru: Iowa Universities Mission to Peru.

_____. 1968c. "Marketing and Price Policy for Beans in Peru." Lima, Peru: Iowa Universities Mission to Peru.

_____. 1969. "How to Set Guaranteed Prices." Lima, Peru: Iowa Universities Mission to Peru.

Shepherd, G. S., J. Cossio, and A. H. Olaechea. 1969. "Is More Storage Needed for Farm Products in Peru?" Lima, Peru: Iowa Universities Mission to Peru.

APPENDIX

The Writings of Geoffrey S. Shepherd

1 9 2 9

Does Iowa "Dump" its Grain? Iowa Agric. Exp. Stn. Circ. 118.
When Shall We Sell Our Corn? Iowa Agric. Exp. Stn. Circ. 113.
When it pays to store corn. *Country Gentleman* 94(4):15, 55–56.

1 9 3 1

Marketing Iowa's Poultry Products. (With W. D. Termohlen.) Iowa Ext. Bull. 173.
The Secular Movement of Corn Prices. Iowa Agric. Exp. Stn. Res. Bull. 140.
The Trend of Corn Prices. Iowa Agric. Exp. Stn. Bull. 284.
Supply and production, demand and consumption. *J. Farm Econ.* 13:639–42.

1 9 3 2

The Agricultural Emergency in Iowa. I. The Situation Today. (Under the name of
   A. G. Black.) Iowa Agric. Exp. Stn. Circ. 139.
The Agricultural Emergency in Iowa. II. The Causes of the Emergency. Iowa Agric.
   Exp. Stn. Circ. 140.
The burden of increased costs of distribution. *J. Farm Econ.* 14:650–61.
Prices, purchasing power, and value. *J. Farm Econ.* 14:491–93.

1 9 3 3

Annual Fluctuations in the Price of Corn. Iowa Agric. Exp. Stn. Res. Bull. 164.
Cooperation in Agriculture, Livestock Marketing. (With P. L. Miller.) Iowa Agric.
   Exp. Stn. Bull. 306.
Prospects for Agricultural Recovery. I. The Economic Situation in 1933. Iowa Agric.
   Exp. Stn. Bull. 310.
Research in Prices of Farm Products. The influence of habit and custom upon price
   (Project 29). Psychological factors affecting price (Project 30). Soc. Sci. Res.
   Counc. 9:165–69.
The Agricultural Emergency in Iowa. VII. Control of the General Price Level. (With
   W. Wright.) Iowa Agric. Exp. Stn. Circ. 143.
The Agricultural Emergency in Iowa. VIII. Monetary Inflation. (with W. Wright.)
   Iowa Agric. Exp. Stn. Circ. 145.
Vertical and horizontal shifts in demand. *J. Farm Econ.* 15:273–79.

1 9 3 4

Prospects for Agricultural Recovery. IV. National Economic Planning. Iowa Agric.
   Exp. Stn. Bull. 313.

Prospects for Agricultural Recovery. VIII. Who Pays for the Hog Reduction Program? Iowa Agric. Exp. Stn. Bull. 317.
The incidence of the cost of the AAA corn-hog program. *J. Farm Econ.* 16:417–30.
Review: Edwin W. Kemmerer, Kemmerer on Money. *J. Farm Econ.* 16:356–58.

1 9 3 5

The Agricultural and Industrial Demand for Corn. (With J. J. Dalton and J. H. Buchanan.) Iowa Agric. Exp. Stn. Bull. 335.
Competition and oligopoly. *J. Farm Econ.* 17:575–79.
Future demand for corn. *Iowa Farm Econ.* 1(4):3–4.
The incidence of the AAA processing tax on hogs. *J. Farm Econ.* 17:321–39.
Paying the processing tax. *Iowa Farm Econ.* (1):9–10.
Marketing corn belt products. Lith. Ames. 275 pp.

1 9 3 6

Vertical and horizontal shifts in demand curves. *Econometrica* 4:361–67.

1 9 3 7

Livestock Marketing Methods in Denmark, Great Britain, and Canada. Iowa Agric. Exp. Stn. Bull. 353.
Stabilizing Corn Supplies by Storage. (With W. W. Wilcox.) Iowa Agric. Exp. Stn. Bull. 368.
The ever-normal granary for corn. (With W. W. Wilcox.) *Iowa Farm Econ.* 3(4):8–9.
Hog selling methods abroad. *Iowa Farm Econ.* 3(1):7–9.

1 9 3 8

Marketing Iowa Cantaloupes. (With A. T. Erwin and N. D. Morgan.) Iowa Agric. Exp. Stn. Bull. 373.
Price discrimination for agricultural products. *J. Farm Econ.* 20:792–806.

1 9 3 9

Demand Curves: Elasticity, Shifts, Rotation, Shape. Cowles Commission. Doc. no. 1219. Washington, D.C.: American Documentation Institute.
Local Hog Marketing Practices in Iowa. (With N. V. Strand.) Iowa Agric. Exp. Stn. Res. Bull. 262.
Selling hogs on carcass grades. (With F. G. Beard.) *Iowa Farm Econ.* 5(4):12–14.
Two prices for farm products. *Iowa Farm Econ.* 5(1):3–5.
Would marketing quotas work? (With W. W. Wilcox.) *Iowa Farm Econ.* 5(2):8–10.

1 9 4 0

Could Hogs Be Sold by Carcass Weight and Grade in the U.S.? (With F. J. Beard, and A. Erickson.) Iowa Agric. Exp. Stn. Res. Bull. 270.
Power Alcohol from Farm Products. (With W. K. McPherson, L. T. Brown, and R. M. Hixon.) Iowa Corn Res. Inst. Bull. 1:281–375.
Alcohol-gasoline. (With W. K. McPherson, L. T. Brown, and R. M. Hixon.) *Iowa Farm Econ.* 6(2):7–10.
Grading hogs on the rail. (With F. J. Beard.) *Country Gentleman,* September 1940.

1 9 4 1

Agricultural Price Analysis. Ames: Iowa State College Press. 402 pp.
Handling and Marketing Iowa Sweet Potatoes. (With A. T. Erwin and P. A. Minges.) Iowa Agric. Exp. Stn. Bull. P32 (n.s.).
How surplus removal programs affect the farmer. (With M. I. Klayman and H. M. Southworth.) *Iowa Farm Econ.* 7(4):10–11, 16.

1 9 4 2

Controlling Corn and Hog Supplies and Prices. USDA Tech. Bull. 826.
Bases for controlling agricultural prices. *J. Farm Econ.* 24:743–60.
Decentralization in agricultural marketing—causes and consequences. *J. Marketing* 6:341–48.
Easing the packer squeeze. (With W. Nicholls.) *Iowa Farm Econ.* 8(11):8, 14.
How the new corn loan is working. *Iowa Farm Econ.* 8(4):15–16.
Rubber from grain. (With R. L. Tontz.) *Iowa Farm Econ.* 8(8):15–16.
Should there be a seasonal movement in the price floor of hogs? (With W. Nicholls and H. O. Drabenstott.) *Iowa Farm Econ.* 8(12):14–15.
Soybeans in season. (With R. C. Bentley.) *Iowa Farm Econ.* 8(10):9, 15.
Stabilization operations of the CCC. *J. Farm Econ.* 24:589–610.

1 9 4 3

The Proper Size and Location of Corn Stabilization Stocks. (With D. G. Paterson.) Iowa Agric. Exp. Stn. Res. Bull. 321.
Wartime Farm and Food Policy. 6. Commodity Loans and Price Floors for Farm Products. Ames: Iowa State College Press.
Controlling hog prices during the transition from war to peace. *J. Farm Econ.* 25:777–92.
Corn price ceilings. *Iowa Farm Econ.* 9(8):10, 12.
Two floors are better than one. *Iowa Farm Econ.* 9(10):8–10.

1 9 4 4

The Coordination of Wheat and Corn Price Controls. Iowa Agric. Exp. Stn. Res. Bull. 330.
Changing emphasis in agricultural price control programs. *J. Farm Econ.* 26:476–502.
Weather vanes in post-war agricultural prices. *Iowa Farm Econ.* 10(11):8–10.

1 9 4 5

Agricultural Price Control. Ames: Iowa State College Press. 361 pp.
Wartime Farm and Food Policy. 11. Agricultural Prices after the War. Ames: Iowa State College Press.
Help them eat! *Iowa Farm Econ.* 11(2):13–15.
How can we support post-war agricultural prices? *Iowa Farm Econ.* 11(1):13–14, 16.
A price policy for agriculture consistent with economic progress, that will promote adequate and more stable income from farming. Honorable Mention. *J. Farm Econ.* 27:886–94.
The problem of removing subsidies. *Iowa Farm Econ.* 11(9):14–16.

1 9 4 6

Marketing Farm Products. Ames: Iowa State College Press. 445 pp.
A bear by the tail. *Iowa Farm Econ.* 12(3):12–13.
The parity formula again. (With L. K. Soth.) *Iowa Farm Econ.* 12(5):5.
A rational system of agricultural price and income controls. *J. Farm Econ.* 28:756–72.

1 9 4 7

Agricultural Price Analysis. 2d ed. Ames: Iowa State College Press. 231 pp.
Agricultural Price Policy. Ames: Iowa State College Press. 440 pp.
Marketing Farm Products. 2d ed. Ames: Iowa State College Press. 461 pp.
How can we support farm prices? *Iowa Farm Science* 1(10):6–7.

1 9 4 8

A farm income stabilization program could be self-financing. *J. Farm Econ.* 30:142–50.
Parity loops the loop. *Iowa Farm Science* 2(8):6.

1 9 4 9

Changes in the Demand for Meat and Dairy Products in the United States since 1910. Iowa Agric. Exp. Stn. Res. Bull. 368.
Long range price policy for Western German agriculture. Bipartite Control Office. Food Agric. and Forestry Group. Frankfurt, Germany.
The field of agricultural marketing research: Objectives, definition, content, criteria. *J. Farm Econ.* 31:444–55.
How much corn should we store? *Iowa Farm Science* 4(4):6–7.
Objectives, effects and costs of feed grain storage. *J. Farm Econ. Proc.* 31:998–1007.
A self-financing farm income stabilizer. *Farm Policy Forum* 2(1):53–56.
Sizing up the new farm price law. *Farm Policy Forum* 2(2):61–64.
Why did the demand for meat go up and butter down? *Iowa Farm Science* 4(2):13–14.

1 9 5 0

Economic Effects of the Missouri River Development Program with Special Reference to Iowa. (With L. Schaffner and P. H. Elwood.) Iowa Agric. Exp. Stn. Res. Bull. 373.
Does marketing cost too much? *Farm Policy Forum* 3(4):28–31.
Food stamps and farm income. *Farm Policy Forum* 3(7):26–29.
The new farm price law. *Iowa Farm Science* 4(7):10–11.
Price supports or direct payments? *Farm Policy Forum* 3(3):6–8.
Price supports or direct payments for hogs? *Farm Policy Forum* 3(5):11–12.

1 9 5 1

Long-range Price Policy for Japanese Agriculture. Tokyo: Ministry of Agriculture and Forestry. 40 pp.
Parity loops again. *Iowa Farm Science* 5(8):11–12.

1 9 5 2

Agricultural Price and Income Policy. Ames: Iowa State College Press. 288 pp.
Butter Pricing and Marketing at Country Points in the North Central Region. (With A. Mathis.) North Central Reg. Pub. 26. Minn. Agric. Exp. Stn. Tech. Bull. 203.
Objective Carcass Grade Standards for Slaughter Hogs. (With E. S. Clifton.) North Central Reg. Pub. 30. Minn. Agric. Exp. Stn. Tech. Bull. 414.
Countervailing power versus the open market. *Farm Policy Forum.* 5(7):21–25.
Methods and procedures in planning regional marketing research. (With A. Goldman.) *J. Farm Econ. Proc.* 34:884–95.
What is average "farm" income? *Farm Policy Forum* 5(11):27–28.

1 9 5 3

Objective grade specifications for slaughter steer carcasses. (With E. S. Clifton.) Iowa Agric. Exp. Stn. Res. Bull. 402.
The feasibility of price supports for perishable farm products. *J. Farm Econ. Proc.* 35:800–810.
Self-service or salesman-service meat retailing. (With F. H. Weigman and E. S. Clifton.) *Iowa Farm Science* 8(2):23–24.
Stabilizing agriculture by storage. *Farm Policy Forum* 6(6):14–16.
What should go into the parity price formula? *J. Farm Econ.* 35:159–72.

1 9 5 4

Economic Analysis of Trends in Beef Cattle and Hog Prices. (With J. C. Purcell and L. V. Manderscheid.) Iowa Agric. Exp. Stn. Res. Bull. 405.
Changes in structure. *Marketing, The Yearbook of Agriculture.* USDA.
Rigid or flexible corn loan rates? *Iowa Farm Science* 8(8):9–11.
There's a bigger job for parity. *Co op Grain Quarterly* 12(4):14–21.
What should go into the parity price formula? State University of Iowa, College of Commerce. *Iowa Business Digest* 25(4):1–7.
When does it pay to store grain? *Iowa Farm Science* 9(2):23–26.

1 9 5 5

Marketing Farm Products—Economic Analysis. 3d ed. Ames: Iowa State College Press. 497 pp.
Agricultural prices and incomes. *Encyclopaedia Britannica.* 1956 ed.
Comparison of Costs of Service and Self-service Methods in Retail Meat Departments. (With F. H. Wiegmann and E. S. Clifton.) Iowa Agric. Stn. Res. Bull. 422.
Methods and Costs of Processing and Delivering Fresh Concentrated Milk in Rural Areas. (With K. L. Utter, W. S. Rosenberger, and H. Homme.) Iowa Agric. Exp. Stn. Spec. Rep. 14.
Objective Grade Specifications for Slaughter Barrow and Gilt Carcasses. (With O. L. Brough.) Iowa Agric. Exp. Stn. Res. Bull. 421.
Surplus disposal and domestic market expansion. *U.S. Agriculture: Perspective and Prospects.* New York: The American Assembly, Graduate College of Business, Columbia Univ.
The analytical problem approach to marketing. *J. Mark.* 19:173–77.
What can a research man do in agricultural price policy? *J. Farm Econ.* 37:305–14.

1 9 5 6

Can we eat up our surpluses? *The Government and the Farmer*. The Reference Shelf 28(5):100–104. New York: H. W. Wilson and Co.

Discussion: Increasing farmers' understanding of public problems and policies and methodological problems in agricultural policy research. *J. Farm Econ.* 37:1329–32.

What can a research man say about values? *J. Farm Econ.* 38:8–16.

Why is the demand for pork dropping? *Iowa Farm Science* 10:263.

1 9 5 7

Agricultural Price Analysis. 4th ed. Ames: Iowa State College Press. 293 pp.

Effects of the U.S. Corn Storage Program on Corn Carryover Stocks and Corn Utilization. (With A. B. Richards.) North Cent. Reg. Pub. 77. Iowa Agric. Exp. Stn. Res. Bull. 446.

Have Agricultural Programs Contributed to Long-run Agricultural Adjustment in Iowa? Basebook for Agricultural Adjustment in Iowa. Iowa Agric. Exp. Stn. Spec. Rep. 22.

Alternative parity formulas for agriculture. (With R. Beneke and W. Fuller.) 85th Congress, 1st Session, Joint Committee Print, *Policy for Commercial Agriculture*. Papers submitted by panelists.

1 9 5 8

Effects of the Federal Programs for Corn and Other Grains on Corn Prices, Feed Grains Production and Livestock Production. (With A. B. Richards.) North Central Reg. Pub. 89. Iowa Agric. Exp. Stn. Res. Bull. 459.

A different base for corn price supports? (With K. Joslin.) *Iowa Farm Science* 13:75–76.

Does the loan and storage program support corn prices? (With A. B. Richards.) *Iowa Farm Science* 13:97–98.

Is corn production leaving the corn belt? *Iowa Farm Science* 13:60–62.

A new gimmick for an old crop. *Co-op Grain Quarterly* 16(3):3.

1 9 5 9

Let's think about hog supplies and prices! (With D. Kaldor and F. A. Kutish.) *Iowa Farm Science* 13:255–58.

Storage and supports have worked, but . . . (With F. A. Kutish, D. Kaldor, R. Heifner, and A. Paulsen.) *Iowa Farm Science* 14:395.

What's happening to our food consumer? *Iowa Farm Science* 14:338–40.

How much too large are the stocks of feed grains? Iowa State University: *Feed-Livestock Workshop Proceedings,* pp. 53–70.

1 9 6 0

Production, Price and Income Estimates and Projections for the Feed-livestock Economy. (With A. Paulsen, F. A. Kutish, D. Kaldor, R. Heifner, and Gene Futrell.) Iowa Agric. and Home Econ. Exp. Stn. Spec. Rep. 27.

Some Effects of Federal Grain Storage Programs. (With A. B. Richards and J. T. Wilkin.) North Cent. Reg. Pub. 114. Purdue Agric. Exp. Stn. Res. Bull. 697.

A barometer of free farm prices. (With A. Paulsen and D. Kaldor.) *Co-op Grain Quarterly* 18(1):7–13.

Farm programs and farm incomes. Federal Reserve Bank of Boston. *Farm Finance News* 15(10):3–4.

Farm programs for farm incomes. *J. Farm Econ.* 42:639–59.

The grain-storage picture. (With A. B. Richards and J. T. Wilkin.) *Iowa Farm Science* 14:519–20.

How low are farm incomes? *Better Farming Methods* 32:12–13, 24–25.

Our corn-hog-cattle belt. (With K. Ullrich.) *Iowa Farm Science* 14:437–38.

Discussion: T. A. Hieronymus, Effects of futures trading on prices. *Futures Trading Seminar, History and Development.* Vol. I. Madison, Wis.: Mimir Publishers, Inc., pp. 181–91.

1 9 6 1

Price Supports and Storage? The Farm Problem — What Are the Choices? Iowa Co op. Ext. Serv. Pam. 276J.

Are big farms more efficient than small ones? *Iowa Farm Science* 16:41–44.

Land values increased, why not farm incomes? *Iowa Farm Science* 15:720–22.

Review: G. R. Allen, Agricultural Marketing Policies. *J. Polit. Econ.* 68:536–37.

A research basis for optimizing world food production and consumption in relation to economic development *J. Agric. Econ. Soc.* (British).

Appraisal of alternative concepts and measures of agricultural parity prices and incomes. Hearings before the Committee on Economic Statistics of the Joint Economic Committee of Congress. Government Price Statistics, pp. 459–502.

1 9 6 2

Marketing Farm Products—Economic Analysis. 4th ed. Ames: Iowa State University Press. 523 pp.

Nutritional Needs by World Regions. (With E. Phipard.) *Food—One Tool in International Economic Development.* Ames: Center for Agriculture and Economics Adjustment, Iowa State University Press, pp. 60–71.

Appraisal of the Federal Feed-grains Programs. North Cent. Reg. Pub. 128. Iowa Agric. and Home Econ. Exp. Stn. Res. Bull.

El mercadeo de productos agropecuarios al mayor y al detal. (With W. Güdel and G. Jiménez. Consejo De Bienestar Rural. Caracas, Venezuela.

What future for our feed-grain exports? *Iowa Farm Science* 16:141–42.

Why the "big farm" trend can't be stopped. *Better Farming Methods* 34(12):11–12, 27.

1 9 6 3

Analysis of Direct-payment Methods for Hogs to Increase Hog Producers' Incomes. (With D. D. Rohdy, J. W. Gruebele, and W. D. Dobson.) Iowa Agric. and Home Econ. Exp. Stn. Res. Bull. 514.

Controlling Agricultural Supplies by Controlling Inputs. (With R. Beneke, R. Heifner, and W. Uhrig.) Interreg. Res. Bull. IR-3. Missouri Agric. Exp. Stn. Bull. 798.

Price Making in Decentralized Markets. Pricing as a Problem for Marketing Research. Western Agric. Econ. Res. Counc. Rep. 5. Berkeley: University of California.

What's the basic farm income problem? *Iowa Farm Science* 17:443–45.

1 9 6 5

Long-run Changes in the Demand for Pork and the Supply of Hogs. (With W. P. Thompson-Barahona.) Iowa Agric. and Home Econ. Exp. Stn. Spec. Rep. 45.

Rice marketing and price policy in Viet-Nam: Problems and alternative solutions. Mimeo. Government of Republic of Viet-Nam and U.S. Operations Mission.

During 1965–1975 G. S. Shepherd spent most of his time on foreign consultative work in several different countries. Publications from that period were usually mimeographed and published both in English and in the language of the foreign country.

1 9 6 6

Low-income People in Peru Need More Protein: Here Is How They Can Get It. Iowa-Peru program staff rep.

1 9 6 7

Are Marketing Margins for Fruits and Vegetables Too Wide? Iowa-Peru program econ. stud. no. 3.

The Economic and Legal Aspects of Price Controls in Peruvian Agriculture. (With D. B. Furnish.) Iowa-Peru program staff rep. no. 2.

Price Policy for Milk in Peru. (With L. Sousa.) Iowa-Peru program staff rep. no. 7.

1 9 6 8

Price Policy for Beef in Peru. Iowa-Peru program staff rep. no. 8.

Rice Marketing Problems and Alternative Solutions. (With G. Prochazka and D. B. Furnish.) Iowa-Peru program staff rep. no. 6.

1 9 6 9

Marketing Farm Products—Economic Analysis. (With Gene A. Futrell.) 5th ed. Ames: Iowa State University Press.

How to Set Guaranteed Prices. (With G. Sanford and J. Cossio.) Iowa-Peru mission rep. B-1.

Is More Storage Needed for Farm Products in Peru? (With J. Cossio and A. Huayanca.) Iowa-Peru econ. stud. no. 12.

Marketing and Price Policy for Beans in Peru. (With G. Sanford and J. Cossio.) Iowa-Peru mission rep. B-1.

Final Report, September 1965 to May 1969. Iowa-Peru program staff rep. no. 31.

1 9 7 2

Rice Storage, Handling and Marketing: Economic and Engineering Study. The Republic of Indonesia. Kansas City, Mo.: Weitz-Hettelsater Engineers, October.

1 9 7 3

Marketing Farm Products—Economic Analysis. (With Gene Futrell and Robert Strain.) 6th ed. Ames: Iowa State University Press.

Marketing Problems of the Alto Llano Occidental Development Project. (With B. Thula and J. Stredel.) Merida, Venezuela: CORPOANDES.

1 9 7 4

Precios minimos, como establescerlos para un producto agricola de exportación. (With R. Henning and T. W. Cook.) Ministerio de Agricultura y Ganaderia, Republica de Paraguay.

1 9 7 5

Plan integral de mejoramiento de comercialización agropecuaria. Parte I: Plan de instalaciones fisicas de mercadeo para granos, frutas y vegetales. (With T. W. Cook.) Ministerio de Agricultura y Ganaderia, Republica de Paraguay.

Plan integral de mejoramiento de comercialización agropecuaria. Parte III: Estudio preliminar de los principales problemas del mercado de ganado. With T. W. Cook.) Ministerio de Agricultura y Ganaderia, Republic de Paraguay.

1 9 8 2

Marketing Farm Products—Economic Analysis. (With Gene A. Futrell.) 7th ed. Ames: Iowa State University Press.

CONTRIBUTORS

G. R. Boddez, Directeur, Centrum voor Landbouweconomisch Onderzoek
Katholieke Universiteit te Leuven
Kardinaal Mercierlaan 92
3030 Heverlee
Belgium

Kenneth E. Boulding, Distinguished Professor of Economics
Institute of Behavioral Science
University of Colorado at Boulder
Boulder, Colorado 80309

Harold F. Breimyer, Perry Foundation Professor of Agricultural Economics
University of Missouri
214B Mumford Hall
Columbia, Missouri 65211

Richard H. Day, Professor of Economics and Director, Modelling Research Group
University of Southern California
University Park
Los Angeles, California 90007

Walter D. Fisher, Professor of Economics
Northwestern University
Center for Mathematical Studies in Economics and Management Science
Evanston, Illinois 60201

Karl A. Fox, Distinguished Professor of Economics
Department of Economics
Iowa State University
Ames, Iowa 50011

Arthur Hanau
Department of Agricultural Economics
Göttingen University
Göttingen, Germany

Earl O. Heady, Distinguished Professor of Economics and Director, The Center for
Agricultural and Rural Development
Iowa State University
578 Heady Hall
Ames, Iowa 50011

Wen-yuan Huang, USDA Collaborator
Department of Economics
Iowa State University
Ames, Iowa 50011

Glenn L. Johnson, Professor of Agricultural Economics
Michigan State University
East Lansing, Michigan 48824

George G. Judge, Professor of Economics
University of Illinois
Box 111
Commerce Building (West)
Urbana, Illinois 61801

Paul L. Kelley, Professor of Economics
Waters Hall
Kansas State University
Manhattan, Kansas 66506

George W. Ladd, Professor of Economics
Iowa State University
Ames, Iowa 50011

W. K. McPherson, Professor Emeritus
University of Florida
Route 2
Box 330
Gainesville, Florida 32601

Frank Meissner
Inter-American Development Bank
Washington, D.C. 20577

G. Edward Schuh, Chairman
Department of Agricultural and Resource Economics
University of Minnesota
St. Paul, Minnesota 55108

Theodore W. Schultz, Nobel Laureate and Professor of Economics
University of Chicago
1126 East 59th Street
Chicago, Illinois 60637

R. T. Shand, Executive Director, Development Studies Centre
The Australian National University
Box 4, P.O. Canberra
A.C.T. 2600
Australia

Geoffrey S. Shepherd, Professor Emeritus
Department of Economics
Iowa State University
Ames, Iowa 50011

Lauren Soth, Journalist
801 State Farm Road
West Des Moines, Iowa 50265

John F. Timmons, Charles F. Curtiss Distinguished Professor of Economics
Iowa State University
Ames, Iowa 50011

Gerhard Tintner, Professor of Economics
Institut für Ökonometrie
Technische Universität Wien
A-1040 Wien
Karlsplatz 13
Vienna
Austria

Reuben Weisz
Land Management Planning Staff
Region 3, Forest Service
517 Gold Ave., SW
Albuquerque, New Mexico 87102

Robert N. Wisner, Professor of Economics
Iowa State University
Ames, Iowa 50011

INDEX

Abstraction, process, 58
Adaptation: institutional, 204; as two-way process, 193
Adaptive economics, 255: and economic development, 258–60
Agg-Norm method, 164–66, 171
Aggregation: activities, 161; constraints, 161; error, 157, 167, 168; exact, 157; inexact, 158; and representative firms, 158–66
Agricultural Adjustment Act, 48
Agricultural development: adjustment problems, 255, 262–63; in agroindustrial complex, 256–57; foreign aid for, 186; and international markets, 278–79; marketing and price policy for (Peru), 334–47
Agricultural economics: analysis and image, 57–58; clouded legitimacy, 57; dichotomy, 60; impact of mathematical techniques, 52; origins, 46–47, 57; social market fundamentals applied to, 283; values, 59
Agricultural economists: generalists, 53; images they think by, 57–65; influence, 47–55; ingredients of their conceptual image, 59–60; and public policy, 46–56; role, 55
Agricultural experiment stations, 186
Agricultural law, German, 299–300
Agricultural policy, 39–43, 140–55: dynamic consequences, 42–43; of European Economic Community, 302–19; implications of international capital markets on U.S., 265–81; normative policy and, 34–45; values, research in connection with, 66–74. See also Economic policy
Agricultural price analysis: role in history of econometrics, 104–8; Shepherd's contribution, 123
Agricultural price policy, 286–87: for agricultural development in Peru, 334–47; for beef in Peru, 342–46; objectives, 24–33; political action in, 51–55
Agricultural research: achievements, 182–83; business, 180–81; centers for international, 183, 185, 192; economics and, 179–91; expenditures, 181–83; in India, 192–208; organized, 180–81; paying for, 183–86; in Peru, 334–47; in price policy, 24–33; by private firms, 184, 187; as public goods, 185–86; Shepherd's contribution, 179–80; value of contributions, 182–83; who benefits, 185
Agricultural sectors, linkage networks between industrial and, 261
Agriculture: development of world, 255; dise-

quilibrium dynamics in, 261–62; foreign capital investment in U.S., 279; image, 64–65; industrialization, 64, 256–57; instability problems, 49; investment in, 84; migration from, 40, 49–50, 287–91, 307–9; permanent adjustment theme, 49; political action in, 51–55; poverty in, 39–40; productivity, 39–40, 298; in social market system, 283–301; technology transfer in India, 192–209; Third World, 278; U.S. and international capital markets, 278–79. See also European Economic Community
Agroindustrial complex: agricultural development, 256–57; crises and structural change, 255–64; networks of linkages, 261; neoclassical interpretation, 257–58; public policy perspective, 262–63
Alcohol: commercial fermentation plans, 231; costs, 232–33; energy requirements, 235, 237; for fuel, 228–30; world food security as policy concern, 236. See also Gasohol
Animal breeding: basic population genetics, 209–13; concepts, 209–15; environmental effects, 211, 212, 221; errors-in-variables model, 221; product-characteristics approach to technical change, 209–27; program, optimal, 225; selection indexes, 213–15. See also Economic value, of animal breeding
Animal products, increased sales, 284–85
Asian Development Bank (ADB), 325, 331

Balance of payments, 267, 272, 273
"Basic needs" strategy, 322–23
Baycsian: approach to inference, 95; procedures to analyze simultaneous equation models, 98
Bayes's posterior density, 95, 96; theorem, 95
Bias: disturbance, 111; Haavelmo, 122; ideological, 58–59; negative, 166; profit, 164, 168
Breeding. See Animal breeding; Economic value, of animal breeding
Bretton Woods Conference, 267, 268, 272
Business: cycle as general speculative short-run equilibrium phenomenon, 126–39; firm, 62–63; fluctuations, theory, 126–39

Capital flows, among countries, 265, 269–70
Center for Agricultural and Rural Development (CARD), 141–42
Clarity, test, 71–72